CTIA

Consolidated Treaties & International Agreements

Current Document Service: United States

2012

VOLUME 5

Containing

Department of State Documents 12-165
through 12-167
and
12-170 through 12-203

Oceana®
NEW YORK

OXFORD
UNIVERSITY PRESS

Oxford University Press is a department of the University of Oxford. It furthers the University's objective of excellence in research, scholarship, and education by publishing worldwide.

Oxford New York
Auckland Cape Town Dar es Salaam Hong Kong Karachi
Kuala Lumpur Madrid Melbourne Mexico City Nairobi
New Delhi Shanghai Taipei Toronto

With offices in
Argentina Austria Brazil Chile Czech Republic France Greece
Guatemala Hungary Italy Japan Poland Portugal Singapore
South Korea Switzerland Thailand Turkey Ukraine Vietnam

Published in the United States of America by
Oxford University Press
198 Madison Avenue, New York, NY 10016

Cataloging-in-Publication information is available from the Library of Congress.

This volume should be cited as **2012-5 CTIA.**

ISSN 1053-9905
ISBN 978-0-19-935003-2

Note to Readers

This publication is designed to provide accurate and authoritative information in regard to the subject matter covered. It is based upon sources believed to be accurate and reliable and is intended to be current as of the time it was written. It is sold with the understanding that the publisher is not engaged in rendering legal, accounting, or other professional services. If legal advice or other expert assistance is required, the services of a competent professional person should be sought. Also, to confirm that the information has not been affected or changed by recent developments, traditional legal research techniques should be used, including checking primary sources where appropriate.

(Based on the Declaration of Principles jointly adopted by a Committee of the American Bar Association and a Committee of Publishers and Associations.)

How to Use Consolidated Treaties & International Agreements

The **Consolidated Treaties & International Agreements** set contains all treaties and agreements in a given year to which the United States is a party. The agreements and treaties are made available by the Department of State and the Senate, as explained below.

The Department of State, under 1 U.S.C. §§ 112a and 112b, is obligated to report to Congress all international agreements and treaties to which the United States is a party within 60 days after the agreement or treaty has entered into force. The Department of State is also required to make available on their website within 180 days after the treaty or agreement has entered into force all reported agreements and treaties meeting the requirements for publication status in the U.S. government publication, *United States Treaties and Other International Agreements.* The Department of State numbers each agreement or treaty with a prefix based on the year reported and a suffix based on the order the agreement or treaty arrived to the Legal Affairs Office. For example, for the year 2008, the agreements were numbered 08-01, 08-02, etc., and for 2009, the agreements were numbered 09-01, 09-02, and so on.

The Senate, on the other hand, has a different procedure for formalizing and numbering treaties. All treaties requiring the Senate's consent to ratification are first submitted to the Senate Foreign Relations Committee for its review and recommendation. Thereafter, the treaty is introduced to the full Senate for its consent to ratification by a two-thirds vote of all members present. Once the Senate consents to its ratification, the treaty is presented to the President for formal ratification. However, the treaty is made available to the public upon the completed review and recommendation of the Foreign Relations Committee, although parts of the treaty text may remain concealed for security reasons. Senate treaty documents may remain in committee for many congressional sessions; thus, a treaty may be negotiated and signed in one year but not ratified until many years later. However, the treaty document is numbered based on the session the treaty was introduced to the Senate. For example, the Treaty between the United States of America and Japan on Mutual Legal Assistance in Criminal Matters was assigned as Senate Document No. 108-12, meaning it was introduced to the Senate during the 108th session of Congress and it was the 12th treaty submitted to the Foreign Relations Committee.

The editorial staff of the Law Division of Oxford University Press, Inc. (*fka* Oceana Publications) monitors the Department of State and the Senate throughout the year and gathers the agreements and treaties as they become available. Each agreement and treaty document is assigned an internal CTIA number and a subject. The CTIA number is used to track the agreement or treaty and its associated amendments, extensions and protocols. Each agreement or treaty document is assigned a CTIA prefix number with a suffix of ".000"; amendments, protocols and/or extensions of the agreement or treaty are assigned the same CTIA prefix, but a sequential CTIA suffix (*i.e.*, 2525.000 (main agreement), 2525.001 (amendment)).

The **Consolidated Treaties & International Agreements** set is organized by document number, beginning with the Department of State agreements and treaties, followed by the Senate treaty documents, and may also include any agreements for the year between the American Institute of Taiwan and the Taipei Economic and Cultural Representative Office. The Table of Contents for each volume provides all the key elements of the treaties published in the volume—agreement or treaty title, date and place of signature and country.

The **Consolidated Treaties & International Agreements** set also contains three indices to help the reader locate documents.

The first index, Appendix I, organizes the treaties published in the volume by country and then by subject. Each treaty title includes the Department of State or Senate document number and the Oceana print citation.

The second index, Appendix II, is a complete listing of all multilateral agreements published in the volume. Each treaty title includes the Department of State or Senate document number and the Oceana print citation.

The third index, Appendix III, is the topical index, organizing each treaty published in the volume under its assigned subject in alphabetical order by country name and with the appropriate Department of State or Senate document number and Oceana print citation.

Table of Contents

* The Department of State did not make these agreements available to the public.

State Department Document Number: 12-165

Development Objective Agreement Between the United States of America and the Republic of Liberia for USAID Development Objective 2: Sustained, Market-Driven Economic Growth to Reduce Poverty, with Annexes

Signed on September 29, 2012
Entered into force September 29, 2012

CTIA DOCUMENT NUMBER: 18074.000

USAID Development Objective Agreement No. 669-DOAG-DO2-12-00

DEVELOPMENT OBJECTIVE AGREEMENT

Dated: September 17, 2012

Between

The United States of America, acting through the United States Agency for International Development ("USAID")

and

The Republic of Liberia (hereinafter referred to as the "Grantee")

Article 1: Purpose.

The purpose of this Development Objective Agreement (the "Agreement") is to set out the understanding of the Parties named above (the "Parties") in connection with the Objective described below.

Article 2: Development Objective and Results.

Section 2.1. Development Objective. In order to further the Development Objective "Sustained, Market-Driven Economic Growth to Reduce Poverty" articulated by the Government of the United States of America in the USAID/Liberia Country Development Cooperation Strategy 2013-2017, the Parties hereto agree to work together by focusing on activities in the areas of Infrastructure, Agriculture, Private Sector Competitiveness and Environment.

Section 2.2. Intermediate Results. In order to achieve the Objective, the Parties agree to work together to achieve the following Intermediate Results:

- Food security enhanced;
- Natural resources managed sustainably;
- Enabling environment supports private enterprise growth.

Within the limits of the definition of the Development Objective in Section 2.1, this Section 2.2 may be changed by written agreement of the authorized representatives of the Parties without formal amendment of this Agreement.

Section 2.3. Annex 1, Amplified Description. Annex 1, attached, amplifies the above Development Objective and describes the Intermediate Results, Sub-results and Indicators that will be used to measure the progress and achievement of the Objective. Within the limits of the definition of the Development Objective set forth in Section 2.1, Annex 1 may be changed by written agreement of the authorized representatives of the Parties without formal amendment of this Agreement.

Article 3: Contributions of the Parties.

Section 3.1. USAID Contribution.

(a) The Grant. To help achieve the Objective set forth in this Agreement, USAID, pursuant to the Foreign Assistance Act of 1961, as amended, hereby grants to the Grantee under the terms of the Agreement an amount not to exceed THIRTY-SEVEN MILLION TWO HUNDRED AND SEVENTY-SIX THOUSAND United States Dollars ($37,276,000).

(b) Total Estimated USAID Contribution. USAID's total estimated contribution to achievement of the Objective will be TWO HUNDRED AND TEN MILLION NINETY-FIVE THOUSAND TWO HUNDRED AND FORTY-FOUR United States Dollars ($210,095,244), which will be provided in increments. Subsequent increments will be subject to the availability of funds to USAID for this purpose and may be provided by USAID upon written notice to the Grantee. The Parties agree that each such incremental contribution provided, if any, shall cumulatively increase the total amount of the Grant set forth in Section 3.1 and consequently may increase the Grantee's contribution under Section 3.2. The Grantee further agrees to acknowledge by written notice to USAID each such incremental contribution, if any.

(c) If at any time USAID determines that its contribution under Section 3.1(a) exceeds the amount which reasonably can be committed for achieving the Objective during the current or next U.S. fiscal year, USAID may, upon written notice to the Grantee, withdraw the excess amount, thereby reducing the amount of the Grant as set forth in Section 3.1(a). Actions taken pursuant to this subsection will not revise USAID's total estimated contribution set forth in 3.1 (b).

(d) The Parties agree that USAID's contribution may be disbursed through mechanisms including grants, cooperative agreements, and contracts with non-governmental organizations and private companies in order to carry out the activities described in Annex 1 of this Agreement or described in Implementation Letters issued in accordance with Section A.2 of Annex 2 of this Agreement. The parties further agree that any such implementing partner carrying out activities in furtherance of the Objective shall receive all of the rights, privileges, and other benefits set forth in this Agreement.

Section 3.2. Grantee Contribution.

(a) The Grantee agrees to provide or cause to be provided all funds, in addition to those provided by USAID and any other donor identified in Annex 1, and all other resources required to complete, on or before the Completion Date, all activities necessary to achieve the Development Objective. The basis for determining the Grantee's contribution and the nature of the contribution will be further described in an Implementation Letter.

(b) The Grantee's financial contributions to the achievement of the Development Objective of this agreement, based on USAID's contribution in Section 3.1(a), will not be less than the equivalent of twenty-five percent of the portion of the Grant that is used to support activities that either directly provides substantial benefit to the Government of the Republic of Liberia or involves the direct and substantial involvement of the Government of the Republic of Liberia in the administration, control or management of such assistance, provided that such amount may be reduced with the written consent of USAID. The Grantee's financial contributions may include either cash or in-kind contributions or both. The dollar equivalent amount of the Grantee's contribution shall be set forth in an Implementation Letter and shall be subsequently included in the Illustrative Financial Plan included in Annex 3 of this Agreement. The amount of the Grantee's contribution shall be adjusted upon any incremental increase in the amount of the Grant set forth in Section 3.1(a), in accordance with the formula described in the first sentence of this paragraph, and the precise amount of such adjustment shall be indicated in an Implementation Letter. The Grantee agrees to maintain a record of its contributions under this Agreement for a period of three years after the Completion Date and will report at least annually in a format to be agreed upon with USAID on its cash and in-kind contributions.

Article 4: Completion Date.

(a) The Completion Date, which is September 30, 2017, or such other date as the Parties may agree to in writing, is the date by which the Parties estimate that all the activities necessary to achieve the Objective will be completed.

(b) Except as USAID may otherwise agree to in writing, USAID will not issue or approve documentation that would authorize disbursement of the Grant for services performed or goods furnished after the Completion Date.

(c) Requests for disbursement, accompanied by necessary supporting documentation prescribed in Implementation Letters, are to be received by USAID no later than nine (9) months before the Completion Date, or such other period as USAID agrees to in writing before or after such period. After such period USAID, at any time or times, may give notice in writing to the Grantee and reduce the amount of the Grant by all or any part thereof for which requests for disbursement, accompanied by necessary supporting documentation prescribed in Implementation Letters, were not received before the expiration of such period.

Article 5: Conditions Precedent to Disbursement.

Section 5.1. First Disbursement. Prior to the first disbursement under the Grant, or to the issuance by USAID of documentation pursuant to which disbursement will be made, the Grantee will, except as the Parties may otherwise agree in writing, furnish to USAID in form and substance satisfactory to USAID:

(a) An opinion of counsel acceptable to USAID that (i) this Agreement has been duly authorized or ratified by, and executed on behalf of the Grantee, (ii) this Agreement constitutes a valid and legally binding obligation of the Grantee in accordance with all of its terms, and (iii) all internal actions and approvals necessary to give effect to this Agreement have been obtained by or on behalf of the Grantee; and

(b) A signed statement in the name of the person holding or acting in the office of the Grantee specified in Section 7.2, which designates by name and title any additional representatives each of whom may act pursuant to Section 7.2.

Section 5.2. Notification. USAID will promptly notify the Grantee when USAID has determined that a condition precedent has been met.

Section 5.3. Terminal Dates for Conditions Precedent.

(a) The terminal date for meeting the conditions specified in Section 5.1 is 60 days from the date of this Agreement or such later date as USAID may agree to in writing before or after the above terminal date. If the conditions precedent in Section 5.1 have not been met by the above terminal date, USAID, at any time, may terminate this Agreement by written notice to the Grantee.

Article 6: Special Covenants.

Section 6.1 The Grantee, in conjunction with the appropriate Government of Liberia Ministries, Agencies and Commissions, hereby covenants and agrees to adopt and implement policies, procedures and systems which are consistent with the Development Objective and conducive to the effective implementation of assistance projects supported by this Grant.

Section 6.2 In addition, the Grantee, in conjunction with the appropriate Government of Liberia Ministries, Agencies and Commissions, covenants and agrees to issue, renew and/or extend free of charge and in a timely manner all official permits, visas, exemptions and any other permissions (including all approvals as may be required from time to time to ensure full access to information, project sites and relevant offices) for the Applicable Persons (as defined below) carrying out activities financed by USAID under this Agreement (collectively, the "Required Documents"). For purposes of these provisions, Applicable Persons is defined as: (1) employees and consultants of any contractors, grantees and other organizations carrying out activities financed by USAID under this Agreement and (b) members of such employees' and consultants' households. Any renewals or extensions of such Required Documents that are required, or become required, in order for such employees, consultants and dependent family members to legally reside in the Republic of Liberia and undertake the activities contemplated by and financed under this Agreement shall also be issued free of charge.

Article 7: Miscellaneous.

Section 7.1. Communications. Any notice, request, document, or other communication submitted by either Party to the other under this Agreement will be in writing and will be deemed duly given or sent when delivered to such Party at the following address:

To USAID:
Mail Address:
Mission Director
United States Agency for International Development
c/o American Embassy

502 Benson St.
Monrovia, Liberia

To Government of Liberia
Mail Address:
Minister
Ministry of Finance
Monrovia, Liberia

All such communications will be in English, unless the Parties otherwise agree in writing. Other contact information may be substituted for the above upon the giving of notice.

Section 7.2. Representatives. For all purposes relevant to this Agreement, the Grantee will be represented by the individual holding or acting in the Office of the Minister of Finance and USAID will be represented by the individual holding or acting in the Office of the Mission Director, USAID/Liberia , each of whom, by written notice, may designate additional representatives for all purposes other than signing formal amendments to the Agreement or exercising the power under Sections 2.2 or 2.3 to revise the results to be achieved. The names and titles of the additional representatives of the Grantee will be provided pursuant to Section 5.1(b) to USAID, which may accept as duly authorized any instrument signed by such additional representatives (or any individuals subsequently holding or acting in the office of such representatives) in accordance with this Section 7.2, until receipt of written notice of revocation of their authority.

Section 7.3. Standard Provisions. A "Standard Provisions Annex" (Annex 2) is attached to and forms part of this Agreement.

Section 7.4. Language of Agreement. This Agreement is prepared in English only.

IN WITNESS WHEREOF, the United States of America and the Grantee, each acting through its duly authorized representative, have caused this Agreement to be signed in their names and delivered as of the day and year first above written.

UNITED STATES OF AMERICA
By:
[Signature]

Name: Patricia Rader
Title: Mission Director

Date: 9/29/12

REPUBLIC OF LIBERIA
By:
[Signature]

Name: Sebastian Muah
Title: Deputy Minister for Budget/
Acting Minister of Finance
Date: September 29, 2012

Annex 1
Amplified Description

I. Introduction.

This Annex describes the activities to be undertaken and the progress and achievements to be made with the funds obligated under this Agreement. Nothing in this annex shall be construed as amending any of the definitions or terms of the Agreement.

II. Development Objective and Intermediate Results

Development Objective 2: Sustained, Market-Driven Economic Growth to Reduce Poverty

Hypothesis: The development hypothesis underlying DO2 is that fostering market-driven, private sector-led agricultural development and food security, strengthening natural resource management, improving rural road infrastructure and increasing renewable energy supplies, and improving the business enabling environment will create the conditions for sustained economic growth that reduces poverty. If Liberian farmers and entrepreneurs are able to increase their productivity, diversify their products, add value to the commodities they produce, and gain better access to input and output markets through the private sector, then rural incomes will increase and fewer Liberians will live in poverty. In order to be sustainable, market-driven growth must create remunerative employment along value chains in rural areas and it must address actual and potential impacts on soil fertility and biodiversity.

An important element of the development hypothesis for this DO is that targeting assistance in the Government of Liberia's (GOL) designated priority development corridors will attract additional investment from the public and private sectors, including other donors, in infrastructure, smallholder forestry, and agricultural production, processing, and marketing that will accelerate, increase, and broaden overall impact. In addition, this geographic focus will capture synergies from co-located USAID investments in health and education that could increase adoption rates for new techniques, improve nutrition behaviors, and promote more effective management of individual and community-based enterprises.

Given the scope of challenges faced and the extensive range of needs in order to achieve results in this sector, USAID assistance must focus, in coordination with the GOL, the private sector, and other donors, on an integrated set of interventions to include:

- Strengthening agricultural commodity value chains for staples in rice and cassava, dietary and income diversification in vegetables and goats, and forest-based products to raise incomes through increased productivity, quality, and commercialization.
- Addressing availability, access, and utilization of more and better quality food for Liberians, including explicit investment in both marketing and behavior change approaches to nutrition behaviors that promote improved food utilization.
- Promoting effective governance, sustainable economic use, and wise stewardship of renewable forest and soil resources to enhance the ecosystem services they provide.
- Rehabilitating rural infrastructure to facilitate transport services and access to markets, by improving the technical and managerial capacity of Liberian private sector contractors to construct and maintain that infrastructure.
- Providing accessible and affordable energy, especially to rural agri-business and in particular using scalable, renewable energy technologies.

- Expanding the availability of credit for micro, small and medium-scale enterprises (MSMEs), to increase competitiveness and facilitate access to profitable markets.
- Expanding the knowledge base and building the skills of the large and growing young workforce to support growing private-sector agricultural production, processing and marketing, road construction, and rural energy supply.

Approach: Consistent with the overall strategic approach of this strategy, USAID/Liberia will take a two-track approach in pursuing DO2. Capacity development assistance will concentrate on supporting GOL reforms to the delivery of extension, market development services, and infrastructure development to rural farmers and forest-based communities, to revitalize agricultural and agroforestry research, and to provide more effective and updated training for its professional cadres. USAID will also assist to develop the private sector in rural communities to better meet needs in linking farmers to markets, including expanding the pool of local firms capable of building and maintaining critical infrastructure. At the policy level, USAID will provide support for reforms needed to promote a more business-friendly enabling environment.

In parallel with these longer-term capacity-building efforts, USAID will also provide direct services and other immediate support to market-driven enterprises in high-priority value chains (rice, cassava, vegetables goats, and forest products), and to public and private partners who deliver improved nutritional products and services. Investments will expand access to improved technologies and market information, introduce improved pre- and post- harvest crop management techniques and better storage, enhance public and private provision of extension services to increase horticulture supplies and quality, and introduce better animal husbandry practices to increase supply in rural and urban markets. These investments will be complemented by improving access to credit and expanding road, energy, and communication networks to support market access. A coordinated set of focused nutrition interventions will address availability, access, and utilization of more and better quality food.

Economic growth activities under this DO will focus in the six counties selected as priorities for the USAID/Liberia strategy: Bong, Lofa, Nimba, Grand Bassa, Montserrado, and Margibi. These counties are home an estimated 75% of all Liberian households; more than two-thirds of all farming households; and nearly 70% of the country's population living below the poverty line. Additionally, they are the counties offering the greatest potential for agricultural development, including Liberia's "breadbasket" counties of Bong, Lofa, and Nimba, which are also focus counties for USAID/Liberia's health portfolio, offering important synergies with DO 2 nutrition interventions.

Together, these six priority counties constitute a critical mass of economic potential as regional development corridors within Liberia. By serving as a focus for new investment, USAID expects these corridors to help create demand for a volume and diversity of goods and services that local and international entrepreneurs will strive to fill, thus generating a dynamic of growth that will be self-sustaining.

As a key organizing principle, all activities will focus on increasing opportunities for women and women-headed households, including in labor-based rural infrastructure. USAID will also make special efforts to engage the participation of youth in economic growth activities. Assistance will leverage the power and collective numbers of producers' associations to ensure new and innovative technologies and inputs can be applied at a level that will foster real change and significant increases in income.

Intermediate Results

Intermediate Result 2.1: Food Security Enhanced

Sub IR 2.1.1 - Nutrition enhanced
Sub IR 2.1.2 - Agriculture sector growth supported

Intermediate Result 2.2: Natural Resources Managed Sustainably

Sub IR 2.2.1 - Forest management systems improved
Sub IR 2.2.2 - Sustainable forestry management enterprises strengthened

Intermediate Result 2.3: Enabling Environment Supports Private Enterprise Growth

Sub IR 2.3.1 Agricultural sector infrastructure improved and maintained
Sub IR 2.3.2 Improved economic policies implemented

III. Funding

Financial Plan. The financial plan for the activities under this Agreement is set forth in the attached Illustrative Financial Plan, Annex 3 to the Agreement. Changes may be made to the Illustrative Financial Plan by representatives of the Parties without formal amendment to the Agreement, if such changes do not cause (1) USAID's contribution to exceed the amount specified in Section 3.1 of the Agreement, or (2) the Grantee's contribution to be less than the amount specified in Section 3.2 of the Agreement.

IV. Roles and Responsibilities of the Parties.

USAID/Liberia

USAID/Liberia will manage and monitor the planned activities in compliance with USAID regulations and procedures. Technical expertise within USAID to advise and direct these efforts will be funded under this Agreement. Additional expertise will be provided in the form of short-term assistance as needed and with the use of funds obligated under this Agreement. USAID in collaboration with the Government of Liberia will lead the selection of the primary implementing partners.

Portfolio review meetings will be held once a year to review objectives, results and activities. Meetings are expected to include the Government of the Republic of Liberia officials, other implementing partners and donors.

Government of Liberia

The Government of Liberia's Ministry of Finance coordinates all activities and is USAID's lead partner in the design and monitoring of activities.

The Liberia Electricity Corporation will be USAID's partner in implementing energy infrastructure activities including providing insights into the selection and management of USAID's direct implementers. The Ministry of Land, Mines and Energy will identify personnel to be trained in policy and regulatory practices, business management systems and technical aspects of energy provision to enhance the capacity of this Ministry to coordinate and oversee needed changes in the policy and regulations regarding Liberia's energy sector. The longer term aim of these efforts is to help rebuild the energy network, restore electricity infrastructure and supply in urban areas, expand electricity supply to rural areas and increase access to affordable energy supplies throughout the country.

USAID's road and institutional infrastructure activities are implemented in accordance with priorities and targets outlined in collaboration with the Ministry of Public Works, the Liberian Reconstruction and Development Committee, and selected Universities and other institutions. The large number of youth in urban and peri-urban areas who are unemployed or who have received training but not follow-on work are to be targeted to rehabilitate or construct physical infrastructure. This effort will create jobs as well as a workforce trained to maintain USAID-funded infrastructure.

USAID will work closely with and support the Ministry of Agriculture to rebuild the infrastructure, develop critical human resources, foster the enabling policy environment and reinstitute a customer-service oriented culture to rebuild Liberia's economy. The Ministry of Agriculture will identify personnel to be trained in policy and regulatory practices, business management systems and technical aspects of agricultural production to enhance the capacity of this Ministry to coordinate and oversee needed changes in policy and regulations regarding Liberia's agriculture sector.

The Government of Liberia's Forestry Development Authority will identify personnel to work with USAID to be trained in policy and regulatory practices, business management systems and natural resource management (biodiversity conservation and sustainable agriculture) practices to enhance forest management and build capacity in community forestry.

V. Monitoring and Evaluation

Except as the Parties may otherwise agree in writing, the Parties stipulate that:

a) USAID and its implementing partners will systematically monitor and report progress on performance indicators during the Agreement period; illustrative indicators are described in the table below;

b) Each contract, grant or cooperative agreement awarded under this Agreement will include a performance and monitoring plan that identifies indicators and targets; the USAID team managing this Agreement will review the data collected from implementing partners and the GOL for inclusion in that plan;

c) Independent audits will be funded under each activity according to regulations set forth in the respective agreements with implementing partners;

d) Funds made available under this Agreement may be used for monitoring and evaluation purposes;

e) The strategy baseline survey conducted by USAID at the beginning of this Agreement will serve as a baseline for measuring progress under this Agreement; and

f) The Grantee will ensure that public sector agencies associated with the Agreement undertake reasonable efforts to produce and/or obtain and provide to USAID all data needed to measure performance of activities under the Agreement.

VI. Indicators

USAID will use the following indicators to measure the impact of programs under this Agreement and track progress towards the goal of "Sustained, Market-Driven Economic Growth to Reduce Poverty". As a group, the indicators capture the intended impact of the development strategy and how this impact will be achieved. Where available USAID will collect baseline values with the assistance of the GOL.

DO2: Sustained, Market-Driven Economic Growth to Reduce Poverty

- Change in household income in target areas
- Proportion of Liberians living below Liberian-defined poverty threshold in target areas

Intermediate Results		IR Indicators
IR 2.1	**Food Security Enhanced**	Prevalence of underweight children under 5
		Household dietary diversity score
		Gross margin per unit of land, kilogram, or animal of selected product (crops/ animals/ fisheries)
SubIR 2.1.1	Nutrition enhanced	Household hunger score
		Proportion of children aged under two years receiving a minimum acceptable diet
SubIR 2.1.2	Agricultural sector growth supported	% increase in yields of crops in target value chains
		Value of incremental sales (collected at farm- level) attributed to FTF implementation
IR 2.2	**Natural Resources Managed Sustainably**	% decrease in deforestation rate in target areas
SubIR 2.2.1	Forest management systems improved	Number of hectares of biological significance and/or natural resources under improved natural resource management as a result of USG assistance
SubIR 2.2.2	Sustainable forestry management enterprises strengthened	Number of people with increased economic benefits derived from sustainable natural resource management and conservation as a result of USG assistance
IR 2.3	**Enabling Environment Supports Private Enterprise Growth**	Number of beneficiaries with improved modem energy services as a result of USG assistance
		Km rural roads maintained by GOL/private sector
		No. of laws and policies implemented to support private enterprise growth thru USG assistance
SubIR 2.3.1	Agricultural sector infrastructure improved and maintained	Kilometers of roads constructed or repaired through USG assistance
SubIR 2.3.2	Improved economic policies implemented	Numerical score on policy matrix

USAID, working with its implementing partners, will identify baseline data, and regularly monitor data on each indicator or track progress and make adjustments as necessary. Specific performance measurements will be identified for achieving targets of each contracting mechanism and a monitoring and evaluation schedule will be set at the time of the award or at a subsequent amendment to the agreement.

Annex 2
Standard Provisions

Table of Contents

Article F: Miscellaneous.

Section F.1. Investment Promotion.

Section F.2. Voluntary Family Planning.

Section F.3. Prohibition on Assistance to Drug Traffickers.

Section F.4. Workers' Rights.

Section F.5 Prohibition on Funding Foreign Government Delegations to International Conferences.

Standard Provisions

Article A: Definitions and Implementation Letters.

Section A.1. Definitions. As used in this Annex, the "Agreement" refers to the Development Objective Agreement to which this Annex is attached and of which this Annex forms a part. Terms used in this Annex have the same meaning or reference as in the Agreement.

Section A.2. Implementation Letters. To assist the Grantee in the implementation of the Agreement, USAID, from time to time, will issue implementation letters ("Implementation Letters") that will furnish additional information about matters stated in this Agreement. The Parties may also issue jointly agreed-upon Implementation Letters to confirm and record their mutual understanding on aspects of the implementation of this Agreement. Implementation Letters can also be issued to record revisions or exceptions which are permitted by the Agreement.

Article B: General Covenants.

Section B.1. Consultation. The Parties will cooperate to assure that the Objective and Program Elements of this Agreement will be accomplished. To this end, the Parties, at the request of either, will exchange views on progress toward the Objective and Program Elements, the performance of obligations under this Agreement, the performance of any consultants, contractors, or suppliers engaged under the Agreement, and other matters relating to the Agreement.

Section B.2. Execution of Agreement. The Grantee will:

(a) Carry out the Agreement and the activities required to be undertaken directly (or caused to be undertaken) by the Grantee, or cause the Agreement and such activities to be carried out with due diligence and efficiency, in conformity with sound technical, financial, and management practices, and in conformity with those documents, plans, specifications, contracts, schedules, or other arrangements, and with any modifications therein, approved by USAID pursuant to this Agreement; and

(b) Provide qualified and experienced management for, and train such staff as may be appropriate for the maintenance and operation of activities financed under the Agreement, and, as applicable for continuing activities, cause those activities to be operated and maintained in such manner as to assure the continuing and successful achievement of the Objective and Program Elements under the Agreement.

Section B.3. Utilization of Goods and Services.

(a) Any goods and services financed under this Agreement, unless otherwise agreed in writing by USAID, will be devoted to the Agreement until the completion or termination of the

Agreement, and thereafter (as well as during any period of suspension of the Agreement) will be used to further the Objective of the Agreement or as USAID may direct in Implementation Letters.

(b) Goods or services financed under this Agreement, except as USAID may otherwise agree in writing, will not be used to promote or assist a foreign aid project or activity associated with or financed by a country not included in USAID Geographic Code 935 as in effect at the time of such use.

Section B.4. Taxation.

(a) General Exemption. The Agreement and the assistance thereunder are free from any taxes imposed under laws in effect in the territory of the Grantee.

(b) Except as provided otherwise in this provision, the General Exemption in subsection (a) applies to, but is not limited to (1) any activity, contract, grant or other implementing agreement financed by USAID under this Agreement; (2) any transaction or supplies, equipment, materials, property or other goods (hereinafter collectively "goods") under (1) above; (3) any contractor, grantee, or other organization carrying out activities financed by USAID under this Agreement; (4) any employee of such organizations; and (5) any individual contractor or grantee carrying out activities financed by USAID under this Agreement.

(c) Except as provided otherwise in this provision, the General Exemption in subsection (a) applies to, but is not limited to, the following taxes:

(1) Exemption 1. Customs duties, tariffs, import taxes, or other levies on the importation, use and re-exportation of goods or the personal belongings and effects (including personally-owned automobiles) for the personal use of non-national individuals or their family members. Exemption 1 includes, but is not limited to, all charges based on the value of such imported goods, but does not include service charges directly related to services performed to transfer goods or cargo.

(2) Exemption 2. Taxes on the income, profits or property of all (i) non-national organizations of any type, (ii) non-national employees of national and non-national organizations, or (iii) non-national individual contractors and grantees. Exemption 2 includes income and social security taxes of all types and all taxes on the property, personal or real, owned by such non-national organizations or persons. The term "national" refers to organizations established under the laws of the Grantee and citizens of the Grantee, other than permanent resident aliens in the United States.

(3) Exemption 3. Taxes levied on the last transaction for the purchase of goods or services financed by USAID under this Agreement, including sales taxes, value-added taxes (VAT), or taxes on purchases or rentals of real or personal property. The term "last transaction" refers to the last transaction by which the goods or services were purchased for use in the activities financed by USAID under this Agreement.

(d) If a tax has been levied and paid contrary to the provisions of an exemption, USAID may, in its discretion, (1) require the Grantee to refund to USAID or to others as USAID may direct the amount of such tax with funds other than those provided under the Agreement, or (2) offset the amount of such tax from amounts to be disbursed under this or any other agreement between the Parties.

(e) In the event of a disagreement about the application of an exemption, the Parties agree to promptly meet and resolve such matters, guided by the principle that the assistance furnished by USAID is free from direct taxation, so that all of the assistance furnished by USAID will contribute directly to the economic development of the country of the Grantee.

Section B.5. Reports and Information, Agreement Books and Records, Audits, and Inspections.

(a) Reports and Information. The Grantee shall furnish USAID accounting records and such other information and reports relating to the Agreement as USAID may reasonably request.

(b) Grantee Agreement Books and Records. The Grantee shall maintain accounting books, records, documents and other evidence relating to the Agreement, adequate to show, without limitation, all costs incurred directly by the Grantee under the Agreement, the receipt and use of goods and services acquired by the Grantee under the Agreement, agreed-upon cost sharing requirements, the nature and extent of solicitations of prospective suppliers of goods and services acquired by the Grantee, the basis of award of contracts and orders made directly by the Grantee, and the overall progress of the Agreement toward completion ("Agreement books and records"). The Grantee shall maintain Agreement books and records in accordance with generally accepted accounting principles prevailing in the United States, or at the Grantee's option, with approval by USAID, other accounting principles, such as those (1) prescribed by the International Accounting Standards Committee (an affiliate of the International Federation of Accountants) or (2) prevailing in the country of the Grantee. Agreement books and records shall be maintained for at least three years after the date of last disbursement by USAID or for such longer period, if any, required to resolve any litigation, claims or audit findings. For the avoidance of doubt, this Section B.5(b) applies solely to Grant funds expended directly by the Grantee.

(c) Grantee Audit. If $300,000 or more of USAID funds are expended directly by the Grantee in its fiscal year under the Agreement, the Grantee shall have financial audits made of the expenditures in accordance with the following terms, except as the Parties may otherwise agree in writing:

(1) With USAID approval, the Grantee shall use its Supreme Audit Institution or select an independent auditor in accordance with the "Guidelines for Financial Audits Contracted by Foreign Recipients" issued by the USAID Inspector General ("Guidelines"), and the audits shall be performed in accordance with the. Guidelines; and

(2) The audit shall determine whether the receipt and expenditure of the funds provided under the Agreement are presented in accordance with generally accepted accounting principles agreed to in subsection (b) above and whether the Grantee has complied with the terms of the Agreement. Each audit shall be completed no later than nine months after the close of the Grantee's year under audit.

(d) Sub-recipient Audits. The Grantee, except as the Parties may otherwise agree in writing, shall submit to USAID, in form and substance satisfactory to USAID, a plan for the audit of the expenditures of "covered" sub-recipients, as defined below, that receive funds in connection with a direct contract or agreement entered into directly with the Grantee pursuant to the activities contemplated by this Agreement.

(1) A "covered" sub-recipient is one who expends $300,000 or more in its fiscal year in "USAID awards" (i.e., as sub-recipients under USAID strategic objective and other grant agreements with foreign governments).

(2) The plan shall describe the methodology to be used by the Grantee to satisfy its audit responsibilities for covered sub-recipients. The Grantee may satisfy such audit responsibilities by relying on independent audits of the sub-recipients; expanding the scope of the independent financial audit of the Grantee to encompass testing of sub-recipients' accounts; or a combination of these procedures.

(3) The plan shall identify the funds made available to covered sub-recipients that will be covered by audits conducted in accordance with other audit provisions that would satisfy the Grantee's audit responsibilities. (A nonprofit organization organized in the United States is required to arrange for its own audits. A for-profit contractor organized in the United States that has a direct contract with USAID is audited by the cognizant U.S. Government Agency. A private voluntary organization organized outside the United States with a direct grant from USAID is required to arrange for its own audits. A host-country contractor should be audited by the Grantee's auditing agency.)

(4) The Grantee shall ensure that covered sub-recipients under direct contracts or agreements with the Grantee take appropriate and timely corrective actions; consider whether sub-recipients' audits necessitate adjustment of its own records; and require each such sub-recipient to permit independent auditors to have access to records and financial statements as necessary.

(e) Audit Reports. The Grantee shall furnish or cause to be furnished to USAID an audit report for each audit arranged for by the Grantee in accordance with this Section within 30 days after completion of the audit and no later than nine months after the end of the period under audit.

(f) Other Covered Sub-recipients. For "covered" sub-recipients who receive funds under the Agreement pursuant to direct contracts or agreements with USAID, USAID will include appropriate audit requirements in such contracts or agreements and will, on behalf of the Grantee, conduct the follow-up activities with regard to the audit reports furnished pursuant to such requirements.

(g) Cost of Audits. Subject to USAID approval in writing, costs of audits performed in accordance with the terms of this Section may be charged to the Agreement.

(h) Audit by USAID. USAID retains the right to perform the audits required under this Agreement on behalf of the Grantee by utilizing funds under the Agreement or other resources available to USAID for this purpose, conduct a financial review, or otherwise ensure accountability of organizations expending USAID funds regardless of the audit requirement.

(i) Opportunity to Audit or Inspect. The Grantee shall afford authorized representatives of USAID the opportunity at all reasonable times to audit or inspect activities financed under the Agreement, the utilization of goods and services financed by USAID, and books, records and other documents relating to the Agreement.

(j) Sub-recipient Books and Records. The Grantee will incorporate paragraphs (a), (b), (d), (e), (g), (h) and (i) of this provision into all sub-agreements with non-U.S. organizations which meet the $300,000 threshold of paragraph (c) of this provision. Sub-agreements with non-U.S. organizations, which do not meet the $300,000 threshold, shall, at a minimum, incorporate paragraphs (h) and (i) of this provision. Sub-agreements with U.S. organizations shall state that the U.S. organization is subject to the audit requirements contained in OMB Circular A-133.

Section B.6. Completeness of Information. The Grantee confirms:

(a) that the facts and circumstances of which it has informed USAID, or caused USAID to be informed, in the course of reaching agreement with USAID on the Agreement, are accurate and complete, and include all facts and circumstances that might materially affect the Agreement and the discharge of responsibilities under this Agreement; and

(b) that it will inform USAID in timely fashion of any subsequent facts and circumstances that might materially affect, or that it is reasonable to believe might so affect, the Agreement or the discharge of responsibilities under this Agreement.

Section B.7. Other Payments. Grantee affirms that no payments have been or will be received by any official of the Grantee in connection with the procurement of goods or services financed under the Agreement, except fees, taxes, or similar payments legally established in the country of the Grantee.

Section B.8. Information and Marking. The Grantee will give appropriate publicity to the Agreement as a program to which the United States has contributed, identify Agreement activity sites, and mark goods financed by USAID, as described in Implementation Letters.

Article C: Procurement Provisions.

Section C.1. Source and Nationality.

C.1. Source and Nationality.

(a) Except as noted herein, or in a sub-agreement issued by USAID, Grant funds will be used to finance the cost of goods and services required for the Agreement in accordance with 22 C.F.R. 228 and having their source, and with respect to suppliers of goods and services, their nationality, in countries included in Geographic Code 937 as in effect at the time orders are placed or contracts entered into for such goods or services except as USAID may otherwise agree in writing and as follows:

(1) Ocean transportation costs shall be financed under the Agreement only on vessels under flag registry of countries included in Code 935. Also see Section C.6 on use of U.S. flag vessels.

(2) The country of the Grantee is an eligible source for foreign exchange cost for marine insurance, if otherwise eligible under Section C.7(a).

(3) Any motor vehicles financed under the Agreement will be of United States manufacture, except as USAID may otherwise agree in writing.

(b) The source and origin of ocean and air shipping will be deemed to be the ocean vessel's or aircraft's country of registry at the time of shipment.

(c) Provisions concerning restricted and ineligible goods and services may be provided in an Implementation Letter.

(d) Transportation by air of property or persons financed under this agreement will be on carriers holding United States certification, to the extent service by such carriers is available under the Fly America Act. This requirement may be further described by USAID in Implementation Letters.

Section C.2. Eligibility Date. No goods or services may be financed under the Agreement which are procured pursuant to orders or contracts firmly placed or entered into prior to the date of this Agreement, except as the Parties may otherwise agree in writing.

Section C.3. Plans, Specifications and Contracts. In order for there to be mutual agreement on the following matters, and except as the Parties may otherwise agree in writing:

(a) The Grantee will furnish to USAID upon preparation:

(1) any plans, specifications, procurement or construction schedules, contracts, or other documentation between the Grantee and third parties, relating to goods or services to be financed under the Agreement, including documentation relating to the prequalification and selection of contractors and to the solicitation of bids and proposals. Material modifications in such documentation will likewise be furnished USAID on preparation; and

(2) such documentation will also be furnished to USAID, upon preparation, relating to any goods or services, which, though not financed under the Agreement, are deemed by USAID to be of major importance to the Agreement. Aspects of the Agreement involving matters under this subsection (a)(2) will be identified in Implementation Letters or Bilateral Project Agreements.

(b) Documents related to the prequalification of contractors, and to the solicitation of bids or proposals for goods and services financed under the Agreement will be approved by USAID in writing prior to their issuance, and their terms will include United States standards and measurements;

(c) Contracts and contractors financed under the Agreement for engineering and other professional services, for construction services, and for such other services, equipment, or materials as may be specified in Implementation Letters, will be approved by USAID in writing prior to execution of the contract. Material modifications in such contracts will also be approved in writing by USAID prior to execution; and

(d) Consulting firms used by the Grantee for the Agreement but not financed under the Agreement, the scope of their services and such of their personnel assigned to activities financed

The attached copy of the Development Objective Assistance Agreement Number 669-DOAG-DO2-12-00 between the United States Agency for International Development (USAID) and the Government of Liberia, is a true copy of the original signed by USAID/Liberia Mission Director Patricia Rader and the Acting Minister of Finance Sebastian Muah.

[Signature]

Djenaba A. Kendrick
Consul
U.S. Embassy Monrovia

Original seen and compared
by a Consular Officer
American Embassy Monrovia

State Department Document Number: 12-166

Development Objective Agreement Between the United States of America and the Republic of Liberia for USAID Development Objective 1: More Effective, Accountable and Inclusive Governance, with Annexes

Signed on September 29, 2012
Entered into force September 29, 2012

CTIA Document Number: 18075.000

USAID Development Objective Agreement No. 669-DOAG-DO1-12-00

DEVELOPMENT OBJECTIVE AGREEMENT

Dated: September 17, 2012

Between

The United States of America, acting through the United States Agency for International Development ("USAID")

and

The Republic of Liberia (hereinafter referred to as the "Grantee")

Article 1: Purpose.

The purpose of this Development Objective Agreement (the "Agreement") is to set out the understanding of the Parties named above (the "Parties") in connection with the Objective described below.

Article 2: Development Objective and Results.

Section 2.1. Development Objective. In order to further the Development Objective "More Effective, Accountable and Inclusive Governance" articulated by the Government of the United States of America in the USAID/Liberia Country Development Cooperation Strategy 2013-2017, the Parties hereto agree to work together by focusing on activities in the areas of Rule of Law and Human Rights, Good Governance, Political Competition and Consensus Building and Civil Society.

Section 2.2. Intermediate Results. In order to achieve the Objective, the Parties agree to work together to achieve the following Intermediate Results:

- Public resources managed more transparently and accountably;
- Improved policies, models and providers increase access to justice;
- Strengthened capacity to implement election processes;
- Civil society and media exercise their advocacy and oversight roles.

Within the limits of the definition of the Development Objective in Section 2.1, this Section 2.2 may be changed by written agreement of the authorized representatives of the Parties without formal amendment of this Agreement.

Section 2.3. Annex 1, Amplified Description. Annex 1, attached, amplifies the above Development Objective and describes the Intermediate Results, Sub-results and Indicators that will be used to measure the progress and achievement of the Objective. Within the limits of the definition of the Development Objective set forth in Section 2.1, Annex 1 may be changed by written agreement of the authorized representatives of the Parties without formal amendment of this Agreement.

Article 3: Contributions of the Parties.

Section 3.1. USAID Contribution.

(a) The Grant. To help achieve the Objective set forth in this Agreement, USAID, pursuant to the Foreign Assistance Act of 1961, as amended, hereby grants to the Grantee under the terms of the Agreement an amount not to exceed THIRTY-FOUR MILLION United States Dollars ($34,000,000).

(b) Total Estimated USAID Contribution. USAID's total estimated contribution to achievement of the Objective will be TWO HUNDRED AND SEVEN MILLION NINE HUNDRED AND FIFTEEN THOUSAND United States Dollars ($207,915,000), which will be provided in increments. Subsequent increments will be subject to the availability of funds to USAID for this purpose and may be provided by USAID upon written notice to the Grantee. The Parties agree that each such incremental contribution provided, if any, shall cumulatively increase the total amount of the Grant set forth in Section 3.1 and consequently may increase the Grantee's contribution under Section 3.2. The Grantee further agrees to acknowledge by written notice to USAID each such incremental contribution, if any.

(c) If at any time USAID determines that its contribution under Section 3.1(a) exceeds the amount which reasonably can be committed for achieving the Objective during the current or next U.S. fiscal year, USAID may, upon written notice to the Grantee, withdraw the excess amount, thereby reducing the amount of the Grant as set forth in Section 3.1(a). Actions taken pursuant to this subsection will not revise USAID's total estimated contribution set forth in 3.1(b).

(d) The Parties agree that USAID's contribution may be disbursed through mechanisms including grants, cooperative agreements, and contracts with non-governmental organizations and private companies in order to carry out the activities described in Annex 1 of this Agreement or described in Implementation Letters issued in accordance with Section A.2 of Annex 2 of this Agreement. The parties further agree that any such implementing partner carrying out activities in furtherance of the Objective shall receive all of the rights, privileges, and other benefits set forth in this Agreement.

Section 3.2. Grantee Contribution.

(a) The Grantee agrees to provide or cause to be provided all funds, in addition to those provided by USAID and any other donor identified in Annex 1, and all other resources required to complete, on or before the Completion Date, all activities necessary to achieve the Objective. The basis for determining the Grantee's contribution and the nature of the contribution will be further described in an Implementation Letter.

(b) The Grantee's financial contributions to the achievement of the Development Objective of this agreement, based on USAID's contribution in Section 3.1(a), will not be less than the equivalent of twenty-five percent of the portion of the Grant that is used to support activities that either directly provide substantial benefit to the Government of the Republic of Liberia or involves the direct and substantial involvement of the Government of the Republic of Liberia in the administration, control or management of such assistance, provided that such amount may be reduced with the written consent of USAID. The Grantee's financial contributions may include either cash or in-kind contributions or both. The dollar equivalent amount of the Grantee's contribution shall be set forth in an Implementation Letter and shall be subsequently included in the Illustrative Financial Plan included in Annex 3 of this Agreement. The amount of the Grantee's contribution shall be adjusted upon any incremental increase in the amount of the Grant set forth in Section 3.1(a), in accordance with the formula described in the first sentence of this paragraph, and the precise amount of such adjustment shall be indicated in an Implementation Letter. The Grantee agrees to maintain a record of its contributions under this Agreement for a period of three years after the Completion Date and will report at least annually in a format to be agreed upon with USAID on its cash and in-kind contributions.

Article 4: Completion Date.

(a) The Completion Date, which is September 30, 2017, or such other date as the Parties may agree to in writing, is the date by which the Parties estimate that all the activities necessary to achieve the Objective will be completed.

(b) Except as USAID may otherwise agree to in writing, USAID will not issue or approve documentation that would authorize disbursement of the Grant for services performed or goods furnished after the Completion Date.

(c) Requests for disbursement, accompanied by necessary supporting documentation prescribed in Implementation Letters, are to be received by USAID no later than nine (9) months before the Completion Date, or such other period as USAID agrees to in writing before or after such period. After such period USAID, at any time or times, may give notice in writing to the Grantee and reduce the amount of the Grant by all or any part thereof for which requests for disbursement, accompanied by necessary supporting documentation prescribed in Implementation Letters, were not received before the expiration of such period.

Article 5: Conditions Precedent to Disbursement.

Section 5.1. First Disbursement. Prior to the first disbursement under the Grant, or to the issuance by USAID of documentation pursuant to which disbursement will be made, the Grantee will, except as the Parties may otherwise agree in writing, furnish to USAID in form and substance satisfactory to USAID:

(a) An opinion of counsel acceptable to USAID that (i) this Agreement has been duly authorized or ratified by, and executed on behalf of the Grantee, (ii) this Agreement constitutes a valid and legally binding obligation of the Grantee in accordance with all of its terms, and (iii) all internal actions and approvals necessary to give effect to this Agreement have been obtained by or on behalf of the Grantee; and

(b) A signed statement in the name of the person holding or acting in the office of the Grantee specified in Section 7.2, which designates by name and title any additional representatives each of whom may act pursuant to Section 7.2.

Section 5.2. Notification. USAID will promptly notify the Grantee when USAID has determined that a condition precedent has been met.

Section 5.3. Terminal Dates for Conditions Precedent.

(a) The terminal date for meeting the conditions specified in Section 5.1 is 60 days from the date of this Agreement or such later date as USAID may agree to in writing before or after the above terminal date. If the conditions precedent in Section 5.1 have not been met by the above terminal date, USAID, at any time, may terminate this Agreement by written notice to the Grantee.

Article 6: Special Covenants.

Section 6.1 The Grantee, in conjunction with the appropriate Government of Liberia Ministries, Agencies and Commissions, hereby covenants and agrees to adopt and implement policies, procedures and systems which are consistent with the Development Objective and conducive to the effective implementation of assistance projects supported by this Grant.

Section 6.2 In addition, the Grantee, in conjunction with the appropriate Government of Liberia Ministries, Agencies and Commissions, covenants and agrees to issue, renew and/or extend free of charge and in a timely manner all official permits, visas, exemptions and any other permissions (including all approvals as may be required from time to time to ensure full access to information, project sites and relevant offices) for the Applicable Persons (as defined below) carrying out activities financed by USAID under this Agreement (collectively, the "Required Documents"). For purposes of these provisions, Applicable Persons is defined as: (1) employees and consultants of any contractors, grantees and other organizations carrying out activities financed by USAID under this Agreement and (b) members of such employees' and consultants' households. Any renewals or extensions of such Required Documents that are required, or become required, in order for such employees, consultants and dependent family members to legally reside in the Republic of Liberia and undertake the activities contemplated by and financed under this Agreement shall also be issued free of charge.

Article 7: Miscellaneous.

Section 7.1. Communications. Any notice, request, document, or other communication submitted by either Party to the other under this Agreement will be in writing and will be deemed duly given or sent when delivered to such Party at the following address:

To USAID:
Mail Address:
Mission Director
United States Agency for International Development
c/o American Embassy
502 Benson St.
Monrovia, Liberia

To Government of Liberia
Mail Address:
Minister
Ministry of Finance
Monrovia, Liberia

All such communications will be in English, unless the Parties otherwise agree in writing. Other contact information may be substituted for the above upon the giving of notice.

Section 7.2. Representatives. For all purposes relevant to this Agreement, the Grantee will be represented by the individual holding or acting in the Office of the Minister of Finance, and USAID will be represented by the individual holding or acting in the Office of the Mission Director, USAID/ Liberia, each of whom, by written notice, may designate additional representatives for all purposes other than signing formal amendments to the Agreement or exercising the power under Sections 2.2 or 2.3 to revise the results to be achieved. The names and titles of the additional representatives of the Grantee will be provided pursuant to Section 5.1(b) to USAID, which may accept as duly authorized any instrument signed by such additional representatives (or any individuals subsequently holding or acting in the office of such representatives) in accordance with this Section 7.2, until receipt of written notice of revocation of their authority.

Section 7.3. Standard Provisions. A "Standard Provisions Annex" (Annex 2) is attached to and forms part of this Agreement.

Section 7.4. Language of Agreement. This Agreement is prepared in English only.

IN WITNESS WHEREOF, the United States of America and the Grantee, each acting through its duly authorized representative, have caused this Agreement to be signed in their names and delivered as of the day and year first above written.

UNITED STATES OF AMERICA	REPUBLIC OF LIBERIA
By:	By:
[Signature]	[Signature]
Name: Patricia Rader	Name: Sebastian Muah
Title: Mission Director	Title: Deputy Minister for Budget/ Acting Minister of Finance
Date: 9/29/12	Date: September 29, 2012

Annex 1
Amplified Description

I. Introduction.

This Annex 1 describes the activities to be undertaken and the progress and achievements to be made with the funds obligated under this Agreement. Nothing in this annex shall be construed as amending any of the definitions or terms of the Agreement.

II. Development Objective and Intermediate Results

Development Objective 1: More Effective, Accountable and Inclusive Governance

Hypothesis: The hypothesis for this Development Objective (DO) is that government institutions must become more effective, accountable, and participatory in order to reverse the destructive legacy of exclusionary politics. This will require sound systems of public administration, competent public sector decision-makers and managers, regular free, fair, and credible elections, peaceful processes for settling disputes, an engaged, active civil society and media, and structures and processes to hold public officials accountable for their actions.

Approach: Activities under DO1 are predominantly focused on long-term capacity building. Capacity building work in this sector will support training, systems development, including information technology to improve management of public resources and service delivery, and organizational strengthening in the priority areas established by the Government of Liberia (GOL) in its National Capacity Development Strategy. USAID will support the GOL's efforts to mobilize and effectively manage public revenues, combat corruption, facilitate the use of alternative dispute resolution in the settlement of disputes over land and other issues, foster constructive, inclusive and participatory political intercourse, and continue to strengthen the electoral process.

USAID/Liberia will also continue to promote capacity-building in local NGOs, the media, and community-based organizations, with the goal of helping these institutions perform a constructive and effective advocacy role in the political process. While prospects for achieving results here are uncertain given the serious shortcomings in the broader non-state sector, the strategic hypothesis is that it is critical to help "grow" this sector as a counterbalance to the historic concentration of power in the executive in Monrovia.

Programs under this DO will be carried out at both national and county levels. At the national level, programs will focus on providing an enabling environment for the DO to be achieved in the six target counties. As the GOL moves forward with political decentralization and deconcentration of public services, USAID will increasingly focus on directly supporting county-level elections and governance of service delivery programs in the six priority counties. USAID will work through the GOL agencies, civil society and media.

Intermediate Results

Intermediate Result 1.1: Public Resources Managed More Transparently and Accountably

Sub IR 1.1.1 – Government of Liberia institutes and utilizes tools of prudent fiscal management

Sub IR 1.1.2 – Increased public and civil society capacity to reduce corruption

Sub IR 1.1.3 – Local systems for governance capacity development strengthened

Intermediate Result 1.2: Improved Policies, Models and Providers Increase Access to Justice

Sub-IR 1.2.1 –Increased capacity of judicial and legal training institutions.

Sub IR 1.2.2 – Formal and informal systems resolve land disputes in an accepted standardized process.

IR 1.3: Strengthened Capacity to Implement Election Processes

Sub IR 1.3.1 – The National Elections Commission (NEC) manages the full election cycle with decreased technical support

Sub IR 1.3.2 – Domestic civil society organizations conduct effective civic and voter education campaigns

IR 1.4: Civil society and media exercise their advocacy and oversight roles

Sub IR 1.4.1 – Civil society strengthened to play a watchdog role

Sub IR 1.4.2 – Increased accuracy and impartiality of target media

III. Funding

Financial Plan. The financial plan for the activities under this Agreement is set forth in the attached Illustrative Financial Plan, Annex 3 to the Agreement. Changes may be made to the Illustrative Financial Plan by representatives of the Parties without formal amendment to the Agreement, if such changes do not cause (1) USAID's contribution to exceed the amount specified in Section 3.1 of the Agreement, or (2) the Grantee's contribution to be less than the amount specified in Section 3.2 of the Agreement.

IV. Roles and Responsibilities of the Parties.

USAID/Liberia

USAID/Liberia will manage and monitor the planned activities in compliance with USAID regulations and procedures. Technical expertise within USAID to advise and direct these efforts will be funded under this Agreement. Additional expertise will be provided in the form of short-term assistance as needed and with the use of funds obligated under this Agreement. USAID will lead the selection of primary implementing partners, in consultation with the Government of Liberia as appropriate

Portfolio review meetings will be held once a year to review objectives, results and activities. Meetings are expected to include the Government of the Republic of Liberia officials, other implementing partners and donors.

Government of Liberia

The Government of Liberia's Ministry of Finance coordinates all activities and is USAID's lead partner in the design and monitoring of activities.

Other key Liberian partners may include the Judicial Institute, the University of Liberia's Louis Arthur Grimes Law School, the Land Commission, the National Elections Commission, the Governance Commission, the Liberia Anti-Corruption Commission, county administrations and selected ministries, agencies and state-owned enterprises the GOL has identified in collaboration with USAID implementing partners. These and other Liberian partners from civil society and the media will benefit from training and technical assistance addressing public resources management, e.g. budget planning, public financial management, logistics, strategic planning, and human resources management, advocacy, information management and data collection, monitoring and evaluation, civic education and participation, leadership, elections administration, implementation of policy reform, rule of law, public outreach, decentralization, the resolution of land and other disputes, policy and regulatory practices, human rights, gender-based violence and mediation, and anti-corruption.

V. Monitoring and Evaluation.

Except as the Parties may otherwise agree in writing, the Parties stipulate that:

a) USAID and its implementing partners will systematically monitor and report progress on performance indicators during the Agreement period; illustrative indicators are described in the table below;

b) Each contract, grant or cooperative agreement awarded under this Agreement will include a performance and monitoring plan that identifies indicators and targets; the USAID team managing this Agreement will review the data collected from implementing partners and the GOL for inclusion in that plan;

c) Independent audits will be funded under each activity according to regulations set forth in the respective agreements with implementing partners;

d) Funds made available under this Agreement may be used for monitoring and evaluation purposes;

e) The strategy baseline survey conducted by USAID at the beginning of this Agreement will serve as a baseline for measuring progress under this Agreement; and

f) The Grantee will ensure that public sector agencies associated with the Agreement undertake reasonable efforts to produce and/or obtain and provide to USAID all data needed to measure performance of activities under the Agreement.

VI. Indicators

USAID will use the following indicators to measure the impact of programs under this Agreement and track progress towards the goal of "More Effective, Accountable and Inclusive Governance". As a group, the indicators capture the intended impact of the development strategy and how this impact will be achieved. Where available USAID will collect baseline values with the assistance of the GOL.

DO1: More Effective, Accountable and Inclusive Governance

- Percent of Ministries and Agencies that have in place expenditure commitment controls that limit commitments to actual cash availability and approved budget allocations
- Corruption perceptions index
- Land policy index

Intermediate Results		**IR Indicators**
IR 1.1	**Public resources managed more transparently and accountably**	Percent of Ministries and Agencies covered by sector strategies with multi-year costs of recurrent and investment expenditure
		Number (or percent) of concessions that are in compliance with the terms of their agreements

Intermediate Results		**IR Indicators**
SubIR 1.1.1	GOL institutes and utilizes tools of prudent fiscal management	Percent of central government entities audited annually, where audits cover revenue, expenditures, assets and liabilities
		Number of central government entities with operational internal audit units
SubIR 1.1.2	Increased public and civil society capacity to reduce corruption	Number of corruption cases referred for prosecution
		Number of corruption cases prosecuted
		Number of corruption cases prosecuted that result in conviction
SubIR 1.1.3	Local systems for governance capacity development strengthened	Number of individuals trained
		Sustainability index for LIPA
IR 1.2	**Improved policies, models and providers increase access to justice**	Number of disputes resolved through ADR
SubIR 1.2.1	Increased capacity of judicial and legal training institutions	Number of new and modified course offerings
		Number of public service system actors trained by JI
		Diversified revenue base
SubIR 1.2.2	Formal and informal systems resolve land disputes in an accepted standardized process	Number of legal and regulatory actions that reform land tenure dispute resolution
		Number of individuals from marginalized groups whose disputes are resolved by USG assistance through ADR
IR 1.3	**Strengthened capacity to implement election processes**	Policy matrix to be developed: Number of revised and new institutional policies and procedures adopted
SubIR 1.3.1	NEC manages full election cycle with decreased technical support	Number of elections infractions reported by CSO observers
SubIR 1.3.2	Domestic CSOs conduct effective civic and voter education campaigns	Number citizens reached through civic and voter education
		Number of domestic monitors trained
IR 1.4	**Civil society and media exercise their advocacy and oversight roles**	Percent of Liberians who report feeling engaged in policy-making
		Amount of airtime community radio stations devote to public affairs programming
SubIR 1.4.1	Civil society strengthened to play watchdog role	Number of CSOs that better understand the policy process (as measured by index)
		Number of CSOs engaging more effectively with government

Intermediate Results		IR Indicators
SubIR 1.4.2	Increased accuracy and impartiality of target media	Percentage of randomly-selected newspaper articles and radio programs that are accurate and impartial (Content analysis)
		Percent of Liberian public who rate media as accurate and impartial (Reader/listener survey)

USAID, working with its implementing partners, will identify baseline data, and regularly monitor data on each indicator or track progress and make adjustments as necessary. Specific performance measurements will be identified for achieving targets of each contracting mechanism and a monitoring and evaluation schedule will be set at the time of the award or at a subsequent amendment to the agreement.

Annex 2
Standard Provisions

Table of Contents

Article F: Miscellaneous.

Section F.1. Investment Promotion.

Section F.2. Voluntary Family Planning.

Section F.3. Prohibition on Assistance to Drug Traffickers.

Section F.4. Workers' Rights.

Section F.5 Prohibition on Funding Foreign Government Delegations to International Conferences.

Standard Provisions

Article A: Definitions and Implementation Letters.

Section A.1. Definitions. As used in this Annex, the "Agreement" refers to the Development Objective Agreement to which this Annex is attached and of which this Annex forms a part. Terms used in this Annex have the same meaning or reference as in the Agreement.

Section A.2. Implementation Letters. To assist the Grantee in the implementation of the Agreement, USAID, from time to time, will issue implementation letters ("Implementation Letters") that will furnish additional information about matters stated in this Agreement. The Parties may also issue jointly agreed-upon Implementation Letters to confirm and record their mutual understanding on aspects of the implementation of this Agreement. Implementation Letters can also be issued to record revisions or exceptions which are permitted by the Agreement.

Article B: General Covenants.

Section B.1. Consultation. The Parties will cooperate to assure that the Objective and Program Elements of this Agreement will be accomplished. To this end, the Parties, at the request of either, will exchange views on progress toward the Objective and Program Elements, the performance of obligations under this Agreement, the performance of any consultants, contractors, or suppliers engaged under the Agreement, and other matters relating to the Agreement.

Section B.2. Execution of Agreement. The Grantee will:

(a) Carry out the Agreement and the activities required to be undertaken directly (or caused to be undertaken) by the Grantee, or cause the Agreement and such activities to be carried out with due diligence and efficiency, in conformity with sound technical, financial, and management practices, and in conformity with those documents, plans, specifications, contracts, schedules, or other arrangements, and with any modifications therein, approved by USAID pursuant to this Agreement; and

(b) Provide qualified and experienced management for, and train such staff as may be appropriate for the maintenance and operation of activities financed under the Agreement, and, as applicable for continuing activities, cause those activities to be operated and maintained in such manner as to assure the continuing and successful achievement of the Objective and Program Elements under the Agreement.

Section B.3. Utilization of Goods and Services.

(a) Any goods and services financed under this Agreement, unless otherwise agreed in writing by USAID, will be devoted to the Agreement until the completion or termination of the

Agreement, and thereafter (as well as during any period of suspension of the Agreement) will be used to further the Objective of the Agreement or as USAID may direct in Implementation Letters.

(b) Goods or services financed under this Agreement, except as USAID may otherwise agree in writing, will not be used to promote or assist a foreign aid project or activity associated with or financed by a country not included in USAID Geographic Code 935 as in effect at the time of such use.

Section B.4. Taxation.

(a) General Exemption. The Agreement and the assistance thereunder are free from any taxes imposed under laws in effect in the territory of the Grantee.

(b) Except as provided otherwise in this provision, the General Exemption in subsection (a) applies to, but is not limited to (1) any activity, contract, grant or other implementing agreement financed by USAID under this Agreement; (2) any transaction or supplies, equipment, materials, property or other goods (hereinafter collectively "goods") under (1) above; (3) any contractor, grantee, or other organization carrying out activities financed by USAID under this Agreement; (4) any employee of such organizations; and (5) any individual contractor or grantee carrying out activities financed by USAID under this Agreement.

(c) Except as provided otherwise in this provision, the General Exemption in subsection (a) applies to, but is not limited to, the following taxes:

(1) Exemption 1. Customs duties, tariffs, import taxes, or other levies on the importation, use and re-exportation of goods or the personal belongings and effects (including personally-owned automobiles) for the personal use of non-national individuals or their family members. Exemption 1 includes, but is not limited to, all charges based on the value of such imported goods, but does not include service charges directly related to services performed to transfer goods or cargo.

(2) Exemption 2. Taxes on the income, profits or property of all (i) non-national organizations of any type, (ii) non-national employees of national and non-national organizations, or (iii) non-national individual contractors and grantees. Exemption 2 includes income and social security taxes of all types and all taxes on the property, personal or real, owned by such non-national organizations or persons. The term "national" refers to organizations established under the laws of the Grantee and citizens of the Grantee, other than permanent resident aliens in the United States.

(3) Exemption 3. Taxes levied on the last transaction for the purchase of goods or services financed by USAID under this Agreement, including sales taxes, value-added taxes (VAT), or taxes on purchases or rentals of real or personal property. The term "last transaction" refers to the last transaction by which the goods or services were purchased for use in the activities financed by USAID under this Agreement.

(d) If a tax has been levied and paid contrary to the provisions of an exemption, USAID may, in its discretion, (1) require the Grantee to refund to USAID or to others as USAID may direct the amount of such tax with funds other than those provided under the Agreement, or (2) offset the amount of such tax from amounts to be disbursed under this or any other agreement between the Parties.

(e) In the event of a disagreement about the application of an exemption, the Parties agree to promptly meet and resolve such matters, guided by the principle that the assistance furnished by USAID is free from direct taxation, so that all of the assistance furnished by USAID will contribute directly to the economic development of the country of the Grantee.

Section B.5. Reports and Information, Agreement Books and Records, Audits, and Inspections.

(a) Reports and Information. The Grantee shall furnish USAID accounting records and such other information and reports relating to the Agreement as USAID may reasonably request.

(b) Grantee Agreement Books and Records. The Grantee shall maintain accounting books, records, documents and other evidence relating to the Agreement, adequate to show, without limitation, all costs incurred directly by the Grantee under the Agreement, the receipt and use of goods and services acquired by the Grantee under the Agreement, agreed-upon cost sharing requirements, the nature and extent of solicitations of prospective suppliers of goods and services acquired by the Grantee, the basis of award of contracts and orders made directly by the Grantee, and the overall progress of the Agreement toward completion ("Agreement books and records"). The Grantee shall maintain Agreement books and records in accordance with generally accepted accounting principles prevailing in the United States, or at the Grantee's option, with approval by USAID, other accounting principles, such as those (1) prescribed by the International Accounting Standards Committee (an affiliate of the International Federation of Accountants) or (2) prevailing in the country of the Grantee. Agreement books and records shall be maintained for at least three years after the date of last disbursement by USAID or for such longer period, if any, required to resolve any litigation, claims or audit findings. For the avoidance of doubt, this Section B.5(b) applies solely to Grant funds expended directly by the Grantee.

(c) Grantee Audit. If $300,000 or more of USAID funds are expended directly by the Grantee in its fiscal year under the Agreement, the Grantee shall have financial audits made of the expenditures in accordance with the following terms, except as the Parties may otherwise agree in writing:

(1) With USAID approval, the Grantee shall use its Supreme Audit Institution or select an independent auditor in accordance with the "Guidelines for Financial Audits Contracted by Foreign Recipients" issued by the USAID Inspector General ("Guidelines"), and the audits shall be performed in accordance with the. Guidelines; and

(2) The audit shall determine whether the receipt and expenditure of the funds provided under the Agreement are presented in accordance with generally accepted accounting principles agreed to in subsection (b) above and whether the Grantee has complied with the terms of the Agreement. Each audit shall be completed no later than nine months after the close of the Grantee's year under audit.

(d) Sub-recipient Audits. The Grantee, except as the Parties may otherwise agree in writing, shall submit to USAID, in form and substance satisfactory to USAID, a plan for the audit of the expenditures of "covered" sub-recipients, as defined below, that receive funds in connection with a direct contract or agreement entered into directly with the Grantee pursuant to the activities contemplated by this Agreement.

(1) A "covered" sub-recipient is one who expends $300,000 or more in its fiscal year in "USAID awards" (i.e., as sub-recipients under USAID strategic objective and other grant agreements with foreign governments).

(2) The plan shall describe the methodology to be used by the Grantee to satisfy its audit responsibilities for covered sub-recipients. The Grantee may satisfy such audit responsibilities by relying on independent audits of the sub-recipients; expanding the scope of the independent financial audit of the Grantee to encompass testing of sub-recipients' accounts; or a combination of these procedures.

(3) The plan shall identify the funds made available to covered sub-recipients that will be covered by audits conducted in accordance with other audit provisions that would satisfy the Grantee's audit responsibilities. (A nonprofit organization organized in the United States is required to arrange for its own audits. A for-profit contractor organized in the United States that has a direct contract with USAID is audited by the cognizant U.S. Government Agency. A private voluntary organization organized outside the United States with a direct grant from USAID is required to arrange for its own audits. A host-country contractor should be audited by the Grantee's auditing agency.)

(4) The Grantee shall ensure that covered sub-recipients under direct contracts or agreements with the Grantee take appropriate and timely corrective actions; consider whether sub-recipients' audits necessitate adjustment of its own records; and require each such sub-recipient to permit independent auditors to have access to records and financial statements as necessary.

(e) Audit Reports. The Grantee shall furnish or cause to be furnished to USAID an audit report for each audit arranged for by the Grantee in accordance with this Section within 30 days after completion of the audit and no later than nine months after the end of the period under audit.

(f) Other Covered Sub-recipients. For "covered" sub-recipients who receive funds under the Agreement pursuant to direct contracts or agreements with USAID, USAID will include appropriate audit requirements in such contracts or agreements and will, on behalf of the Grantee, conduct the follow-up activities with regard to the audit reports furnished pursuant to such requirements.

(g) Cost of Audits. Subject to USAID approval in writing, costs of audits performed in accordance with the terms of this Section may be charged to the Agreement.

(h) Audit by USAID. USAID retains the right to perform the audits required under this Agreement on behalf of the Grantee by utilizing funds under the Agreement or other resources available to USAID for this purpose, conduct a financial review, or otherwise ensure accountability of organizations expending USAID funds regardless of the audit requirement.

(i) Opportunity to Audit or Inspect. The Grantee shall afford authorized representatives of USAID the opportunity at all reasonable times to audit or inspect activities financed under the Agreement, the utilization of goods and services financed by USAID, and books, records and other documents relating to the Agreement.

(j) Sub-recipient Books and Records. The Grantee will incorporate paragraphs (a), (b), (d), (e), (g), (h) and (i) of this provision into all sub-agreements with non-U.S. organizations which meet the $300,000 threshold of paragraph (c) of this provision. Sub-agreements with non-U.S. organizations, which do not meet the $300,000 threshold, shall, at a minimum, incorporate paragraphs (h) and (i) of this provision. Sub-agreements with U.S. organizations shall state that the U.S. organization is subject to the audit requirements contained in OMB Circular A-133.

Section B.6. Completeness of Information. The Grantee confirms:

(a) that the facts and circumstances of which it has informed USAID, or caused USAID to be informed, in the course of reaching agreement with USAID on the Agreement, are accurate and complete, and include all facts and circumstances that might materially affect the Agreement and the discharge of responsibilities under this Agreement; and

(b) that it will inform USAID in timely fashion of any subsequent facts and circumstances that might materially affect, or that it is reasonable to believe might so affect, the Agreement or the discharge of responsibilities under this Agreement.

Section B.7. Other Payments. Grantee affirms that no payments have been or will be received by any official of the Grantee in connection with the procurement of goods or services financed under the Agreement, except fees, taxes, or similar payments legally established in the country of the Grantee.

Section B.8. Information and Marking. The Grantee will give appropriate publicity to the Agreement as a program to which the United States has contributed, identify Agreement activity sites, and mark goods financed by USAID, as described in Implementation Letters.

Article C: Procurement Provisions.

Section C.1. Source and Nationality.

C.1. Source and Nationality.

(a) Except as noted herein, or in a sub-agreement issued by USAID, Grant funds will be used to finance the cost of goods and services required for the Agreement in accordance with 22 C.F.R. 228 and having their source, and with respect to suppliers of goods and services, their nationality, in countries included in Geographic Code 937 as in effect at the time orders are placed or contracts entered into for such goods or services except as USAID may otherwise agree in writing and as follows:

(1) Ocean transportation costs shall be financed under the Agreement only on vessels under flag registry of countries included in Code 935. Also see Section C.6 on use of U.S. flag vessels.

(2) The country of the Grantee is an eligible source for foreign exchange cost for marine insurance, if otherwise eligible under Section C.7(a).

(3) Any motor vehicles financed under the Agreement will be of United States manufacture, except as USAID may otherwise agree in writing.

(b) The source and origin of ocean and air shipping will be deemed to be the ocean vessel's or aircraft's country of registry at the time of shipment.

(c) Provisions concerning restricted and ineligible goods and services may be provided in an Implementation Letter.

(d) Transportation by air of property or persons financed under this agreement will be on carriers holding United States certification, to the extent service by such carriers is available under the Fly America Act. This requirement may be further described by USAID in Implementation Letters.

Section C.2. Eligibility Date. No goods or services may be financed under the Agreement which are procured pursuant to orders or contracts firmly placed or entered into prior to the date of this Agreement, except as the Parties may otherwise agree in writing.

Section C.3. Plans, Specifications and Contracts. In order for there to be mutual agreement on the following matters, and except as the Parties may otherwise agree in writing:

(a) The Grantee will furnish to USAID upon preparation:

(1) any plans, specifications, procurement or construction schedules, contracts, or other documentation between the Grantee and third parties, relating to goods or services to be financed under the Agreement, including documentation relating to the prequalification and selection of contractors and to the solicitation of bids and proposals. Material modifications in such documentation will likewise be furnished USAID on preparation; and

(2) such documentation will also be furnished to USAID, upon preparation, relating to any goods or services, which, though not financed under the Agreement, are deemed by USAID to be of major importance to the Agreement. Aspects of the Agreement involving matters under this subsection (a)(2) will be identified in Implementation Letters or Bilateral Project Agreements.

(b) Documents related to the prequalification of contractors, and to the solicitation of bids or proposals for goods and services financed under the Agreement will be approved by USAID in writing prior to their issuance, and their terms will include United States standards and measurements;

(c) Contracts and contractors financed under the Agreement for engineering and other professional services, for construction services, and for such other services, equipment, or materials as may be specified in Implementation Letters, will be approved by USAID in writing prior to execution of the contract. Material modifications in such contracts will also be approved in writing by USAID prior to execution; and

(d) Consulting firms used by the Grantee for the Agreement but not financed under the Agreement, the scope of their services and such of their personnel assigned to activities financed under the Agreement as USAID may specify, and construction contractors used by the Grantee for the Agreement but not financed under the Agreement, shall be acceptable to USAID.

Section C.4. Reasonable Price. No more than reasonable prices will be paid for any goods or services financed, in whole or in part, under the Agreement. Such items will be procured on a fair and, to the maximum extent practicable, competitive basis.

Section C.5. Notification to Potential Suppliers. To permit all United States firms to have the opportunity to participate in furnishing goods and services to be financed under the Agreement, the Grantee will furnish USAID such information with regard thereto, and at such times, as USAID may request in Implementation Letters.

Section C.6. Transportation

(a) In addition to the requirements in Section C.1(a), costs of ocean or air transportation and related delivery services may not be financed under the Agreement, if the costs are for transportation under an ocean vessel or air charter which has not received prior USAID approval.

(b) Unless USAID determines that privately owned United States-flag commercial ocean vessels are not available at fair and reasonable rates for such vessels, or otherwise agrees in writing:

(1) at least fifty percent (50%) of the gross tonnage of all goods (computed separately for dry bulk carriers, dry cargo liners and tankers) financed by USAID which may be transported on ocean vessels will be transported on privately owned United States-flag commercial vessels; and

(2) at least fifty percent (50%) of the gross freight revenue generated by all shipments financed by USAID and transported to the territory of the Grantee on dry cargo liners shall be paid to or for the benefit of privately owned United States-flag commercial vessels. Compliance with the requirements of (1) and (2) of this subsection must be achieved with respect to both any cargo transported from U.S. ports and any cargo transported from non-U.S. ports, computed separately.

Section C.7. Insurance.

(a) Marine insurance on goods financed by USAID which are to be transported to the territory of the Grantee may be financed as a foreign exchange cost under this Agreement provided

(1) such insurance is placed at the most advantageous competitive rate;

(2) such insurance is placed in a country which is authorized under Section C.1(a); and

(3) claims there under are payable in U.S. dollars or any freely convertible currency unless USAID agrees otherwise in writing.

If the Grantee (or government of the Grantee), by statute, decree, rule, regulation, or practice discriminates with respect to USAID-financed procurement against any marine insurance company authorized to do business in any State of the United States, then all goods shipped to the territory of the Grantee financed by USAID hereunder shall be insured against marine risks and such insurance shall be placed in the United States with a company or companies authorized to do marine insurance business in the United States.

(b) Except as USAID may otherwise agree in writing, the Grantee will insure, or cause to be insured, goods financed under the Agreement imported for the Agreement against risks incident to their transit to the point of their use under the Agreement; such insurance will be issued on terms and conditions consistent with sound commercial practice and will insure the full value of the goods. Any indemnification received by the Grantee under such insurance will be used to replace or repair any material damage or any loss of the goods insured or will be used to reimburse the Grantee for the replacement or repair of such goods. Any such replacement will be of source and origin of countries listed in USAID Geographic Code 935 as in effect at the time of replacement and, except as the Parties may agree in writing, will be otherwise subject to the provisions of the Agreement.

Section C.8. U.S. Government-Owned Excess Property. The Grantee agrees that wherever practicable United States Government-owned excess personal property, in lieu of new items financed under the Agreement, should be utilized. Funds under the Agreement may be used to finance the costs of obtaining such property.

Article D: Disbursements.

Section D.1. Disbursement for Foreign Exchange Costs.

(a) After satisfaction of conditions precedent, if any, the Grantee may obtain disbursements of funds under the Agreement for the foreign exchange costs of goods or services required for the

Agreement in accordance with its terms, by such of the following methods as may be mutually agreed upon:

(1) by submitting to USAID, with necessary supporting documentation as prescribed in Implementation Letters, (A) requests for reimbursement for such goods or services, or, (B) requests for USAID to procure commodities or services in Grantee's behalf for the Agreement; or,

(2) by requesting USAID to issue letters of commitment for specified amounts directly to one or more contractors or suppliers, committing USAID to pay such contractors or suppliers for such goods or services.

(b) Banking charges incurred by the Grantee in connection with letters of commitment will be financed under the Agreement unless the Grantee instructs USAID to the contrary. Such other charges as the Parties may agree to may also be financed under the Agreement.

Section D.2. Disbursement for Local Currency Costs.

(a) After satisfaction of conditions precedent, if any, the Grantee may obtain disbursements of funds under the Agreement for Local Currency Costs required for the Agreement in accordance with terms of this Agreement, by submitting to USAID, with necessary supporting documentation as prescribed in Implementation Letters, requests to finance such costs.

(b) The local currency needed for such disbursements may be purchased by USAID with U.S. Dollars. The U.S. Dollar equivalent of the local currency made available hereunder will be the amount of U.S. Dollars required by USAID to obtain the local currency.

Section D.3. Other Forms of Disbursement. Disbursements may also be made through such other means as the Parties may agree to in writing.

Section D.4. Rate of Exchange. If funds provided under the Agreement are introduced into the Cooperating Country by USAID or any public or private agency for purposes of carrying out obligations of USAID hereunder, the Grantee will make such arrangements as may be necessary so that such funds may be converted into local currency at the highest rate of exchange which, at the time the conversion is made, is not unlawful in the country of the Grantee to any person for any purpose.

Article E: Termination; Remedies.

Section E.1. Suspension and Termination.

(a) Either Party may terminate this Agreement in its entirety by giving the other Party thirty (30) days written notice. USAID also may terminate this Agreement in part by giving the Grantee thirty (30) days written notice, and suspend this Agreement in whole or in part upon giving the Grantee written notice. In addition, USAID may terminate this Agreement in whole or in part, upon giving the Grantee written notice, if (i) the Grantee fails to comply with any provision of this Agreement, (ii) an event occurs that USAID determines makes it improbable that the Objective or Program Elements of the Agreement or the assistance program will be attained or that the Grantee will be able to perform its obligations under this Agreement, or (iii) any disbursement or use of funds in the manner herein contemplated would be in violation of the legislation governing USAID, whether now or hereafter in effect.

(b) Except for payment which the Parties are committed to make pursuant to non-cancellable commitments entered into with third parties prior to such suspension or termination, suspension or termination of this entire Agreement or part thereof will suspend (for the period of the suspension) or terminate, as applicable, any obligation of the Parties to provide financial or other resources to the Agreement, or to the suspended or terminated portion of the Agreement, as applicable. Any portion of this Agreement which is not suspended or terminated shall remain in full force and effect.

(c) In addition, upon such full or partial suspension or termination, USAID may, at USAID's expense, direct that title to goods financed under the Agreement, or under the applicable portion of the Agreement, be transferred to USAID if the goods are in a deliverable state.

Section E.2. Refunds.

(a) In the case of any disbursement which is not supported by valid documentation in accordance with this Agreement, or which is not made or used in accordance with this Agreement, or which was for goods or services not used in accordance with this Agreement, USAID, notwithstanding the availability or exercise of any other remedies under this Agreement, may require the Grantee to refund the amount of such disbursement in U.S. Dollars to USAID within sixty (60) days after receipt of a request therefore.

(b) If the failure of Grantee to comply with any of its obligations under this Agreement has the result that goods or services financed or supported under the Agreement are not used effectively in accordance with this Agreement, USAID may require the Grantee to refund all or any part of the amount of the disbursements under this Agreement for or in connection with such goods or services in U.S. Dollars to USAID within sixty (60) days after receipt of a request therefore.

(c) The right under subsections (a) or (b) to require a refund of a disbursement will continue, notwithstanding any other provision of this Agreement, for three years from the date of the last disbursement under this Agreement.

(d) (1) Any refunds under subsections (a) or (b), or (2) any refund to USAID from a contractor, supplier, bank or other third party with respect to goods or services financed under the Agreement, which refund relates to an unreasonable price for or erroneous invoicing of goods or services, or to goods that did not conform to specifications, or to services that were inadequate, will (A) be made available first for the Agreement, to the extent justified, and (B) the remainder, if any, will be applied to reduce the amount of the Grant.

(e) Any interest or other earnings on funds disbursed by USAID to the Grantee under this Agreement prior to the authorized use of such funds for the Agreement will be returned to USAID in U.S. Dollars by the Grantee, unless USAID otherwise agrees in writing.

Section E.3. Non-waiver of Remedies. No delay in exercising any right or remedy accruing to a Party in connection with its financing under this Agreement will be construed as a waiver of such right or remedy.

Section E.4. Assignment. The Grantee agrees, upon request, to execute an assignment to USAID of any cause of action which may accrue to the Grantee in connection with or arising out of the contractual performance or breach of performance by a Party to a direct U.S. Dollar contract which USAID financed in whole or in part out of funds granted by USAID under this Agreement.

Article F: Miscellaneous.

Section F.1. Investment Promotion.

(a) Except as specifically set forth in the Agreement or otherwise authorized by USAID in writing, no funds or other support provided hereunder may be used for any activity that involves investment promotion in a foreign country.

(b) In the event the Grantee is requested or wishes to provide assistance in the above area or requires clarification from USAID as to whether the activity would be consistent with the limitation set forth above, the Grantee must notify USAID and provide a detailed description of the proposed activity. The Grantee must not proceed with the activity until advised by USAID that it may do so.

(c) The Grantee must ensure that its employees and subcontractors and sub-recipients providing investment promotion services hereunder are made aware of the restrictions set forth in this clause and must include this clause in all subcontracts and other sub-agreements entered into hereunder.

Section F.2. Voluntary Family Planning.

The Parties agree that all USAID funds provided under this Agreement shall be used in accordance with applicable United States policy and statutory requirements relating to voluntary family planning projects, and that none of the USAID funds provided under this Agreement, or goods or services financed by such funds, may be used for:

(a) the performance of abortion as a method of family planning or to motivate or coerce any person to practice abortions;

(b) the performance of involuntary sterilizations as a method of family planning or to coerce or provide any financial incentive to any person to undergo sterilizations; or

(c) any biomedical research which relates, in whole or in part, to methods of, or the performance of, abortions or involuntary sterilizations as a method family planning.

(d) USAID will issue implementation letters that more fully describe the requirements of this section.

Section F.3. Prohibition on Assistance to Drug Traffickers.

(a) USAID reserves the right to terminate this Agreement or take other appropriate measures if the Grantee or a key individual of the Grantee is found to have been convicted of a narcotics offense or to have been engaged in drug trafficking as defined in 22 CFR Part 140.

(b) USAID reserves the right to terminate assistance to, or take or take other appropriate measures with respect to, any participant approved by USAID who is found to have been convicted of a narcotics offense or to have been engaged in drug trafficking as defined in 22 CFR Part 140.

Section F.4. Workers' Rights.

(a) Except as specifically set forth in the Agreement or otherwise authorized by USAID in writing, no funds or other support provided hereunder may be used for any activity that involves workers' rights in a foreign country.

(b) In the event the Grantee is requested or wishes to provide assistance in the above area or requires clarification from USAID as to whether the activity would be consistent with the limitation set forth above, the Grantee must notify the USAID and provide a detailed description of the proposed activity. The Grantee must not proceed with the activity until advised by USAID that it may do so.

(c) The Grantee must ensure that all employees and subcontractors and sub-recipients providing employment-related services hereunder are made aware of the restrictions set forth in this clause and must include this clause in all subcontracts and other sub-agreements entered into hereunder.

Section F.5. Prohibition on Funding Foreign Government Delegations to International Conferences. Except as USAID may otherwise agree in writing, funds obligated under this Agreement may not be used to finance the travel, per diem, hotel expenses, meals, conference fees or other conference costs for any member of a foreign government's delegation to an international conference sponsored by a public international organization. This restriction may be further described by USAID in Implementation Letters.

Annex 3
Illustrative Financial Plan

Program Area		Program Element		This Obligation FY 2012	Estimated Future Obligations	Total Planned Funding Level
				US$	US$	US$
Development Objective Agreement						
A07	**Rule of Law and Human Rights**			**6,000,000**	**29,020,000**	**35,020,000**
		A031	Justice System	6,000,000		
A08	**Good Governance**			**18,000,000**	**97,045,000**	**115,045,000**
		A035	Public Sector Executive Function	10,000,000		
		A036	Local Government and Decentralization	4,000,000		
		A037	Anti-Corruption Reforms	4,000,000		
		A140 A141	Program Design and Learning; Administration and Oversight			
A09	**Political Competition and Consensus-Building**			**6,000,000**	**27,440,000**	**33,440,000**
		A041	Elections and Political Processes	5,250,000		
		A140 A141	Program Design and Learning; Administration and Oversight	750,000		
A10	**Civil Society**			**4,000,000**	**20,410,000**	**24,410,000**
		A044	Civic Participation	2,880,000		
		A045	Media Freedom and Freedom of Information	1,120,000		
		A140 A141	Program Design and Learning; Administration and Oversight			
	Total Development Objective Agreement			**34,000,000**	**173,915,000**	**207,915,000**
				This Obligation FY 2012	**Estimated Future Obligations**	**Total Planned Funding Level**
				US$	**US$**	**US$**
			Total USG Contribution	**34,000,000**	**173,915,000**	**207,915,000**

Program Area		Program Element		This Obligation FY 2012	Estimated Future Obligations	Total Planned Funding Level
				US$	US$	US$
Government of the Republic of Liberia Contribution to the Development Objective 1 Agreement				In Support of FY 2012 Obligations	Estimated Support for Future Obligations	Total Planned Contribution
				US$	US$	US$
			Total Expected GOL Contribution	8,500,000	43,478,750	51,978,750

The attached copy of the Development Objective Assistance Agreement Number 669-DOAG-DO1-12-00 between the United States Agency for International Development (USAID) and the Government of Liberia, is a true copy of the original signed by USAID/Liberia Mission Director Patricia Rader and the Acting Minister of Finance Sebastian Muah.

[Signature]

Djaraba A. Kendrick
Consul
U.S. Embassy Monrovia

Original seen and compared
by a Consular Officer
American Embassy Monrovia

STATE DEPARTMENT DOCUMENT NUMBER: 12-167

DEVELOPMENT OBJECTIVE AGREEMENT BETWEEN THE UNITED STATES OF AMERICA AND THE REPUBLIC OF LIBERIA FOR USAID DEVELOPMENT OBJECTIVE 4: BETTER-EDUCATED LIBERIANS, WITH ANNEXES

SIGNED ON SEPTEMBER 29, 2012
ENTERED INTO FORCE SEPTEMBER 29, 2012

CTIA DOCUMENT NUMBER: 18076.000

USAID Development Objective Agreement No. 669-DOAG-DO4-12-00

DEVELOPMENT OBJECTIVE AGREEMENT

Dated: September 17, 2012

Between

The United States of America, acting through the United States Agency for International Development ("USAID")

and

The Republic of Liberia (hereinafter referred to as the "Grantee")

Article 1: Purpose.

The purpose of this Development Objective Agreement (the "Agreement") is to set out the understanding of the Parties named above (the "Parties") in connection with the Objective described below.

Article 2: Development Objective and Results.

Section 2.1. Development Objective. In order to further the Development Objective "Better-Educated Liberians" articulated by the Government of the United States of America in the USAID/Liberia Country Development Cooperation Strategy 2013-2017, the Parties hereto agree to work together by focusing on activities in Basic and Higher Education.

Section 2.2. Intermediate Results. In order to achieve the Objective, the Parties agree to work together to achieve the following results:

- Improved basic education opportunities;
- Improved higher education opportunities.

Within the limits of the definition of the Development Objective in Section 2.1, this Section 2.2 may be changed by written agreement of the authorized representatives of the Parties without formal amendment of this Agreement.

Section 2.3. Annex 1, Amplified Description. Annex 1, attached, amplifies the above Objective and describes the Intermediate Results, Sub-results and Indicators that will be used to measure the progress and achievement of the Objective. Within the limits of the definition of the Development Objective set forth in Section 2.1, Annex 1 may be changed by written agreement of the authorized representatives of the Parties without formal amendment of this Agreement.

Article 3: Contributions of the Parties.

Section 3.1. USAID Contribution.

(a) The Grant. To help achieve the Objective set forth in this Agreement, USAID, pursuant to the Foreign Assistance Act of 1961, as amended, hereby grants to the Grantee under the terms of the Agreement an amount not to exceed THIRTY-TWO MILLION FIVE HUNDRED THOUSAND United States Dollars ($32,500,000).

(b) Total Estimated USAID Contribution. USAID's total estimated contribution to achievement of the Objective will be ONE HUNDRED AND SEVENTY-TWO MILLION THREE HUNDRED AND EIGHTY-SEVEN THOUSAND AND TWENTY United States Dollars ($172,387,020), which will be provided in increments. Subsequent increments will be subject to the availability of funds to USAID for this purpose and may be provided by USAID upon written notice to the Grantee. The Parties agree that each such incremental contribution provided, if any, shall cumulatively increase the total amount of the Grant set forth in Section 3.1 and consequently may increase the Grantee's contribution under Section 3.2. The Grantee further agrees to acknowledge by written notice to USAID each such incremental contribution, if any.

(c) If at any time USAID determines that its contribution under Section 3.1 (a) exceeds the amount which reasonably can be committed for achieving the Objective during the current or next U.S. fiscal year, USAID may, upon written notice to the Grantee, withdraw the excess amount, thereby reducing the amount of the Grant as set forth in Section 3.1(a). Actions taken pursuant to this subsection will not revise USAID's total estimated contribution set forth in 3.1(b).

(d) The Parties agree that USAID's contribution may be disbursed through mechanisms including grants, cooperative agreements, and contracts with non-governmental organizations and private companies in order to carry out the activities described in Annex 1 of this Agreement or described in Implementation Letters issued in accordance with Section A.2 of Annex 2 of this Agreement. The parties further agree that any such implementing partner carrying out activities in furtherance of the Objective shall receive all of the rights, privileges, and other benefits set forth in this Agreement.

Section 3.2. Grantee Contribution.

(a) The Grantee agrees to provide or cause to be provided all funds, in addition to those provided by USAID and any other donor identified in Annex 1, and all other resources required to complete, on or before the Completion Date, all activities necessary to achieve the Objective. The basis for determining the Grantee's contribution and the nature of the contribution will be further described in an Implementation Letter.

(b) The Grantee's financial contributions to the achievement of this Development Objective, based on USAID's contribution in Section 3.1(a), will not be less than the equivalent of twenty-five percent of the portion of the Grant that is used to support activities that either directly provide substantial benefit to the Government of the Republic of Liberia or involve the direct and substantial involvement of the Government of the Republic of Liberia in the administration, control or management of such assistance, provided that such amount may be reduced with the written consent of USAID. The Grantee's financial contributions may include either cash or in-kind contributions or both. The dollar equivalent amount of the Grantee's contribution shall be set forth in an Implementation Letter and shall be subsequently included in the Illustrative Financial Plan included in Annex 3 of this Agreement. The amount of the Grantee's contribution shall be adjusted upon any incremental increase in the amount of the Grant set forth in Section 3.1(a), in accordance with the formula described in the first sentence of this paragraph, and the precise amount of such adjustment shall be indicated in an Implementation Letter. The Grantee agrees to maintain a record of its contributions under this Agreement for a period of three years after the Completion Date and will report at least annually in a format to be agreed upon with USAID on its cash and in-kind contributions.

Article 4: Completion Date.

(a) The Completion Date, which is September 30, 2017, or such other date as the Parties may agree to in writing, is the date by which the Parties estimate that all the activities necessary to achieve the Objective will be completed.

(b) Except as USAID may otherwise agree to in writing, USAID will not issue or approve documentation that would authorize disbursement of the Grant for services performed or goods furnished after the Completion Date.

(c) Requests for disbursement, accompanied by necessary supporting documentation prescribed in Implementation Letters, are to be received by USAID no later than nine (9) months before the Completion Date, or such other period as USAID agrees to in writing before or after such period. After such period USAID, at any time or times, may give notice in writing to the Grantee and reduce the amount of the Grant by all or any part thereof for which requests for disbursement, accompanied by necessary supporting documentation prescribed in Implementation Letters, were not received before the expiration of such period.

Article 5: Conditions Precedent to Disbursement.

Section 5.1. First Disbursement. Prior to the first disbursement under the Grant, or to the issuance by USAID of documentation pursuant to which disbursement will be made, the Grantee will, except as the Parties may otherwise agree in writing, furnish to USAID in form and substance satisfactory to USAID:

(a) An opinion of counsel acceptable to USAID that (i) this Agreement has been duly authorized or ratified by, and executed on behalf of the Grantee, (ii) this Agreement constitutes a valid and legally binding obligation of the Grantee in accordance with all of its terms, and (iii) all internal actions and approvals necessary to give effect to this Agreement have been obtained by or on behalf of the Grantee; and

(b) A signed statement in the name of the person holding or acting in the office of the Grantee specified in Section 7.2, which designates by name and title any additional representatives each of whom may act pursuant to Section 7.2.

Section 5.2. Notification. USAID will promptly notify the Grantee when USAID has determined that a condition precedent has been met.

Section 5.3. Terminal Dates for Conditions Precedent.

The terminal date for meeting the conditions specified in Section 5.1 is 60 days from the date of this Agreement or such later date as USAID may agree to in writing before or after the above terminal date. If the conditions precedent in Section 5.1 have not been met by the above terminal date, USAID, at any time, may terminate this Agreement by written notice to the Grantee.

Article 6: Special Covenants.

Section 6.1 The Grantee, in conjunction with the appropriate Government of Liberia Ministries, Agencies and Commissions, hereby covenants and agrees to adopt and implement policies, procedures and systems which are consistent with the Development Objective and conducive to the effective implementation of assistance projects supported by this Grant.

Section 6.2 In addition, the Grantee, in conjunction with the appropriate Government of Liberia Ministries, Agencies and Commissions, covenants and agrees to issue, renew and/or extend free of charge and in a timely manner all official permits, visas, exemptions and any other permissions (including all approvals as may be required from time to time to ensure full access to information, project sites and relevant offices) for the Applicable Persons (as defined below) carrying out activities financed by USAID under this Agreement (collectively, the "Required Documents"). For purposes of these provisions, Applicable Persons is defined as: (1) employees and consultants of any contractors, grantees and other organizations carrying out activities financed by USAID under this Agreement and (b) members of such employees' and consultants' households. Any renewals or extensions of such Required Documents that are required, or become required, in order for such employees, consultants and dependent family members to legally reside in the Republic of Liberia and undertake the activities contemplated by and financed under this Agreement shall also be issued free of charge.

Article 7: Miscellaneous.

Section 7.1. Communications. Any notice, request, document, or other communication submitted by either Party to the other under this Agreement will be in writing and will be deemed duly given or sent when delivered to such Party at the following address:

To USAID:
Mail Address:
Mission Director
United States Agency for International Development
c/o American Embassy
502 Benson St.
Monrovia, Liberia

To Government of Liberia
Mail Address:
Minister
Ministry of Finance
Monrovia, Liberia

All such communications will be in English, unless the Parties otherwise agree in writing. Other contact information may be substituted for the above upon the giving of notice.

Section 7.2. Representatives. For all purposes relevant to this Agreement, the Grantee will be represented by the individual holding or acting in the Office of the Minister of Finance and USAID will be represented by the individual holding or acting in the Office of the Mission Director, each of whom, by written notice, may designate additional representatives for all purposes other than signing formal amendments to the Agreement. The names and titles of the additional representatives of the Grantee will be provided pursuant to Section 5.1(b) to USAID, which may accept as duly authorized any instrument signed by such additional representatives (or any individuals subsequently holding or acting in the office of such representatives) in accordance with this Section 7.2, until receipt of written notice of revocation of their authority.

Section 7.3. Standard Provisions. A "Standard Provisions Annex" (Annex 2) is attached to and forms part of this Agreement.

Section 7.4. Language of Agreement. This Agreement is prepared in English only.

IN WITNESS WHEREOF, the United States of America and the Grantee, each acting through its duly authorized representative, have caused this Agreement to be signed in their names and delivered as of the day and year first above written.

UNITED STATES OF AMERICA	REPUBLIC OF LIBERIA
By:	By:
[Signature]	[Signature]
Name: Patricia Rader	Name: Sebastian Muah
Title: Mission Director	Title: Deputy Minister for Budget/ Acting Minister of Finance
Date:	Date:
9/29/12	September 29, 2012

Annex 1
Amplified Description

I. Introduction.

This Annex 1 describes the activities to be undertaken and the progress and achievements to be made with the funds obligated under this Agreement. Nothing in this annex shall be construed as amending any of the definitions or terms of the Agreement.

II. Development Objective and Intermediate Results

Development Objective 4: Better Educated Liberians

Hypothesis: USAID/Liberia aims to increase educational achievement in Liberia by improving the educational opportunities provided to Liberian children, youth, and young adults. To achieve this will require: first, getting more children and youth, especially girls and young women in the rural areas, into primary schools and alternative basic education programs and keeping them there; and second, improving the quality of the education they receive.

The development hypothesis underpinning USAID's education program is that by increasing the number of trained teachers in Liberian schools, improving teachers' and pupils' access to modem pedagogical resources and tools and safe learning environments, and systemically strengthening the management and oversight of Liberia's educational system as a whole, more children and youth will attend and complete primary school or alternative basic education programs. Through improved instruction, especially in reading, these pupils will acquire the foundational skills they need to succeed at higher levels of schooling. USAID also hypothesizes that, through these improvements in basic education, youth and adults coming out of higher levels of the Liberian educational system will have acquired cognitive and life skills that will help to improve health results for themselves and their households, increase their potential economic productivity and employability, strengthen their ability and desire to participate constructively in the democratic process, and otherwise improve their living standards and quality of life.

As mentioned above, low age-appropriate enrollments represent a serious problem in Liberia, and the factors which contribute to this pattern are not clearly understood. USAID/Liberia's hypothesis is that, in response to tangible improvements in the availability and quality of educational services, parents will be more willing to enroll their children as soon as they are eligible to begin school and keep their children in school longer. This hypothesis will be closely studied during the initial period of this strategy. In the event that the program interventions are not having the desired effect on enrollment and retention rates, USAID will explore alternative approaches.

At the tertiary level, Liberia's ability to direct its own development, and succeed in an increasingly competitive global economy largely depends on the quality and relevance of professional and technical education and training. The sheer magnitude of the gap between demand for, and supply of, qualified professionals would make it prohibitively expensive to attempt to fill these gaps by sending students outside Liberia. Therefore, tertiary education institutions must be strengthened within Liberia.

In this context, the development hypothesis underpinning USAID's investments in tertiary education is that unmet demands for professional and technical graduates in agriculture, engineering, health care, and education can be better filled by strengthening Liberian universities so that these local institutions can increase equitable access for and offer high quality advanced education and training to capable secondary school graduates.

Approach: USAID will take a two-track approach to achieve our objective in education, supporting direct interventions to boost educational access and outcomes in selected counties in the shorter term, while also building the capacity of the Ministry of Education (MOE) and the educational system in general to deliver more effective and efficient educational services on a sustained basis over the longer term. Direct, short-term interventions will include rapid dissemination of improved curricula, teaching and learning materials and other pedagogical resources and tools, and public outreach and stakeholder engagement to promote increased enrollment, retention and learning outcomes, particularly for girls. Medium- and long-term capacity development work in this sector will focus on teachers' professional development, management and curricular reforms, and improving MOE decision-making, planning and policy development, accountability, community outreach and engagement, management and administration, and monitoring and evaluation capabilities.

USAID's capacity development efforts will support decentralization of decision-making, management, and administration of the education system. Decentralization of education services can lead to greater community engagement by bringing education decision-making closer to the people and strengthening accountability in the use of education funds. USAID expects that greater community engagement in the learning process will improve student enrollment and the quality of basic education services.

Higher education programs under this DO will focus on expanding access to education opportunities for young adults. Active recruitment for pre-service teacher training, as well as participation in USAID-supported higher education programs, will be carried out throughout the country. MOE systems reforms, including information and resource management, are national in scope.

The principal beneficiaries of USAID's education program in Liberia will be basic education-level school children, over-age and out-of-school youth and young adults (including ex-combatants), students enrolled in tertiary education programs, in-service and teachers in training, and administrators within Liberia's educational system, at central, county and community levels. In all of these categories, we will particularly seek to engage girls and women, and promote their increased participation in and contributions to the development of Liberia's educational system.

Details of Intermediate Results and Illustrative Activities

Intermediate Result 4.1: Improved Basic Education Opportunities.

Sub IR 4.1.1 - Improved quality
Sub IR 4.1.2 - Increased equitable access
Sub IR 4.1.3 - Strengthened human and institutional capacity

Intermediate Result 4.2: Improved Higher Education Opportunities

Sub IR 4.2.1 - Improved quality
Sub IR 4.2.2 - Increased equitable access
Sub IR 4.2.3 - Strengthened human and institutional capacity

III. Funding.

Financial Plan. The financial plan for the activities under this Agreement is set forth in the attached Illustrative Financial Plan, Annex 3 to the Agreement. Changes may be made to the Illustrative Financial Plan by representatives of the Parties without formal amendment to the Agreement, if such changes do not cause (1) USAID's contribution to exceed the amount specified in Section 3.1 of the Agreement, or (2) the Grantee's contribution to be less than the amount specified in Section 3.2 of the Agreement.

IV. Roles and Responsibilities of the Parties.

USAID/Liberia

USAID/Liberia will manage and monitor the planned activities in compliance with USAID regulations and procedures. Technical expertise within USAID to advise and direct these efforts will be funded under this Agreement. Additional expertise will be provided in the form of short-term assistance as needed and with the use of funds obligated under this Agreement. USAID will lead the selection of the primary implementing partners in consultation with the Ministry of Education.

Portfolio review meetings will be held once a year to review objectives, results and activities. Meetings are expected to include the Government of the Republic of Liberia officials, other implementing partners and donors.

Government of Liberia

The Government of Liberia's Ministry of Finance coordinates all activities and is USAID's lead partner in the planning and monitoring of project activities.

The Government of Liberia's Ministry of Education serves as USAID's lead partner for activities under this Development Objective in the technical design, monitoring and coordination of project activities. The Ministry of Education convenes monthly donor coordination meetings to present strategic issues and outline key priorities, and chairs monthly implementing partner meetings to keep all stakeholders informed of new developments.

The Ministry of Education of the Government of Liberia will provide access to critical national educational data so as to provide insight into local and national realities and facilitate program monitoring and evaluation.

V. Monitoring and Evaluation.

Except as the Parties may otherwise agree in writing, the Parties stipulate that:

a) USAID and its implementing partners will systematically monitor and report progress on performance indicators during the Agreement period; illustrative indicators are described in the table below;

b) Each contract, grant or cooperative agreement awarded under this Agreement will include a performance and monitoring plan that identifies indicators and targets; the USAID team managing this Agreement will review the data collected from implementing partners and the GOL for inclusion in that plan;

c) Independent audits will be funded under each activity according to regulations set forth in the respective agreements with implementing partners;

d) Funds made available under this Agreement may be used for monitoring and evaluation purposes;

e) The strategy baseline survey conducted by USAID at the beginning of this Agreement will serve as a baseline for measuring progress under this Agreement; and

f) The Grantee will ensure that public sector agencies associated with the Agreement undertake reasonable efforts to produce and/or obtain and provide to USAID all data needed to measure performance of activities under the Agreement.

VI. Indicators

USAID will use the following indicators to measure the impact of programs under this Agreement and track progress towards the goal of "Better-Educated Liberians". As a group, the indicators capture the intended impact of the development strategy and how this impact will be achieved. Where available USAID will collect baseline values with the assistance of the GOL.

DO4: Better-Educated Liberians

- Proportion of students who, by the end of two grades of primary schooling, demonstrate that they can read and understand the meaning of grade level text
- Women's literacy rate (ages 15-34)
- Percentage change in Primary Net Enrollment Ratio (Gross)
- Girls' Gross Primary Completion ratio (Net)

Intermediate Results		**IR Indicators**
IR 4.1	**Improved basic education opportunities**	Proportion of students who after two/three years of schooling reach benchmark in reading fluency due to USG interventions
		% of trained public primary education school teachers
		% of youth in USG-supported alternative basic education programs who transit to post-program academic or livelihood options
SubIR 4.1.1	Improved quality	Number of learners receiving USG supported reading interventions at the primary level
		Number of textbooks and other teaching and learning materials (TLM) provided with USG assistance
		Number of teachers, administrators and officials trained in improved reading/ classroom instructional delivery
SubIR 4.1.2	Increased equitable access	Number of learners enrolled in primary schools and/or equivalent non-school based settings
		Gender Parity Index
		Number of teachers in USG supported programs trained on how to support learners' psychosocial well-being
SubIR 4.1.3	Strengthened institutional capacity	MOE institutional capacity index
		# of laws, policies, regulations, or guidelines developed or modified to improve primary grade reading programs or increase equitable access
		Number of PTAs or similar school governance structures supported

Intermediate Results		IR Indicators
IR 4.2	**Improved higher education opportunities**	Percentage of USG-supported graduates from tertiary education programs reporting themselves as employed
		Number of individuals from underserved and/or disadvantaged groups accessing tertiary education programs
SubIR 4.2.1	Improved quality	Number of USG-funded tertiary education programs that include experiential and/or applied learning opportunities
		Number of USG-supported tertiary programs with curricula revised with private and/or public sector employers' input or on the basis of market research
		Number of tertiary institution faculty or teaching staff whose qualifications are strengthened through USG-supported tertiary education programs
SubIR 4.2.2	Increased equitable access	Number of students awarded merit and need-based scholarships to study in tertiary programs that support country development goals
		Number of students who participate in internships through linkages with private and public entities
SubIR 3.2.3	Strengthened institutional capacity	# of USG-supported tertiary educational programs that develop or implement industry-recognized skills certification
		Number of USG-supported organizational improvements that strengthen the institutional capacity of host-country tertiary institutions

Progress toward achieving the Development Objective "Better-Educated Liberians" will be measured against indicators such as those listed in this Agreement. USAID, working with its implementing partners, will identify baseline data, and regularly monitor data on each indicator or track progress and make adjustments as necessary. Specific performance measurements will be identified for achieving targets of each implementation mechanism and a monitoring and evaluation schedule will be set at the time of the award or at a subsequent amendment to the agreement.

Annex 2
Standard Provisions

Table of Contents

Article F: Miscellaneous.

Section F.1. Investment Promotion.

Section F.2. Voluntary Family Planning.

Section F.3. Prohibition on Assistance to Drug Traffickers.

Section F.4. Workers' Rights.

Section F.5 Prohibition on Funding Foreign Government Delegations to International Conferences.

Standard Provisions

Article A: Definitions and Implementation Letters.

Section A.1. Definitions. As used in this Annex, the "Agreement" refers to the Development Objective Agreement to which this Annex is attached and of which this Annex forms a part. Terms used in this Annex have the same meaning or reference as in the Agreement.

Section A.2. Implementation Letters. To assist the Grantee in the implementation of the Agreement, USAID, from time to time, will issue implementation letters ("Implementation Letters") that will furnish additional information about matters stated in this Agreement. The Parties may also issue jointly agreed-upon Implementation Letters to confirm and record their mutual understanding on aspects of the implementation of this Agreement. Implementation Letters can also be issued to record revisions or exceptions which are permitted by the Agreement.

Article B: General Covenants.

Section B.1. Consultation. The Parties will cooperate to assure that the Objective and Program Elements of this Agreement will be accomplished. To this end, the Parties, at the request of either, will exchange views on progress toward the Objective and Program Elements, the performance of obligations under this Agreement, the performance of any consultants, contractors, or suppliers engaged under the Agreement, and other matters relating to the Agreement.

Section B.2. Execution of Agreement. The Grantee will:

(a) Carry out the Agreement and the activities required to be undertaken directly (or caused to be undertaken) by the Grantee, or cause the Agreement and such activities to be carried out with due diligence and efficiency, in conformity with sound technical, financial, and management practices, and in conformity with those documents, plans, specifications, contracts, schedules, or other arrangements, and with any modifications therein, approved by USAID pursuant to this Agreement; and

(b) Provide qualified and experienced management for, and train such staff as may be appropriate for the maintenance and operation of activities financed under the Agreement, and, as applicable for continuing activities, cause those activities to be operated and maintained in such manner as to assure the continuing and successful achievement of the Objective and Program Elements under the Agreement.

Section B.3. Utilization of Goods and Services.

(a) Any goods and services financed under this Agreement, unless otherwise agreed in writing by USAID, will be devoted to the Agreement until the completion or termination of the

Agreement, and thereafter (as well as during any period of suspension of the Agreement) will be used to further the Objective of the Agreement or as USAID may direct in Implementation Letters.

(b) Goods or services financed under this Agreement, except as USAID may otherwise agree in writing, will not be used to promote or assist a foreign aid project or activity associated with or financed by a country not included in USAID Geographic Code 935 as in effect at the time of such use.

Section B.4. Taxation.

(a) General Exemption. The Agreement and the assistance thereunder are free from any taxes imposed under laws in effect in the territory of the Grantee.

(b) Except as provided otherwise in this provision, the General Exemption in subsection (a) applies to, but is not limited to (1) any activity, contract, grant or other implementing agreement financed by USAID under this Agreement; (2) any transaction or supplies, equipment, materials, property or other goods (hereinafter collectively "goods") under (1) above; (3) any contractor, grantee, or other organization carrying out activities financed by USAID under this Agreement; (4) any employee of such organizations; and (5) any individual contractor or grantee carrying out activities financed by USAID under this Agreement.

(c) Except as provided otherwise in this provision, the General Exemption in subsection (a) applies to, but is not limited to, the following taxes:

(1) Exemption 1. Customs duties, tariffs, import taxes, or other levies on the importation, use and re-exportation of goods or the personal belongings and effects (including personally-owned automobiles) for the personal use of non-national individuals or their family members. Exemption 1 includes, but is not limited to, all charges based on the value of such imported goods, but does not include service charges directly related to services performed to transfer goods or cargo.

(2) Exemption 2. Taxes on the income, profits or property of all (i) non-national organizations of any type, (ii) non-national employees of national and non-national organizations, or (iii) non-national individual contractors and grantees. Exemption 2 includes income and social security taxes of all types and all taxes on the property, personal or real, owned by such non-national organizations or persons. The term "national" refers to organizations established under the laws of the Grantee and citizens of the Grantee, other than permanent resident aliens in the United States.

(3) Exemption 3. Taxes levied on the last transaction for the purchase of goods or services financed by USAID under this Agreement, including sales taxes, value-added taxes (VAT), or taxes on purchases or rentals of real or personal property. The term "last transaction" refers to the last transaction by which the goods or services were purchased for use in the activities financed by USAID under this Agreement.

(d) If a tax has been levied and paid contrary to the provisions of an exemption, USAID may, in its discretion, (1) require the Grantee to refund to USAID or to others as USAID may direct the amount of such tax with funds other than those provided under the Agreement, or (2) offset the amount of such tax from amounts to be disbursed under this or any other agreement between the Parties.

(e) In the event of a disagreement about the application of an exemption, the Parties agree to promptly meet and resolve such matters, guided by the principle that the assistance furnished by USAID is free from direct taxation, so that all of the assistance furnished by USAID will contribute directly to the economic development of the country of the Grantee.

Section B.5. Reports and Information, Agreement Books and Records, Audits, and Inspections.

(a) Reports and Information. The Grantee shall furnish USAID accounting records and such other information and reports relating to the Agreement as USAID may reasonably request.

(b) Grantee Agreement Books and Records. The Grantee shall maintain accounting books, records, documents and other evidence relating to the Agreement, adequate to show, without limitation, all costs incurred directly by the Grantee under the Agreement, the receipt and use of goods and services acquired by the Grantee under the Agreement, agreed-upon cost sharing requirements, the nature and extent of solicitations of prospective suppliers of goods and services acquired by the Grantee, the basis of award of contracts and orders made directly by the Grantee, and the overall progress of the Agreement toward completion ("Agreement books and records"). The Grantee shall maintain Agreement books and records in accordance with generally accepted accounting principles prevailing in the United States, or at the Grantee's option, with approval by USAID, other accounting principles, such as those (1) prescribed by the International Accounting Standards Committee (an affiliate of the International Federation of Accountants) or (2) prevailing in the country of the Grantee. Agreement books and records shall be maintained for at least three years after the date of last disbursement by USAID or for such longer period, if any, required to resolve any litigation, claims or audit findings. For the avoidance of doubt, this Section B.5(b) applies solely to Grant funds expended directly by the Grantee.

(c) Grantee Audit. If $300,000 or more of USAID funds are expended directly by the Grantee in its fiscal year under the Agreement, the Grantee shall have financial audits made of the expenditures in accordance with the following terms, except as the Parties may otherwise agree in writing:

(1) With USAID approval, the Grantee shall use its Supreme Audit Institution or select an independent auditor in accordance with the "Guidelines for Financial Audits Contracted by Foreign Recipients" issued by the USAID Inspector General ("Guidelines"), and the audits shall be performed in accordance with the Guidelines; and

(2) The audit shall determine whether the receipt and expenditure of the funds provided under the Agreement are presented in accordance with generally accepted accounting principles agreed to in subsection (b) above and whether the Grantee has complied with the terms of the Agreement. Each audit shall be completed no later than nine months after the close of the Grantee's year under audit.

(d) Sub-recipient Audits. The Grantee, except as the Parties may otherwise agree in writing, shall submit to USAID, in form and substance satisfactory to USAID, a plan for the audit of the expenditures of "covered" sub-recipients, as defined below, that receive funds in connection with a direct contract or agreement entered into directly with the Grantee pursuant to the activities contemplated by this Agreement.

(1) A "covered" sub-recipient is one who expends $300,000 or more in its fiscal year in "USAID awards" (i.e., as sub-recipients under USAID strategic objective and other grant agreements with foreign governments).

(2) The plan shall describe the methodology to be used by the Grantee to satisfy its audit responsibilities for covered sub-recipients. The Grantee may satisfy such audit responsibilities by relying on independent audits of the sub-recipients; expanding the scope of the independent financial audit of the Grantee to encompass testing of sub-recipients' accounts; or a combination of these procedures.

(3) The plan shall identify the funds made available to covered sub-recipients that will be covered by audits conducted in accordance with other audit provisions that would satisfy the Grantee's audit responsibilities. (A nonprofit organization organized in the United States is required to arrange for its own audits. A for-profit contractor organized in the United States that has a direct contract with USAID is audited by the cognizant U.S. Government Agency. A private voluntary organization organized outside the United States with a direct grant from USAID is required to arrange for its own audits. A host-country contractor should be audited by the Grantee's auditing agency.)

(4) The Grantee shall ensure that covered sub-recipients under direct contracts or agreements with the Grantee take appropriate and timely corrective actions; consider whether sub-recipients' audits necessitate adjustment of its own records; and require each such sub-recipient to permit independent auditors to have access to records and financial statements as necessary.

(e) Audit Reports. The Grantee shall furnish or cause to be furnished to USAID an audit report for each audit arranged for by the Grantee in accordance with this Section within 30 days after completion of the audit and no later than nine months after the end of the period under audit.

(f) Other Covered Sub-recipients. For "covered" sub-recipients who receive funds under the Agreement pursuant to direct contracts or agreements with USAID, USAID will include appropriate audit requirements in such contracts or agreements and will, on behalf of the Grantee, conduct the follow-up activities with regard to the audit reports furnished pursuant to such requirements.

(g) Cost of Audits. Subject to USAID approval in writing, costs of audits performed in accordance with the terms of this Section may be charged to the Agreement.

(h) Audit by USAID. USAID retains the right to perform the audits required under this Agreement on behalf of the Grantee by utilizing funds under the Agreement or other resources available to USAID for this purpose, conduct a financial review, or otherwise ensure accountability of organizations expending USAID funds regardless of the audit requirement.

(i) Opportunity to Audit or Inspect. The Grantee shall afford authorized representatives of USAID the opportunity at all reasonable times to audit or inspect activities financed under the Agreement, the utilization of goods and services financed by USAID, and books, records and other documents relating to the Agreement.

(j) Sub-recipient Books and Records. The Grantee will incorporate paragraphs (a), (b), (d), (e), (g), (h) and (i) of this provision into all sub-agreements with non-U.S. organizations which meet the $300,000 threshold of paragraph (c) of this provision. Sub-agreements with non-U.S. organizations, which do not meet the $300,000 threshold, shall, at a minimum, incorporate paragraphs (h) and (i) of this provision. Sub-agreements with U.S. organizations shall state that the U.S. organization is subject to the audit requirements contained in OMB Circular A-133.

Section B.6. Completeness of Information. The Grantee confirms:

(a) that the facts and circumstances of which it has informed USAID, or caused USAID to be informed, in the course of reaching agreement with USAID on the Agreement, are accurate and complete, and include all facts and circumstances that might materially affect the Agreement and the discharge of responsibilities under this Agreement; and

(b) that it will inform USAID in timely fashion of any subsequent facts and circumstances that might materially affect, or that it is reasonable to believe might so affect, the Agreement or the discharge of responsibilities under this Agreement.

Section B.7. Other Payments. Grantee affirms that no payments have been or will be received by any official of the Grantee in connection with the procurement of goods or services financed under the Agreement, except fees, taxes, or similar payments legally established in the country of the Grantee.

Section B.8. Information and Marking. The Grantee will give appropriate publicity to the Agreement as a program to which the United States has contributed, identify Agreement activity sites, and mark goods financed by USAID, as described in Implementation Letters.

Article C: Procurement Provisions.

Section C.1. Source and Nationality.

C.1. Source and Nationality.

(a) Except as noted herein, or in a sub-agreement issued by USAID, Grant funds will be used to finance the cost of goods and services required for the Agreement in accordance with 22 C.F.R. 228 and having their source, and with respect to suppliers of goods and services, their nationality, in countries included in Geographic Code 937 as in effect at the time orders are placed or contracts entered into for such goods or services except as USAID may otherwise agree in writing and as follows:

(1) Ocean transportation costs shall be financed under the Agreement only on vessels under flag registry of countries included in Code 935. Also see Section C.6 on use of U.S. flag vessels.

(2) The country of the Grantee is an eligible source for foreign exchange cost for marine insurance, if otherwise eligible under Section C.7(a).

(3) Any motor vehicles financed under the Agreement will be of United States manufacture, except as USAID may otherwise agree in writing.

(b) The source and origin of ocean and air shipping will be deemed to be the ocean vessel's or aircraft's country of registry at the time of shipment.

(c) Provisions concerning restricted and ineligible goods and services may be provided in an Implementation Letter.

(d) Transportation by air of property or persons financed under this agreement will be on carriers holding United States certification, to the extent service by such carriers is available under the Fly America Act. This requirement may be further described by USAID in Implementation Letters.

Section C.2. Eligibility Date. No goods or services may be financed under the Agreement which are procured pursuant to orders or contracts firmly placed or entered into prior to the date of this Agreement, except as the Parties may otherwise agree in writing.

Section C.3. Plans, Specifications and Contracts. In order for there to be mutual agreement on the following matters, and except as the Parties may otherwise agree in writing:

(a) The Grantee will furnish to USAID upon preparation:

(1) any plans, specifications, procurement or construction schedules, contracts, or other documentation between the Grantee and third parties, relating to goods or services to be financed under the Agreement, including documentation relating to the prequalification and selection of contractors and to the solicitation of bids and proposals. Material modifications in such documentation will likewise be furnished USAID on preparation; and

(2) such documentation will also be furnished to USAID, upon preparation, relating to any goods or services, which, though not financed under the Agreement, are deemed by USAID to be of major importance to the Agreement. Aspects of the Agreement involving matters under this subsection (a)(2) will be identified in Implementation Letters or Bilateral Project Agreements.

(b) Documents related to the prequalification of contractors, and to the solicitation of bids or proposals for goods and services financed under the Agreement will be approved by USAID in writing prior to their issuance, and their terms will include United States standards and measurements;

(c) Contracts and contractors financed under the Agreement for engineering and other professional services, for construction services, and for such other services, equipment, or materials as may be specified in Implementation Letters, will be approved by USAID in writing prior to execution of the contract. Material modifications in such contracts will also be approved in writing by USAID prior to execution; and

(d) Consulting firms used by the Grantee for the Agreement but not financed under the Agreement, the scope of their services and such of their personnel assigned to activities financed under the Agreement as USAID may specify, and construction contractors used by the Grantee for the Agreement but not financed under the Agreement, shall be acceptable to USAID.

Section C.4. Reasonable Price. No more than reasonable prices will be paid for any goods or services financed, in whole or in part, under the Agreement. Such items will be procured on a fair and, to the maximum extent practicable, competitive basis.

Section C.5. Notification to Potential Suppliers. To permit all United States firms to have the opportunity to participate in furnishing goods and services to be financed under the Agreement, the Grantee will furnish USAID such information with regard thereto, and at such times, as USAID may request in Implementation Letters.

Section C.6. Transportation

(a) In addition to the requirements in Section C.1(a), costs of ocean or air transportation and related delivery services may not be financed under the Agreement, if the costs are for transportation under an ocean vessel or air charter which has not received prior USAID approval.

(b) Unless USAID determines that privately owned United States-flag commercial ocean vessels are not available at fair and reasonable rates for such vessels, or otherwise agrees in writing:

(1) at least fifty percent (50%) of the gross tonnage of all goods (computed separately for dry bulk carriers, dry cargo liners and tankers) financed by USAID which may be transported on ocean vessels will be transported on privately owned United States-flag commercial vessels; and

(2) at least fifty percent (50%) of the gross freight revenue generated by all shipments financed by USAID and transported to the territory of the Grantee on dry cargo liners shall be paid to or for the benefit of privately owned United States-flag commercial vessels. Compliance with the requirements of (1) and (2) of this subsection must be achieved with respect to both any cargo transported from U.S. ports and any cargo transported from non-U.S. ports, computed separately.

Section C.7. Insurance.

(a) Marine insurance on goods financed by USAID which are to be transported to the territory of the Grantee may be financed as a foreign exchange cost under this Agreement provided

(1) such insurance is placed at the most advantageous competitive rate;

(2) such insurance is placed in a country which is authorized under Section C.1(a); and

(3) claims there under are payable in U.S. dollars or any freely convertible currency unless USAID agrees otherwise in writing.

If the Grantee (or government of the Grantee), by statute, decree, rule, regulation, or practice discriminates with respect to USAID-financed procurement against any marine insurance company authorized to do business in any State of the United States, then all goods shipped to the territory of the Grantee financed by USAID hereunder shall be insured against marine risks and such insurance shall be placed in the United States with a company or companies authorized to do marine insurance business in the United States.

(b) Except as USAID may otherwise agree in writing, the Grantee will insure, or cause to be insured, goods financed under the Agreement imported for the Agreement against risks incident to their transit to the point of their use under the Agreement; such insurance will be issued on terms and conditions consistent with sound commercial practice and will insure the full value of the goods. Any indemnification received by the Grantee under such insurance will be used to replace or repair any material damage or any loss of the goods insured or will be used to reimburse the Grantee for the replacement or repair of such goods. Any such replacement will be of source and origin of countries listed in USAID Geographic Code 935 as in effect at the time of replacement and, except as the Parties may agree in writing, will be otherwise subject to the provisions of the Agreement.

Section C.8. U.S. Government-Owned Excess Property. The Grantee agrees that wherever practicable United States Government-owned excess personal property, in lieu of new items financed under the Agreement, should be utilized. Funds under the Agreement may be used to finance the costs of obtaining such property.

Article D: Disbursements.

Section D.1. Disbursement for Foreign Exchange Costs.

(a) After satisfaction of conditions precedent, if any, the Grantee may obtain disbursements of funds under the Agreement for the foreign exchange costs of goods or services required for the

Agreement in accordance with its terms, by such of the following methods as may be mutually agreed upon:

(1) by submitting to USAID, with necessary supporting documentation as prescribed in Implementation Letters, (A) requests for reimbursement for such goods or services, or, (B) requests for USAID to procure commodities or services in Grantee's behalf for the Agreement; or,

(2) by requesting USAID to issue letters of commitment for specified amounts directly to one or more contractors or suppliers, committing USAID to pay such contractors or suppliers for such goods or services.

(b) Banking charges incurred by the Grantee in connection with letters of commitment will be financed under the Agreement unless the Grantee instructs USAID to the contrary. Such other charges as the Parties may agree to may also be financed under the Agreement.

Section D.2. Disbursement for Local Currency Costs.

(a) After satisfaction of conditions precedent, if any, the Grantee may obtain disbursements of funds under the Agreement for Local Currency Costs required for the Agreement in accordance with terms of this Agreement, by submitting to USAID, with necessary supporting documentation as prescribed in Implementation Letters, requests to finance such costs.

(b) The local currency needed for such disbursements may be purchased by USAID with U.S. Dollars. The U.S. Dollar equivalent of the local currency made available hereunder will be the amount of U.S. Dollars required by USAID to obtain the local currency.

Section D.3. Other Forms of Disbursement. Disbursements may also be made through such other means as the Parties may agree to in writing.

Section D.4. Rate of Exchange. If funds provided under the Agreement are introduced into the Cooperating Country by USAID or any public or private agency for purposes of carrying out obligations of USAID hereunder, the Grantee will make such arrangements as may be necessary so that such funds may be converted into local currency at the highest rate of exchange which, at the time the conversion is made, is not unlawful in the country of the Grantee to any person for any purpose.

Article E: Termination; Remedies.

Section E.1. Suspension and Termination.

(a) Either Party may terminate this Agreement in its entirety by giving the other Party thirty (30) days written notice. USAID also may terminate this Agreement in part by giving the Grantee thirty (30) days written notice, and suspend this Agreement in whole or in part upon giving the Grantee written notice. In addition, USAID may terminate this Agreement in whole or in part, upon giving the Grantee written notice, if (i) the Grantee fails to comply with any provision of this Agreement, (ii) an event occurs that USAID determines makes it improbable that the Objective or Program Elements of the Agreement or the assistance program will be attained or that the Grantee will be able to perform its obligations under this Agreement, or (iii) any disbursement or use of funds in the manner herein contemplated would be in violation of the legislation governing USAID, whether now or hereafter in effect.

(b) Except for payment which the Parties are committed to make pursuant to non-cancellable commitments entered into with third parties prior to such suspension or termination, suspension or termination of this entire Agreement or part thereof will suspend (for the period of the suspension) or terminate, as applicable, any obligation of the Parties to provide financial or other resources to the Agreement, or to the suspended or terminated portion of the Agreement, as applicable. Any portion of this Agreement which is not suspended or terminated shall remain in full force and effect.

(c) In addition, upon such full or partial suspension or termination, USAID may, at USAID's expense, direct that title to goods financed under the Agreement, or under the applicable portion of the Agreement, be transferred to USAID if the goods are in a deliverable state.

Section E.2. Refunds.

(a) In the case of any disbursement which is not supported by valid documentation in accordance with this Agreement, or which is not made or used in accordance with this Agreement, or which was for goods or services not used in accordance with this Agreement, USAID, notwithstanding the availability or exercise of any other remedies under this Agreement, may require the Grantee to refund the amount of such disbursement in U.S. Dollars to USAID within sixty (60) days after receipt of a request therefore.

(b) If the failure of Grantee to comply with any of its obligations under this Agreement has the result that goods or services financed or supported under the Agreement are not used effectively in accordance with this Agreement, USAID may require the Grantee to refund all or any part of the amount of the disbursements under this Agreement for or in connection with such goods or services in U.S. Dollars to USAID within sixty (60) days after receipt of a request therefore.

(c) The right under subsections (a) or (b) to require a refund of a disbursement will continue, notwithstanding any other provision of this Agreement, for three years from the date of the last disbursement under this Agreement.

(d) (1) Any refunds under subsections (a) or (b), or (2) any refund to USAID from a contractor, supplier, bank or other third party with respect to goods or services financed under the Agreement, which refund relates to an unreasonable price for or erroneous invoicing of goods or services, or to goods that did not conform to specifications, or to services that were inadequate, will (A) be made available first for the Agreement, to the extent justified, and (B) the remainder, if any, will be applied to reduce the amount of the Grant.

(e) Any interest or other earnings on funds disbursed by USAID to the Grantee under this Agreement prior to the authorized use of such funds for the Agreement will be returned to USAID in U.S. Dollars by the Grantee, unless USAID otherwise agrees in writing.

Section E.3. Non-waiver of Remedies. No delay in exercising any right or remedy accruing to a Party in connection with its financing under this Agreement will be construed as a waiver of such right or remedy.

Section E.4. Assignment. The Grantee agrees, upon request, to execute an assignment to USAID of any cause of action which may accrue to the Grantee in connection with or arising out of the contractual performance or breach of performance by a Party to a direct U.S. Dollar contract which USAID financed in whole or in part out of funds granted by USAID under this Agreement.

Article F: Miscellaneous.

Section F.1. Investment Promotion.

(a) Except as specifically set forth in the Agreement or otherwise authorized by USAID in writing, no funds or other support provided hereunder may be used for any activity that involves investment promotion in a foreign country.

(b) In the event the Grantee is requested or wishes to provide assistance in the above area or requires clarification from USAID as to whether the activity would be consistent with the limitation set forth above, the Grantee must notify USAID and provide a detailed description of the proposed activity. The Grantee must not proceed with the activity until advised by USAID that it may do so.

(c) The Grantee must ensure that its employees and subcontractors and sub-recipients providing investment promotion services hereunder are made aware of the restrictions set forth in this clause and must include this clause in all subcontracts and other sub-agreements entered into hereunder.

Section F.2. Voluntary Family Planning.

The Parties agree that all USAID funds provided under this Agreement shall be used in accordance with applicable United States policy and statutory requirements relating to voluntary family planning projects, and that none of the USAID funds provided under this Agreement, or goods or services financed by such funds, may be used for:

(a) the performance of abortion as a method of family planning or to motivate or coerce any person to practice abortions;

(b) the performance of involuntary sterilizations as a method of family planning or to coerce or provide any financial incentive to any person to undergo sterilizations; or

(c) any biomedical research which relates, in whole or in part, to methods of, or the performance of, abortions or involuntary sterilizations as a method family planning.

(d) USAID will issue implementation letters that more fully describe the requirements of this section.

Section F.3. Prohibition on Assistance to Drug Traffickers.

(a) USAID reserves the right to terminate this Agreement or take other appropriate measures if the Grantee or a key individual of the Grantee is found to have been convicted of a narcotics offense or to have been engaged in drug trafficking as defined in 22 CFR Part 140.

(b) USAID reserves the right to terminate assistance to, or take or take other appropriate measures with respect to, any participant approved by USAID who is found to have been convicted of a narcotics offense or to have been engaged in drug trafficking as defined in 22 CFR Part 140.

Section F.4. Workers' Rights.

(a) Except as specifically set forth in the Agreement or otherwise authorized by USAID in writing, no funds or other support provided hereunder may be used for any activity that involves workers' rights in a foreign country.

(b) In the event the Grantee is requested or wishes to provide assistance in the above area or requires clarification from USAID as to whether the activity would be consistent with the limitation set forth above, the Grantee must notify the USAID and provide a detailed description of the proposed activity. The Grantee must not proceed with the activity until advised by USAID that it may do so.

(c) The Grantee must ensure that all employees and subcontractors and sub-recipients providing employment-related services hereunder are made aware of the restrictions set forth in this clause and must include this clause in all subcontracts and other sub-agreements entered into hereunder.

Section F.5. Prohibition on Funding Foreign Government Delegations to International Conferences. Except as USAID may otherwise agree in writing, funds obligated under this Agreement may not be used to finance the travel, per diem, hotel expenses, meals, conference fees or other conference costs for any member of a foreign government's delegation to an international conference sponsored by a public international organization. This restriction may be further described by USAID in Implementation Letters.

Annex 3

Illustrative Financial Plan

Program Area		Program Element		This Obligation FY2012	Estimated Future Obligations	Total Planned Funding Level
				US$	US$	US$
Development Objective Agreement						
A12	**Education**			**32,500,000**	**139,887,020**	**172,387,020**
		A055	Basic Education	27,850,000		
		A056	Higher Education	3,350,000		
		A140 A141	Program Design and Learning; Administration and Oversight	1,300,000		
Total Development Objective Agreement				**32,500,000**	**139,887,020**	**172,387,020**
Program Area		**Program Element**		**This Obligation FY2012**	**Estimated Future Obligations**	**Total Planned Funding Level**
				US$	**US$**	**US$**
Field Support and Food for Peace						
A18	**Agriculture**			**2,000,000**	**4,292,980**	**6,292,980**
		A055	Basic Education	2,000,000		
		A140 A141	Program Design and Learning; Administration and Oversight			
		Total Field Support and Food for Peace		**2,000,000**	**4,292,980**	**6,292,980**
				This Obligation FY2012	**Estimated Future Obligations**	**Total Planned Funding Level**
				US$	**US$**	**US$**
			Total USG Contribution	**34,500,000**	**144,180,000**	**178,680,000**
Government of the Republic of Liberia Contribution to the Development Objective 4 Agreement				**In Support of FY 2012 Obligations**	**Estimated Support for Future Obligations**	**Total Planned Contribution**
				US$	**US$**	**US$**
			Total Expected GOL Contribution	**8,125,000**	**34,971,755**	**43,096,755**

The attached copy of the Development Objective Assistance Agreement Number between the United States Agency for International Development (USAID) and the Government of Liberia, is a true copy of the original signed by USAID/Liberia Mission Director Patricia Rader and the Acting Minister of Finance Sebastian Muah.

[Signature]
Djenaba A. Kendrick
Consul
U. S. Embassy Monrovia

Original seen and compared
by a Consular Officer
American Embassy Monrovia

State Department Document Number: 12-170

Agreement Between the United States of America and the State of Qatar Concerning Security Measures for the Protection of Classified Military Information, with Appendix

Signed on July 17, 2012
Entered into force August 15, 2012

CTIA DOCUMENT NUMBER: 18077.000

The Government of the United States of America and the Government of the State of Qatar hereinafter referred to as "the Parties," and separately as "a Party",

In furtherance of mutual cooperation to ensure the protection of classified military information;

Have agreed as follows:

ARTICLE 1

Classified military information provided directly or indirectly by one Party to the other Party or to an officer or other representative of the other Party, shall be protected according to the ternes set forth herein and in accordance with the laws and regulations of the Parties.

ARTICLE 2

Each Party shall promptly notify the other of any changes to its laws and regulations that would affect the protection of classified military information under this Agreement. In such case, the Parties shall consult, as provided for in Article 22, to consider possible amendments to this Agreement. In the interim, classified military information shall continue to be protected as described in this Agreement, unless otherwise agreed in writing by the releasing Party.

ARTICLE 3

For the purpose of this Agreement, classified military information is information that is generated by or for the Department of Defense of the United States of America or the Ministry of Defense of Qatar, or that is under their jurisdiction or control, and which requires protection in the interests of national security of the Party by or for whom the information was generated.

For the Government of the United States of America, classified military information is marked **CONFIDENTIAL, SECRET,** or **TOP SECRET.** For the Government of the State of Qatar, it is marked [Arabic text omitted], [Arabic text omitted], [Arabic text omitted], or [Arabic text omitted]. Each Party shall stamp, mark or designate the name of the originating government on all classified military information received from the other Party. The information may be in oral, visual, electronic, magnetic, or documentary form, or in the form of equipment or technology. The Parties shall, consistent with their national laws and regulations employ the following equivalent classification levels and markings:

Table of Equivalent Security Classification Categories

Government of the State of Qatar	**Government of the United States of America**
(TOP SECRET) [Arabic text omitted]	TOP SECRET
(SECRET) [Arabic text omitted]	SECRET
(CONFIDENTIAL) [Arabic text omitted]	CONFIDENTIAL
(RESTRICTED) [Arabic text omitted]	No equivalent (See Appendix A)

ARTICLE 4

No individual shall be entitled to access to classified military information solely by virtue of rank, appointment, or security clearance. Access to the information shall be granted only to those individuals whose official duties require such access and who have been granted a personnel security clearance in accordance with the prescribed standards of the Parties. The Parties shall ensure that:

A. The recipient Party shall not release the information to a government, person, firm, institution, organization or other entity of a third country without the prior written approval of the releasing Party;

B. The recipient Party shall afford the information a degree of protection equivalent to that afforded it by the releasing Party;

C. The recipient Party shall not use the information for any other purpose than that for which it was provided without the prior written approval of the releasing Party;

D. The recipient Party shall respect private rights, such as patents, copyrights, or trade secrets, which are involved in the information; and

E. Each facility or establishment that handles classified military information shall maintain a registry of the clearance of individuals at the facility or establishment who are authorized to have access to such information.

ARTICLE 5

The determination on the granting of a personnel security clearance to an individual shall be consistent with the interests of national security and shall be based upon all available information indicating whether the individual is of unquestioned loyalty, integrity, trustworthiness, and excellent character, and of such habits and associates as to cast no doubt upon his or her discretion or good judgment in the handling of classified military information.

ARTICLE 6

An appropriate investigation, in sufficient detail to provide assurance that the above criteria have been met, shall be conducted by the parties with respect to any individual granted access to classified military information covered by this Agreement.

ARTICLE 7

Before a representative of a Party releases classified military information to an officer or representative of the other Party, the receiving Party shall provide to the releasing Party an assurance that the officer or representative possesses the necessary level of security clearance and requires access for official purposes, and that the information will be protected by the receiving Party as required by the releasing Party.

ARTICLE 8

Authorizations for visits by representatives of one Party to facilities and establishments of the other Party, where access to classified military information is required, shall be limited to those necessary for official purposes. Authorization to visit a facility or establishment shall be granted only by the Party in whose territory the facility or establishment is located or by government officials designated by that Party. The visited Party or the designee shall be responsible for advising the facility or establishment of the proposed visit, and the scope and highest level of classified military information that may be furnished to the visitor. Requests for visits by representatives of the Parties shall be submitted through the United States Defense Attaché Office in Qatar, in the case of United States visitors, and through the Qatari Defense Attaché Office in Washington, D.C., in the case of Qatari visitors.

ARTICLE 9

Each Party shall be responsible for all classified military information of the other Party while the information is in transit or storage within its territory.

ARTICLE 10

Each Party shall be responsible for the security of all government and private facilities and establishments where the information of the other Party is kept and shall assure for each such facility or establishment that qualified individuals are appointed who shall have the responsibility and authority for the control and protection of the information.

ARTICLE 11

The information shall be stored in a manner that assures access only by those individuals who have been authorized access pursuant to Articles 4, 5, 6, and 7 of this Agreement.

ARTICLE 12

Classified military information shall be transmitted between the Parties through government-to-government channels. The minimum requirements for the security of the information during transmission shall be as follows:

A. ***Documents.***

(1) Documents or other media containing classified military information shall be transmitted in double, sealed envelopes, the innermost envelope bearing only the classification of the documents or other media and the organizational address of the intended recipient, the outer envelope bearing the organizational address of the recipient, the organizational address of the sender, and the registry number, if applicable.

(2) No indication of the classification of the enclosed documents or other media shall be made on the outer envelope. The sealed envelope shall then be transmitted according to the prescribed regulations and procedures of the releasing Party.

(3) Receipts shall be prepared for packages containing classified documents or other media that are transmitted between the Parties, and a receipt for the enclosed documents or media shall be signed by the final recipient and returned to the sender.

B. ***Classified Equipment.***

(1) Classified equipment shall be transported in sealed, covered vehicles, or be securely packaged or protected in order to prevent identification of its details, and kept under continuous control to prevent access by unauthorized persons.

(2) Classified equipment which must be stored temporarily awaiting shipment shall be placed in protected storage areas. The area shall be protected by intrusion-detection equipment or guards with security clearances who shall maintain continuous surveillance of the storage area. Only authorized personnel with the requisite security clearance shall have access to the storage area.

(3) Receipts shall be obtained on every occasion when classified equipment changes hands en route.

(4) Receipts shall be signed by the final recipient and returned to the sender.

C. ***Electronic Transmissions.*** Classified military information transmitted by electronic means shall be protected during transmission using encryption appropriate for that level of classified information. Information systems processing, storing or conveying classified information shall receive security accreditation by the appropriate authority of the Party employing the system.

ARTICLE 13

Accountability and control procedures shall be established to manage the dissemination of and access to classified military information.

ARTICLE 14

Each Party shall stamp or mark the name of the originating government on all classified military information received from the other Party. The information shall be marked with a national security classification marking of the recipient Party that will afford a degree of protection equivalent to that afforded to it by the releasing Party.

ARTICLE 15

Classified documents and other media containing classified military information shall be destroyed by burning, shredding, pulping, or other means preventing reconstruction of the classified military information contained therein.

ARTICLE 16

Classified equipment shall be destroyed beyond recognition or modified so as to preclude reconstruction of the classified military information in whole or in part.

ARTICLE 17

When classified documents or other media are reproduced, all original security markings thereon shall also be reproduced or marked on each copy. Such reproduced documents or media shall be placed under the same controls as the original document or media. The number of copies shall be limited to that required for official purposes.

ARTICLE 18

All translations of classified military information shall be made by individuals with security clearances pursuant to Articles 5, 6, and 7. The number of copies shall be kept to a minimum and the distribution thereof shall be controlled. Such translations shall bear appropriate security classification markings and a suitable notation in the language into which it is translated, indicating that the document or media contains classified military information of the releasing Party.

ARTICLE 19

Prior to the release to a contractor or prospective contractor of any classified military information received from the other Party, the recipient Party shall:

A. Ensure that such contractor or prospective contractor and the contractor's facility have the capability to protect the information;

B. Grant to the facility an appropriate facility security clearance. A facility security clearance is not required for a Contractor to undertake contracts that require the receipt or production of Classified Information at the RESTRICTED level;

C. Grant appropriate personnel security clearances for all individuals whose duties require access to the information;

D. Ensure that all individuals having access to the information are informed of their responsibilities to protect the information in accordance with applicable laws and regulations;

E. Carry out periodic security inspections of cleared facilities to ensure that the information is protected as required herein; and

F. Ensure that access to the information is limited to those persons who have a need to know for official purposes.

ARTICLE 20

The releasing Party shall be informed immediately of all losses or compromises, as well as possible losses or compromises, of its classified military information, and the recipient Party shall initiate an investigation to determine the circumstances. The results of the investigation and information regarding measures taken to prevent recurrence shall be forwarded to the releasing Party by the Party that conducts the investigation.

ARTICLE 21

Implementation of the foregoing security requirements can be advanced through reciprocal visits by security personnel of the Parties. Accordingly, security representatives of each Party, after prior consultation, shall be permitted to visit the other Party, to discuss and view firsthand the implementing procedures of the other Party in the interest of achieving reasonable comparability of the security systems. Each Party shall assist the security representatives in determining whether classified military information provided by the other Party is being adequately protected.

ARTICLE 22

A. This Agreement shall enter into force from the date of the last written notification given by one Party to another, which states that all the necessary legal procedures for the entry into force of this Agreement have been completed in accordance with internal procedures.

B. Amendments to this Agreement shall be made by mutual consent of the Parties. Such amendments shall enter into force in accordance with the procedures set forth in paragraph A. of this Article.

C. Supplemental annexes under this Agreement may be concluded by the designated implementing agencies. For the Government of the United States of America, the implementing agency shall be the Department of Defense. For the Government of Qatar, the implementing agency shall be the Qatar Armed Forces.

D. This Agreement shall remain in force for a period of five years and shall be automatically extended annually thereafter, unless either Party notifies the other in writing through diplomatic channels, ninety days in advance, of its intention to terminate the Agreement.

E. Notwithstanding the termination of this Agreement, all classified military information provided pursuant to this Agreement shall continue to be protected in accordance with the provisions set forth herein.

F. Disagreements between the Parties arising under or relating to this Agreement shall be settled through consultations between the Parties and shall not be referred to a national court, to an international tribunal, or to any other person or entity for settlement.

IN WITNESS WHEREOF, the undersigned, being duly authorized by their respective Governments, have signed this Agreement.

DONE in duplicate at ________ on this ________ day of ________, in the English and Arabic languages, both texts being equally authentic.

FOR THE GOVERNMENT OF THE UNITED STATES OF AMERICA:

[Signature]

Her Excellency Susan L. Ziadeh
United States Ambassador

FOR THE GOVERNMENT OF THE STATE OF QATAR:

[Signature]

Staff Major General Hamad Bin Ali Al-Attiyah
Chief of Staff of the Qatar Armed Forces

APPENDIX
PROCEDURES FOR HANDLING RESTRICTED INFORMATION WITHIN THE UNITED STATES

A. Upon receipt, Qatar documents or material bearing the classification "RESTRICTED" shall be handled in the United States as U.S. UNCLASSIFIED information that is exempt from public release under one or more U.S. laws. These laws include the Freedom of Information Act (FOIA) and Title 10 U.S.C. Section 130(c), "Nondisclosure of Information: Certain Sensitive Information of Foreign Governments and International Organizations." Documents or Material so marked shall be stored in locked containers affording the appropriate protection or closed spaces or areas that will prevent access by unauthorized personnel.

B. RESTRICTED documents shall be handled in a manner that will preclude open publication and access or use for other than official government purposes of the United States or the releasing country.

C. RESTRICTED information shall be transmitted or accessed electronically via a public network (e.g., Internet), using government or commercial encryption devices mutually accepted by the Parties' government security authorities.

D. Before any communications and information system is allowed to store, process, or forward RESTRICTED information, it must be given security approval, known as Accreditation. An Accreditation is defined as a formal statement by the appropriate authority confirming that the use of a system meets the appropriate security requirement and does not present an unacceptable risk. For stand-alone automated information systems such as desktop and laptop computers utilized in DoD establishments the system registration document together with the Security Operating Procedures fulfils the role of the required Accreditation. For Contractors, guidance on the use of Communications and Information Systems will be incorporated within the Restricted Conditions Requirements Clause in the Contract.

E. RESTRICTED documents shall be transmitted by first class mail within the United States in one secure cover. Transmission outside the United States shall be in two secure covers, the inner cover marked "RESTRICTED." Such transmissions shall be by traceable means such as Commercial Courier or other means agreed upon in writing.

F. Otherwise, unclassified U.S. documents originated by a U.S. Government agency that contain information that Qatar has classified RESTRICTED shall bear on the cover and the first page the marking "RESTRICTED - Exempt from Public Disclosure under (insert citation for applicable U.S. law here)." The portion of the document containing RESTRICTED information also shall be identified in the documents.

G. Telephone conversations, video conferencing, or facsimile transmissions containing RESTRICTED information may be in clear text, if an approved encryption system is not available.

H. A facility security clearance is not required for a Contractor to undertake contracts that require the receipt or production of Classified Information at the RESTRICTED level.

I. Access to RESTRICTED information shall be granted only to those individuals whose official duties require such access. A personnel security clearance is not required to access RESTRICTED information.

STATE DEPARTMENT DOCUMENT NUMBER: 12-171

EXTENSION OF THE AGREEMENT OF SEPTEMBER 19, 1997 BETWEEN THE UNITED STATES OF AMERICA AND THE REPUBLIC OF MALI CONCERNING THE IMPOSITION OF IMPORT RESTRICTIONS ON ARCHAEOLOGICAL MATERIAL FROM MALI FROM THE PALEOLITHIC ERA (STONE AGE) TO APPROXIMATELY THE MID-EIGHTEENTH CENTURY, WITH ATTACHMENT

EFFECTED BY EXCHANGE OF NOTES AT BAMAKO,
AUGUST 15 AND SEPTEMBER 5, 2012
ENTERED INTO FORCE SEPTEMBER 5, 2012,
EFFECTIVE SEPTEMBER 19, 2012

CTIA DOCUMENT NUMBER: 9385.003

U.S. Department of State
Office of Language Services
Translating Division

LS No. 10-2013-0015
French/English
GPG/ALK

TRANSLATION

Republic of Mali
Ministry of Culture
Office of the Secretary General

Minister of Culture

No. 0835/MC-SG

Bamako, September 5, 2012

Her Excellency Mary Beth Leonard
Ambassador of the United States of America to Mali
Bamako

c/o
Mr. Tieman Coulibaly
Minister of Foreign Affairs and International Cooperation
Koulouba

***Subject**: Extension of the Agreement between the Government of the United States of America and the Government of the Republic of Mali Concerning the Imposition of Export Restrictions on Archaeological Material from Mali*

Madam Ambassador:

The Ministry of Culture of the Republic of Mali presents its compliments to the Embassy of the United States of America and has the honor to acknowledge receipt of Note No. 110 of August 15, 2012 regarding the Agreement Between the Government of the United States of America and the Government of the Republic of Mali Concerning the Imposition of Import Restrictions on Archaeological Material from Mali from the Paleolithic Era (Stone Age) to Approximately the Mid-Eighteenth Century, done at Washington September 19, 1997, as amended and extended (hereinafter referred to as "the Agreement"), which reads as follows:

> "The Embassy of the United States of America presents its compliments to the Ministry of Culture of the Republic of Mali and has the honor to refer to the Agreement Between the Government of the United States of America and the Government of the Republic of Mali Concerning the Imposition of Import Restrictions on Archaeological Material from Mali from the Paleolithic Era (Stone Age) to Approximately the Mid-Eighteenth Century, done at Washington September 19, 1997, as amended and extended (hereinafter referred to as "the Agreement"). The Embassy, on behalf of the Government of the United States of America, proposes that, pursuant to Article IV.A of the Agreement, the Agreement be extended for an additional five-year period.
>
> The Embassy further proposes that, pursuant to Article IV. B of the Agreement, the Agreement be amended by replacing Article II with the attached revised Article II.
>
> If the foregoing proposals are acceptable to the Ministry of Culture, the Embassy proposes that this note, including the attached revised Article II, and the Ministry's note in reply, shall constitute an agreement to extend and amend the Agreement, which shall enter into force on the date of your note in reply and shall take effect on September 19, 2012."

The Ministry of Culture of the Republic of Mali has the honor to inform the Embassy of the United States of America that the foregoing proposal is acceptable to the Government of the Republic of Mali and to confirm that the Note No. 110 and this Note in reply shall constitute an agreement between our two Governments which shall enter into force on this date and be effective on September 19, 2012.

[Seal: Ministry of Culture]
[Signature]
Boubacar Hamadou Kébé
Minister of Culture

Attachments:

- Copy of the Note Verbale
- Copy of Draft Article II, as amended
- Copy of the Agreement

Ministry of Culture,

Bamako, September 5, 2012.

DIPLOMATIC NOTE

No. 110

The Embassy of the United States of America presents its compliments to the Ministry of Culture of the Republic of Mali and has the honor to refer to the Agreement Between the Government of the United States of America and the Government of the Republic of Mali Concerning the Imposition of Import Restrictions on Archaeological Material from Mali from the Palcolithic Era (Stone Age) to Approximately the Mid-Eighteenth Century, done at Washington September 19, 1997, as amended and extended (hereinafter referred to as "the Agreement"). The Embassy, on behalf of the Government of the United States of America, proposes that, pursuant to Article IV.A of the Agreement, the Agreement be extended for an additional five-year period.

The Embassy further proposes that, pursuant to Article IV. B of the Agreement, the Agreement be amended by replacing Article II with the attached revised Article II.

If the foregoing proposals are acceptable to the Ministry of Culture, the Embassy proposes that this note, including the attached revised Article II, and the Ministry's note in reply, shall constitute an agreement to extend and amend the Agreement, which shall enter into force on the date of your note in reply and shall take effect on September 19, 2012.

The Embassy of the United States of America takes this opportunity to renew to the Ministry of Culture of the Republic of Mali the assurances of its highest consideration.

Attachment: as stated.

Embassy of the United States of America.
Bamako, August 15, 2012.

2012 Extension—Amended Article II

A. Representatives of the Government of the United States of America and representatives of the Government of the Republic of Mali shall take steps to publicize this Agreement.

B. Recognizing the successful initiatives of the Government of the Republic of Mali through the establishment of Cultural Missions that carry out research, site management, and educational programs among local populations at major archaeological sites, the Government of the United States of America encourages the continuation of such measures as part of an effort toward sustainable strategies for protecting cultural resources.

C. The Government of the United States of America recognizes that the Government of the Republic of Mali has a history of permitting the interchange of archaeological materials for exhibition and educational purposes to enable public appreciation of and access to Mali's cultural heritage. The Government of the Republic of Mali agrees to use its best efforts to encourage further interchange through consideration of accommodating requests for extended international loans of archaeological material to United States museums and academic institutions for educational, cultural, and scientific purposes under circumstances in which such exchange does not jeopardize Mali's cultural patrimony.

D. As appropriate under existing programs in the public and/or private sectors, the Government of the United States of America shall use its best efforts to 1) respond to requests from the Republic of Mali for technical assistance in cultural resource management and security, and 2) promote professional exchanges to enhance capacity of the Republic of Mali in exhibition preparation and conservation science.

E. Both Governments shall seek to encourage academic institutions, non-governmental institutions, and other organizations to cooperate in the interchange of knowledge and information about the cultural patrimony of the Republic of Mali, and to collaborate in the preservation and protection of Mali's cultural patrimony through appropriate technical assistance, training, and resources.

F. The Government of the Republic of Mali shall seek to develop and promote professional training programs for archaeologists, museum staff, and public institution administrators responsible for cultural patrimony.

G. The Government of the Republic of Mali shall initiate the work of its authorized interministerial committee to coordinate activities to preserve cultural heritage, strengthen efforts to reduce the internal sale and export of the restricted antiquities, and sensitize tour operators and others about the need to protect archaeological sites against looting in regions such as the Sahara. This inter-ministerial committee and the U.S. Embassy shall meet once a year to review the status of the Agreement.

H. The Government of the Republic of Mali shall endeavor to strengthen cooperation with its neighboring states, for the protection of the cultural patrimony of the region.

I. The Government of the Republic of Mali shall seek the cooperation of other nations where there is a market for illicit Malian archaeological material to reduce the importation into those countries of such material.

J. The Government of the Republic of Mali shall endeavor to identify and record the locations of undocumented archaeological sites through field surveys, and to use its best efforts to protect these sites. The Government of the Republic of Mali shall continue its registration and monitoring of known archaeological sites.

K. The Government of the Republic of Mali shall develop and maintain a comprehensive record of reported incidents of looting of archaeological sites. Such record shall include an indication of the eventual outcome of cases that result in prosecution or penalties.

L. Each Government shall keep the other informed of the effectiveness of the measures agreed to in this Agreement; reports shall be exchanged in October 2014 to coincide with an interim review, and in March 2017, should there be a proposal to extend the Agreement.

STATE DEPARTMENT DOCUMENT NUMBER: 12-172

ARRANGEMENT BETWEEN THE UNITED STATES NUCLEAR REGULATORY COMMISSION AND THE TURKISH ATOMIC ENERGY AUTHORITY FOR THE EXCHANGE OF TECHNICAL INFORMATION AND COOPERATION IN NUCLEAR SAFETY MATTERS, WITH ADDENDUMS

SIGNED AT VIENNA, SEPTEMBER 18, 2012
ENTERED INTO FORCE SEPTEMBER 18, 2012

CTIA DOCUMENT NUMBER: 18078.000

September 18, 2012

The United States Nuclear Regulatory Commission (hereinafter called the USNRC) and the Turkish Atomic Energy Authority (hereinafter called the TAEK), both hereinafter referred to as the Parties and individually as a "Party;

Desiring to have extensive mutual cooperation in the nuclear safety and regulatory matters and also to have a mutual benefit in a continuing exchange of information relating to regulations of safety and environmental impact of nuclear facilities;

Recognizing the Agreement for the Peaceful Uses of Nuclear Energy between the Government of the United States of America and the Government of Turkey, signed at Ankara, on July 26, 2000, and entered into force on June 2, 2008;

Have agreed as follows:

I. SCOPE OF THE ARRANGEMENT

A. Technical Information Exchange

To the extent that the Parties are permitted to do so under the laws, regulations, and policy directives of their respective countries, they shall exchange the following types of unclassified technical information relating to the regulation of safety, safeguards, physical security, waste management, radiological safety, and environmental impact of designated nuclear energy facilities and to nuclear safety research programs:

1. Topical reports concerning safety, , waste management, radiological safety, and environmental effects written by or for one of the Parties as a basis for, or in support of, regulatory decisions and policies;

2. Documents relating to significant licensing actions and safety and environmental decisions affecting nuclear facilities;

3. Detailed documents describing the USNRC process for licensing and regulating certain U.S. facilities designated by the TAEK as similar to certain facilities being built or planned in Turkey and equivalent documents on such Turkish facilities;

4. Information in the field of reactor safety research that the Parties have the right to disclose, either in the possession of one of the Parties or available to it, including light water reactor safety information from the technical areas described in Addenda "A" and "B", attached hereto and made integral parts of this Arrangement. Cooperation in these itemized research areas may require a separate agreement, as determined to be necessary by the research organizations of one or both of the Parties. Each Party shall transmit immediately to the other information concerning research results that requires early attention in the interest of public safety, along with an indication of significant implications.

5. Reports on operating experience, such as reports on nuclear incidents, accidents and shutdowns, and compilations of historical reliability data on components and systems;

6. Regulatory procedures for the safety, waste management, radiological safety and environmental impact evaluation of nuclear facilities;

7. Early advice of important events, such as serious operating incidents, government-directed reactor shutdowns, and emerging technical issues, that are of immediate interest to the Parties;

8. Copies of regulatory standards required to be used, or proposed for use, by the regulatory organizations of the Parties; and

9. Any other forms of technical information exchange that may be mutually agreed upon by the Parties.

B. Cooperation in Nuclear Safety Research

The terms of cooperation for joint programs and projects of nuclear safety research and development, or those programs and projects under which activities are divided between the two Parties, including the use of test facilities and/or computer programs owned by either Party, shall be considered on a case-by-case basis and may be the subject of a separate agreement, as determined to be necessary by the research organizations of one or both of the Parties. When not the subject of a separate agreement, the terms of cooperation may be established by an exchange of letters between the research organizations of the Parties and shall be subject to the terms and conditions of the present Arrangement.

Technical areas specified by such exchanges of letters may be modified subsequently by mutual consent. Temporary assignments of personnel by one Party in the other Party's agency shall also be considered on a case-by-case basis and shall, in general, require a separate letter of agreement between the research organizations of the Parties.

C. Training and Assignments

Within the limits of available resources and subject to the availability of appropriated funds, the USNRC shall cooperate with the TAEK in providing certain training and experience for TAEK safety personnel. Unless otherwise agreed, costs of salary, allowances, and travel of TAEK participants shall be paid by the TAEK. The following are typical of, but not necessarily exclusive of, the kinds of training and experience that may be provided:

1. TAEK-designated inspector accompaniment of USNRC inspectors on reactor operation and (if available) reactor construction inspections in the United States, including extended briefings at USNRC regional inspection offices.

2. Participation by TAEK employees in USNRC staff training courses.

3. Assignment of TAEK experts for certain periods (to be determined by the Parties) to work on USNRC staff duties and gain on-the-job experience.

4. Training assignments of the TAEK within the radiation control program in the United States.

5. Assignment of USNRC experts for certain periods (to be determined by the Parties) to work on TAEK staff duties and gain on-the-job experience. Cost of salary, allowances, and travel of USNRC experts for the entire period shall be paid by USNRC unless otherwise agreed.

II. ADMINISTRATION

A. The exchange of information under this Arrangement shall be accomplished through letters, reports, and other documents, and by visits and meetings arranged in advance on a case-by-case basis. Periodic meetings shall be held at such times as mutually agreed to review the exchange of information and cooperation under this Arrangement, to recommend revisions to the provisions of the Arrangement, and to discuss topics coming within the scope of the cooperation. The time, place, and agenda for such meetings shall be agreed upon in advance. Visits which take place under the Arrangement, including their schedules, shall have the prior approval of the administrators referred to in paragraph II.B.

B. An administrator shall be designated by each Party to coordinate its participation in the overall exchange under this Arrangement. The administrators shall be the recipients of all documents transmitted under the exchange, including copies of all letters unless otherwise agreed. Within the terms of the exchange, the administrators shall be responsible for developing the scope of the exchange, including agreement on the designation of the nuclear energy facilities subject to the exchange, and on specific documents and standards to be exchanged. One or more technical coordinators may be appointed as direct contacts for specific disciplinary areas. These technical coordinators shall ensure that both administrators receive copies of all transmittals. These detailed arrangements are intended to ensure, among other things, that a reasonably balanced exchange giving access to equivalent available information is achieved and maintained.

C. The administrators shall determine the number of copies to be provided of the documents exchanged. Each document shall be accompanied by an abstract in English, 250 words or less, describing its scope and content.

D. The application or use of any information exchanged or transferred between the Parties under this Arrangement shall be the responsibility of the receiving Party, and the transmitting Party does not warrant the suitability of such information for any particular use or application.

E. Recognizing that some information of the type covered in this Arrangement is not available within the agencies that are Parties to this Arrangement, but is available from other agencies of the governments of the Parties, each Party shall assist the other to the maximum extent possible by organizing visits and directing inquiries concerning such information to appropriate agencies of the government concerned. The foregoing shall not constitute a commitment of other agencies to furnish such information or to receive such visitors.

III. EXCHANGE AND USE OF INFORMATION

A. General

The Parties support the widest possible dissemination of information provided or exchanged under this Arrangement, subject to the requirements of each Party's national laws, regulations and policies and the need to protect proprietary and other sensitive or privileged information as may be exchanged hereunder, and subject to the provisions of the Intellectual Property Annex, which is an integral part of this Arrangement.

B. Definitions

1. The term "information" means unclassified nuclear energy-related regulatory, safety, safeguards, waste management, scientific or technical data, including information on results or methods of assessment, research, and any other knowledge provided, created or exchanged under this Arrangement.

2. The term "proprietary information" means information made available under this Arrangement that contains trade secrets or other privileged or confidential commercial information (such that the person having the information may derive a commercial benefit from it or may have a commercial advantage over those who do not have it), and may only include information that:

a. has been held in confidence by its owner;

b. is of a type which is customarily held in confidence by its owner;

c. has not been transmitted by the owner to other entities (including the receiving Party), except on the basis that it be held in confidence;

d is not otherwise available to the receiving Party from another source without restriction on its further dissemination; and

e. is not already in the possession of the receiving Party.

3. The term "other confidential or privileged information" means information, other than "proprietary information," that has been transmitted and received in confidence under this Arrangement and is protected from public disclosure under the laws, regulations, or policies of the country of the Party providing the information, or is otherwise restricted by the provider.

4. All information described subparagraph 1,2,3 above that constitutes the state secret of the Parties shall not be exchanged under this Arrangement.

C. Marking Procedures for Documentary Proprietary Information

A Party receiving documentary proprietary information pursuant to this Arrangement shall respect the privileged nature of such information, provided that such proprietary information is clearly marked with the following (or substantially similar) restrictive legend:

> "This document contains proprietary information furnished in confidence under an Arrangement dated September 18th, 2012, between the United States Nuclear Regulatory Commission and the Turkey Atomic Energy Authority and shall not be disseminated outside these organizations, their consultants, contractors, and licensees, or concerned departments and agencies of the Government of the United

States and the Government of Turkey, without the prior written approval of (name of transmitting Party). This notice shall be marked on each page of any reproduction hereof, in whole or in part. These limitations shall automatically terminate when the proprietary information is disclosed by the owner without restriction."

This restrictive legend shall be respected by the Parties to this Arrangement. Proprietary information bearing this restrictive legend shall not be made public or otherwise disseminated in any manner unspecified by or contrary to the terms of this Arrangement without the prior written consent of the transmitting Party. Proprietary information bearing this restrictive legend shall not be used by the receiving Party or its contractors and consultants for any commercial purposes without the prior written consent of the transmitting Party.

D. Dissemination of Documentary Proprietary Information

1. In general, proprietary information received under this Arrangement may be disseminated by the receiving Party without prior consent to persons within or employed by the receiving Party, and to concerned Government departments and Government agencies in the country of the receiving Party, provided:

a. such dissemination is made on a case-by-case basis; and

b. such proprietary information bears the restrictive legend appearing in Section III.C. of this Arrangement.

2. Proprietary information received under this Arrangement may be disseminated by the receiving Party without prior consent to contractors and consultants of the receiving Party located within the geographical limits of that Party's country provided:

a. that the proprietary information is used by such contractors and consultants only for work within the scope of their contracts with the receiving Party relating to the subject matter of the proprietary information, and shall not be used by such contractors and consultants for any other private commercial purposes;

b. that such dissemination is made on a case-by-case basis to contractors and consultants who have executed a non-disclosure agreement; and

c. that such proprietary information shall bear the restrictive legend appearing in Section III.C. of this Arrangement.

3. With the prior written consent of the Party furnishing proprietary information under this Arrangement, the receiving Party may disseminate such proprietary information more widely than otherwise permitted under the terms set forth in this Arrangement. The Parties shall endeavor to grant such approval to the extent permitted by their respective national laws, regulations and policies, provided:

a. that the entities receiving proprietary information under Section III.D.3. of this Arrangement, including domestic organizations permitted or licensed by the receiving Party to construct or operate nuclear production or utilization facilities, or to use nuclear and materials radiation sources, have executed a non-disclosure agreement;

b. that the entities receiving proprietary information under Section III.D.3. of this Arrangement, including domestic organizations permitted or licensed by the receiving Party to construct or operate nuclear production or utilization facilities, shall not use such proprietary information for any private commercial purposes; and

c. that those entities receiving proprietary information under Section III.D.3. of this Arrangement that are domestic organizations permitted or licensed by the receiving Party agree to use the proprietary information only for activities carried out under or within the terms of their specific permit or license.

E. Marking Procedures for Other Confidential or Privileged Information of a Documentary Nature

A Party receiving under this Arrangement other confidential or privileged information shall respect its confidential nature, provided such information is clearly marked so as to indicate its confidential or privileged nature and is accompanied by a statement indicating:

1. that the information is protected from public disclosure by the government of the transmitting Party; and

2. that the information is transmitted under the condition that it be maintained in confidence.

F. Dissemination of Other Confidential or Privileged Information of a Documentary Nature

Other confidential or privileged information may be disseminated in the same manner as that set forth in Section III.D, "Dissemination of Documentary Proprietary Information."

G. Non-Documentary Proprietary or Other Confidential or Privileged Information

Non-documentary proprietary or other confidential or privileged information provided in seminars and other meetings organized under this Arrangement, or information arising from the attachments of staff, use of facilities, or joint projects, shall be treated by the Parties according to the principles specified for documentary information in this Arrangement; provided, however, that the Party communicating such proprietary or other confidential or privileged information has placed the recipient on notice as to the character of the information communicated.

H. Consultation

If, for any reason, one of the Parties becomes aware that it will be, or may reasonably be expected to become, unable to meet the non-dissemination provisions of this Arrangement, it shall immediately inform the other Party. The Parties shall thereafter consult to define an appropriate course of action.

I. Other

Nothing contained in this Arrangement shall preclude a Party from using or disseminating information received without restriction by a Party from sources outside of this Arrangement.

IV. FINAL PROVISIONS

A. Nothing contained in this Arrangement shall require either Party to take any action that would be inconsistent with its existing laws, regulations, or policy directives. Should any conflict arise between the terms of this Arrangement and those laws, regulations, or policy directives, the Parties agree to consult before any action is taken. No nuclear information related to proliferation-sensitive technologies shall be exchanged under this Arrangement.

B. Unless otherwise agreed, all costs resulting from cooperation pursuant to this Arrangement shall be the responsibility of the Party that incurs them. The ability of the Parties to carry out their obligations is subject to the appropriation of funds by the appropriate governmental authority and to the laws, regulations and policies applicable to the Parties.

C. Cooperation under this Arrangement shall be in accordance with the laws and regulations of the Parties. Any dispute or questions between the Parties concerning the interpretation or application of this Arrangement shall be settled by mutual agreement of the Parties.

D. This Arrangement shall enter into force upon signature and, subject to paragraph E of this Section, shall remain in force for a period of five years. It may be extended for a further period of time by written agreement of the Parties.

E. Either Party may terminate this Arrangement after providing the other Party written notice 180 days prior to its intended date of termination.

DONE at Vienna, Austria on this 18th day of September 2012, in the English language.

FOR THE UNITED STATES NUCLEAR REGULATORY COMMISSION:	FOR THE TURKISH ATOMIC ENERGY AUTHORITY:
[Signature]	[Signature]
Allison Macfarlane, Chairman	Zafer Alper, President

CERTIFIED A TRUE COPY
BY [Signature]
Office of the Secretary

Addendum A

USNRC-TAEK Safety Research Areas In Which the USNRC Is Performing Safety Research

1. Digital Instrumentation and Control
2. Reactor and Electrical Equipment Qualification
3. Environmental Transport
4. Radionuclide Transport and Waste Management
5. Dry Cask Storage and Transport
6. Fire Safety Research
7. Nuclear Fuel Analysis
8. Severe Accident Analysis
9. Operating Experience and Generic Issues
10. Human Factors Engineering
11. Organizational Factors/Safety Culture
12. Human Reliability Analysis (HRA)
13. Probabilistic Risk Assessments
14. Radiation Protection and Health Effects
15. Seismic Safety
16. State of the Art Risk Consequences
17. Reactor Containment Structural Safety
18. Reactor Vessel and Piping Integrity
19. Regulatory Guide Update
20. New and Advanced Reactor Designs
21. Decommissioning
22. Thermal Hydraulic Code Applications and Maintenance
23. Uncertainty Analysis for Thermal Hydraulic Kinetics
24. Coupled 3D Neutronic and Plant Thermal Hydraulics
25. Medical Isotope Production
26. Long-term Operational Management
27. Plant and Systems Operations

Addendum B

USNRC-TAEK Safety Research Areas In Which the TAEK Is Envisaging Safety Research

1. Research Test Reactors
2. Safety Regulation of Nuclear Facilities
3. Licensing Procedure and Regulatory Inspection
4. Radiological Safety Controls
5. Nuclear Reactor Safety Research
6. Computer Codes
7. Radiation Protection and Health Effects
8. Environmental Protection

INTELLECTUAL PROPERTY RIGHTS ANNEX

I. General Obligation

The Parties shall ensure adequate and effective protection of intellectual property created or furnished under this Arrangement and relevant implementing arrangements. Rights to such intellectual property shall be allocated as provided in this Annex.

II. Scope

A. This Annex is applicable to all cooperative activities undertaken pursuant to this Arrangement, except as otherwise specifically agreed by the Parties or their designees.

B. For purposes of this Arrangement, "intellectual property" shall mean the subject matter listed in Article 2 of the Convention Establishing the World Intellectual Property Organization, done at Stockholm, July 14, 1967, and may include other subject matter as agreed by the Parties.

C. Each Party shall ensure, through contracts or other legal means with its own participants, if necessary, that the other Party can obtain the rights to intellectual property allocated in accordance with this Annex. This Annex does not otherwise alter or prejudice the allocation between a Party and its nationals, which shall be determined by that Party's laws and practices.

D. Except as otherwise provided in this Arrangement, disputes concerning intellectual property arising under this Arrangement shall be resolved through discussions between the concerned participating institutions, or, if necessary, the Parties or their designees. Upon mutual Arrangement of the Parties, a dispute shall be submitted to an arbitral tribunal for binding arbitration in accordance with the applicable rules of international law. Unless the Parties or their designees agree otherwise in writing, the arbitration rules of UNCITRAL shall govern.

E. Termination or expiration of this Arrangement shall not affect rights or obligations under this Annex.

III. Allocation of Rights

A. Each Party shall be entitled to a non-exclusive, irrevocable, royalty-free license in all countries to translate, reproduce, and publicly distribute scientific and technical journal articles, reports, and books directly arising from cooperation under this Arrangement. All publicly distributed copies of a copyrighted work prepared under this provision shall indicate the names of the authors of the work unless an author explicitly declines to be named.

B. Rights to all forms of intellectual property, other than those rights described in Section III.A above, shall be allocated as follows:

1. Visiting researchers shall receive rights, awards, bonuses and royalties in accordance with the policies of the host institution.

2. (a) Any intellectual property created by persons employed or sponsored by one Party under cooperative activities other than those covered by paragraph III.(B)(1) shall be owned by that Party. Intellectual property created by persons employed or sponsored by both Parties shall be jointly owned by the Parties. In addition, each creator shall be entitled to awards, bonuses and royalties in accordance with the policies of the institution employing or sponsoring that person.

(b) Unless otherwise agreed in an implementing or other arrangement, each Party shall have within its territory a right to exploit or license intellectual property created in the course of the cooperative activities.

(c) The rights of a Party outside its territory shall be determined by mutual Arrangement considering the relative contributions of the Parties and their participants to the cooperative activities, the degree of commitment in obtaining legal protection and licensing of the intellectual property and such other factors deemed appropriate.

(d) Notwithstanding paragraphs III.B(2)(a) and (b) above, if either Party believes that a particular project is likely to lead to or has led to the creation of intellectual property not protected by the laws of the other Party, the Parties shall immediately hold discussions to determine the allocation of rights to the intellectual property. If an Arrangement cannot be reached within three months of the date of the initiation of the discussions, cooperation on the project in question shall be terminated at the request of either Party. Creators of intellectual property shall nonetheless be entitled to awards, bonuses and royalties as provided in paragraph III.B(2)(a).

(e) For each invention made under any cooperative activity, the Party employing or sponsoring the inventor(s) shall disclose the invention promptly to the other Party together with any documentation and information necessary to enable the other Party to establish any rights to which it may be entitled. Either Party may ask the other Party in writing to delay publication or public disclosure of such documentation or information for the purpose of protecting its rights in the invention. Unless otherwise agreed in writing, the delay shall not exceed a period of six months from the date of disclosure by the inventing Party to the other Party.

IV. Business Confidential Information

In the event that information identified in a timely fashion as business-confidential is furnished or created under this Arrangement, each Party and its participants shall protect such information in accordance with applicable laws, regulations, and administrative practices. Information may be identified as "business-confidential" if a person having the information may derive an economic benefit from it or may obtain a competitive advantage over those who do not have it, and the information is not generally known or publicly available from other sources, and the owner has not previously made the information available without imposing in a timely manner an obligation to keep it confidential.

State Department Document Number: 12-173

Arrangement Between the United States Nuclear Regulatory Commission and the Nuclear Safety and Security Commission of the Republic of Korea for the Exchange of Technical Information and Cooperation in Nuclear Safety Matters, with Addendums

Signed at Vienna, September 18, 2012
Entered into force September 18, 2012

CTIA DOCUMENT NUMBER: 18079.000

September 18, 2012

The Nuclear Regulatory Commission of the United States of America (hereinafter called the USNRC), and the Nuclear Safety and Security Commission of the Republic of Korea (hereinafter called the NSSC); both hereinafter referred to as the Parties;

Having a mutual interest in a continuing exchange of information pertaining to regulatory matters and of standards required or recommended by their organizations for the regulation of safety and environmental impact of nuclear facilities;

Having in mind the spirit of mutual cooperation of the Agreement for Cooperation Between the Government of the Republic of Korea and the Government of the United States of America Concerning Civil Uses of Atomic Energy done at Washington on November 24, 1972, and amended on May 15, 1974;

Have agreed as follows:

I. SCOPE OF THE ARRANGEMENT

A. Technical Information Exchange

To the extent that the Parties are permitted to do so under the laws, regulations, and policy directives of their respective countries, they will exchange the following types of unclassified technical information relating to the regulation of safety, safeguards, physical protection, waste management, radiological safety, and environmental impact of designated nuclear energy facilities and to nuclear safety research programs:

1. Topical reports concerning safety, safeguards, physical protection, waste management, radiological safety, and environmental effects written by or for one of the Parties as a basis for, or in support of, regulatory decisions and policies.

2. Documents relating to significant licensing actions and safety and environmental decisions affecting nuclear facilities.

3. Detailed documents describing the USNRC process for licensing and regulating certain U.S. facilities designated by the NSSC as similar to certain facilities being built or planned in the Republic of Korea and equivalent documents on such facilities owned by the Republic of Korea.

4. Information in the field of reactor safety research that the Parties have the right to disclose, either in the possession of one of the Parties or available to it, including light water reactor safety information from the technical areas described in Addenda "A" and "B", attached hereto and made integral parts of this Arrangement. Cooperation in these itemized research areas may require a separate agreement, as determined to be necessary by the research organizations of one or both of the Parties. Each Party will transmit immediately to the other information concerning research results that requires early attention in the interest of public safety, along with an indication of significant implications.

5. Reports on operating experience, such as reports on nuclear incidents, accidents and shutdowns, and compilations of historical reliability data on components and systems.

6. Regulatory procedures for the safety, safeguards, physical protection, waste management, radiological safety, and environmental impact evaluation of nuclear facilities.

7. Early advice of important events, such as serious operating incidents, government-directed reactor shutdowns, and emerging technical issues, that are of immediate interest to the Parties.

B. Cooperation in Nuclear Safety Research

The terms of cooperation for joint programs and projects of nuclear safety research and development, or those programs and projects under which activities are divided between the two Parties, including the use of test facilities and/or computer programs owned by either Party, will be considered on a case-by-case basis and may be the subject of a separate letter of agreement, if determined to be necessary by the research organizations of one or both of the Parties. When not the subject of a separate agreement, the terms of cooperation may be established by an exchange of letters between the research organizations of the Parties, and will be subject to the terms and conditions of the present Arrangement.

Technical areas specified by such exchanges of letters may be modified subsequently by mutual consent. Temporary assignments of personnel by one Party in the other Party's Agency will also be considered on a case-by-case basis and will, in general, require a separate letter of agreement between the research organizations of the Parties.

C. Training and Assignments

Within the limits of available resources and subject to the availability of appropriated funds, the Parties will cooperate in providing certain training and experience for safety personnel of the Parties. Unless otherwise agreed, costs of salary, allowances, and travel of participants will be paid by the sending country. The following are typical of, but not necessarily exclusive of, the kinds of training and experience that may be provided:

1. One Party's designated inspector accompaniment of the other Party's inspectors on reactor operation and reactor construction inspection visits in the United States and the Republic of Korea, including extended briefings at regional inspection offices.

2. Participation by one Party's employees in the other Party's staff training courses.

3. Assignment of one Party's experts for certain periods to be determined by the Parties within the staff of the other Party's to work on staff duties of the Parties and gain on the job experience.

4. Training assignments of the Parties within the radiation control program in the United States and Republic of Korea.

II. ADMINISTRATION

A. The exchange of information under this Arrangement will be accomplished through letters, reports, and other documents, and by visits and meetings arranged in advance on a case-by-case basis. Annual meetings will be held at such times as mutually agreed to review the exchange of information and cooperation under this Arrangement, to recommend revisions to the provisions of the Arrangement, and to discuss topics coming within the scope of the cooperation. The time, place, and agenda for such meetings will be agreed upon in advance. Visits which take place under the Arrangement, including their schedules, will have the prior approval of the administrators referred to in paragraph II.B.

B. An administrator will be designated by each Party to coordinate its participation in the overall exchange under this Arrangement. The administrators will be the recipients of all documents transmitted under the exchange, including copies of all letters unless otherwise agreed. Within the terms of the exchange, the administrators will be responsible for developing the scope of the exchange, including agreement on the designation of the nuclear energy facilities subject to the exchange, and on specific documents and standards to be exchanged. One or more technical coordinators may be appointed as direct contacts for specific disciplinary areas. These technical coordinators will ensure that both administrators receive copies of all transmittals. These detailed arrangements are intended to ensure, among other things, that a reasonably balanced exchange giving access to equivalent available information is achieved and maintained.

C. The administrators will determine the number of copies to be provided of the documents exchanged. Each document will be accompanied by an abstract in English, 250 words or less, describing its scope and content.

D. The application or use of any information exchanged or transferred between the Parties under this Arrangement will be the responsibility of the receiving Party, and the transmitting Party does not warrant the suitability of such information for any particular use or application.

E. Recognizing that some information of the type covered in this Arrangement is not available within the agencies that are Parties to this Arrangement, but is available from other agencies of the governments of the Parties, each Party will assist the other to the maximum extent possible by organizing visits and directing inquiries concerning such information to appropriate agencies of the government concerned. The foregoing will not constitute a commitment of other agencies to furnish such information or to receive such visitors.

III. EXCHANGE AND USE OF INFORMATION

A. General

The Parties support the widest possible dissemination of information provided or exchanged under this Arrangement, subject to the requirements of each Party's national laws, regulations and policies and the need to protect proprietary and other confidential or privileged information, and subject to the provisions of the Intellectual Property Rights Annex, which is an integral part of this Arrangement.

B. Definitions

1. The term "information" means unclassified nuclear energy-related regulatory, safety, safeguards, waste management, scientific or technical data, including information on results or methods of assessment, research, and any other knowledge provided, created or exchanged under this Arrangement.

2. The term "proprietary information" means information made available under this Arrangement that contains trade secrets or other privileged or confidential commercial information (such that the person having the information may derive a commercial benefit from it or may have a commercial advantage over those who do not have it), and may only include information that:

a. has been held in confidence by its owner;

b. has not been transmitted by the owner to other entities (including the receiving Party), except on the basis that it be held in confidence;

c. is not otherwise available to the receiving Party from another source without restriction on its further dissemination; and

d. is not already in the possession of the receiving Party.

3. The term "other confidential or privileged information" means information, other than "proprietary information," that has been transmitted and received in confidence under this Arrangement and is protected from public disclosure under the laws, regulations, or policies of the country of the Party providing the information.

C. Marking Procedures for Documentary Proprietary Information

A Party receiving documentary proprietary information pursuant to this Arrangement will respect the privileged nature of such information, provided that such proprietary information is clearly marked with the following (or substantially similar) restrictive legend:

> "This document contains proprietary information furnished in confidence under an Arrangement dated September 18th, 2012, between the Nuclear Safety and Security Commission (NSSC) of Republic of Korea and the United States Nuclear Regulatory Commission (USNRC) will not be disseminated outside these organizations, their consultants, contractors, and licensees, or concerned departments and agencies of the Government of the Republic of Korea and the Government of the of the United States without the prior written approval of (name of transmitting Party). This notice will be marked on each page of any reproduction hereof, in whole or in part. These limitations will automatically terminate when the proprietary information is disclosed by the owner without restriction."

This restrictive legend will be respected by the Parties to this Arrangement. Proprietary information bearing this restrictive legend will not be made public or otherwise disseminated in any manner unspecified or contrary to the terms of this Arrangement without the prior written consent of the transmitting Party. Proprietary information bearing this restrictive legend will not be used by the receiving Party or its contractors and consultants for any commercial purposes without the prior written consent of the transmitting Party.

D. Dissemination of Documentary Proprietary Information

1. In general, proprietary information received under this Arrangement may be disseminated by the receiving Party without prior consent to persons within or employed by the receiving Party, and to concerned Government departments and Government agencies in the country of the receiving Party, provided:

a. such dissemination is made on a case-by-case basis; and

b. such proprietary information bears the restrictive legend appearing in Section III.C. of this Arrangement.

2. Proprietary information received under this Arrangement may be disseminated by the receiving Party without prior consent to contractors and consultants of the receiving Party located within the geographical limits of that Party's country provided:

a. that the proprietary information is used by such contractors and consultants only for work within the scope of their contracts with the receiving Party relating to the subject matter of the proprietary information, and will not be used by such contractors and consultants for any other private commercial purposes;

b. that such dissemination is made on a case-by-case basis to contractors and consultants who have executed a non-disclosure agreement; and

c. that such proprietary information will bear the restrictive legend appearing in Section III.C. of this Arrangement.

3. With the prior written consent of the Party furnishing proprietary information under this Arrangement, the receiving Party may disseminate such proprietary information more widely than otherwise permitted under the terms set forth in this Arrangement. The Parties will endeavor to grant such approval to the extent permitted by their respective national laws, regulations and policies, provided:

a. that the entities receiving proprietary information under Section III.D.3. of this Arrangement, including domestic organizations permitted or licensed by the receiving Party to construct or operate nuclear production or utilization facilities, or to use nuclear and materials radiation sources, have executed a non-disclosure agreement;

b. that the entities receiving proprietary information under Section III.D.3. of this Arrangement, including domestic organizations permitted or licensed by the receiving Party to construct or operate nuclear production or utilization facilities, will not use such proprietary information for any private commercial purposes; and

c. that those entities receiving proprietary information under Section III.D.3. of this Arrangement that are domestic organizations permitted or licensed by the receiving Party, agree to use the proprietary information only for activities carried out under or within the terms of their specific permit or license.

E. Marking Procedures for Other Confidential or Privileged Information of a Documentary Nature

A Party receiving under this Arrangement other confidential or privileged information will respect its confidential nature, provided such information is clearly marked so as to indicate its confidential or privileged nature and is accompanied by a statement indicating:

1. that the information is protected from public disclosure by the government of the transmitting Party; and

2. that the information is transmitted under the condition that it be maintained in confidence.

F. Dissemination of Other Confidential or Privileged Information of a Documentary Nature

Other confidential or privileged information may be disseminated in the same manner as that set forth in Section III.D, "Dissemination of Documentary Proprietary Information."

G. Non-Documentary Proprietary or Other Confidential or Privileged Information

Non-documentary proprietary or other confidential or privileged information provided in seminars and other meetings organized under this Arrangement, or information arising from the attachments of staff, use of facilities, or joint projects, shall be treated by the Parties according to the principles specified for documentary information in this Arrangement; provided, however, that the Party communicating such proprietary or other confidential or privileged information has placed the recipient on notice as to the character of the information communicated.

H. Consultation

If, for any reason, one of the Parties becomes aware that it will be, or may reasonably be expected to become, unable to meet the non-dissemination provisions of this Arrangement, it shall immediately inform the other Party. The Parties shall thereafter consult to define an appropriate course of action.

I. Other

Nothing contained in this Arrangement shall preclude a Party from using or disseminating information received without restriction by a Party from sources outside of this Arrangement.

IV. FINAL PROVISIONS

A. Nothing contained in this Arrangement shall require either Party to take any action that would be inconsistent with its existing laws, regulations, or policy directives. Should any conflict arise between the terms of this Arrangement and those laws, regulations, or policy directives, the Parties agree to consult before any action is taken. No nuclear information related to proliferation-sensitive technologies shall be exchanged under this Arrangement.

B. Unless otherwise agreed, all costs resulting from cooperation pursuant to this Arrangement shall be the responsibility of the Party that incurs them. The ability of the Parties to carry out their obligations is subject to the appropriation of funds by the appropriate governmental authority and to the laws, regulations and policies applicable to the Parties.

C. Cooperation under this Arrangement shall be in accordance with the laws and regulations of the Parties. Any dispute or questions between the Parties concerning the interpretation or application of this Arrangement shall be settled by mutual agreement of the Parties.

D. This Arrangement shall enter into force upon signature and, subject to paragraph E of this Section, shall remain in force for a period of five years. It may be extended for a further period of time by written agreement of the Parties.

E. Either Party may terminate this Arrangement after providing the other Party written notice 180 days prior to its intended date of termination.

DONE at Vienna, Austria on this 18th day of September, 2012.

FOR THE NUCLEAR REGULATORY COMMISSION OF THE UNITED STATES OF AMERICA

[Signature]
Allison M. Macfarlane,
Chairman

FOR THE NUCLEAR SAFETY AND SECURITY COMMISSION OF THE REPUBLIC OF KOREA

[Signature]
Chang Sun Kang,
Chairman and Chief Regulatory Officer

CERTIFIED A TRUE COPY
BY [Signature]

Office of the Secretary

Addendum A

NRC-NSSC Safety Research Exchange
Areas in Which the NRC Is Performing or Sponsoring Safety Research

1. Digital Instrumentation and Control
2. Reactor and Electrical Equipment Qualification
3. Environmental Transport
4. Radionuclide Transport and Waste Management
5. Dry Cask Storage and Transport
6. Fire Safety Research
7. Nuclear Fuel Analysis
8. Severe Accident Analysis
9. Operating Experience and Generic Issues
10. Human Factors Engineering
11. Organizational Factors/Safety Culture
12. Human Reliability Analysis (HRA)
13. Probabilistic Risk Assessments
14. Radiation Protection and Health Effects
15. Seismic Safety
16. State of the Art Risk Consequences
17. Reactor Containment Structural Safety
18. Reactor Vessel and Piping Integrity
19. Regulatory Guide Update
20. New and Advanced Reactor Designs
21. Decommissioning
22. Thermal Hydraulic Code Applications and Maintenance
23. Uncertainty Analysis for Thermal Hydraulic Kinetics
24. Coupled 3D Neutronic and Plant Thermal Hydraulics
25. Medical Isotope Production
26. Long-term Operational Management
27. Plant and Systems Operations

Addendum B

NRC-NSSC Safety Research Exchange
Areas in Which the NSSC Is Performing or Sponsoring Safety Research

1. Regulatory Research on Nuclear Safety
    - Risk-informed Regulation
    - Plant Aging and Life Extension
    - Accident Analysis
    - Severe Accident Evaluation
    - Digital Instrumentation and Control
    - Structural Integrity and Seismic Safety
    - Regulatory Effectiveness
    - Code & Standard
2. Regulatory Research on Radiation and the Environment
    - Radiation Protection
    - Radioactive Waste Management
    - Environmental Protection and Emergency Preparedness
    - Radiation Monitoring and Survey
    - Electric Motor Condition Monitoring
3. Aircraft Impact Assessments
4. Advanced Reactor Designs (VHTR and SFR)
5. Spent Fuel Management
6. Interface between Safety and Security
7. Cyber Security Plan
8. Transportation Security Plan
9. Performance based Regulation
10. Nuclear Forensics
11. Force on Force Implementation

Intellectual Property Rights Annex

I. General Obligation

The Parties will ensure adequate and effective protection of intellectual property created or furnished under this Arrangement and relevant implementing arrangements. Rights to such intellectual property will be allocated as provided in this Annex.

II. Scope

A. This Annex is applicable to all cooperative activities undertaken pursuant to this Arrangement, except as otherwise specifically agreed by the Parties or their designees.

B. For purposes of this Arrangement, "intellectual property" will mean the subject matter listed in Article 2 of the Convention Establishing the World Intellectual Property Organization, done at Stockholm, July 14, 1967 and may include other subject matter as agreed by the Parties.

C. Each Party will ensure, through contracts or other legal means with its own participants, if necessary, that the other Party can obtain the rights to intellectual property allocated in accordance with this Annex. This Annex does not otherwise alter or prejudice the allocation between a Party and its nationals, which will I be determined by that Party's laws and practices.

D. Except as otherwise provided in this Arrangement, disputes concerning intellectual property arising under this Arrangement will be resolved through discussions between the concerned participating institutions, or, if necessary, the Parties or their designees. Upon mutual Arrangement of the Parties, a dispute will be submitted to an arbitral tribunal for binding arbitration in accordance with the applicable rules of international law. Unless the Parties or their designees agree otherwise in writing, the arbitration rules of UNCITRAL will govern.

E. Termination or expiration of this Arrangement will not affect rights or obligations under this Annex.

III. Allocation of Rights

A. Each Party will be entitled to a non-exclusive, irrevocable, royalty-free license in all countries to translate, reproduce, and publicly distribute scientific and technical journal articles, reports, and books directly arising from cooperation under this Arrangement. All publicly distributed copies of a copyrighted work prepared under this provision will indicate the names of the authors of the work unless an author explicitly declines to be named.

B. Rights to all forms of intellectual property, other than those rights described in paragraph III.A. above, will be allocated as follows:

(1) Visiting researchers will receive rights, awards, bonuses and royalties in accordance with the policies of the host institution.

(2) (a) Any intellectual property created by persons employed or sponsored by one Party under cooperative activities other than those covered by paragraph III.(B)(1) will be owned by that Party. Intellectual property created by persons employed or sponsored by both Parties will be jointly owned by the Parties. In addition, each creator will be entitled to awards, bonuses and royalties in accordance with the policies of the institution employing or sponsoring that person.

(b) Unless otherwise agreed in an implementing or other arrangement, each Party will have within its territory a right to exploit or license intellectual property created in the course of the cooperative activities.

(c) The rights of a Party outside its territory will be determined by mutual Arrangement considering the relative contributions of the Parties and their participants to the cooperative activities, the degree of commitment in obtaining legal protection and licensing of the intellectual property and such other factors deemed appropriate.

(d) Notwithstanding paragraphs III.B(2)(a) and (b) above, if either Party believes that a particular project is likely to lead to or has led to the creation of intellectual property not protected by the laws of the other Party, the Parties will immediately hold discussions to determine the allocation of rights to the intellectual property. If an Arrangement cannot be reached within three months of the date of the initiation of the discussions, cooperation on the project in question will be terminated at the request of either Party. Creators of intellectual property will nonetheless be entitled to awards, bonuses and royalties as provided in paragraph III.B(2)(a).

(e) For each invention made under any cooperative activity, the Party employing or sponsoring the inventor(s) will disclose the invention promptly to the other Party together with any documentation and information necessary to enable the other Party to establish any rights to which it may be entitled. Either Party may ask the other Party in writing to delay publication or public disclosure of such documentation or information for the purpose of protecting its rights in the invention. Unless otherwise agreed in writing, the delay will not exceed a period of six months from the date of disclosure by the inventing Party to the other Party.

IV. Business Confidential Information

In the event that information identified in a timely fashion as business-confidential is furnished or created under this Arrangement, each Party and its participants will protect such information in accordance with applicable laws, regulations, and administrative practices. Information may be identified as "business-confidential" if a person having the information may derive an economic benefit from it or may obtain a competitive advantage over those who do not have it, and the information is not generally known or publicly available from other sources, and the owner has not previously made the information available without imposing in a timely manner an obligation to keep it confidential.

State Department Document Number: 12-174

Arrangement Between the Nuclear Regulatory Commission of the United States of America and the Comision Nacional de Seguridad Nuclear y Salvaguardias of the United Mexican States for the Exchange of Technical Information and Cooperation in Nuclear Safety and Research Matters, with Addendums

Signed at Vienna, September 18, 2012
Entered into force September 18, 2012

CTIA Document Number: 18080.000

September 18, 2012

The United States Nuclear Regulatory Commission (hereinafter called the USNRC) and the *Comision Nacional de Seguridad Nuclear y Salvaguardias* of the United Mexican States (hereinafter called the CNSNS), both hereinafter referred to as the Parties;

Having a mutual interest in a continuing exchange of information pertaining to regulatory matters and of standards required or recommended by their organizations for the regulation of safety and environmental impact of nuclear facilities;

Having similarly cooperated under an Arrangement effected by an exchange of letters of July 30 and October 15, 1980, with Implementing Procedures for the Exchange of Technical Information and Cooperation in Nuclear Safety Matters, signed on April 8, 1981;

Having replaced their initial implementing procedures by other implementing procedures signed on September 8 and October 6, 1989;

Having continued that cooperation under an Arrangement signed on March 5, 1997, and amended and extended on November 12, 2002, and an Arrangement signed on September 19, 2007, and having indicated their mutual desire to continue the cooperation so established for another five years;

Have agreed as follows:

I. SCOPE OF THE ARRANGEMENT

A. Technical Information Exchange

To the extent that the Parties are permitted to do so under the laws, regulations, and policy directives of their respective countries, they shall exchange the following types of unclassified technical information relating to the regulation of nuclear safety, waste management, radiological safety, and environmental impact of designated nuclear energy facilities and to nuclear safety research programs:

1. Topical reports concerning safety, waste management, radiological safety, and environmental effects written by or for one of the Parties as a basis for, or in support of, regulatory decisions and policies.

2. Documents relating to significant licensing actions and safety and environmental decisions affecting nuclear facilities.

3. Detailed documents describing the USNRC process for licensing and regulating certain U.S. facilities designated by the CNSNS as similar to certain facilities being built or planned in Mexico and equivalent documents on such facilities owned by Mexico.

4. Information in the field of reactor safety research that the Parties have the right to disclose, either in the possession of one of the Parties or available to it, including reactor safety information from the technical areas described in Addenda "A" and "B", attached hereto and made a part of this Arrangement. Cooperation in these itemized research areas may require a separate agreement, as determined to be necessary by the research organizations of one or both of the Parties. Each Party shall transmit immediately to the other information concerning research results that requires early attention in the interest of public safety, along with an indication of significant implications.

5. Reports on operating experience, such as reports on nuclear incidents, accidents and shutdowns, and compilations of historical reliability data on components and systems.

6. Regulatory procedures for the safety, waste management, radiological safety, and environmental impact evaluation of nuclear facilities.

7. Early advice of important events, such as serious operating incidents, government-directed reactor shutdowns, and emerging technical issues, that are of immediate interest to the Parties.

B. Cooperation in Nuclear Safety Research

The terms of cooperation for joint programs and projects of nuclear safety research and development, or those programs and projects under which activities are divided between the two Parties, including the use of test facilities and/or computer programs owned by either Party, shall be considered on a case-by-case basis and may be the subject of a separate agreement, if determined to be necessary by the research organizations of one or both of the Parties. When not the subject of a separate agreement, the terms of cooperation may be established by an exchange of letters between the research organizations of the Parties, and shall be subject to the terms and conditions of the present Arrangement.

Technical areas specified by such exchanges of letters may be modified subsequently by mutual consent. Temporary assignments of personnel by one Party in the other Party's Agency shall also be considered on a case-by-case basis and shall, in general, require a separate agreement between the research organizations of the Parties.

C. Training and Assignments

Within the limits of available resources and subject to the availability of appropriated funds, the USNRC shall cooperate with the CNSNS in providing certain training and experience for CNSNS safety personnel. Unless otherwise agreed, costs of salary, allowances, and travel of CNSNS participants shall be paid by the CNSNS. The following are typical of, but not necessarily exclusive of, the kinds of training and experience that may be provided:

1. CNSNS designated inspector accompaniment of USNRC inspectors on reactor operation and reactor construction inspection visits in the United States, including extended briefings at USNRC regional inspection offices.

2. Participation by CNSNS employees in USNRC staff training courses.

3. Assignment of CNSNS staff for certain periods to be determined by the Parties within the USNRC staff to work on USNRC staff duties and gain on the job experience.

4. Training assignments of the CNSNS within the radiation control program in the United States.

II. ADMINISTRATION

A. The exchange of information under this Arrangement shall be accomplished through letters, reports, and other documents, and by visits and meetings arranged in advance on a case-by-case basis. Periodic meetings shall be held at such times as mutually agreed to review the exchange of information and cooperation under this Arrangement, to recommend revisions to the provisions of the Arrangement, and to discuss topics coming within the scope of the cooperation. The time, place, and agenda for such meetings shall be agreed upon in advance. Visits which take place under the Arrangement, including their schedules, shall have the prior approval of the administrators referred to in paragraph II.B.

B. An administrator shall be designated by each Party to coordinate its participation in the overall exchange under this Arrangement. The administrators shall be the recipients of all documents transmitted under the exchange, including copies of all letters unless otherwise agreed. Within the terms of the exchange, the administrators will be responsible for developing the scope of the exchange, including agreement on the designation of the nuclear energy facilities subject to the exchange, and on specific documents and standards to be exchanged. One or more technical coordinators may be appointed as direct contacts for specific disciplinary areas. These technical coordinators shall ensure that both administrators receive copies of all transmittals. These detailed arrangements are intended to ensure, among other things, that a reasonably balanced exchange giving access to equivalent available information is achieved and maintained.

C. The administrators shall determine the number of copies to be provided of the documents exchanged. Each document shall be accompanied by an abstract in English, 250 words or less, describing its scope and content.

D. The application or use of any information exchanged or transferred between the Parties under this Arrangement shall be the responsibility of the receiving Party, and the transmitting Party does not warrant the suitability of such information for any particular use or application.

E. Recognizing that some information of the type covered in this Arrangement is not available within the agencies that are Parties to this Arrangement, but is available from other agencies of the governments of the Parties, each Party shall assist the other to the maximum extent possible by organizing visits and directing inquiries concerning such information to appropriate agencies of the government concerned. The foregoing shall not constitute a commitment of other agencies to furnish such information or to receive such visitors.

III. EXCHANGE AND USE OF INFORMATION

A. General

The Parties support the widest possible dissemination of information provided or exchanged under this Arrangement, subject to the requirements of each Party's national laws, regulations and policies and the need to protect proprietary and other confidential or privileged information, and subject to the provisions of the Intellectual Property Annex, which is an integral part of this Arrangement.

B. Definitions

1. The term "information" means unclassified nuclear energy-related regulatory, safety, waste management, scientific or technical data, including information on results or methods of assessment, research, and any other knowledge provided, created or exchanged under this Arrangement.

2. The term "proprietary information" means information made available under this Arrangement that contains trade secrets or other privileged or confidential commercial information (such that the person having the information may derive a commercial benefit from it or may have a commercial advantage over those who do not have it), and may only include information that:

a. has been held in confidence by its owner;

b. has not been transmitted by the owner to other entities (including the receiving Party), except on the basis that it be held in confidence;

c. is not otherwise available to the receiving Party from another source without restriction on its further dissemination; and

d. is not already in the possession of the receiving Party.

3. The term "other confidential or privileged information" means information, other than "proprietary information," that has been transmitted and received in confidence under this Arrangement and is protected from public disclosure under the laws, regulations, or policies of the country of the Party providing the information.

C. Marking Procedures for Documentary Proprietary Information

A Party receiving documentary proprietary information pursuant to this Arrangement shall respect the privileged nature of such information, provided that such proprietary information is clearly marked with the following (or substantially similar) restrictive legend:

> "This document contains proprietary information furnished in confidence under an Arrangement dated September 18th, 2012, between the United States Nuclear Regulatory Commission and the Nuclear Safety and Security Commission of the United Mexican States and shall not be disseminated outside these organizations, their consultants, contractors, and licensees, or concerned departments and agencies of the Government of the United States and the Government of Mexico, without the prior written approval of (name of transmitting Party). This notice shall be marked on each page of any reproduction hereof, in whole or in part. These limitations shall automatically terminate when the proprietary information is disclosed by the owner without restriction."

This restrictive legend shall be respected by the Parties to this Arrangement. Proprietary information bearing this restrictive legend shall not be made public or otherwise disseminated in any manner unspecified or contrary to the terms of this Arrangement without the prior written consent of the transmitting Party. Proprietary information bearing this restrictive legend shall not be used by the receiving Party or its contractors and consultants for any commercial purposes without the prior written consent of the transmitting Party.

D. Dissemination of Documentary Proprietary Information

1. In general, proprietary information received under this Arrangement may be disseminated by the receiving Party without prior consent to persons within or employed by the receiving Party, and to concerned Government departments and Government agencies in the country of the receiving Party, provided:

a. such dissemination is made on a case-by-case basis; and

b. such proprietary information bears the restrictive legend appearing in Section III.C. of this Arrangement.

2. Proprietary information received under this Arrangement may be disseminated by the receiving Party without prior consent to contractors and consultants of the receiving Party located within the geographical limits of that Party's country provided:

a. that the proprietary information is used by such contractors and consultants only for work within the scope of their contracts with the receiving Party relating to the subject matter of the proprietary information, and shall not be used by such contractors and consultants for any other private commercial purposes;

b. that such dissemination is made on a case-by-case basis to contractors and consultants who have executed a non-disclosure agreement; and

c. that such proprietary information shall bear the restrictive legend appearing in Section III.C. of this Arrangement.

3. With the prior written consent of the Party furnishing proprietary information under this Arrangement, the receiving Party may disseminate such proprietary information more widely than otherwise permitted under the terms set forth in this Arrangement. The Parties shall endeavor to grant such approval to the extent permitted by their respective national laws, regulations and policies, provided:

a. that the entities receiving proprietary information under Section III.D.3. of this Arrangement, including domestic organizations permitted or licensed by the receiving Party to construct or operate nuclear production or utilization facilities, or to use nuclear and materials radiation sources, have executed a non-disclosure agreement;

b. that the entities receiving proprietary information under Section III.D.3. of this Arrangement, including domestic organizations permitted or licensed by the receiving Party to construct or operate nuclear production or utilization facilities, shall not use such proprietary information for any private commercial purposes; and

c. that those entities receiving proprietary information under Section III.D.3. of this Arrangement that are domestic organizations permitted or licensed by the receiving Party, agree to use the proprietary information only for activities carried out under or within the terms of their specific permit or license.

E. Marking Procedures for Other Confidential or Privileged Information of a Documentary Nature

A Party receiving under this Arrangement other confidential or privileged information shall respect its confidential nature, provided such information is clearly marked so as to indicate its confidential or privileged nature and is accompanied by a statement indicating:

1. that the information is protected from public disclosure by the government of the transmitting Party; and

2. that the information is transmitted under the condition that it be maintained in confidence.

F. Dissemination of Other Confidential or Privileged Information of a Documentary Nature

Other confidential or privileged information may be disseminated in the same manner as that set forth in Section III.D, "Dissemination of Documentary Proprietary Information."

G. Non-Documentary Proprietary or Other Confidential or Privileged Information

Non-documentary proprietary or other confidential or privileged information provided in seminars and other meetings organized under this Arrangement, or information arising from the attachments of staff, use of facilities, or joint projects, shall be treated by the Parties according to the principles specified for documentary information in this Arrangement; provided, however, that the Party communicating such proprietary or other confidential or privileged information has placed the recipient on notice as to the character of the information communicated.

H. Consultation

If, for any reason, one of the Parties becomes aware that it will be, or may reasonably be expected to become, unable to meet the non-dissemination provisions of this Arrangement, it shall immediately inform the other Party. The Parties shall thereafter consult to define an appropriate course of action.

I. Other

Nothing contained in this Arrangement shall preclude a Party from using or disseminating information received without restriction by a Party from sources outside of this Arrangement.

IV. FINAL PROVISIONS

A. Nothing contained in this Arrangement shall require either Party to take any action that would be inconsistent with its existing laws, regulations, or policy directives. Should any conflict arise between the terms of this Arrangement and those laws, regulations, or policy directives, the Parties agree to consult before any action is taken. No nuclear information related to proliferation-sensitive technologies shall be exchanged under this Arrangement.

B. Unless otherwise agreed, all costs resulting from cooperation pursuant to this Arrangement shall be the responsibility of the Party that incurs them. The ability of the Parties to carry out their obligations is subject to the appropriation of funds by the appropriate governmental authority and to the laws, regulations and policies applicable to the Parties.

C. Cooperation under this Arrangement shall be in accordance with the laws and regulations of the Parties. Any dispute or questions between the Parties concerning the interpretation or application of this Arrangement shall be settled by mutual agreement of the Parties.

D. This Arrangement shall enter into force upon signature and, subject to paragraph E of this Section, shall remain in force for a period of five years. It may be extended for a further period of time by written agreement of the Parties.

E. Either Party may terminate this Arrangement after providing the other Party written notice 180 days prior to its intended date of termination.

DONE at Vienna, Austria on this 18th day of September, 2012, in duplicate in the English and Spanish languages, both texts being equally authentic.

FOR THE NUCLEAR REGULATORY COMMISSION OF THE UNITED STATES OF AMERICA

[Signature]

Allison M. Macfarlane, Chairman

FOR THE COMISION NACIONAL DE SEGURIDAD NUCLEAR Y SALVAGUARDIAS OF THE UNITED MEXICAN STATES

[Signature]

Juan Eibenschutz, Director General

CERTIFIED A TRUE COPY
BY [Signature]

Office of the Secretary

Addendum A

USNRC-CNSNS Safety Research Exchange
Areas in Which the USNRC Is Performing or Sponsoring Safety Research

1. Digital Instrumentation and Control
2. Reactor and Electrical Equipment Qualification
3. Environmental Transport
4. Radionuclide Transport and Waste Management
5. Dry Cask Storage and Transport
6. Fire Safety Research
7. Nuclear Fuel Analysis
8. Severe Accident Analysis
9. Operating Experience and Generic Issues
10. Human Factors Engineering
11. Organizational Factors/Safety Culture
12. Human Reliability Analysis (HRA)
13. Probabilistic Risk Assessments
14. Radiation Protection and Health Effects
15. Seismic Safety
16. State of the Art Risk Consequences
17. Reactor Containment Structural Safety
18. Reactor Vessel and Piping Integrity
19. Regulatory Guide Update
20. New and Advanced Reactor Designs
21. Decommissioning
22. Thermal Hydraulic Code Applications and Maintenance
23. Uncertainty Analysis for Thermal Hydraulic Kinetics
24. Coupled 3D Neutronic and Plant Thermal Hydraulics
25. Medical Isotope Production
26. Long-term Operational Management
27. Plant and Systems Operations

Addendum B

USNRC-CNSNS Nuclear Safety Research Exchange Areas in Which the CNSNS is Performing or Sponsoring Safety Research

1. Transient Analysis
2. Reactor Fuel and Coolant Behavior analysis
3. Evaluation and Applications of Integral and Best Estimate Codes for Severe Accident Analysis
4. Development of Basis for Severe Accident Management Guidelines
5. PSA for Low Power and Shutdown
6. Containment Response Analysis
7. PSA Applications
8. PSA for Radioactive Installations
9. Integral Safety Margins Assessment

INTELLECTUAL PROPERTY RIGHTS

I. General Obligationa

The Parties shall ensure adequate and effective protection of intellectual property created or furnished under this Arrangement and relevant implementing arrangements. Rights to such intellectual property shall be allocated as provided in this Annex.

II. Scope

A. This Annex is applicable to all cooperative activities undertaken pursuant to this Arrangement, except as otherwise specifically agreed by the Parties or their designees.

B. For purposes of this Arrangement, "intellectual property" shall mean the subject matter listed in Article 2 of the Convention Establishing the World Intellectual Property Organization, done at Stockholm, July 14, 1967 and may include other subject matter as agreed by the Parties.

C. Each Party shall ensure, through contracts or other legal means with its own participants, if necessary, that the other Party can obtain the rights to intellectual property allocated in accordance with this Annex. This Annex does not otherwise alter or prejudice the allocation between a Party and its nationals, which shall be determined by that Party's laws and practices.

D. Except as otherwise provided in this Arrangement, disputes concerning intellectual property arising under this Arrangement shall be resolved through discussions between the concerned participating institutions, or, if necessary, the Parties or their designees. Upon mutual agreement of the Parties, a dispute shall be submitted to an arbitral tribunal for binding arbitration in accordance with the applicable rules of international law. Unless the Parties or their designees agree otherwise in writing, the arbitration rules of United Nations Commission on International Trade Law UNCITRAL shall govern.

E. Termination or expiration of this Arrangement shall not affect rights or obligations under this Annex.

III. Allocation of Rights

A. Each Party shall be entitled to a non-exclusive, irrevocable, royalty-free license in all countries to translate, reproduce, and publicly distribute scientific and technical journal articles, reports, and books directly arising from cooperation under this Arrangement. All publicly distributed copies of a copyrighted work prepared under this provision shall indicate the names of the authors of the work unless an author explicitly declines to be named.

B. Rights to all forms of intellectual property, other than those rights described in paragraph III.A. above, shall be allocated as follows:

(1) Visiting researchers shall receive rights, awards, bonuses and royalties in accordance with the policies of the host institution.

(2)(a) Any intellectual property created by persons employed or sponsored by one Party under cooperative activities other than those covered by paragraph III.(B)(1) shall be owned by that Party. Intellectual property created by persons employed or sponsored by both Parties shall be jointly owned by the Parties. In addition, each creator shall be entitled to awards, bonuses and royalties in accordance with the policies of the institution employing or sponsoring that person.

(b) Unless otherwise agreed in an implementing or other arrangement, each Party shall have within its territory a right to exploit or license intellectual property created in the course of the cooperative activities.

(c) The rights of a Party outside its territory shall be determined by mutual agreement considering the relative contributions of the Parties and their participants to the cooperative activities, the degree of commitment in obtaining legal protection and licensing of the intellectual property and such other factors deemed appropriate.

(d) Notwithstanding paragraphs III.B(2)(a) and (b) above, if either Party believes that a particular project is likely to lead to or has led to the creation of intellectual property not protected by the laws of the other Party, the Parties shall immediately hold discussions to determine the allocation of rights to the intellectual property. If an agreement cannot be reached within three months of the date of the initiation of the discussions, cooperation on the project in question shall be terminated at the request of either Party. Creators of intellectual property shall nonetheless be entitled to awards, bonuses and royalties as provided in paragraph III.B(2)(a).

(e) For each invention made under any cooperative activity, the Party employing or sponsoring the inventor(s) shall disclose the invention promptly to the other Party together with any documentation and information necessary to enable the other Party to establish any rights to which it may be entitled. Either Party may ask the other Party in writing to delay publication or public disclosure of such documentation or information for the purpose of protecting its rights in the invention. Unless otherwise agreed in writing, the delay shall not exceed a period of six months from the date of disclosure by the inventing Party to the other Party.

IV. Business Confidential Information

In the event that information identified in a timely fashion as business-confidential is furnished or created under this Arrangement, each Party and its participants shall protect such information in accordance with applicable laws, regulations, and administrative practices. Information may be identified as "business-confidential" if a person having the information may derive an economic benefit from it or may obtain a competitive advantage over those who do not have it, and the information is not generally known or publicly available from other sources, and the owner has not previously made the information available without imposing in a timely manner an obligation to keep it confidential.

STATE DEPARTMENT DOCUMENT NUMBER: 12-175

ARRANGEMENT BETWEEN THE UNITED STATES NUCLEAR REGULATORY COMMISSION AND THE SWISS FEDERAL NUCLEAR SAFETY INSPECTORATE OF SWITZERLAND FOR THE EXCHANGE OF TECHNICAL INFORMATION AND COOPERATION IN NUCLEAR SAFETY MATTERS, WITH ADDENDUMS

SIGNED AT VIENNA, SEPTEMBER 19, 2012
ENTERED INTO FORCE SEPTEMBER 19, 2012

CTIA DOCUMENT NUMBER: 18081.000

SEPTEMBER 19, 2012

The United States Nuclear Regulatory Commission (hereinafter called the USNRC) and the Swiss Federal Nuclear Safety Inspectorate of Switzerland (hereinafter called the ENSI), both hereinafter called the Parties;

Having a mutual interest, within the framework of their competence, in the exchange of information and cooperation pertaining to regulatory matters and of standards required or recommended by their organizations for the regulation of safety and environmental impact of nuclear facilities;

Having similarly cooperated under the terms of a five-year Arrangement for the Exchange of Technical Information and Cooperation in Nuclear Safety Matters, signed on December 9, 1974, between their predecessor agencies, the United States Atomic Energy Commission and the Swiss Federal Office of Energy;

They or their predecessor agencies having already continued such cooperation for five-year periods on August 10, 1982, September 23, 1987, September 23, 1992, September 30, 1997, September 18, 2002, and September 18, 2007; and having indicated their mutual desire to continue the cooperation for another five years;

Have agreed as follows:

I. SCOPE OF THE ARRANGEMENT

A. Technical Information Exchange

To the extent that the Parties are permitted to do so under the laws, regulations, and policy directives of their respective countries, they shall exchange the following types of unclassified technical information relating to the regulation of safety, waste management, radiological safety, and environmental impact of designated nuclear energy facilities and to nuclear safety research programs:

1. Topical reports concerning safety, waste management, radiological safety, and environmental effects written by or for one of the Parties as a basis for, or in support of, regulatory decisions and policies.

2. Documents relating to significant licensing actions and safety and environmental decisions affecting nuclear facilities.

3. Detailed documents describing the USNRC process for licensing and regulating certain U.S. facilities designated by the ENSI as similar to certain facilities being built or planned in Switzerland and equivalent documents on such Swiss facilities.

4. Information in the field of reactor safety research that the Parties have the right to disclose, either in the possession of one of the Parties or available to it, including light water reactor safety information from the technical areas described in Addenda "A" and "B", attached hereto and made a part of this Arrangement. Cooperation in these itemized research areas may require a separate agreement, as determined to be necessary by the research organizations of one or both of the Parties. Each Party shall transmit immediately to the other information concerning research results that requires early attention in the interest of public safety, along with an indication of significant implications.

5. Reports on operating experience, such as reports on nuclear incidents, accidents and shutdowns, and compilations of historical reliability data on components and systems.

6. Regulatory procedures for the safety, waste management, radiological safety, and environmental impact evaluation of nuclear facilities.

7. Early advice of important events, such as serious operating incidents, government-directed reactor shutdowns, and emerging technical issues, that are of immediate interest to the Parties.

B. Cooperation in Nuclear Safety Research

The terms of cooperation for joint programs and projects of nuclear safety research and development, or those programs and projects under which activities are divided between the two Parties, including the use of test facilities and/or computer programs owned by either Party, shall be considered on a case-by-case basis and may be the subject of a separate letter of agreement, if determined to be necessary by the research organizations of one or both of the Parties. When not the subject of a separate letter of agreement, the terms of cooperation may be established by an exchange of letters between the research organizations of the Parties, and shall be subject to the terms and conditions of the present Arrangement.

Technical areas specified by such exchanges of letters may be modified subsequently by mutual consent. Temporary assignments of personnel by one Party in the other Party's Agency shall also be considered on a case-by-case basis and shall, in general, require a separate letter of agreement between the research organizations of the Parties.

C. Training and Assignments

Within the limits of available resources and subject to the availability of appropriated funds, the USNRC shall cooperate with the ENSI in providing certain training and experience for ENSI safety personnel. Unless otherwise agreed, costs of salary, allowances, and travel of ENSI participants shall be paid by the ENSI. The following are typical of, but not necessarily restricted to, the kinds of training and experience that may be provided:

1. ENSI designated inspector accompaniment of USNRC inspectors on reactor operation and reactor construction inspection visits in the United States, including extended briefings at USNRC regional inspection offices.

2. Participation by ENSI employees in USNRC staff training courses.

3. Assignment of ENSI experts for certain periods to be determined by the Parties within the USNRC staff to work on USNRC staff duties and gain on the job experience.

4. Training assignments of the ENSI within the radiation control program in the United States.

II. ADMINISTRATION

A. The exchange of information under this Arrangement shall be accomplished through letters, reports, and other documents, and by visits and meetings arranged in advance on a case-by-case basis. Periodic meetings shall be held at such times as mutually agreed to review the exchange of information and cooperation under this Arrangement, to recommend revisions to the provisions of the Arrangement, and to discuss topics coming within the scope of the cooperation. The time, place, and agenda for such meetings shall be agreed upon in advance. Visits which take place under the Arrangement, including their schedules, shall have the prior approval of the administrators referred to in paragraph II.B.

B. An administrator shall be designated by each Party to coordinate its participation in the overall exchange under this Arrangement. The administrators shall be the recipients of all documents transmitted under the exchange, including copies of all letters unless otherwise agreed. Within the terms of the exchange, the administrators will be responsible for developing the scope of the exchange, including agreement on the designation of the nuclear energy facilities subject to the exchange, and on specific documents and standards to be exchanged. One or more technical coordinators may be appointed as direct contacts for specific disciplinary areas. These technical coordinators shall ensure that both administrators receive copies of all transmittals. These detailed arrangements are intended to ensure, among other things, that a reasonably balanced exchange giving access to equivalent available information is achieved and maintained.

C. The administrators shall determine the number of copies to be provided of the documents exchanged. Each document shall be accompanied by an abstract in English, 250 words or less, describing its scope and content.

D. The application or use of any information exchanged or transferred between the Parties under this Arrangement shall be the responsibility of the receiving Party, and the transmitting Party does not warrant the suitability of such information for any particular use or application.

E. Recognizing that some information of the type covered in this Arrangement is not available within the agencies that are Parties to this Arrangement, but is available from other agencies of the governments of the Parties, each Party shall assist the other to the maximum extent possible by organizing visits and directing inquiries concerning such information to appropriate agencies of the government concerned. The foregoing shall not constitute a commitment of other agencies to furnish such information or to receive such visitors.

III. EXCHANGE AND USE OF INFORMATION

A. General

The Parties support the widest possible dissemination of information provided or exchanged under this Arrangement, subject to the requirements of each Party's national laws, regulations and policies and the need to protect proprietary and other confidential or privileged information, and subject to the provisions of the Intellectual Property Annex, which is an integral part of this Arrangement.

B. Definitions

1. The term "information" means unclassified nuclear energy-related regulatory, safety, waste management, scientific or technical data, including information on results or methods of assessment, research, and any other knowledge provided, created or exchanged under this Arrangement.

2. The term "proprietary information" means information made available under this Arrangement that contains trade secrets or other privileged or confidential commercial information (such that the person having the information may derive a commercial benefit from it or may have a commercial advantage over those who do not have it), and may only include information that:

a. has been held in confidence by its owner;

b. has not been transmitted by the owner to other entities (including the receiving Party), except on the basis that it be held in confidence;

c. is not otherwise available to the receiving Party from another source without restriction on its further dissemination; and

d. is not already in the possession of the receiving Party.

3. The term "other confidential or privileged information" means information, other than "proprietary information," that has been transmitted and received in confidence under this Arrangement and is protected from public disclosure under the laws, regulations, or policies of the country of the Party providing the information.

C. Marking Procedures for Documentary Proprietary Information

A Party receiving documentary proprietary information pursuant to this Arrangement shall respect the privileged nature of such information, provided that such proprietary information is clearly marked with the following (or substantially similar) restrictive legend:

> "This document contains proprietary information furnished in confidence under an Arrangement dated September 19th, 2012, between the United States Nuclear Regulatory Commission and the Swiss Federal Nuclear Safety Inspectorate (ENSI) and shall not be disseminated outside these organizations, their consultants, contractors, and licensees, or concerned departments and agencies of the Government of the United States and the Government of Switzerland, without the prior written approval of (name of transmitting Party). This notice shall be marked on each page of any reproduction hereof, in whole or in part. These limitations shall automatically terminate when the proprietary information is disclosed by the owner without restriction."

This restrictive legend shall be respected by the Parties to this Arrangement. Proprietary information bearing this restrictive legend shall not be made public or otherwise disseminated in any manner unspecified or contrary to the terms of this Arrangement without the prior written consent of the transmitting Party. Proprietary information bearing this restrictive legend shall not be used by the receiving Party or its contractors and consultants for any commercial purposes without the prior written consent of the transmitting Party.

D. Dissemination of Documentary Proprietary Information

1. In general, proprietary information received under this Arrangement may be disseminated by the receiving Party without prior consent to persons within or employed by the receiving Party, and to concerned Government departments and Government agencies in the country of the receiving Party, provided:

a. such dissemination is made on a case-by-case basis; and

b. such proprietary information bears the restrictive legend appearing in Section III.C. of this Arrangement.

2. Proprietary information received under this Arrangement may be disseminated by the receiving Party without prior consent to contractors and consultants of the receiving Party located within the geographical limits of that Party's country provided:

a. that the proprietary information is used by such contractors and consultants only for work within the scope of their contracts with the receiving Party relating to the subject matter of the proprietary information, and shall not be used by such contractors and consultants for any other private commercial purposes;

b. that such dissemination is made on a case-by-case basis to contractors and consultants who have executed a non-disclosure agreement; and

c. that such proprietary information shall bear the restrictive legend appearing in Section III.C. of this Arrangement.

3. With the prior written consent of the Party furnishing proprietary information under this Arrangement, the receiving Party may disseminate such proprietary information more widely than otherwise permitted under the terms set forth in this Arrangement. The Parties shall endeavor to grant such approval to the extent permitted by their respective national laws, regulations and policies, provided:

a. that the entities receiving proprietary information under Section III.D.3. of this Arrangement, including domestic organizations permitted or licensed by the receiving Party to construct or operate nuclear production or utilization facilities, or to use nuclear and materials radiation sources, have executed a non-disclosure agreement;

b. that the entities receiving proprietary information under Section III.D.3. of this Arrangement, including domestic organizations permitted or licensed by the receiving Party to construct or operate nuclear production or utilization facilities, shall not use such proprietary information for any private commercial purposes; and

c. that those entities receiving proprietary information under Section III.D.3. of this Arrangement that are domestic organizations permitted or licensed by the receiving Party, agree to use the proprietary information only for activities carried out under or within the terms of their specific permit or license.

E. Marking Procedures for Other Confidential or Privileged Information of a Documentary Nature

A Party receiving under this Arrangement other confidential or privileged information shall respect its confidential nature, provided such information is clearly marked so as to indicate its confidential or privileged nature and is accompanied by a statement indicating:

1. that the information is protected from public disclosure by the government of the transmitting Party; and
2. that the information is transmitted under the condition that it be maintained in confidence.

F. Dissemination of Other Confidential or Privileged Information of a Documentary Nature

Other confidential or privileged information may be disseminated in the same manner as that set forth in Section III.D, "Dissemination of Documentary Proprietary Information."

G. Non-Documentary Proprietary or Other Confidential or Privileged Information

Non-documentary proprietary or other confidential or privileged information provided in seminars and other meetings organized under this Arrangement, or information arising from the attachments of staff, use of facilities, or joint projects, shall be treated by the Parties according to the principles specified for documentary information in this Arrangement; provided, however, that the Party communicating such proprietary or other confidential or privileged information has placed the recipient on notice as to the character of the information communicated.

H. Consultation

If, for any reason, one of the Parties becomes aware that it will be, or may reasonably be expected to become, unable to meet the non-dissemination provisions of this Arrangement, it shall immediately inform the other Party. The Parties shall thereafter consult to define an appropriate course of action.

I. Other

Nothing contained in this Arrangement shall preclude a Party from using or disseminating information received without restriction by a Party from sources outside of this Arrangement.

IV. FINAL PROVISIONS

A. Nothing contained in this Arrangement shall require either Party to take any action that would be inconsistent with its existing laws, regulations, or policy directives. Should any conflict arise between the terms of this Arrangement and those laws, regulations, or policy directives, the Parties agree to consult before any action is taken. No nuclear information related to proliferation-sensitive technologies shall be exchanged under this Arrangement.

B. Unless otherwise agreed, all costs resulting from cooperation pursuant to this Arrangement shall be the responsibility of the Party that incurs them. The ability of the Parties to carry out their obligations is subject to the appropriation of funds by the appropriate governmental authority and to the laws, regulations and policies applicable to the Parties.

C. All information protected by provisions of this Arrangement as proprietary or other confidential or privileged information shall remain so protected for the duration of this Arrangement and after this Arrangement has expired or been terminated, unless otherwise agreed by the Parties in writing.

D. Cooperation under this Arrangement shall be in accordance with the laws and regulations of the Parties. Any dispute or questions between the Parties concerning the interpretation or application of this Arrangement shall be settled by mutual agreement of the Parties.

E. This Arrangement shall enter into force upon signature and, subject to paragraph F. of this Section, shall remain in force for a period of five years. It may be extended for a further period of time by written agreement of the Parties.

F. Either Party may terminate this Arrangement after providing the other Party written notice 180 days prior to its intended date of termination.

DONE at Vienna, Austria on this 19th day of September, 2012, in the English language.

FOR THE US NUCLEAR REGULATORY COMMISSION OF THE UNITED STATES

[Signature]

Allison M. Macfarlane, Chairman

FOR THE SWISS FEDERAL NUCLEAR SAFETY INSPECTORATE

[Signature]

Hans Wanner, Director General

CERTIFIED A TRUE COPY
BY [Signature]

Office of the Secretary

Addendum A

USNRC-ENSI Safety Research Exchange
Areas in Which the USNRC Is Performing or Sponsoring Safety Research

1. Digital Instrumentation and Control
2. Reactor and Electrical Equipment Qualification
3. Environmental Transport
4. Radionuclide Transport and Waste Management
5. Dry Cask Storage and Transport
6. Fire Safety Research
7. Nuclear Fuel Analysis
8. Severe Accident Analysis
9. Operating Experience and Generic Issues
10. Human Factors Engineering
11. Organizational Factors/Safety Culture
12. Human Reliability Analysis (HRA)
13. Probabilistic Risk Assessments
14. Radiation Protection and Health Effects
15. Seismic Safety
16. State of the Art Risk Consequences
17. Reactor Containment Structural Safety
18. Reactor Vessel and Piping Integrity
19. Regulatory Guide Update
20. New and Advanced Reactor Designs
21. Decommissioning
22. Thermal Hydraulic Code Applications and Maintenance
23. Uncertainty Analysis for Thermal Hydraulic Kinetics
24. Coupled 3D Neutronic and Plant Thermal Hydraulics
25. Medical Isotope Production
26. Long-term Operational Management
27. Plant and Systems Operations

Addendum B

Areas in Which the ENSI Is Performing or Sponsoring Nuclear Safety Research

1. Fuel safety criteria and ageing of structural materials
2. Internal events and damage occurrences
3. External events
4. Human factors
5. Systems behaviour and accident sequences
6. Radiological protection
7. Waste disposal

ANNEX
Intellectual Property Rights

I. General Obligation

The Parties shall ensure adequate and effective protection of intellectual property created or furnished under this Arrangement and relevant implementing arrangements. Rights to such intellectual property shall be allocated as provided in this Annex.

II. Scope

A. This Annex is applicable to all cooperative activities undertaken pursuant to this Arrangement, except as otherwise specifically agreed by the Parties or their designees.

B. For purposes of this Arrangement, "intellectual property" shall mean the subject matter listed in Article 2 of the Convention Establishing the World Intellectual Property Organization, done at Stockholm, July 14, 1967 and may include other subject matter as agreed by the Parties.

C. Each Party shall ensure, through contracts or other legal means with its own participants, if necessary, that the other Party can obtain the rights to intellectual property allocated in accordance with this Annex. This Annex does not otherwise alter or prejudice the allocation between a Party and its nationals, which shall be determined by that Party's laws and practices.

D. Except as otherwise provided in this Arrangement, disputes concerning intellectual property arising under this Arrangement shall be resolved through discussions between the concerned participating institutions, or, if necessary, the Parties or their designees. Upon mutual Arrangement of the Parties, a dispute shall be submitted to an arbitral tribunal for binding arbitration in accordance with the applicable rules of international law. Unless the Parties or their designees agree otherwise in writing, the arbitration rules of UNCITRAL shall govern.

E. Termination or expiration of this Arrangement shall not affect rights or obligations under this Annex.

III. Allocation of Rights

A. Each Party shall be entitled to a non-exclusive, irrevocable, royalty-free license in all countries to translate, reproduce, and publicly distribute scientific and technical journal articles, reports, and books directly arising from cooperation under this Arrangement. All publicly distributed copies of a copyrighted work prepared under this provision shall indicate the names of the authors of the work unless an author explicitly declines to be named.

B. Rights to all forms of intellectual property, other than those rights described in paragraph IIIA above, shall be allocated as follows:

(1) Visiting researchers shall receive rights, awards, bonuses and royalties in accordance with the policies of the host institution.

(2)(a) Any intellectual property created by persons employed or sponsored by one Party under cooperative activities other than those covered by paragraph III.(B)(1) shall be owned by that Party. Intellectual property created by persons employed or sponsored by both Parties shall be jointly owned by the Parties. In addition, each creator shall be entitled to awards, bonuses and royalties in accordance with the policies of the institution employing or sponsoring that person.

(b) Unless otherwise agreed in an implementing or other arrangement, each Party shall have within its territory a right to exploit or license intellectual property created in the course of the cooperative activities.

(c) The rights of a Party outside its territory shall be determined by mutual Arrangement considering the relative contributions of the Parties and their participants to the cooperative activities, the degree of commitment in obtaining legal protection and licensing of the intellectual property and such other factors deemed appropriate.

(d) Notwithstanding paragraphs III.B(2)(a) and (b) above, if either Party believes that a particular project is likely to lead to or has led to the creation of intellectual property not protected by the laws of the other Party, the Parties shall immediately hold discussions to determine the allocation of rights to the intellectual property. If an Arrangement cannot be reached within three months of the date of the initiation of the discussions, cooperation on the project in question shall be terminated at the request of either Party. Creators of intellectual property shall nonetheless be entitled to awards, bonuses and royalties as provided in paragraph III.B(2)(a).

(e) For each invention made under any cooperative activity, the Party employing or sponsoring the inventor(s) shall disclose the invention promptly to the other Party together with any documentation and information necessary to enable the other Party to establish any rights to which it may be entitled. Either Party may ask the other Party in writing to delay publication or public disclosure of such documentation or information for the purpose of protecting its rights in the invention. Unless otherwise agreed in writing, the delay shall not exceed a period of six months from the date of disclosure by the inventing Party to the other Party.

IV. Business Confidential Information

In the event that information identified in a timely fashion as business-confidential is furnished or created under this Arrangement, each Party and its participants shall protect such information in accordance with applicable laws, regulations, and administrative practices. Information may be identified as "business-confidential" if a person having the information may derive an economic benefit from it or may obtain a competitive advantage over those who do not have it, and the information is not generally known or publicly available from other sources, and the owner has not previously made the information available without imposing in a timely manner an obligation to keep it confidential.

STATE DEPARTMENT DOCUMENT NUMBER: 12-176

ARRANGEMENT BETWEEN THE UNITED STATES NUCLEAR REGULATORY COMMISSION AND THE JORDAN NUCLEAR REGULATORY COMMISSION FOR THE EXCHANGE OF TECHNICAL INFORMATION AND COOPERATION IN NUCLEAR SAFETY MATTERS, WITH ADDENDUMS

SIGNED AT VIENNA, SEPTEMBER 20, 2012
ENTERED INTO FORCE SEPTEMBER 20, 2012

CTIA DOCUMENT NUMBER: 18082.000

September 20, 2012

The Nuclear Regulatory Commission of the United States of America (hereinafter called the USNRC), and the Jordan Nuclear Regulatory Commission (hereinafter called the USNRC), both hereinafter referred to as the Parties;

Having a mutual interest in a continuing exchange of information pertaining to regulatory matters and of standards required or recommended by their organizations for the regulation of safety and environmental impact of nuclear facilities;

Have agreed as follows:

I. SCOPE OF THE ARRANGEMENT

A. Technical Information Exchange

To the extent that the Parties are permitted to do so under the laws, regulations, and policy directives of their respective countries, they shall exchange the following types of unclassified technical information relating to the regulation of safety, waste management, radiological safety, and environmental impact of designated nuclear energy facilities and to nuclear safety research programs:

1. Topical reports concerning safety, waste management, radiological safety, and environmental effects written by or for one of the Parties as a basis for, or in support of, regulatory decisions and policies.

2. Documents relating to significant licensing actions and safety and environmental decisions affecting nuclear facilities.

3. Detailed documents describing the USNRC process for licensing and regulating certain U.S. facilities designated by the JNRC as similar to certain facilities being built or planned in Jordan and equivalent documents on such facilities owned by Jordan.

4. Information in the field of reactor safety research that the Parties have the right to disclose, either in the possession of one of the Parties or available to it, including light water reactor safety information from the technical areas described in Addenda "A" and "B", attached hereto and made integral parts of this Arrangement. Cooperation in these itemized research areas may require a separate agreement, as determined to be necessary by the research organizations of one or both of the Parties. Each Party shall transmit immediately to the other information concerning research results that requires early attention in the interest of public safety, along with an indication of significant implications.

5. Reports on operating experience, such as reports on nuclear incidents, accidents and shutdowns, and compilations of historical reliability data on components and systems.

6. Regulatory procedures for the safety, waste management, radiological safety, and environmental impact evaluation of nuclear facilities.

7. Early advice of important events, such as serious operating incidents, government-directed reactor shutdowns, and emerging technical issues, that are of immediate interest to the Parties.

B. Cooperation in Nuclear Safety Research

The terms of cooperation for joint programs and projects of nuclear safety research and development, or those programs and projects under which activities are divided between the two Parties, including the use of test facilities and/or computer programs owned by either Party, shall be considered on a case-by-case basis and may be the subject of a separate agreement, if determined to be necessary by the research organizations of one or both of the Parties. When not the subject of a separate agreement, the terms of cooperation may be established by an exchange of letters between the research organizations of the Parties, and shall be subject to the terms and conditions of the present Arrangement.

Technical areas specified by such exchanges of letters may be modified subsequently by mutual consent. Temporary assignments of personnel by one Party in the other Party's Agency shall also be considered on a case-by-case basis and shall, in general, require a separate agreement between the research organizations of the Parties.

C. Training and Assignments

Within the limits of available resources and subject to the availability of appropriated funds, the USNRC shall cooperate with the JNRC in providing certain training and experience for JNRC safety personnel. Unless otherwise agreed, costs of salary, allowances, and travel of JNRC participants shall be paid by the JNRC. The following are typical of, but not necessarily exclusive of, the kinds of training and experience that may be provided:

1. JNRC designated inspector accompaniment of USNRC inspectors on reactor operation and reactor construction inspection visits in the United States, including extended briefings at USNRC regional inspection offices.

2. Participation by JNRC employees in USNRC staff training courses.

3. Assignment of JNRC experts for certain periods to be determined by the Parties within the USNRC staff to work on USNRC staff duties and gain on the job experience.

4. Training assignments of the JNRC within the radiation control program in the United States.

II. ADMINISTRATION

A. The exchange of information under this Arrangement shall be accomplished through letters, reports, and other documents, and by visits and meetings arranged in advance on a case-by-case basis. Periodic meetings shall be held at such times as mutually agreed to review the exchange of information and cooperation under this Arrangement, to recommend revisions to the provisions of the Arrangement, and to discuss topics coming within the scope of the cooperation. The time, place, and agenda for such meetings shall be agreed upon in advance. Visits which take place under the Arrangement, including their schedules, shall have the prior approval of the administrators referred to in paragraph II.B.

B. An administrator shall be designated by each Party to coordinate its participation in the overall exchange under this Arrangement. The administrators shall be the recipients of all documents transmitted under the exchange, including copies of all letters unless otherwise agreed. Within the terms of the exchange, the administrators will be responsible for developing the scope of the exchange, including agreement on the designation of the nuclear energy facilities subject to the exchange, and on specific documents and standards to be exchanged. One or more technical coordinators may be appointed as direct contacts for specific disciplinary areas. These technical coordinators shall ensure that both administrators receive copies of all transmittals. These detailed arrangements are intended to ensure, among other things, that a reasonably balanced exchange giving access to equivalent available information is achieved and maintained.

C. The administrators shall determine the number of copies to be provided of the documents exchanged. Each document shall be accompanied by an abstract in English, 250 words or less, describing its scope and content.

D. The application or use of any information exchanged or transferred between the Parties under this Arrangement shall be the responsibility of the receiving Party, and the transmitting Party does not warrant the suitability of such information for any particular use or application.

E. Recognizing that some information of the type covered in this Arrangement is not available within the agencies that are Parties to this Arrangement, but is available from other agencies of the governments of the Parties, each Party shall assist the other to the maximum extent possible by organizing visits and directing inquiries concerning such information to appropriate agencies of the government concerned. The foregoing shall not constitute a commitment of other agencies to furnish such information or to receive such visitors.

III. EXCHANGE AND USE OF INFORMATION

A. General

The Parties support the widest possible dissemination of information provided or exchanged under this Arrangement, subject to the requirements of each Party's national laws, regulations and policies and the need to protect proprietary and other confidential or privileged information, and subject to the provisions of the Intellectual Property Annex, which is an integral part of this Arrangement.

B. Definitions

1. The term "information" means unclassified nuclear energy-related regulatory, safety, waste management, scientific or technical data, including information on results or methods of assessment, research, and any other knowledge provided, created or exchanged under this Arrangement.

2. The term "proprietary information" means information made available under this Arrangement that contains trade secrets or other privileged or confidential commercial information (such that the

person having the information may derive a commercial benefit from it or may have a commercial advantage over those who do not have it), and may only include information that:

a. has been held in confidence by its owner;

b. has not been transmitted by the owner to other entities (including the receiving Party), except on the basis that it be held in confidence;

c. is not otherwise available to the receiving Party from another source without restriction on its further dissemination; and

d. is not already in the possession of the receiving Party.

3. The term "other confidential or privileged information" means information, other than "proprietary information," that has been transmitted and received in confidence under this Arrangement and is protected from public disclosure under the laws, regulations, or policies of the country of the Party providing the information.

C. Marking Procedures for Documentary Proprietary Information

A Party receiving documentary proprietary information pursuant to this Arrangement shall respect the privileged nature of such information, provided that such proprietary information is clearly marked with the following (or substantially similar) restrictive legend:

> "This document contains proprietary information furnished in confidence under an Arrangement dated September 20th, 2012, between the United States Nuclear Regulatory Commission and the Jordan Nuclear Regulatory Commission and shall not be disseminated outside these organizations, their consultants, contractors, and licensees, or concerned departments and agencies of the Government of the United States and the Government of Jordan, without the prior written approval of (name of transmitting Party). This notice shall be marked on each page of any reproduction hereof, in whole or in part. These limitations shall automatically terminate when the proprietary information is disclosed by the owner without restriction."

This restrictive legend shall be respected by the Parties to this Arrangement. Proprietary information bearing this restrictive legend shall not be made public or otherwise disseminated in any manner unspecified or contrary to the terms of this Arrangement without the prior written consent of the transmitting Party. Proprietary information bearing this restrictive legend shall not be used by the receiving Party or its contractors and consultants for any commercial purposes without the prior written consent of the transmitting Party.

D. Dissemination of Documentary Proprietary Information

1. In general, proprietary information received under this Arrangement may be disseminated by the receiving Party without prior consent to persons within or employed by the receiving Party, and to concerned Government departments and Government agencies in the country of the receiving Party, provided:

a. such dissemination is made on a case-by-case basis; and

b. such proprietary information bears the restrictive legend appearing in Section III.C. of this Arrangement.

2. Proprietary information received under this Arrangement may be disseminated by the receiving Party without prior consent to contractors and consultants of the receiving Party located within the geographical limits of that Party's country provided:

a. that the proprietary information is used by such contractors and consultants only for work within the scope of their contracts with the receiving Party relating to the subject matter of the proprietary information, and shall not be used by such contractors and consultants for any other private commercial purposes;

b. that such dissemination is made on a case-by-case basis to contractors and consultants who have executed a non-disclosure agreement; and

c. that such proprietary information shall bear the restrictive legend appearing in Section III.C. of this Arrangement.

3. With the prior written consent of the Party furnishing proprietary information under this Arrangement, the receiving Party may disseminate such proprietary information more widely than otherwise permitted under the terms set forth in this Arrangement. The Parties shall endeavor to grant such approval to the extent permitted by their respective national laws, regulations and policies, provided:

a. that the entities receiving proprietary information under Section III.D.3. of this Arrangement, including domestic organizations permitted or licensed by the receiving Party to construct or operate nuclear production or utilization facilities, or to use nuclear and materials radiation sources, have executed a non-disclosure agreement;

b. that the entities receiving proprietary information under Section III.D.3. of this Arrangement, including domestic organizations permitted or licensed by the receiving Party to construct or operate nuclear production or utilization facilities, shall not use such proprietary information for any private commercial purposes; and

c. that those entities receiving proprietary information under Section III.D.3. of this Arrangement that are domestic organizations permitted or licensed by the receiving Party agree to use the proprietary information only for activities carried out under or within the terms of their specific permit or license.

E. Marking Procedures for Other Confidential or Privileged Information of a Documentary Nature

A Party receiving under this Arrangement other confidential or privileged information shall respect its confidential nature, provided such information is clearly marked so as to indicate its confidential or privileged nature and is accompanied by a statement indicating:

1. that the information is protected from public disclosure by the government of the transmitting Party; and

2. that the information is transmitted under the condition that it be maintained in confidence.

F. Dissemination of Other Confidential or Privileged Information of a Documentary Nature

Other confidential or privileged information may be disseminated in the same manner as that set forth in Section III.D, "Dissemination of Documentary Proprietary Information."

G. Non-Documentary Proprietary or Other Confidential or Privileged Information

Non-documentary proprietary or other confidential or privileged information provided in seminars and other meetings organized under this Arrangement, or information arising from the attachments of staff, use of facilities, or joint projects, shall be treated by the Parties according to the principles specified for documentary information in this Arrangement; provided, however, that the Party communicating such proprietary or other confidential or privileged information has placed the recipient on notice as to the character of the information communicated.

H. Consultation

If, for any reason, one of the Parties becomes aware that it will be, or may reasonably be expected to become, unable to meet the non-dissemination provisions of this Arrangement, it shall immediately inform the other Party. The Parties shall thereafter consult to define an appropriate course of action.

I. Other

Nothing contained in this Arrangement shall preclude a Party from using or disseminating information received without restriction by a Party from sources outside of this Arrangement.

IV. FINAL PROVISIONS

A. Nothing contained in this Arrangement shall require either Party to take any action that would be inconsistent with its existing laws, regulations, or policy directives. Should any conflict arise between the terms of this Arrangement and those laws, regulations, or policy directives, the Parties agree to consult before any action is taken. No nuclear information related to proliferation-sensitive technologies shall be exchanged under this Arrangement.

B. Unless otherwise agreed, all costs resulting from cooperation pursuant to this Arrangement shall be the responsibility of the Party that incurs them. The ability of the Parties to carry out their obligations is subject to the appropriation of funds by the appropriate governmental authority and to the laws, regulations and policies applicable to the Parties.

C. Cooperation under this Arrangement shall be in accordance with the laws and regulations of the Parties. Any dispute or questions between the Parties concerning the interpretation or application of this Arrangement shall be settled by mutual agreement of the Parties.

D. This Arrangement shall enter into force upon signature and, subject to paragraph E of this Section, shall remain in force for a period of five years. It may be extended for a further period of time by written agreement of the Parties.

E. Either Party may terminate this Arrangement after providing the other Party written notice 180 days prior to its intended date of termination.

DONE at Vienna, Austria on this 20th day of September, 2012, in the English language.

FOR THE UNITED STATES NUCLEAR REGULATORY COMMISSION

[Signature]

Allison M. Macfarlane, Chairman

FOR THE JORDAN NUCLEAR REGULATORY COMMISSION

[Signature]

Jamal M. Sharaf, Director General

CERTIFIED A TRUE COPY
BY [Signature]

Office of the Secretary

Addendum A

USNRC-JNRC Safety Research Exchange
Areas in Which the USNRC Is Performing or Sponsoring Safety Research

1. Digital Instrumentation and Control
2. Reactor and Electrical Equipment Qualification
3. Environmental Transport
4. Radionuclide Transport and Waste Management
5. Dry Cask Storage and Transport
6. Fire Safety Research
7. Nuclear Fuel Analysis
8. Severe Accident Analysis
9. Operating Experience and Generic Issues
10. Human Factors Engineering
11. Organizational Factors/Safety Culture
12. Human Reliability Analysis (HRA)
13. Probabilistic Risk Assessments
14. Radiation Protection and Health Effects
15. Seismic Safety
16. State of the Art Risk Consequences
17. Reactor Containment Structural Safety
18. Reactor Vessel and Piping Integrity
19. Regulatory Guide Update
20. New and Advanced Reactor Designs
21. Decommissioning
22. Thermal Hydraulic Code Applications and Maintenance
23. Uncertainty Analysis for Thermal Hydraulic Kinetics
24. Coupled 3D Neutronic and Plant Thermal Hydraulics
25. Medical Isotope Production
26. Long-term Operational Management
27. Plant and Systems Operations

JNRC-NRC Safety Research Exchange

Areas In Which the JNRC Is Performing Safety Research

1. Safety Regulation of Nuclear Facilities
2. Licensing of Research Reactors
3. Licensing Procedure and Regulatory Inspection
4. Radiological Safety Controls
5. Radiological Safety of Nuclear Facilities
6. Radiation Protection (medical & industrial)
7. Transport
8. Safety Culture and Public Awareness
9. Human Resources Development
10. Seismic Safety
11. Probabilistic Risk Assessments
12. Thermal Hydraulic Code Applications and Maintenance
13. Plant and Systems Operations
14. SSAC
15. Export and import of nuclear material and radioactive material, sources, equipment, information and technology.
16. Radiological and nuclear emergency preparedness
17. Contamination/decontamination
18. Border Control
19. Computer Codes
20. Laboratory (Radiological & Chemical)
21. Environmental Monitoring
22. Training and education

INTELLECTUAL PROPERTY RIGHTS ANNEX

I. General Obligation

The Parties shall ensure adequate and effective protection of intellectual property created or furnished under this Arrangement and relevant implementing arrangements. Rights to such intellectual property shall be allocated as provided in this Annex.

II. Scope

A. This Annex is applicable to all cooperative activities undertaken pursuant to this Arrangement, except as otherwise specifically agreed by the Parties or their designees.

B. For purposes of this Arrangement, "intellectual property" shall mean the subject matter listed in Article 2 of the Convention Establishing the World Intellectual Property Organization, done at Stockholm, July 14, 1967 and may include other subject matter as agreed by the Parties.

C. Each Party shall ensure, through contracts or other legal means with its own participants, if necessary, that the other Party can obtain the rights to intellectual property allocated in accordance with this Annex. This Annex does not otherwise alter or prejudice the allocation between a Party and its nationals, which shall be determined by that Party's laws and practices.

D. Except as otherwise provided in this Arrangement, disputes concerning intellectual property arising under this Arrangement shall be resolved through discussions between the concerned participating institutions, or, if necessary, the Parties or their designees. Upon mutual agreement of the Parties, a dispute shall be submitted to an arbitral tribunal for binding arbitration in accordance with the applicable rules of international law. Unless the Parties or their designees agree otherwise in writing, the arbitration rules of United Nations Commission on International Trade Law (UNCITRAL) shall govern.

E. Termination or expiration of this Arrangement shall not affect rights or obligations under this Annex.

III. Allocation of Rights

A. Each Party shall be entitled to a non-exclusive, irrevocable, royalty-free license in all countries to translate, reproduce, and publicly distribute scientific and technical journal articles, reports, and books directly arising from cooperation under this Arrangement. All publicly distributed copies of a copyrighted work prepared under this provision shall indicate the names of the authors of the work unless an author explicitly declines to be named.

B. Rights to all forms of intellectual property, other than those rights described in paragraph IIIA above, shall be allocated as follows:

(1) Visiting researchers shall receive rights, awards, bonuses and royalties in accordance with the policies of the host institution.

(2) (a) Any intellectual property created by persons employed or sponsored by one Party under cooperative activities other than those covered by paragraph III.(B)(1) shall be owned by that Party. Intellectual property created by persons employed or sponsored by both Parties shall be jointly owned by the Parties. In addition, each creator shall be entitled to awards,

bonuses and royalties in accordance with the policies of the institution employing or sponsoring that person.

(b) Unless otherwise agreed in an implementing or other arrangement, each Party shall have within its territory a right to exploit or license intellectual property created in the course of the cooperative activities.

(c) The rights of a Party outside its territory shall be determined by mutual agreement considering the relative contributions of the Parties and their participants to the cooperative activities, the degree of commitment in obtaining legal protection and licensing of the intellectual property and such other factors deemed appropriate.

(d) Notwithstanding paragraphs III.B(2)(a) and (b) above, if a particular project has led to the creation of intellectual property protected by the laws of one Party but not the other, the Party whose laws provide for this type of protection shall be entitled to all rights to exploit or license intellectual property worldwide although creators of intellectual property shall nonetheless be entitled to awards, bonuses and royalties as provided in paragraph III.B(2)(a).

(e) For each invention made under any cooperative activity, the Party employing or sponsoring the inventor(s) shall disclose the inventions promptly to the other Party together with any documentation and information necessary to enable the other Party to establish any rights to which it may be entitled. Either Party may ask the other Party in writing to delay publication or public disclosure of such documentation or information for the purpose of protecting its rights in the invention. Unless otherwise agreed in writing, the delay shall not exceed a period of six months from the date of disclosure by the inventing Party to the other Party.

IV. Business Confidential Information

In the event that information identified in a timely fashion as business-confidential is furnished or created under this Arrangement, each Party and its participants shall protect such information in accordance with applicable laws, regulations, and administrative practices. Information may be identified as "business-confidential" if a person having the information may derive an economic benefit from it or may obtain a competitive advantage over those who do not have it, and the information is not generally known or publicly available from other sources, and the owner has not previously made the information available without imposing in a timely manner an obligation to keep it confidential.

State Department Document Number: 12-177

Adherence Agreement Between the United States of America and the Council of Europe Development Bank with Respect to the Regional Housing Programme Fund, with Annexes

Signed at Washington D.C. and Paris,
August 26 and September 24, 2012
Entered into force September 24, 2012

CTIA Document Number: 18083.000

THIS ADHERENCE AGREEMENT (the **"Adherence Agreement"**) is made between

The **GOVERNMENT OF THE UNITED STATES OF AMERICA** (the **"Donor"**); and

The **COUNCIL OF EUROPE DEVELOPMENT BANK,** International Organisation, with its headquarters at 55 Avenue Kléber, 75116 Paris, France (the **"CEB"**, or the **"Fund Manager"**);

Jointly referred to hereinafter as the **"Parties",** or individually as the **"Party";**

In respect of the Donor's participation and contribution to the Regional Housing Programme Fund (the **"RHP Fund"**);

WHEREAS

(A) As part of the joint initiative of Bosnia and Herzegovina, Republic of Croatia, Montenegro and Republic of Serbia (the **"Partner Countries"**) under the Sarajevo process on refugees and displaced persons to create 'Durable Solutions for Refugees and Displaced Persons (DPs) in the Western Balkans' (the **"Regional Housing Programme"** or **"RHP"**), the RHP Fund has been established to be managed by the CEB.

(B) The purpose of the RHP Fund is to pool resources, contributed by states and institutions, to be used for the purposes of making Grants to the Partner Countries in respect of their respective Regional Housing Project under the Regional Housing Programme.

(C) The CEB shall manage the RHP Fund, and all Fund Resources shall be accepted, held, used, committed, expended or otherwise disposed of, in accordance with the General Conditions of the RHP Fund (attached) as may be amended, from time to time, in accordance with the terms for amendment, provided therein (the **"General Conditions"**).

(D) The Donor now wishes to confirm (i) its commitment to contribute to the RHP Fund; (ii) that it agrees that the use and management of any Contribution made by it to the RHP Fund shall be done in accordance with the General Conditions and this Adherence Agreement; (iii) its participation in the Assembly of Donors in accordance with the General Conditions and (iv) its participation in the RHP Steering Committee in accordance with the Rules of Procedure of the RHP Steering Committee.

NOW THEREFORE the Parties hereto agree as follows:

1. General Conditions of the RHP Fund

The Donor hereby (i) acknowledges receipt of a copy of the General Conditions (comprising its Annex), as in force as of the date of entry into force of this Adherence Agreement; and (ii) agrees that the General Conditions shall apply to any Contribution made by it to the RHP Fund (any such Contribution to be made by way of a Contribution Agreement, substantially in the form of the Annex I hereto), as if incorporated therein in full, with the following derogations:

(a) Clause 7 (Dispute resolution) of the General Conditions shall be replaced as follows:

> "If a disagreement should arise between the CEB and the Donor in connection with the Contribution of the Donor, such dispute will be resolved by the Parties through consultation. If consultation fails to resolve the disagreement, the CEB and the Donor may, subject to mutual agreement, resort to arbitration in accordance with the Permanent Court of Arbitration Optional Rules for Arbitration Involving International Organizations and States in force at the date of the Contribution Agreement."

2. Contributions

The Donor confirms its commitment to contribute to the RHP Fund, for the purposes of which it shall enter into a Contribution Agreement with the CEB in the form of the Annex I hereto.

3. Notices

All matters relating to the RHP Fund shall be addressed, as and when required, to the following representatives of the Parties, as appropriate:

For the Donor:

Nancy Iris
Deputy Director, Bureau of Population, Refugees, and Migration, Office for
Assistance of Europe, Central Asia & Americas
Department of State
United States of America
2201 C Street Northwest, Washington, DC 20520

Tel: 202-453-9297
Email: irisnr@state.gov

For the Fund Manager:

Director, Central Directorate for Studies and International Relations
Council of Europe Development Bank
55, avenue Kléber
75116 Paris, France

Tel: +331 47 55 71 51
Fax: +331 47 55 71 55
Email: CEB-donor-relations@coebank.org

4. General

(a) All capitalised terms used herein have the meaning attributed to them in the General Conditions as in force at the time of entry into force of this Adherence Agreement.

(b) In the event of discrepancies, inconsistencies and/or conflicts between the terms of the General Conditions, this Adherence Agreement and/or any Contribution Agreement, the documents shall prevail in the following order: (i) this Adherence Agreement; (ii) the General Conditions; and (iii) the Contribution Agreement.

(c) Any disputes arising out of or in connection with this Adherence Agreement shall be resolved in accordance with the terms of Clause 7 (Dispute Resolution) of the General Conditions, as replaced under Clause 1 above.

(d) This Adherence Agreement shall enter into force on upon signature by both Parties.

Signed in duplicate in the English language.

For the Department of State,
Bureau of Population, Refugees, and Migration
United States of America:

[Signature]

David Robinson
Principal Deputy Assistant Secretary

Date: 9/24/2012

Place: WASHINGTON, D.C.

For the Council of Europe Development Bank:

[Signature]

Mikolaj Dowgielewicz
Vice-Governor

Date: 26/08/2012

Place: Paris

CEB
COUNCIL OF EUROPE DEVELOPMENT BANK
BANQUE DE DEVELOPPEMENT DU CONSEIL DE L'EUROPE

GENERAL CONDITIONS

OF THE

REGIONAL HOUSING PROGRAMME FUND

Dated: 24 September 2012

WHEREAS

(A) The 'Joint Regional Programme on Durable Solutions for Refugees and Displaced Persons' (the **"Regional Housing Programme"** or the **"RHP"**) is a joint initiative of Bosnia and Herzegovina, Republic of Croatia, Montenegro and Republic of Serbia (each a **"Partner Country"** and together the **"Partner Countries"**).

(B) The aim of this regional initiative, which is an integral part of the 'Sarajevo Process on refugees and displaced persons' initiated in 2005, re-launched in March 2010 at the Belgrade conference, and to which the Partner Countries have re-committed themselves with the November 2011 Belgrade Declaration, is to contribute towards resolving the protracted displacement situation of the most vulnerable refugees and displaced persons (DPs) following the 1991-1995 conflicts on the territory of former Yugoslavia, including internally displaced persons (IDPs) in Montenegro from 1999, by, inter alia, providing them with durable housing solutions.

(C) The RHP aims to benefit close to 74,000 people or 27,000 households and its cost is estimated to be approximately €584 million over a five-year period. It will comprise four country housing projects, one in each Partner Country each of which will be implemented by the relevant Partner Country in several sub-projects and in several phases (each a **"Country Housing Project"** or a **"CHP"**).

(D) The regional initiative, as part of the overall 'Sarajevo process', is endorsed by the international community, including the European Union represented by the European Commission (the **"Commission"**), the United States of America (**"USA"**), the Council of Europe Development Bank (**"CEB"**), the United Nations High Commissioner for Refugees (**"UNHCR"**) and the Organization for Security and Cooperation in Europe (**"OSCE"**).

(E) A donors' conference took place in Sarajevo on 24 April 2012 (the **"Donors' Conference"**) where the Commission, the Governments of the USA, Germany, Italy, the Kingdom of Norway, the Swiss Federation, the Kingdom of Denmark, Turkey, Luxembourg, Cyprus, Czech Republic, Romania, Hungary, Slovak Republic and the former United Nations High Commissioner for Refugees, Ms. Sadako Ogata pledged contributions for the Regional Housing Programme in a total of EUR 261 million.

(F) The CEB was established on 16 April 1956 by the adoption of its Articles of Agreement, as amended, (the **"Articles"**) by the Committee of Ministers of the Council of Europe, the decision-making body of the Council of Europe and has its origins in a Partial Agreement originally entered into between eight Council of Europe member states. The CEB is governed by the Third Protocol to the General Agreement on Privileges and Immunities of the Council of Europe of March 6, 1959 (the **"Protocol"**), by its Articles and by regulations issued pursuant to the Articles.

(G) The CEB is empowered under Article VII Section 3 of the Articles to open and manage trust accounts and such accounts may receive contributions from CEB, members of the CEB and of the Council of Europe.

(H) The participation of CEB to the RHP and the establishment of a fund named 'Regional Housing Programme Fund' (the **"RHP Fund"**) were approved on 27 January 2012 by the CEB's Administrative Council by Resolution 1543(2012).

(I) By Resolution 399 (2012) of its Governing Board of 30 March 2012 the CEB is authorised to receive voluntary contributions from non-member states of the CEB and international institutions in the framework of the Regional Housing Programme.

(J) CEB's role in respect of the RHP shall be that of RHP Secretariat, Fund Manager and Finance Institution as further detailed herein.

(K) CEB's management fee (as defined in Paragraph 3.6 below) has been determined so as to cover, together with the bilateral contributions the CEB receives from the Commission directly, the total of CEB's management costs in respect of the RHP until the termination date (as defined in Paragraph 4.2(a) below).

ACCORDINGLY, the CEB accepted to administer the RHP Fund, in accordance with these General Conditions.

1. GENERAL PROVISIONS

1.1 Definitions

In these General Conditions the following defined terms and expressions shall bear the following meaning, unless the context requires otherwise:

"Adherence Agreement" means the agreement to be entered into between each Donor and the Fund Manager, pursuant to which the parties to any such Adherence Agreement agree that the General Conditions shall govern the management of the RHP Fund;

"Assembly of Donors" means the Assembly of Donors described in Paragraph 3.2 of these General Conditions;

"CEB Procurement Guidelines" means the CEB's 'Guidelines for Procurement of supplies, works and services' as publically available on its website: www.coebank.org;

"CEB Public Information Policy" means CEB's Public Information Policy as publically available on its website: www.coebank.org;

"Contribution/s" means resources contributed to the RHP Fund, subject to the conclusion of a Contribution Agreement and governed by the terms set out therein and as described in Paragraph 2.2 of these General Conditions;

"Contribution Agreement" means the written understanding or agreement to be entered into between a Donor and the CEB, which will specify the amount committed by the Donor, the currency of such Contribution, the date(s) on which and the manner in which payments thereof will be made to the Fund Account and may contain such other administrative matters as may be required and are permitted by the General Conditions, and will be in the form attached to the Adherence Agreement;

"Donor/s" means any state and / or institution that has made a Contribution to the RHP Fund;

"Donor Group" means group of Donors whose Contributions taken together amount to €5,000,000 or in excess thereof;

"Effective Date" means the date on which the first Contribution has been received by the RHP Fund as confirmed by the CEB to the Donors who as at such date have entered into a Contribution Agreement.

"Euro", **"€"**, **"euro"** and **"EUR"** each means the lawful currency of the member states of the European Union that adopt the single currency in accordance with the Treaty on the Functioning of the European Union (TFEU);

"Finance Institution" means the CEB in its capacity as the finance institution where it (i) shall appraise Grant Requests and/or Loan Requests, (ii) shall disburse Grants to the Partner Countries, (iii) may provide Loans, subject to all CEB's conditions for financing being met and (iv) shall monitor the implementation of sub-projects under the Country Housing Projects financed by either Grants and Loans or Grants;

"Fund Account" means the account/s and, to the extent applicable, the sub-account/s, opened and maintained by the Fund Manager in CEB's books, to which Contributions will be transferred and out of which the Fund Manager shall disburse the Fund Resources, as required;

"Fund Manager" means the CEB in its capacity as fund manager as further described in Paragraph 3.4;

"Fund Resources" means the Contributions made to the RHP Fund and other amounts as described in Paragraph 2.1 of these General Conditions;

"General Conditions" means the general conditions of the RHP Fund set out herein;

"Grant/s" means any investment subsidy grant to be disbursed by the Finance Institution from the Fund Resources to the Partner Countries for any sub-project under the Country Housing Projects that fulfils the Eligibility Criteria set out in Paragraph 1.3 of these General Conditions upon the decision of the Assembly of Donors;

"Grant Request" means any Partner Country's request for a Grant;

"Grant Request Assessment Criteria" means the grant request assessment criteria, as described in Paragraph 1.3(f) of these General Conditions;

"Initial Contribution Minimum Amount" means the minimum amount of €250,000 in respect of the initial Contribution by each Donor;

"Loan" means a loan to be disbursed upon the decision of the CEB by the CEB from its resources to such Partner Country for financing any sub-project under the Country Housing Projects;

"Loan Request" means any Partner Country's request for a loan to be disbursed upon the decision of the CEB by the CEB from its resources to such Partner Country for financing any sub-project under the Country Housing Projects;

"Project Implementation Unit" or **"PIU"** means any unit which will implement sub-projects under any Country Housing Project;

"Regional Coordination Forum" means the regional coordination forum coordinating the RHP activities within the Partner Countries;

"RHP Secretariat" means the CEB in its capacity as RHP secretariat as described in Paragraph 3.5 of these General Conditions;

"RHP Steering Committee" means the RHP steering committee comprising the Partner Countries, UNHCR, OSCE, the Donors and the RHP Secretariat;

"Subsequent Contribution Minimum Amount" means the minimum amount of €250,000 in respect of each subsequent Contribution by each Donor;

"Technical Committee" means the technical committee, as described in Paragraph 3.3 of these General Conditions;

"U.S. dollars", "$" or **"USD"** are references to United States dollars.

1.2 Purpose of the RHP Fund

(a) The purpose of the RHP Fund is to allocate Fund Resources within the framework of the Regional Housing Programme as follows:

(i) for providing support in the form of Grants;

(ii) for such other activities as the Assembly of Donors may approve, from time to time, on recommendation of the Technical Committee,

(b) Grant Requests will be made by each Partner Country via the RHP Secretariat and subject to assessment by the Technical Committee after pre-assessment by the Finance Institution. The allocation of Fund Resources for financing such sub-projects under the Country Housing Projects will be subject to a decision to that effect, taken by the Assembly of Donors in accordance with the decision-making procedure set out in Paragraph 3.2(g).

(c) The Fund Resources will also be used to pay (i) the Management Fee in accordance with Paragraph 3.5, (ii) the costs of the audit of the financial statements of the RHP Fund in accordance with Paragraph 3.8(b) and costs of recovery in accordance with Paragraph 3.4(c) of these General Conditions.

1.3 Eligibility Criteria of Grant Requests

To be eligible for the support by the RHP Fund, Grant Requests shall comply with the following eligibility criteria (the **"Eligibility Criteria"**):

(a) *Geographical coverage*: The sub-projects under any of the Country Housing Projects must be implemented on the territory of the Partner Countries.

(b) *Eligible beneficiaries*: The sub-projects under any of the Country Housing Projects must benefit vulnerable refugees and/or displaced persons, including internally displaced persons (IDPs) in Montenegro from 1999, within Partner Countries who fit one of the following six categories (the **"Eligible Beneficiaries"**):

(i) Category I: All 1991-1995 refugees, regardless of their status, who are residents of collective centres or other forms of collective accommodations, either formal or informal.

(ii) Category II: All 1991-1995 vulnerable refugees accommodated privately and all former occupancy right holders without a durable solution in their country of origin or reception country. For the purpose of the Regional Housing Programme, the vulnerability criteria applied by UNHCR in countries in the region are also to be applied here.

(iii) Category III: All vulnerable returnees to Bosnia and Herzegovina and Croatia and all vulnerable returnees who have already returned to Croatia but who do not have a durable solution either in the country of origin or in the reception country.

(iv) Category IV: Displaced persons accommodated in collective centres and private accommodations in Croatia.

(v) Category V: Vulnerable displaced persons outside collective centres in Bosnia and Herzegovina.

(vi) Category VI: Vulnerable persons displaced in Montenegro in 1999. This was especially agreed by the participating countries given that the Regional Housing Programme in other countries deals only with 1991-1995 refugees.

(c) *Eligible housing solutions*: The sub-projects under any of the Country Housing Projects must provide the Eligible Beneficiaries with a durable housing solution. The housing solutions to be provided include:

(i) Provision of flats and houses through building, reconstruction, renovation or purchase;

(ii) Provision of construction materials;

(iii) Accommodation in social welfare institutions.

Refugees and displaced persons will be provided with the choice of either: voluntary return and reintegration in their place of origin, or integration in their place of current residence.

(d) *Eligible costs*: The following represents a non-exhaustive list of cost elements of the sub-projects which are eligible:

(i) the cost of surveys or studies (technical, economic or commercial, engineering) as well as the cost of technical supervision of the sub-projects;

(ii) the preparation of the land;

(iii) the construction/renovation/modernization or purchase of buildings or provision of building material directly linked to a sub-project;

(iv) the installation of basic infrastructure such as sewerage, water supply, electricity and telecommunications networks, waste disposal and waste water treatment, roads, etc.;

(v) the purchase of materials and equipment;

(vi) contingencies for unanticipated costs (technical and/or price increases) in respect of possible changes in the quantity of work required, in the type and quantity of equipment to be purchased or in the method of carrying out the sub-project which may represent up to 10 per cent of the total cost of the sub-project.

(e) *Non-eligible costs*: The following represents a non-exhaustive list of cost elements of the sub-projects which are not eligible:

(i) the acquisition of land;

(ii) financial costs of investments (payment of debts, refinancing, interest charges etc.);

(iii) value added tax paid in the EU Member States or in the Partner Countries; and

(iv) any other costs which are not eligible under CEB's policy for loans and project financing.

(f) *Grant request assessment criteria*: Specific technical information on each sub-project shall be further detailed in the relevant Grant Request based on and in compliance with the grant request assessment criteria to be prepared by the Technical Committee in consultation with the

Partner Countries and approved by the Assembly of Donors (the **"Grant Request Assessment Criteria"**).

(g) *Blending Grants and own resources*: The Fund Resources are intended to be used within the framework of the Regional Housing Programme to support sub-projects co-financed by the Partner Countries. The relevant Partner Country shall allocate to its sub-project its own financial and/or in-kind contribution in an amount at least equal to the corresponding own contribution specified in the "Budget" set out in Annex 2 to the "Joint Regional Programme on Durable Solutions for Refugees and Displaced Persons". For the avoidance of doubt, Grant Requests shall be approved, only if the available funding covers the cost of the relevant sub-project.

1.4 Application of General Conditions

(a) As and from the Effective Date, the operation of the RHP Fund and the Fund Resources will be governed by, and such Fund Resources will be received, administered, used and disposed of in accordance with these General Conditions. The General Conditions may be supplemented by Procedures and Implementing Guidelines to be adopted by the Assembly of Donors in agreement with the Fund Manager. Without prejudice to the foregoing, where discrepancies or conflicts are identified between or among the provisions of the General Conditions and the provisions of any supplementary Procedures and/or Implementing Guidelines, adopted by the Assembly of Donors, the General Conditions will prevail.

(b) Each Donor will conclude with the Fund Manager an Adherence Agreement at the time when it makes its first Contribution to the RHP Fund. The conclusion of the Adherence Agreement will be a prerequisite for making a Contribution to the RHP Fund and participation in the RHP Fund. By adhering to the General Conditions each Donor agrees to participate in the Assembly of Donors according to the provisions set out herein.

2. FUND RESOURCES

2.1 Fund Resources

The Fund Resources will consist of:

(a) Contributions made by Donors pursuant to Paragraphs 2.2 and 2.3 below;

(b) interest accrued on the Fund Resources in accordance with Paragraph 3.7; and

(c) amounts recovered under proceedings taken pursuant to Paragraph 3.4(c) below.

2.2 Contributions

(a) Subject to the provisions of Paragraphs 1.4(b) above and 2.2(b) below, any Donor may make a Contribution to the RHP Fund by entering into a Contribution Agreement. By entering into a Contribution Agreement the relevant Donor irrevocably undertakes to make the Contribution described therein available on the relevant date/s specified therein in accordance with Paragraph 2.3 below.

(b) The minimum amount of the initial Contributions by each Donor will be €250,000 (the **"Initial Contribution Minimum Amount"**) and each subsequent Contribution will be made in an amount of at least €250,000 (the **"Subsequent Contribution Minimum Amount"**).

(c) A Donor may, at any time, increase the amount of its Contribution. The provisions of the General Conditions relating to the Contribution will apply equally to any additional amounts so contributed.

2.3 Payment of Contributions

(a) Each Contribution will be in Euro or U.S. dollars and will be transferred to the Fund Account within three months following the signing of the relevant Contribution Agreement at the latest. Payments may be made (i) as a single instalment, or (ii) where the Contributions are of €5,000,000 or in excess thereof in several instalments with a maximum of two per calendar year, whereby the first instalment is payable within three months following the signing of the relevant Contribution Agreement as set out in the relevant Contribution Agreement.

(b) All payments made in U.S. dollars will be converted upon receipt into Euro by the Fund Manager and the amount of Euro so received will be deemed to be the amount of the relevant Contribution.

2.4 Earmarking of Contributions

Un-earmarked Contributions to the RHP Fund (covering all four Country Housing Projects) are preferred. However, a Donor may earmark its Contribution for a specific Country Housing Project or specific Country Housing Projects, by specifying the earmarking in the Contribution Agreement.

2.5 The Fund Manager's acknowledgment of Contributions

First Contribution: Following receipt of the first Contribution in the Fund Account, the Fund Manager shall issue to each Donor who at such date has entered into a Contribution Agreement a statement including (a) details of such first Contribution and (b) a confirmation of the commencement of the RHP Fund's activities specifying the Effective Date.

Further Contributions: Following receipt of any further signed Contribution Agreement, the Fund Manager shall issue to each Donor a statement including details of such Contribution.

On the occasion of each Assembly of Donors, the Fund Manager shall issue a table showing the aggregate Contributions effectively received from each Donor and the voting rights thus acquired in the Assembly of Donors (see Paragraph 3.2(g)).

2.6 Separation of Resources

(a) The Fund Resources will at all times and in all respects be kept in a separate Fund Account.

(b) Under no circumstances will the resources of the CEB be charged with, or used to discharge, losses or liabilities arising out of the operations or other activities of the RHP Fund.

(c) In the operation and other activities of the RHP Fund, the liability of the CEB shall be limited to the Fund Resources which are at the disposal of the CEB.

3. GOVERNANCE AND ADMINISTRATION OF THE RHP FUND

3.1 General Principles of Governance

The RHP Fund has no separate legal personality and thus will be managed by the Fund Manager on behalf of the Donors in accordance with these General Conditions and under the supervision of the Assembly of Donors and the RHP Steering Committee.

The Assembly of Donors is the governing body of the RHP Fund and, in particular, decides on the use and allocation of the Fund Resources.

The RHP Steering Committee is the high coordinating body of the RHP.

The role and the functioning of the RHP Steering Committee is described in the Rules of Procedure of the RHP Steering Committee which will be endorsed by the participants to the RHP Steering Committee prior to the RHP Steering Committee's first meeting.

3.2 The Assembly of Donors

(a) The Assembly of Donors of the RHP Fund will be composed of the following:

(i) one (1) representative of each Donor;

(ii) the Fund Manager having a non-voting status, and it will be co-chaired by the Commission on a permanent basis (the **"Chair of the Assembly of Donors"**) and another Donor on an annual rotation basis being, at any given time, the same Donor who will act as co-chair of the RHP Steering Committee (the **"Co-Chair of the Assembly of Donors"**).

(b) The Assembly of Donors of the RHP Fund will:

(i) approve Grants in accordance with the decision making procedure described in Paragraph 3.2(g) below.

(ii) monitor the payment of the committed Contributions to the RHP Fund, having regard to implementation of Country Housing Projects to be supported with Fund Resources;

(iii) decide on measures to be taken, pursuant to Paragraph 3.2(i) below;

(iv) approve the annual financial statements of the RHP Fund;

(v) monitor financial flows of the RHP Fund, including upon the cancellation of any Contribution Agreement and/or the winding up of the RHP Fund;

(vi) take decisions pursuant to Paragraph 3.2(j) below; and

(vii) on an exceptional basis, approve the use of Fund Resources by the Finance Institution for such other activities as the Assembly of Donors may decide within the framework of the Regional Housing Programme in accordance with the decision making procedure described in Paragraph 3.2(g) below.

(c) Subject to Paragraph 2.2(b), each Donor will have the right to be represented in the Assembly of Donors of the RHP Fund, to participate in their meetings provided that such Donor has, on the date of the meeting of the Assembly of Donors of the RHP Fund, met its obligations under its Contribution Agreement(s).

(d) Each Donor's representative to the Assembly of Donors of the RHP Fund will be at the service of such Donor without remuneration from the RHP Fund. Each representative may be accompanied by up to one (1) advisory staff while the Chair of the Assembly of Donors and the Co-Chair of the Assembly of Donors may be accompanied by up to two (2) advisory staff each also without remuneration from the RHP Fund. The same representative of each Donor to the Assembly of Donors of the RHP Fund will act as its representative to the RHP Steering Committee. Participants to the Assembly of Donors of the RHP Fund will cover their own costs of participation. An individual may at the same time serve as representative of more than one Donor in the Assembly of Donors of the RHP Fund if such Donors will have so agreed and notified the Fund Manager, in writing and in advance of the meeting.

(e) The Assembly of Donors of the RHP Fund will meet a minimum of two (2) times per year, except for in the first and last year of the operation of the RHP Fund where the Assembly of Donors will meet a minimum of one (1) time per year, to perform the activities set out in Paragraph 3.2(b).

(f) In addition, the Assembly of Donors of the RHP Fund may hold special meetings to review the implementation of the RHP Fund. Such meetings of the Assembly of Donors may be called by the Chair of the Assembly of Donors, at the request of CEB or of the Donors, which account for not less than one-third of the aggregate amount of all paid in Contributions to the RHP Fund at the date on which such request will have been made to the CEB.

(g) As and when required, the Assembly of Donors will endeavour to take decisions by consensus of all Donors present at the meeting when the relevant decision is taken.

Where consensus cannot be reached, such decision will be taken by the Assembly of Donors by vote. *Quorum*: The quorum is established at the start of each Assembly of Donors meeting. The Assembly of Donors shall be quorate if the Donors in attendance (A) account for at least one fourth of the Donors who have delivered a Contribution Agreement to the Fund Manager and (B) represent at least 2/3 of the total amount of the paid-in Contributions at the time of the meeting. *Voting Rules*: A decision will be adopted if a majority of not less than 2/3 of the Donors voting, vote in favour of such a decision, provided that the total amount of all paid-in Contributions to the RHP Fund by the Donors voting in favour of a decision represents not less than 2/3 of the total amount of the paid-in Contributions.

(h) *Written Procedure*: On an exceptional basis, for any urgent business concerning the RHP Fund, the Assembly of Donors may take decisions, in accordance with the decision-making procedure described in Paragraph 3.2(g) above, on the basis of written resolutions, in the absence of a meeting.

Such a resolution will be approved if all Donors entitled to participate in the decision-making process, confirm their agreement with the written resolution. If a Donor does not submit its response with respect to the written resolution within the timeframe provided for this purpose, its vote will be counted in favour of the written resolution. A minimum of fifteen (15) calendar days will be given for each request for response.

If one or more Donors reject the proposal within fifteen (15) calendar days following receipt of the written request for a decision accompanied by relevant supporting documents, such rejection to be made in writing addressed to the Chair of the Assembly of Donors and the Fund Manager, the Chair of the Assembly of Donors shall upon receipt of such a rejection call for a meeting of the Assembly of Donors to discuss the relevant resolution.

(i) If failure by a Donor to meet its obligations under its Contribution Agreement will, in the judgement of the Fund Manager, materially interfere with or prejudice the operations of the RHP Fund, in whole or in part, the Fund Manager may request that the Chair of the preceding Assembly of Donors call a special meeting of the Assembly of Donors to consider the taking of appropriate measures.

(j) Subject to the provisions of Paragraph 3.2(g), the Assembly of Donors of the RHP Fund may decide on its own rules of procedure and guidelines. Such rules of procedure and guidelines will be in line with the General Conditions.

3.3 The Technical Committee

(a) The Technical Committee will consist of one (1) representative of the following:

(i) the Commission;

(ii) each Donor who has made one or more Contributions totalling €5,000,000 or in excess thereof;

(iii) each Donor Group; and

(iv) RHP Secretariat, and it will be chaired by the RHP Secretariat (the **"Chair of the Technical Committee"**).

(b) The Technical Committee will:

(i) prepare the Grant Request Assessment Criteria;

(ii) screen and assess Grant Requests;

(iii) submit Grant Requests for approval to the Assembly of Donors; and

(iv) discuss implementation related issues based on information provided by RHP Secretariat, including the progress of the Programme.

(c) Except for the RHP Secretariat, each member's representative to the Technical Committee will be at the service of such member without remuneration from the RHP/RHP Fund. Each representative may be accompanied by advisory staff also without remuneration from the RHP/RHP Fund. Participants to the Technical Committee will cover their own costs of participation. An individual may at the same time serve as representative of more than one member in the Technical Committee if such members will have so agreed and notified the RHP Secretariat, in writing and in advance of the meeting.

(d) The Technical Committee will meet a minimum of two (2) times per year, except for in the first and last year of the operation of the RHP Fund where the Technical Committee will meet a minimum of one (1) time per year, to perform the activities set out in Paragraph 3.3(b). The meetings will be called by the Chair of the Technical Committee. The meetings will be held in the headquarters of the CEB in Paris. The RHP Secretariat shall draft the agenda for these meetings and distribute it to the members of the Technical Committee no later than one week prior the scheduled date of the meeting.

(e) The Technical Committee, in consultation with the Chair of the Technical Committee, may invite representatives of governments, other institutions and entities to attend specific agenda items of meetings of the Technical Committee as observers.

3.4 Management and Administration of the RHP Fund—Role of the Fund Manager

(a) The Fund Manager will manage the RHP Fund in accordance with these General Conditions. In particular, it will fulfil its role as follows, it will:

(i) open and maintain the Fund Account for the RHP Fund in which it will record the receipt of Contributions, the disbursement of the Fund Resources, all remuneration received and payment of the Management Fee in accordance with Paragraph 3.6 and all other operations affecting the Fund Resources;

(ii) prepare the annual financial statements of the RHP Fund and report on the activities financed with the Fund Resources for review and approval by the Assembly of Donors;

(iii) liaise with the Donors, to the extent necessary to fulfil its managerial role with respect to all issues related to the Assembly of Donors, including maintaining the records of contributions, voting rights and grants;

(iv) prepare the meetings of the Assembly of Donors;

(v) submit to the Assembly of Donors all necessary reports and technical documentation, including an Annual Report of Fund operations, which will include information provided by the RHP Secretariat and audited financial statements;

(vi) submit to Donors written resolutions for approval and inform the Donors of the results from such approval process; and

(vii) carry out such other functions as may be necessary for the efficient administration of the RHP Fund as deemed necessary by the Assembly of Donors.

(b) In managing the RHP Fund and the Fund Resources, the CEB will exercise the same amount of care and diligence as it exercises with respect to its own capital resources and shall have no further liability to any Donor in respect thereof.

(c) In case of misuse, or alleged misuse of Fund Resources, the Fund Manager, after consultation with the Assembly of Donors, may undertake recovery proceedings as are approved by the Assembly of Donors, in accordance with the provisions of Paragraphs 3.2(g) herein above, in a manner consistent with the care and diligence applied in CEB projects financed out of its resources and taking into consideration any concerns, opinions, views, recommendations, advice of the Assembly of Donors. The cost of such proceedings will be charged to the Fund Resources, pro-rata to each Donor based on the size of its Contribution to the RHP Fund.

(d) The Fund Manager may adopt such operating procedures, compatible with the General Conditions, as may be considered necessary or appropriate for the efficient administration of the RHP Fund.

(e) Documents and materials, compiled by the Fund Manager, relating to individual sub-projects submitted for financing by the RHP Fund or relating to activities of the RHP Fund will be provided to the Donors to the extent that such disclosure will be consistent with CEB Public Information Policy.

3.5 The Role of the RHP Secretariat

The RHP Secretariat will:

(a) prepare the meetings of and provide support to the RHP Steering Committee as further detailed in the Rules of Procedure of the RHP Steering Committee;

(b) liaise with the Partner Countries, the Donors, the UNHCR and the OSCE to the extent necessary to fulfil its role with respect to all issues related to the RHP Steering Committee;

(c) prepare the meetings of and provide support to the Technical Committee, including as described in Paragraph 3.3(d) above;

(d) chair the Technical Committee;

(e) collect all incoming Grant Requests as described in Paragraph 1.2(b) above which it will transmit to the Technical Committee;

(f) ensure that in relevant CEB publications, communications with recipient Partner Countries, other entities and the media, appropriate visibility is given to the RHP Fund and its Donors, save that, when developing and implementing such visibility measures, the RHP Secretariat, as informed by the Fund Manager, will take due account of the relative size of the Contributions to the RHP Fund made by each Donor;

(g) in the context of the RHP prepare the meetings of and provide support to the Regional Coordination Forum as further detailed in the Regional Coordination Forum's terms of reference;

(h) in the context of the RHP co-chair the Regional Coordination Forum as further detailed in the Regional Coordination Forum's terms of reference; and

(i) any other tasks deemed necessary by the RHP Steering Committee and/or the Technical Committee and/or the Assembly of Donors to achieve efficient implementation of the Regional Housing Programme.

3.6 Management Fee

In order to defray the costs to the CEB in its capacity as Fund Manager and RHP Secretariat as well as all ancillary costs for the management and administrative support of the RHP Fund and the RHP, the CEB will receive a management fee, corresponding to 2.5 per cent. of the total amount of Contributions paid into the RHP Fund (the **"Management Fee"**). The Management Fee will be payable to the CEB out of each Contribution upon its transfer to the Fund Account.

Given that any costs CEB incurs prior to 1 January 2013 in respect of the management and administrative support of the RHP Fund and the RHP will be funded by bilateral contributions to the CEB from the Commission, only costs incurred by CEB in its capacity as Fund Manager and RHP Secretariat from 1 January 2013 will be funded by the Management Fee.

The Management Fee may be reviewed pursuant to the Paragraph 3.11 herein below.

3.7 Remuneration of the Fund Account

The Fund Manager shall pay interest to the Fund Account on the daily outstanding credit balances. Such interest is calculated on the basis of the monthly average of the Euro Overnight Index Average (EONIA) defined as the reference rate calculated by the European Central Bank and published on Reuters page "EONIA" minus 30 basis points (–0.30%). For non-business days the reference EONIA rate of the preceding working business day shall apply. The interest amount is calculated on an actual/360 day-count-fraction. Interest is credited at the end of each month as the sole remuneration.

In case of negative interest resulting from the remuneration formula stated above, Fund Resources will decrease accordingly.

3.8 Accounts and Audit

(a) The Fund Manager will maintain the accounts of the RHP Fund in Euro in accordance with the same accounting principles it follows in respect of its other fiduciary accounts.

(b) The financial statements of the RHP Fund will be audited on an annual basis before the end of June of the following year by CEB's external auditors in a manner consistent with that applied to CEB's resources. The costs of the audit will be paid from the Fund Resources.

(c) The fiscal year of the RHP Fund will be the calendar year. Unless otherwise agreed with the Assembly of Donors, the first fiscal period of the RHP Fund will end on 31 December immediately following the Effective Date.

3.9 Policies and procedures applicable to the implementation of Grants approved for financing with the Fund Resources

Grants approved by the Assembly of Donors for financing from the Fund Resources will be implemented and monitored in accordance with the applicable policies and procedures of the Finance

Institution. This includes the procurement of goods, works and services, including consulting services, necessary for the implementation of the CHPs and financed with the Fund Resources.

Partner Countries will carry out procurement in accordance with CEB Procurement Guidelines.

Procurement under each CHP shall comply with the principles of transparency, proportionality, sound financial management, equal treatment and non-discrimination, lack of conflicts of interests and respect of internationally accepted standards.

The contracting authorities of the Partner Countries shall in particular guarantee that non-discrimination is ensured among tenderers in all stages of the public procurement procedure and regarding in particular circumstances which might lead to locational, material or personal discrimination of tenderers, or discrimination originating from the classification of activities performed by the tenderer.

CEB will ensure that partner countries set up systems that will allow them to provide reasonable assurance of the respect of the above mentioned principles. In particular CEB will carry out regular checks throughout the procurement cycle, ranging from pre-reviews (ex-ante) with the issuance of no-objection, to post-reviews (ex-post). These verifications will entail both desk reviews and field missions. CEB will establish specific circuits for the approval of procurement plans and of all steps of procurement procedures.

CEB will require the Partner Countries to set up systems which will guarantee an adequate control environment and ensure that their contracting authorities carry out public procurement in such a manner that it guarantees economic, effective and efficient use of the financing provided by the RHP Fund and successfully attains the goals of the RHP

Monitoring and evaluation: With respect to monitoring and evaluation of the CHPs, CEB will perform both regular desk reviews and field visits in line with CEB's policy for loans and project financing. On-site monitoring missions will be carried out jointly with Donors upon request.

The RHP monitoring and evaluation framework will be based on a two-tier structure:

(a) Internal monitoring will be carried out by:

(i) the UNHCR and the OSCE who will monitor beneficiary-related issues and the CEB who will supervise overall implementation of the CHPs;

(ii) consultants, who will be deployed on short- or long-term missions to provide support to the project implementation units (the **"PIUs"**) and / or address specific issues;

(iii) the four (4) PIUs, who will be in charge of implementing the Country Housing Projects in accordance with best practices.

(b) External monitoring will be carried out by:

(i) independent auditors, who will conduct regular audits;

(ii) specialised consultants and/or institutions, who will provide independent evaluation of CHPs' outcomes.

Monitoring and evaluation outcomes and reports will also be outlined with agreed key development impact indicators (baseline data and targets for each country), to be provided periodically during the whole implementation period and at the project completion.

An independent evaluation of the results will take place at the completion of each CHP. A mid-term review, the timing and scope of which are to be decided by the Assembly of Donors, may be carried out.

3.10 Liability

No Donor will assume liability in respect of (i) any third party claims for damages arising out of the implementation of sub-project financed from the Fund Resources, or (ii) any damage or injury sustained by the staff or property of CEB arising out of the management and/or administration of the RHP Fund.

3.11 Review

The Fund Manager may, *inter alia,* at any time, add as an item on the agenda of a meeting of the Assembly of Donors a review regarding:

(a) the amount of the Management Fee being paid by the Donors, with a view of adjusting such amount, if required, taking into account:

(i) the actual costs for management and administration of the RHP Fund, incurred by the Fund Manager and the RHP Secretariat for the period from the Effective Date until the date of the review, and the total value of all Contributions made for the same period; and/or

(ii) the actual duration of the RHP following a possible extension of the termination date (as defined in Paragraph 4.2(a) below); and/or

(iii) the actual Contributions to the extent that they exceed the amounts pledged at the Donors' Conference; and/or

(b) changes required to the governance of the RHP Fund, if any; and/or

(c) the total value of all Contributions made to the RHP Fund for the period from the Effective Date until the date of the review.

Any decisions taken by the Assembly of Donors shall be taken in accordance with the decision-making procedure, described in Paragraph 3.2(g) of these General Conditions. If such decisions are inconsistent with, or in any other way necessitate changes to, the terms of these General Conditions, then the decisions and the resulting changes to the General Conditions shall only become effective upon the entry into force of a formal amendment to the General Conditions, executed pursuant to the provisions of Clause 6 herein below.

4. TERMINATION

4.1 Termination of a Contribution Agreement

(a) Subject to Paragraph 4.1(b) and Paragraph 4.4 below, each Donor may at any time terminate its Contribution Agreement upon sixty (60) days prior written notice.

(b) As from the effective date of termination of a Contribution Agreement, the relevant Donor will have no rights or obligations in respect of the RHP Fund except those set forth in this Clause 4. The Donor will be relieved of any liability to pay to the RHP Fund any amounts of its Contribution under the relevant Contribution Agreement, not yet fully committed. "Fully committed" means commitments in respect of subprojects, approved by the Assembly of Donors regardless of whether a transfer from the Fund Account has been made by the CEB.

4.2 Termination of the RHP Fund

(a) The RHP Fund will remain active until 30 June 2018 (the **"Termination Date"**), subject to extension upon the Assembly of Donors' approval following the Fund Manager's request based on a request from the RHP Secretariat. If not all of the Fund Resources have been disbursed by the

Termination Date, the Fund Manager will make a final re-distribution of the Fund Resources to all Donors on the Termination Date.

(b) Notwithstanding Paragraph 4.2(a) above and subject to Paragraph 4.3 below, the RHP Fund may be terminated at any time by a decision of the Assembly of Donors, taken with the unanimous consent of Donors, and the agreement of the Fund Manager.

(c) The RHP Fund will terminate automatically upon termination by CEB of its operations pursuant to Article XV of the Articles.

(d) The Fund Manager may cease to perform the functions conferred upon it pursuant to these General Conditions upon six (6) months' notice to the Assembly of Donors, given following consultation with the RHP Steering Committee.

4.3 Disposal of the Resources on Termination of the RHP Fund

Upon termination of the RHP Fund, the following provisions will apply with respect to the disposal of the Fund Resources:

(a) CEB will immediately cease all activities relating to such Fund Resources, except those incidental to the orderly realisation, conservation and preservation of such Fund Resources and the settlement of the direct or contingent obligations to which they may be subject.

(b) Subject to Paragraph 4.3(c) below, CEB will distribute the total net assets of the RHP Fund (as shown in the books of the CEB as of the date of termination) among the Donors in proportion to the amounts respectively contributed to the RHP Fund. Such distribution will be effected at such times and in such currencies and types of assets as CEB determines, and as approved by the Assembly of Donors. For the avoidance of doubt, the currency of such distribution may be Euro even if the relevant Contribution/s was/were made in U.S. dollars. If an amount in Euro is converted into its U.S. dollars equivalent by the CEB before effecting the distribution, the exchange rate as at the day of conversion shall be applicable.

(c) No distribution will be made until all liabilities of the RHP Fund (including payments due to CEB) will have been discharged or provided for. Any distribution to a Donor will be subject to prior settlement of all outstanding claims by CEB against such Donor in respect of its Contribution.

(d) Until final distribution of the net assets of the RHP Fund, all rights and obligations of CEB under these General Conditions and of the Donors under this Clause 4 of the General Conditions will continue unimpaired.

4.4 Disposal of Fund Resources on Termination of a Contribution Agreement

Upon termination of a Contribution Agreement, the following provisions will apply with respect to the Contribution made pursuant to such Contribution Agreement:

(a) CEB will immediately cease all activities relating to such Contribution, except those incidental to the orderly realisation, conservation and preservation of such Contribution and the settlement of the direct or contingent obligations to which it may be subject.

(b) Subject to Paragraph 4.4(c) below, CEB will distribute any funds received pursuant to the relevant Contribution Agreement and not yet committed at the time of termination of the Contribution Agreement to the relevant Donor. Such distribution will be effected at such times and in such currencies as CEB determines, and as approved by the Assembly of Donors. For the avoidance of doubt, the currency of such distribution may be Euro even if the relevant Contribution/s was/were made in U.S. dollars. If an amount in Euro is converted into its U.S. dollars equivalent by the CEB before effecting the distribution, the exchange rate as at the day of conversion shall be applicable.

(c) No distribution will be made until the pro-rata share of all liabilities (including payments due to CEB) in respect of such Contribution have been discharged or provided for. Any distribution to a Donor will be subject to prior settlement of all outstanding claims by CEB against such Donor in respect of its Contribution.

(d) In the event of release or return to the RHP Fund of any funds committed to a subproject, approved for financing with Fund Resources, such Donor's pro-rata share of such released or returned funds will be disbursed to such Donor.

(e) Until final reimbursement to the relevant Donor, all rights and obligations of CEB under these General Conditions and of the Donors under this Clause 4 of the General Conditions will continue unimpaired.

5. COMMUNICATIONS AND NOTICES

All communications and notices required or permitted under the General Conditions will be sent in writing by the most expedient means available. All communications and notices, required or permitted under the General Conditions, may be submitted by means of electronic mail.

6. AMENDMENTS

A proposal to amend these General Conditions may be made by any member of the Assembly of Donors. Such proposal, including the rationale and justifications for the proposed amendment of the General Conditions, shall be submitted to the Assembly of Donors by the Fund Manager.

These General Conditions may be amended only pursuant to a decision of the Assembly of Donors taken by consensus and with the agreement of the Fund Manager. Amendments to the General Conditions will be implemented in accordance with their provisions or, absent any particular provision, upon the later of the approval by the Assembly of Donors and the agreement of the Fund Manager to such amendments.

7. DISPUTE RESOLUTION

7.1 Disputes with members of CEB

If a disagreement should arise between the CEB and any Donor who is a member of the CEB concerning any matter arising out of or in connection with the Contribution of the Donor, and such dispute cannot be amicably settled by consultation between them, such disagreement will be resolved between the Governor of the CEB and the representative of the Donor concerned.

7.2 Disputes with non-members of CEB

If a disagreement should arise between the CEB, and a Donor who is not a member of the CEB in connection with the Contribution of that Donor, and such dispute cannot be settled amicably by the parties, such disagreement will be settled by arbitration in accordance with the Permanent Court of Arbitration Optional Rules for Arbitration Involving International Organisations and States in force at the date of the Contribution Agreement.

ANNEX—FORM OF ADHERENCE AGREEMENT

ADHERENCE AGREEMENT

with respect to the Regional Housing Programme Fund

THIS ADHERENCE AGREEMENT (the **"Adherence Agreement"**) is made between

The [*NAME OF COUNTRY/ENTITY*] (the **"Donor"**); and

The **COUNCIL OF EUROPE DEVELOPMENT BANK,** International Organisation, with its headquarters at 55 Avenue Kléber, 75116 Paris, France (the **"CEB"**, or the **"Fund Manager"**);

jointly referred to hereinafter as the **"Parties"**, each a **"Party"**;

in respect of the Donor's participation and contribution to the Regional Housing Programme Fund (the **"RHP Fund"**);

WHEREAS

(A) As part of the joint initiative of Bosnia and Herzegovina, Republic of Croatia, Montenegro and Republic of Serbia (the **"Partner Countries"**) under the Sarajevo process on refugees and displaced persons to create 'Durable Solutions for Refugees and Displaced Persons (DPs) in the Western Balkans' (the **"Regional Housing Programme"** or **"RHP"**), the RHP Fund has been established to be managed by the CEB.

(B) The purpose of the RHP Fund is to pool resources, contributed by states and institutions, to be used for the purposes of providing Grants to the Partner Countries in respect of their respective Country Housing Project under the Regional Housing Programme.

(C) The CEB shall manage the RHP Fund, and all Fund Resources shall be accepted, held, used, committed, expended or otherwise disposed of, in accordance with the General Conditions of the RHP Fund (attached) as may be amended, from time to time, in accordance with the terms for amendment, provided therein (the **"General Conditions"**).

(D) The Donor now wishes to confirm (i) its commitment to contribute to the RHP Fund; (ii) that it agrees that the use and management of any Contribution made by it to the RHP Fund shall be done in accordance with the General Conditions and this Adherence Agreement; (iii) its participation in the Assembly of Donors in accordance with the General Conditions and (iv) its participation in the RHP Steering Committee in accordance with the Rules of Procedure of the RHP Steering Committee.

NOW THEREFORE the Parties hereto agree as follows:

1. General Conditions of the RHP Fund

The Donor hereby (i) acknowledges receipt of a copy of the General Conditions (comprising its Annex), as in force as of the date of entry into force of this Adherence Agreement; and (ii) agrees that the General Conditions shall apply to any Contribution made by it to the RHP Fund (any such Contribution to be made by way of a Contribution Agreement, substantially in the form of the Annex I hereto), as if incorporated therein in full.

2. Contributions

The Donor confirms its commitment to contribute to the RHP Fund, for the purposes of which it shall enter into a Contribution Agreement with the CEB in the form of the Annex I hereto.

3. Notices

All matters relating to the RHP Fund shall be addressed, as and when required, to the following representatives of the Parties, as appropriate:

For the Donor:

[NAME]
[TITLE]
[NAME OF COUNTRY/ENTITY]
[ADDRESS]

Tel: [•]
Fax: [•]
Email: [•]

For the Fund Manager:

Director of the Central Directorate for Studies
and International Relations
Council of Europe Development Bank
55, avenue Kléber
75116 Paris, France

Tel: +331 47 55 71 51
Fax: +331 47 55 71 55
Email: CEB-donor-relations@coebank.org

4. General

(a) All capitalised terms used herein have the meaning attributed to them in the General Conditions as in force at the time of entry into force of this Adherence Agreement.

(b) Any disputes arising out of or in connection with this Adherence Agreement shall be resolved in accordance with the terms of Clause 7 (Dispute Resolution) of the General Conditions.

(c) This Adherence Agreement shall enter into force on upon signature by both Parties.

Signed in the English language, in two originals, one for each of the Parties,

For the [DONOR'S NAME]

____

Name :
Title :
Date :

For the Council of Europe Development Bank

____

Name :
Title :
Date :

(Annex I to the Adherence Agreement)

FORM OF CONTRIBUTION AGREEMENT
with respect to the Regional Housing Programme Fund

[LETTERHEAD OF DONOR]

Director of the Central Directorate for Studies and International Relations
Council of Europe Development Bank
55, avenue Kléber
75116 Paris
France

Date:

Dear Mr [ ],

I refer to the Adherence Agreement in respect to the Regional Housing Programme Fund (the **"RHP Fund"**) between [*NAME OF COUNTRY/ENTITY*] (the **"Donor"**) and the Council of Europe Development Bank, in force as of [*date*].

[NOTE (to be deleted): if the Contribution Agreement pertains to an increase of Contribution, the following reference should also be made here, separated by a comma from the reference to the Adherence Agreement: "our Contribution Agreement(s) dated [. . .], [. . .] and [. . .]."]

I am pleased to inform you that [*NAME OF COUNTRY/ENTITY*] wishes to [make a Contribution] *OR* [increase its Contribution] to the RHP Fund [in] *OR* [with] the aggregate amount of [*AMOUNT*] [Euro][U.S. dollars].

The Contribution will be paid in cash, in [Euro] [U.S. dollars]
[in one instalment on [*DATE*]]* *OR*
[in *[X]* instalments, with the first one of *[AMOUNT]* on [*DATE*], the second one of [*AMOUNT*] on [*DATE*] etc.]* *OR*
[in *[X]* instalments, of [*AMOUNT*] each on *[DATES/PERIOD, E.G. QUARTERLY ON...]*]* *OR*
[in several instalments, with the first one of [*AMOUNT*] on [*DATE*] and the amount/s and payment date/s of all subsequent instalments to be notified by the Donor to the Fund Manager as soon as possible in advance of making the payment and no later than [two weeks] in advance of making the payment]* (the **"Payment Date/s"**).

**DELETE THE OPTION WHICH DOES NOT APPLY.*

The Donor will notify the Fund Manager two business days prior the [relevant] Payment Date that its Contribution will be made with value date on the Payment Date. Such notice shall be made by email and shall be addressed to the Fund Manager:

Director of the Central Directorate for Studies and International Relations
Council of Europe Development Bank
55, avenue Kléber
75116 Paris, France

Tel: +331 47 55 71 51
Fax: +331 47 55 71 55
Email: CEB-donor-relations@coebank.org

[The Contribution will be deposited into the Fund Account via the Euro account opened in the name of the Council of Europe Development Bank:
SWIFT code CEFP FR PP
IBAN DE44500700100928738400
BIC code DEUTDEFF
with DEUTSCHE BANK AG FRANKFURT
Taunusanlange 12,
60325 Frankfurt am Main
with indication for further credit in EUR on the "RHP Fund Account".] *OR*

[The Contribution will be deposited into the Fund Account via the U.S. dollar account opened in the name of the Council of Europe Development Bank:
SWIFT code CEFP FR PP
Account number 04405734
BIC code BKTRUS33
with DEUTSCHE BANK TRUST COMPANY AMERICAS NEW YORK
60 Wall Street
New York NY 10005
with indication for further credit in EUR on the "RHP Fund Account".]

The Contribution is made without earmarking for a specific Country Housing Project. *OR* [The Contribution is earmarked for the/ following Country Housing Project/s in [*NAME OF PARTNER COUNTRY/COUNTRIES*].

I confirm that the terms used herein have the meaning attributed to them in the General Conditions of the RHP Fund (the **"General Conditions"**). [*NAME OF COUNTRY/ENTITY*] acknowledges that this Contribution Agreement is subject to and incorporates by reference the terms and conditions of the General Conditions in full.

Sincerely yours,

____

Name :
Title :
Date :

State Department Document Number: 12-178

Implementation Letter Amending the Development Cooperation Agreement of September 27, 2011 Between the United States of America and the Republic of Zambia

Signed at Lusaka, September 25, 2012
Entered into force September 25, 2012

CTIA DOCUMENT NUMBER: 18084.001

September 25, 2012

Mr. Felix Nkulukusa
Permanent Secretary
Ministry of Finance
Lusaka

SUBJECT: USAID/Zambia Development Cooperation Agreement Number 611-000-G-11-0000: Implementation Letter Number 1 Incremental Contribution to the Development Objectives

Dear Mr. Permanent Secretary:

This Implementation Letter (1L) is issued in accordance with the Development Cooperation Agreement number 611-000-G-11-0000, dated September 27, 2011, which was entered into by the Government of the Republic of Zambia (GRZ) and the Government of the United States of America (USG) acting through the United States Agency for International Development (USAID) (hereinafter the "DCA").

Pursuant to Article 3.1(b) of the DCA, this IL seeks your acknowledgement and records our mutual agreement on an incremental contribution by USAID to be obligated under this IL in the amount of Forty-Six Million Nine Hundred Forty-Nine Thousand Eight Hundred Four U.S. Dollars ($46,949,804) which increases the total grant amount in Article 3.1 (a) from One Hundred Seventy Million Seven Hundred Thirty-Nine Thousand Seven Hundred Ten U.S. Dollars ($170,739,710) to Two Hundred Seventeen Million Six Hundred Eighty-Nine Thousand Five Hundred Fourteen U.S. Dollars ($217,689,514) consistent with Annex 5 of the DCA.

This incremental funding will support Development Objective 2: Rural Poverty Reduced in Targeted Areas ($6,900,000); and Development Objective 3: Human Capital Improved ($40,049,804). This brings the total amount by DO to:

DO1 Enabling Governance Environment Improved	$1,626,000
DO2 Rural Poverty Reduced in Targeted Areas	$26,592,728
DO3 Human Capital Improved	$189,470,786

The attached illustrative financial plan has been modified to reflect this incremental contribution and replaces the prior illustrative financial plan in its entirety.

Please acknowledge to USAID concurrence with this IL by signing two originals of this IL in the space provided. One original should be returned to USAID with the other to be retained for your files.

USAID/Zambia appreciates the opportunity to work with the GRZ to achieve the development objectives mentioned above. We look forward to our continued collaboration.

Sincerely,
[Signature]
Susan K. Brems, Ph.D.
Mission Director

Concurrence: [Signature] Date: 26th Sept. 2012.
Mr. Felix Nkulukula
Permanent Secretary
Ministry of Finance

Cc: Dr. Peter Mwaba
Permanent Secretary
Ministry of Health

Ms. Mirriam Chinyama Chonya
Permanent Secretary
Ministry of Education

Dr. Patrick Nkanza
Permanent Secretary
Ministry of Education

Dr. David Shamulenge
Permanent Secretary
Ministry of Agriculture

Embassy of The United States of America
Subdivision 694/Stand 100
Kabulonga District, Ibex Hill Road
P O Box 32481

Telephone +260.211.357.000
Fax +260.357.041
+260.357.042
URL http://www.usaid.gov/zm

Development Cooperation Agreement and USAID Assistance FY2012

Illustrative Financial Plan

DO 1 Enabling Governance Environment Improved	Obligation To-Date	Planned Obligation Through This Action	Total Obligations as of this Action
2.4 Civil Society	1,626,000		1,626,000
Total DO 1 Development Cooperation Agreement	**1,626,000**		**1,626,000**

DO 2 Rural Poverty Reduced in Targeted Areas	Obligation To-Date	Planned Obligation Through This Action	Total Obligations as of this Action
3.1 Health	**858,628**	-	**858,628**
3.1.1 HIV/AIDS	858,628		858,628
4 Economic Growth	**18,834,100**	**6,900,000**	**25,734,100**
4.5 Agriculture	14,000,000	6,900,000	20,900,000
4.8 Environment	4,834,100		4,834,100
Total DO [?] Development Cooperation Agreement	**19,692,728**	**6,900,000**	**26,592,728**

DO [?] Human Capital Improved	Obligation To-Date	Planned Obligation Through This Action	Total Obligations as of this Action
3.1 Health	**139,420,982**	**30,049,804**	**169,470,786**
3.1.1 HIV/AIDS	111,719,489	4,365,252	116,084,741
3.1.2 Tuberculosis	84,000	104,000	188,000
3.1.3 Malaria	9,375,493	5,891,552	15,267,045
3.1.6 Maternal and Child Health	7,387,000	8,002,000	15,389,000
3.1.7 Family Planning and Reproductive Health	7,561,000	7,987,000	15,548,000
3.1.8 Water Supply and Sanitation	200,000	100,000	300,000
3.1.9 Nutrition	3,094,000	3,600,000	6,694,000
3.2 Education	**10,000,000**	**10,000,000**	**20,000,000**
3.2.1 Basic Education	10,000,000	10,000,000	20,000,000
Total DO 2 Development Cooperation Agreement	**149,420,982**	**40,049,804**	**189,470,786**
Total Development Cooperation Agreement	**170,739,710**	**46,949,804**	**217,689,514**

State Department Document Number: 12-179

Twenty-seventh Amendment to the Development Assistance Grant Agreement of August 19, 2003 Between the United States of America and the Republic of Kenya for Reduced Fertility and the Risk of HIV/AIDS Transmission Through Sustainable, Integrated Family Planning and Health Services

Signed on September 28, 2012
Entered into force September 28, 2012

CTIA Document Number: 13275.007

DATE: 28 SEP 2012

TWENTY-SEVENTH AMENDMENT TO THE DEVELOPMENT ASSISTANCE GRANT AGREEMENT NO. 615-003

Between

The United States of America, acting through the United States Agency for International Development ("USAID")

And

The Republic of Kenya (hereinafter referred to as the "GOK" or "Grantee")

Article 1: Purpose of Amendment

The purpose of this Twenty-Seventh Amendment is to: 1) grant additional USAID resources; and 2) increase the current "in-kind" contribution of the Grantee.

This Twenty-Seventh Amendment to the Development Assistance Grant Agreement No. 615-003 dated the 19th day of August 2003, is hereby entered into between the parties above named as follows:

Article 2: Contributions of the Parties

Section 3.1 USAID Contribution.

Section 3.1 (a) is deleted in its entirety and replaced with the following:

(a) The Grant: To help achieve the Objective and Results set forth in this Agreement, USAID, pursuant to the Foreign Assistance Act of 1961, as amended, has previously obligated the sum of One Billion,

Eight Hundred and Fifty-Two Million, Three Hundred and Ninety-Two Thousand, and Twenty-Two U.S. Dollars ($1,852,392,022). In order to further help achieve the Objective and Results set forth in this Agreement, USAID hereby further grants to the Grantee under the terms of this Agreement an additional amount not to exceed Forty-One Million, Nine Hundred and Nine Thousand, Four Hundred and Sixty-Five U.S. Dollars ($41,909,465) via this Twenty-Seventh Amendment. This funding through the Twenty-Seventh Amendment shall be used for activities to support USAID Program Area Health: Program Elements Tuberculosis ($3,970,000), Malaria ($14,375,000), Maternal and Child Health ($4,945,172), Family Planning and Reproductive Health ($15,500,000) and Nutrition ($1,500,000); and Program Area Program Element Administration and Oversight ($1,619,293). The total amount of the Grant is now One Billion, Eight Hundred and Ninety-Four Million, Three Hundred and One Thousand, Four Hundred and Eighty-Seven U.S. Dollars ($1,894,301,487).

Section 3.2 The Grantee Contribution

Section 3.2 (a) is deleted in its entirety and replaced with the following:

(a) The Grantee contribution for the Strategic Objective under this Twenty-Seventh Amendment is equivalent to Thirteen Million, Nine Hundred and Sixty-Nine Thousand, Eight Hundred and Twenty U.S. Dollars ($13,969,820) making the total contribution to date Five Hundred and Fifty-Eight Million, One Hundred and Eighty-Six Thousand, Four Hundred and Sixty-Four U.S. Dollars ($558,186,464). The contribution will be in kind support including personnel, office space, and other facilities necessary to successful implementation of the objective. The GOK will report at least annually in a format to be agreed upon with USAID on its in-kind cash equivalent contributions.

Article 3: Attachments

Attachment 1 to Annex 1, Illustrative Budget, Amendment 26 is hereby deleted and Attachment 1 to Annex 1, Illustrative Budget, Amendment 27 is substituted in its stead.

Article 4: Other Terms and Conditions

All other terms and conditions of the original Development Assistance Grant Agreement as amended shall remain in full force and effect.

IN WITNESS WHEREOF, the United States of America and the Grantee, each acting through its duly authorized representatives, have caused this Twenty-Seventh Amendment to be signed in their names and delivered as of the day and year written below.

FOR THE GOVERNMENT OF THE REPUBLIC OF KENYA

BY: [Signature]

NAME: MUTUA KILAKA CBS, SS

TITLE: FINANCIAL SECRETARY

FOR THE GOVERNMENT OF THE UNITED STATES OF AMERICA

BY: [Signature]

NAME: JAMES HOPE

TITLE: ACTING MISSION DIRECTOR

Development Assistance Grant Agreement Number 615-003
Reduced Fertility and the Risk of HIV/ASIDS Transmission
Through sustainable, Intergrated [*sic*] Family Planning and Health Services
Attachement [*sic*] 1 to Annex 1 Amendment 27

ILLUSTRATIVE BUDGET
(In US Dollars)

	Prior Obligations		This Obligation		Cumulative Obligations		Future Planned Obligations		Planned Life of Activity Funding	
	USAID	Implementing Agency Cont (Equiv.)	USAID	Implementing Agency Cont (Equiv.)	USAID	Implementing Agency Cont (Equiv.)	USAID	Implementing Agency Cont (Equiv.)	USAID	Implementing Agency Cont (Equiv.)
A. FY 2006 and Prior Years Obligations										
Integrated Service Delivery	25,786,000	478,500	-	-	25,786,000	478,500	-	-	25,786,000	478,500
Health Care Fin. & Sustainability	3,875,000	503,000	-	-	3,875,000	503,000	-	-	3,875,000	503,000
Child Survival & Diseases	12,774,000	382,400	-	-	12,774,000	382,400	-	-	12,774,000	382,400
Management & Coordination	9,757,283	366,450	-	-	9,757,283	366,450	-	-	9,757,283	366,450
HIV/AIDS	185,763,996	4,341,100	-	-	185,763,996	4,341,100	-	-	185,763,996	4,341,100
Sub-Total	**237,956,279**	**6,071,450**			**237,956,279**	**6,071,450**			**237,956,279**	**6,071,450**
B. FY 2007 and Beyond Obligations										
Program Area: Health **Program Elements**										
HIV/AIDS-Programs	1,430,279,828	-	-	-	1,430,279,828	-	1,004,356,212	-	2,434,636,040	-
HIV/AIDS-Administration & Oversight (A&O)	11,887,879	-		-	11,887,879	-	0	-	11,887,879	-
Tuberculosis	9,162,000	-	3,970,000	-	13,132,000	-	4,124,000	-	17,256,000	-

	Prior Obligations		This Obligation		Cumulative Obligations		Future Planned Obligations		Planned Life of Activity Funding	
	USAID	Implementing Agency Cont (Equiv.)	USAID	Implementing Agency Cont (Equiv.)	USAID	Implementing Agency Cont (Equiv.)	USAID	Implementing Agency Cont (Equiv.)	USAID	Implementing Agency Cont (Equiv.)
Malaria	57,846,162	-	14,375,000	-	72,221,162	-	34,678,838	-	106,900,000	-
Maternal and Child Health	19,700,081	-	4,945,172	-	24,645,253	-	4,824,747	-	29,470,000	-
Family Planning & Reproductive Health	65,241,092	-	15,500,000	-	80,741,092	-	12,208,908	-	92,950,000	-
Nutrition	3,744,000	-	1,500,000	-	5,244,000	-	2,006,000	-	7,250,000	-
Program Area: Social & Economic Services **Protection for Vulnerable POP Health**										
Program Elements Social Services	1,573,181	-	-	-	1,573,181	-	1,326,819	-	2,900,000	-
Program Area: Adminstraion [*sic*] and Oversight										
Program Elements Adminstraion [*sic*] and Oversight	15,001,520	-	1,619,293	-	16,620,813	-	7,585,695	-	24,206,508	-
Implementing Agency Contribution: 33.3% of Obligations	-	538,145,194	-	13,969,820	-	552,115,014	-	357,037,037	-	909,152,051
Sub-Total	**1,614,435,743**	**538,145,194**	**41,909,465**	**13,969,820**	**1,656,345,208**	**552,115,014**	**1,071,111,219**	**357,037,037**	**2,727,456,427**	**909,152,051**
Grand-Total	**1,852,392,022**	**544,216,644**	**41,909,465**	**13,969,820**	**1,894,301,487**	**558,186,464**	**1,071,111,219**	**357,037,037**	**2,965,412,706**	**915,223,501**

State Department Document Number: 12-180

Eighteenth Amendment to the Development Assistance Grant Agreement of August 19, 2002, as Amended, Between the United States of America and the Republic of Kenya for Increased Rural Household Income

Signed on September 28, 2012
Entered into force September 28, 2012

CTIA DOCUMENT NUMBER: 13795.003

DATE: 28 SEP 2012

EIGHTEENTH AMENDMENT TO THE DEVELOPMENT ASSISTANCE GRANT

AGREEMENT NO. 615-007

Between

The United States of America, acting through the
United States Agency for International Development ("USAID")

And

The Republic of Kenya (hereinafter referred to as the "GOK" or "Grantee")

Article 1
Purpose of Amendment

The purpose of this Eighteenth Amendment is to: 1) Grant additional USAID resources and 2) increase the current "in-kind" contribution of the Grantee.

This Eighteenth Amendment to the Development Assistance Grant Agreement No. 615-007, dated the 19th day of August 2002, is hereby entered into between the parties above as follows:

Article 2
Contributions of the Parties

Section 3.1 USAID Contribution.

Section 3.1 (a) is deleted in its entirety and replaced with the following:

a) The Grant: To help achieve the Objective and Results set forth in this Agreement, USAID, pursuant to the Foreign Assistance Act of 1961, as amended, has previously obligated the sum of One Hundred and Sixty-One Million, Four Hundred and Sixty-Six Thousand, Two Hundred and Thirty-Seven U.S. Dollars ($161,466,237). In order to further help achieve the Objective and Results set forth in this Agreement, USAID hereby further grants to the Grantee under the terms of this Agreement an additional amount not to exceed Fifty-Four Million, Four Hundred and Twelve Thousand, and Four U.S. Dollars ($54,412,004) via this Eighteenth Amendment. The funding in the Eighteenth Amendment shall be used to support activities under USAID's Program Area Agriculture, Program Element Agricultural Sector Capacity ($46,991,015), Program Element Agricultural Enabling Environment ($5,524,847); and Program Area and Program Element Administration and Oversight ($1,896,142). The total amount of the Grant is now Two Hundred and Fifteen Million, Eight Hundred and Seventy-Eight Thousand, Two Hundred and Forty-One U.S. Dollars ($215,878,241).

Section 3.2 The Grantee Contribution.

Section 3.2 (a) is deleted in its entirety and replaced with the following:

(a) The Grantee contribution for the Strategic Objective under this Eighteenth Amendment is equivalent to eighteen Million Fifty-Four Thousand, and One U.S. Dollars ($18,054,001), making the total contribution to date to Sixty-Six Million, Six Hundred and Twenty-Eight Thousand, and Sixty U.S. Dollars ($66,628,060). The contribution will be in kind support including personnel, office space, and other facilities necessary to successful implementation of the objective. The GOK will report at least annually in a format to be agreed upon with USAID on its in-kind cash equivalent contributions.

Article 3
Attachments

Attachment 1 to Annex 1, Illustrative Budget, Amendment 17 is hereby deleted and Attachment 1 to Annex 1, Illustrative Budget, Amendment 18 is substituted in its stead.

Article 4
Other Terms and Conditions

All other terms and conditions of the Development Assistance Grant Agreement as amended shall remain in full force and effect.

IN WITNESS WHEREOF, the United States of America and the Grantee, each acting through its duly authorized representatives, have caused this Eighteenth Amendment to be signed in their names and delivered as of the day and year written below.

FOR THE GOVERNMENT OF THE REPUBLIC OF KENYA

BY: [Signature]

NAME: MUTUA KILAKA CBS, SS

TITLE: FINANCIAL SECRETARY

FOR THE GOVERNMENT OF THE UNITED STATES OF AMERICA

BY: [Signature]

NAME: JAMES M. HOPE

TITLE: Actg Mission Director

Development Assistance Grant Agreement Number 615-007
Increased Rural Housohold Incomes
Attachment 1 to Annex 1 Amendment 17

ILLUSTRATIVE BUDGET
(In US Dollars)

	Prior Obligations		This Obligation		Cumulative Obligations		Future Planned Obligations		Planned Life of Activity Funding	
	USAID	Implementing Agency Cont (Equiv.)	USAID	Implementing Agency Cont (Equiv.)	USAID	Implementing Agency Cont (Equiv.)	USAID	Implementing Agency Cont (Equiv.)	USAID	Implementing Agency Cont (Equiv.)
A. FY 2006 and Prior Years Obligations										
Input Distribution Development	250,810	83,603	-	-	250,810	83,603	-	-	250,810	83,603
Agricultural Policy	1,362,100	1,375,496	-	-	1,362,100	1,375,496	-	-	1,362,100	1,375,496
Microenterprise Development	4,665,778	654,583	-	-	4,665,778	654,583	-	-	4,665,778	654,583
Institutional Capacity Building	257,528	169,364	-	-	257,528	169,364	-	-	257,528	169,364
Biotechnology Program	2,596,400	856,812	-	-	2,596,400	856,812	-	-	2,596,400	856,812
Horticulture Program	5,051,200	12,540	-	-	5,051,200	12,540	-	-	5,051,200	12,540
Dairy Program	5,341,320	116,286	-	-	5,341,320	116,286	-	-	5,341,320	116,286
Maize Program	3,644,100	128,210	-	-	3,644,100	128,210	-	-	3,644,100	128,210
Program Support	2,820,500	-	-	-	2,820,500	-	-	-	2,820,500	-
Evaluation and Audits	195,005	-	-	-	195,005	-	-	-	195,005	-
Sub-Total	**26,184,741**	**3,396,894**	**-**	**-**	**26,184,741**	**3,396,894**	**-**	**-**	**26,184,741**	**3,396,894**
B. FY 2007 and Beyond Obligations										
Program Area: Health					**19,976,880**		-		**19,976,880**	
Program Elements: Water Supply and Sanitation	19,976,880	-		-	19,976,880	-		-		-

	Prior Obligations		This Obligation		Cumulative Obligations		Future Planned Obligations		Planned Life of Activity Funding	
	USAID	Implementing Agency Cont (Equiv.)	USAID	Implementing Agency Cont (Equiv.)	USAID	Implementing Agency Cont (Equiv.)	USAID	Implementing Agency Cont (Equiv.)	USAID	Implementing Agency Cont (Equiv.)
Program Area: Agriculture					**147,279,836**		**11,026,284**		**158,306,120**	
Program Elements: Agriculture Enabling Environment	10,165,000	-	5,524,847	-	15,689,847	-		-		-
Agricultural Sector Capacity	76,215,999	-	46,991,015		123,207,014	-		-		-
Agricultural Sector Productivity	5,750,000	-	-	-	5,750,000	-		-		-
Program Support (Agriculture)	1,232,975	-	-	-	1,232,975	-		-		-
Program Design and Learning	300,000	-	-	-	300,000	-		-		-
Administration and Oversight	1,100,000	-	-	-	1,100,000	-		-		-
Program Area: Private Sector Competitiveness					**2,938,939**		**5,616,061**		**8,555,000**	
Program Elements: Private Sector Productivity	250,000	-	-	-	250,000	-		-		-
Private Sector Capacity	2,688,939	-	-	-	2,688,939	-		-		-
Program Area: Economic Oppportunity					**8,283,626**		**7,919,297**		**16,202,923**	
Program Elements: Policy Environment for Micro & Small Enterprise	200,000	-	-	-	200,000	-		-		-
Strengthen Micro Enterprise Productivity	4,533,626	-	-	-	4,533,626	-		-		-
Program Support (Econ Opportunity)	150,000	-	-	-	150,000	-		-		-
Inclusive Financial Markets	3,250,000	-	-	-	3,250,000	-		-		-

	Prior Obligations		This Obligation		Cumulative Obligations		Future Planned Obligations		Planned Life of Activity Funding	
	USAID	Implementing Agency Cont (Equiv.)	USAID	Implementing Agency Cont (Equiv.)	USAID	Implementing Agency Cont (Equiv.)	USAID	Implementing Agency Cont (Equiv.)	USAID	Implementing Agency Cont (Equiv.)
Program Design and Learning	50,000	-	-	-	50,000	-		-		-
Administration and Oversight	100,000	-	-	-	100,000	-		-		-
Program Area: Disaster Readiness					**200,000**		**500,000**		**700,000**	
Program Elements: Capacity Building, Preparedness and Planning	200,000	-	-	-	200,000	-		-		-
Program Area: Protection, Assistance and Solutions					**2,608,077**		**0**		**2,608,077**	
Program Element: Assistance and Recovery	2,608,077	-	-	-	2,608,077	-		-		-
Program Area: Administration and Oversight					**8,406,142**		**7,093,858**		**15,500,000**	
Program Elements: Administration and Oversight	6,510,000	-	1,896,142		8,406,142					
Implementing Agency Contribution: 33.3% of Obligations	-	45,093,832	-	18,137,334	-	63,231,166	-	10,718,500	-	73,949,666
Sub-Total	**135,281,496**	**45,093,832**	**54,412,004**	**18,137,334**	**189,693,500**	**63,231,166**	**32,155,500**	**10,718,500**	**221,849,000**	**73,949,666**
Grand-Total	**161,466,237**	**48,490,726**	**54,412,004**	**18,137,334**	**215,878,241**	**66,628,060**	**32,155,500**	**10,718,500**	**248,033,741**	**77,346,560**

STATE DEPARTMENT DOCUMENT NUMBER: 12-181

SECOND AMENDMENT TO THE PARTNERSHIP AGREEMENT OF SEPTEMBER 30, 2010, AS AMENDED, BETWEEN THE UNITED STATES OF AMERICA AND INDIA, FOR HEALTH, WITH ADDENDUM AND ATTACHMENT

SIGNED AT NEW DELHI, SEPTEMBER 28 AND OCTOBER 1, 2012
ENTERED INTO FORCE OCTOBER 1, 2012

CTIA DOCUMENT NUMBER: 18085.001

CONFORMED COPY

USAID Assistance Agreement No. 386-0547

Certified to be a true copy of the original signed by Mr. William Hammink, Director, USAID/New Delhi and Mr. Rajesh Khullar, Joint Secretary, Department of Economic Affairs, Ministry of Finance, Government of India.

[Signature]
William Hammink
Mission Director
USAID/India

Date: September 28, 2012

Article 1
Purpose of Amendment

The purpose of this Second Amendment to the Partnership Agreement for Health Project, entered into on September 30, 2010, (the "Agreement") is to: (1) grant incremental funding of Thirty-Eight Million Nine Hundred Fifty-Nine Thousand Five Hundred Thirty-One United States (U.S.) Dollars ($38,959,531) to the Government of India (GOI); (2) revise the GOI contribution in concert with revisions to the USAID grant; and (3) revise Annex 1, the Amplified Description of Planned Activities under the USAID-GOI Health Partnership Agreement, and Attachment A to Annex 1, the Illustrative Summary of Current and Planned Bilateral Obligations.

Article 2
Contributions of the Parties

A. Under Section 3.1, USAID Contribution, subsections 3.1 (a) of the Agreement is hereby deleted in its entirety and the following substituted in their stead:

(a) *The Grant.* To help achieve the objective set forth in this Agreement, USAID, pursuant to the Foreign Assistance Act of 1961, as amended, hereby grants to the GOI under the terms of this Agreement an amount not to exceed One Hundred Million Five Hundred Sixty Four Thousand Six Hundred Ten U.S. Dollars ($100,564,610) (the "Grant").

B. Under Section 3.2, GOI Contribution, the second paragraph of subsection 3.2(a) and subsection 3.2(b) of the Agreement are hereby deleted in their entireties and the following new subsection 3.2(b) is substituted in their stead:

(b) The GOI's contribution, based on USAID's contribution in Section 3.1(a), will not be less than the equivalent of Thirty-Three Million Five Hundred Twenty-One Thousand Five Hundred Thirty-Seven U.S. Dollars ($33,521,537), including in-kind contributions, calculated at the exchange rate in effect on the date of the agreement and the relevant amendment providing incremental funding. If USAID increases the amount of the Grant in Section 3.1 (a) incrementally, as contemplated herein, the GOI's contribution shall increase with each increment accordingly, such that the GOI's contribution will not be less than the equivalent of one-third of that portion of the Grant that is used to support activities that either directly provides substantial benefit to the GOI or involves the direct and substantial involvement of the GOI in the administration, control or management of such assistance. The precise amount of GOI contribution shall be indicated in USAID's written notice of each incremental contribution. The GOI's total estimated planned contribution to the Objective will be subject to availability of funds to the GOI for this purpose and to USAID providing the total estimated amount in Section 3.1(b). The Grantee will report at least annually in a format to be agreed upon with USAID on its contributions.

Article 3
Amplified Description

A. The attached Addendum to this Second Amendment revises Annex 1 of the Agreement, the Amplified Description of Planned Activities under the USAID-GOI Health Partnership Agreement.

B. The financial plan, entitled "Illustrative Summary of Current and Planned Bilateral Obligations Up To and Including This First Amendment," as shown in Attachment A to Annex 1 of the Agreement, is hereby deleted in its entirety and is replaced by the revised "Illustrative Summary of Current Bilateral Obligations Up to and Including This Second Amendment", included as Attachment A to this Second Amendment.

Article 4
Other Terms and Conditions

All other terms and conditions of the Agreement shall, except as amended herein, remain in full force and effect.

IN WITNESS WHEREOF, the Grantee and the United States of America, each acting through its duly authorized representative, have caused this Second Amendment to be signed in their names and delivered as of the day and year first above written.

THE GOVERNMENT OF INDIA

[Signature]

Rajesh Khullar
Joint Secretary
Department of Economic Affairs
Ministry of Finance

THE UNITED STATES OF AMERICA

[Signature]

William Hammink
Director
United States Agency for International Development, Mission to India

Counter-signed on October 1, 2012

Health Partnership Program (HPP) Agreement Addendum No. 2 to Annex 1, the Amplified Description of Planned Activities under the USAID-GOI Health Partnership Agreement

This addendum revises the Amplified Description of Planned Activities to establish a process for identifying the geographic focus of project activities, by adding the new paragraph provided below:

> **Geographic Focus:** The focus states for non-HIV/AIDS health programs are to be jointly identified by Department of Health and Family Welfare and USAID. The focus states for HIV/AIDS programs are to be jointly identified by Department of AIDS Control/NACO and USAID.

ATTACHMENT A

HEALTH PARTNERSHIP PROGRAM (386-0547)
ILLUSTRATIVE SUMMARY OF BILATERAL OBLIGATIONS
UP TO AND INCLUDING THIS SECOND AMENDMENT
(In Thousands of U.S. Dollars)

Intermediate Result[1]	Obligation This Amendment			Cumulative Obligations Through This Amendment		
	U.S. FY 2012			U.S. FY 2010-FY 2012		
	USAID Contribution	HCC[2]	Program Total	USAID Contribution	HCC[2]	Program Total
1. *Increased Access to Quality Services*						
– Quality Improvement	9,350	3,696	13,046	21,076	8,046	29,122
– Health of the Urban Poor[3] (On-going)	3,000	1,000	4,000	4,870	1,624	6,494
2. *Strengthened Policy and Regulatory Environment*	-	-	-	-	-	-
3. *Increased Healthy Behavior*						
– Behavior Change Communication	6,500	2,167	8,667	18,000	6,500	24,000
(of which for HIV/ AIDS activities)	**(2,500)**	**(833)**	**(3,333)**	**(4,903)**	**(1,634)**	**(6,537)**
4. *Increased Use of Data for Decision-Making*						
– Strategic Information/Policy	810	270	1,080	6,711	2,237	8,948
5. *Increased Private Sector Engagement in Health*						
– Public-Private Partnership for Health	2,300	767	3,067	7,617	2,539	10,156
HIV/AIDS	**11,491**	**3,830**	**15,321**	**33,977**	**11,326**	**45,303**
Tuberculosis	3,750	1,250	5,000	3,750	1,250	5,000
Evaluation	1,759	-	1,759	4,564	-	4,564
(of which for HIV/AIDS activities)	**(759)**	**-**	**(759)**	**(1,809)**	**-**	**(1,809)**
Other Technical Assistance	-	-	-	-	-	-
BILATERAL PROGRAM TOTAL	**38,960**	**12,980**	**51,940**	**100,565**	**33,522**	**134,087**

1/ Representatives of the Parties, as defined in Section 8.2 of the Agreement, may unilaterally, with written notice to the other Party, adjust the line item obligated amounts in this budget to a maximum of fifteen percent (15%) of their respective total cumulative obligation amount, provided, however, that the adjustments in line item obligated amounts may not result in a change to their respective total cumulative obligation amount.

2/ Host Country Contribution (HCC): Exchange rates to be used for calculation of HCC will be the rate which is in effect on the date of the Agreement and the date of any subsequent amendment providing incremental funding.

3/ The planned total USAID obligation for the Health of the Urban Poor is $10.779 million, subject to the availability of funds and agreement of USAID and the program implementer to proceed. Of this, $3.140 million was obligated directly by USAID in FY 2009 and FY 2010. The planned balance of $7.639 million is expected to be provided as sub-obligations under this agreement.

STATE DEPARTMENT DOCUMENT NUMBER: 12-182

AGREEMENT BETWEEN THE UNITED STATES OF AMERICA AND IRELAND ON ENHANCING COOPERATION IN PREVENTING AND COMBATING SERIOUS CRIME

SIGNED AT DUBLIN, JULY 21, 2011
ENTERED INTO FORCE OCTOBER 19, 2012

CTIA DOCUMENT NUMBER: 18086.000

The Government of the United States of America and the Government of Ireland (hereinafter "the Parties"),

Desiring to step up co-operation to prevent and combat serious crime, particularly terrorism,

Recognizing that information sharing is an essential component in the fight against serious crime, particularly terrorism,

Recognizing the importance of preventing and combating serious crime, particularly terrorism, while respecting fundamental rights and freedoms, notably privacy,

Inspired by the EU Council Decision 2008/615/JHA of 23 June 2008 on the stepping up of cross-border cooperation, particularly in combating terrorism and cross-border crime, and the Treaty done at Prüm on 27 May 2005, and

Seeking to enhance and encourage cooperation between the Parties in the spirit of partnership,

Have agreed as follows:

Article 1
Definitions

For the purposes of this Agreement,

1. DNA profiles (DNA identification patterns) shall mean a letter or numerical code representing a number of identifying features of the non-coding part of an analyzed human DNA sample.

2. Personal data shall mean any information relating to an identified or identifiable natural person (the "data subject").

3. Processing of personal data shall mean any operation or set of operations which is performed upon personal data, whether or not by automated means, such as collection, recording, organization, storage, adaptation or alteration, sorting, retrieval, consultation, use, disclosure by supply,

dissemination or otherwise making available, combination or alignment, blocking, or deletion through erasure or destruction of personal data.

4. Reference data shall mean a DNA profile and the related reference (DNA reference data) or fingerprinting data and the related reference (fingerprinting reference data). Reference data must not contain any data from which the data subject can be directly identified. Reference data not traceable to any individual (untraceables) must be recognisable as such.

Serious crime, for the purposes of this Agreement, shall mean conduct constituting a criminal offence which is not a minor offence in accordance with Irish law or a misdemeanour under United States law.

Article 2
Purpose and Scope of this Agreement

1. The purpose of this Agreement is to enhance the cooperation between the United States and Ireland in preventing and combating serious crime.

2. The querying powers provided for under this Agreement shall be used only for prevention, detection and investigation of crime because particular circumstances give reason to inquire whether the data subject will commit or has committed an offence referred to in Article 2, paragraph 3.

3. The offences in respect of which the querying powers provided for under this Agreement shall be used shall be serious offences as defined in Article 1.

To ensure compliance with the Parties' respective national laws, the Parties may agree to specify particular serious crimes for which a Party shall not be obligated to supply personal data as described in Articles 6 and 9 of the Agreement.

Article 3
Fingerprinting data

For the purpose of implementing this Agreement, the Parties shall ensure the availability of reference data from the file for the national automated fingerprint identification systems established for the prevention and investigation of criminal offences. Reference data shall only include fingerprinting data and a reference.

Article 4
Automated querying of fingerprint data

1. For the prevention, detection and investigation of serious crime, each Party shall allow the other Party's national contact points, as referred to in Article 7, access to the reference data in the automated fingerprint identification system, which it has established for that purpose, with the power to conduct automated queries by comparing fingerprinting data. Queries may be conducted only in individual cases and in compliance with the querying Party's national law.

2. Comparison of fingerprinting data with reference data held by the Party in charge of the file shall be carried out by the querying national contact points by means of the automated supply of the reference data required for a clear match.

Article 5
Alternative means to query using identifying data

Until Ireland has a fully operational and automated fingerprint identification system that links to individual criminal records and is prepared to provide the United States with automated access to such a system, it shall provide an alternative means to conduct a query using other identifying data to determine a clear match linking the individual to additional data. Query powers shall be exercised in the same manner as provided in Article 4 to allow for the supply of additional data as provided for in Article 6.

Article 6
Supply of further personal and other data

Should the procedure referred to in Article 4 show a match between fingerprinting data, or should the procedure utilized pursuant to Article 5 show a match, the supply of any available further personal data and other data relating to the reference data shall be governed by the national law, including the legal assistance rules, of the requested Party and shall be supplied in accordance with Article 7.

Article 7
National contact points and implementing agreements

1. For the purpose of the supply of data as referred to in Articles 4 and 5, and the subsequent supply of further personal data as referred to in Article 6, each Party shall designate one or more national contact points. The contact point shall supply such data in accordance with the national law of the Party designating the contact point. Other available legal assistance channels need not be used unless necessary, for instance to authenticate such data for purposes of its admissibility in judicial proceedings of the requesting Party.

2. The technical and procedural details for the queries conducted pursuant to Articles 4 and 5 shall be set forth in one or more implementing agreements or arrangements.

Article 8
Automated querying of DNA profiles

1. If permissible under the national law of both Parties and on the basis of reciprocity, the Parties may allow each other's national contact point, as referred to in Article 10, access to the reference data in their DNA analysis files, with the power to conduct automated queries by comparing DNA profiles for the investigation of serious crime. Queries may be made only in individual cases and in compliance with the querying Party's national law.

2. Should an automated query show that a DNA profile supplied matches a DNA profile entered in the other Party's file, the querying national contact point shall receive by automated notification the reference data for which a match has been found. If no match can be found, automated notification of this shall be given.

Article 9
Supply of further personal and other data

Should the procedure referred to in Article 8 show a match between DNA profiles, the supply of any available further personal data and other data relating to the reference data shall be governed by the national law, including the legal assistance rules, of the requested Party and shall be supplied in accordance with Article 10.

Article 10
National contact point and implementing agreements

1. For the purposes of the supply of data as set forth in Article 8, and the subsequent supply of further personal data as referred to in Article 9, each Party shall designate a national contact point. The contact point shall supply such data in accordance with the national law of the Party designating the contact point. Other available legal assistance channels need not be used unless necessary, for instance to authenticate such data for purposes of its admissibility in judicial proceedings of the requesting Party.

2. The technical and procedural details for the queries conducted pursuant to Article 8 shall be set forth in one or more implementing agreements or arrangements.

Article 11
Supply of personal and other data in order to prevent serious criminal and terrorist offences

1. For the prevention of serious criminal and terrorist offences, the Parties may, in compliance with their respective national law, in individual cases, even without being requested to do so, supply the other Party's relevant national contact point, as referred to in paragraph 6, with the personal data specified in paragraph 2, in so far as is necessary because particular circumstances give reason to believe that the data subject(s) will commit or has committed an offence referred to in Article 2, paragraph 3 and, in particular, terrorist activity, terrorist-linked activity and offences related to the activities of a criminal organisation.

2. The personal data to be supplied may include, if available, surname, first names, former names, other names, aliases, alternative spelling of names, sex, date and place of birth, current and former nationalities, passport number, numbers from other identity documents, and fingerprinting data, as well as a description of any conviction or of the circumstarices giving rise to the belief referred to in paragraph 1.

3. The supplying Party may, in compliance with its national law, impose conditions on the use that may be made of such data by the receiving Party. If the receiving Party accepts such data, it shall be bound by any such conditions.

4. Generic restrictions with respect to the legal standards of the receiving Party for processing personal data may not be imposed by the transmitting Party as a condition under paragraph 3 to providing data.

5. In addition to the personal data referred to in paragraph 2, the Parties may provide each other with non-personal data related to the offences set forth in paragraph 1.

6. Each Party shall designate one or more national contact points for the exchange of personal and other data under this Article with the other Party's contact points. The powers of the national contact points shall be governed by the national law applicable.

Article 12
Privacy and Data Protection

1. The Parties recognise that the handling and processing of personal data that they acquire from each other is of critical importance to preserving confidence in the implementation of this Agreement.

2. The Parties commit themselves to processing personal data fairly and in accordance with their respective national laws and:

a. to ensuring that the personal data provided are adequate and relevant in relation to the specific purpose of the transfer;

b. to retaining personal data only so long as necessary for the specific purpose for which the data were provided or further processed in accordance with this Agreement; and

c. to ensuring that possibly inaccurate personal data are brought to the attention of the receiving Party without delay in order that appropriate corrective action is taken.

3. This Agreement shall not give rise to rights on the part of any private person, including to obtain, suppress, or exclude any evidence, or to impede the sharing of personal data. Rights existing independently of this Agreement, however, are not affected.

Article 13
Limitation on processing to protect personal and other data

1. Each Party may process data obtained under this Agreement:

a. for the purposes set out in Article 2;

b. for the purposes set out in Article 11;

c. for preventing a serious threat to its public security

d. for any other purpose, only with the prior consent of the Party which has transmitted the data; or

e. in other proceedings directly related to the purposes set out in Article 2.

2. The Parties shall not communicate data provided under this Agreement to any third State, international body or private entity without the consent of the Party that provided the data and without the appropriate safeguards.

3. A Party may conduct an automated query of the other Party's fingerprint or DNA files under Articles 4 or 8, and process data received in response to such a query, including the communication whether or not a hit exists, solely in order to:

a. establish whether the compared DNA profiles or fingerprint data match;

b. prepare and submit a follow-up request for assistance in compliance with national law, including the legal assistance rules, if those data match; or

c. conduct record-keeping, as required or permitted by its national law.

The Party administering the file may process the data supplied to it by the querying Party during the course of an automated query in accordance with Articles 4 and 8 solely where this is necessary for the purposes of comparison, providing automated replies to the query or record-keeping pursuant to Article 16. The data supplied for comparison shall be deleted immediately following data comparison or automated replies to queries unless further processing is necessary for the purposes mentioned under this Article, paragraph 3, subparagraphs (b) or (c).

Article 14
Correction, blockage and deletion of data

1. At the request of the supplying Party, the receiving Party shall be obliged to correct, block, or delete, consistent with its national law, data received under this Agreement that are incorrect or incomplete or if its collection or further processing contravenes this Agreement or the rules applicable to the supplying Party.

2. Where a Party becomes aware that data it has received from the other Party under this Agreement are not accurate, it shall take all appropriate measures to safeguard against erroneous reliance on such data, which shall include in particular supplementation, deletion, or correction of such data.

3. Each Party shall notify the other if it becomes aware that material data it has transmitted to the other Party or received from the other Party under this Agreement are inaccurate or unreliable or are subject to significant doubt.

Article 15
Documentation

1. Each Party shall maintain a record of the transmission and receipt of data communicated to the other Party under this Agreement. This record shall serve to:

 a. ensure effective monitoring of data protection in accordance with the national law of the respective Party;

 b. enable the Parties to effectively make use of the rights granted to them according to Articles 14 and 18; and

 c. ensure data security.

2. The record shall include:

 a. information on the data supplied;

 b. the reason for the supply of the data;

 c. the date of supply; and

 d. the recipient of the data in case the data are supplied to other entities.

3. The recorded data shall be protected with suitable measures against inappropriate use and other forms of improper use and shall be kept for two years. After the conservation period the recorded data shall be deleted immediately, unless this is inconsistent with national law, including applicable data protection and retention rules.

Article 16
Data Security

1. The Parties shall ensure that the necessary technical measures and organisational arrangements are utilised to protect personal data against accidental or unlawful destruction, loss or unauthorised disclosure, alteration, access or any unauthorised form of processing. The Parties in particular shall reasonably take measures to ensure that only those authorised to access personal data can have access to such data.

2. The implementing agreements or arrangements that govern the procedures for automated querying of fingerprint and DNA files pursuant to Articles 4 and 8 shall provide:

a. that appropriate use is made of modern technology to ensure data protection, security, confidentiality and integrity;

b. that encryption and authorisation procedures recognised by the competent authorities are used when having recourse to generally accessible networks; and

c. for a mechanism to ensure that only permissible queries are conducted.

Article 17
Transparency—Providing information to the data subjects

1. Nothing in this Agreement shall be interpreted to interfere with the Parties' legal obligations, as set forth by their respective national laws, to provide data subjects with information as to the purposes of the processing and the identity of the data controller, the recipients or categories of recipients, the existence of the right of access to and the right to rectify the data concerning him or her and any further information such as the legal basis of the processing operation for which the data are intended, the time limits for storing the data and the right of recourse, in so far as such further information is necessary, having regard for the purposes and the specific circumstances in which the data are processed, to guarantee fair processing with respect to data subjects.

2. Such information may be denied in accordance with the respective national laws of the Parties, including if providing this information may jeopardise:

a. the purposes of the processing;

b. investigations or prosecutions conducted by the competent authorities in the United States or by the competent authorities in Ireland; or

c. the rights and freedoms of third parties.

3. Nothing in this Agreement shall be interpreted to interfere with the rights of a data subject, as set out in the Parties' respective national laws, to seek redress for any breach of their data protection or data privacy rights, as set out in the Parties' respective national laws.

Article 18
Information

Upon request, the receiving Party shall inform the supplying Party of the processing of supplied data and the result obtained. The receiving Party shall ensure that its answer is communicated to the supplying Party in a timely manner.

Article 19
Relation to Other Agreements

Nothing in this Agreement shall be construed to limit or prejudice the provisions of any treaty, other agreement, working law enforcement relationship, or domestic law allowing for information sharing between Ireland and the United States.

Article 20
Consultations

1. The Parties shall consult each other regularly on the implementation of the provisions of this Agreement.

2. In the event of any dispute regarding the interpretation or application of this Agreement, the Parties shall consult each other in order to facilitate its resolution.

Article 21
Expenses

Each Party shall bear the expenses incurred by its authorities in implementing this Agreement. In special cases, the Parties may agree on different arrangements.

Article 22
Termination of the Agreement

This Agreement may be terminated by either Party with three months' notice in writing to the other Party. The provisions of this Agreement shall continue to apply to data supplied prior to such termination.

Article 23
Amendments

1. The Parties shall enter into consultations with respect to the amendment of this Agreement at the request of either Party.

2. This Agreement may be amended by written agreement of the Parties at any time.

Article 24
Entry into force

1. This Agreement shall enter into force, with the exception of Articles 8 through 10, on the date of the later note completing an exchange of diplomatic notes between the Parties indicating that each has taken any steps necessary to bring the agreement into force.

2. Articles 8 through 10 of this Agreement shall enter into force following the conclusion of the implementing agreement(s) or arrangement(s) referenced in Article 10 and on the date of the later note completing an exchange of diplomatic notes between the Parties indicating that each Party is

able to implement those articles on a reciprocal basis. This exchange shall occur if the national laws of both Parties permit the type of DNA screening contemplated by Articles 8 through 10.

Done at Dublin, this 21st day of July 2011, in duplicate, in the English language.

FOR THE GOVERNMENT OF THE UNITED STATES OF AMERICA:

[Signature]

FOR THE GOVERNMENT OF IRELAND:

[Signature]

STATE DEPARTMENT DOCUMENT NUMBER: 12-183

EXTENSION OF THE AGREEMENT OF OCTOBER 24, 1996, AS AMENDED, BETWEEN THE UNITED STATES OF AMERICA AND JAPAN CONCERNING COOPERATION ON THE ADVANCED SPACEBORNE THERMAL EMISSION AND REFLECTION RADIOMETER (ASTER) PROGRAM

EFFECTED BY EXCHANGE OF NOTES AT WASHINGTON D.C.,
OCTOBER 19, 2012
ENTERED INTO FORCE OCTOBER 19, 2012,
EFFECTIVE OCTOBER 24, 2012

CTIA DOCUMENT NUMBER: 9192.001

EMBASSY OF JAPAN
WASHINGTON, D. C.

Washington, October 19, 2012

Her Excellency
Hillary Rodham Clinton
The Secretary of State

Excellency,

I have the honor to refer to the agreement between the Government of Japan and the Government of the United States of America concerning the cooperation between the Ministry of Economy, Trade and Industry of Japan and the National Aeronautics and Space Administration of the United States of America on the Advanced Spaceborne Thermal Emission and Reflection Radiometer (ASTER) Program (hereinafter referred to as "the Program"), which was effected by the Exchange of Notes dated October 24, 1996 and extended for a period of eight years from October 24, 2004 (hereinafter referred to as "the Present Agreement").

In consideration of the continuing mutually beneficial relationship between the two Governments in the field of peaceful exploration and use of outer space; taking into account the Agreement between the Government of Japan and the Government of the United States of America on Cooperation in Research and Development in Science and Technology, signed at Toronto on June 20, 1988, as extended and amended; and reaffirming that the provisions of the Agreement between the Government of Japan and the Government of the United States of America Concerning Cross-Waiver of Liability for Cooperation in the Exploration and Use of Space for Peaceful Purposes, signed at Washington on April 24, 1995, and the Exchange of Notes of the same date between the two Governments concerning subrogated claims shall apply to the Program, I have further the honor to propose, on behalf of the Government of Japan, that the Present Agreement shall be extended for a period of seven years from October 24, 2012.

I have further the honor to propose that, if the foregoing is acceptable to the Government of the United States of America, this Note and Your Excellency's Note in reply shall constitute an agreement between the two Governments, which shall enter into force on the date of Your Excellency's reply.

Accept, Excellency, the renewed assurances of my highest consideration.

For the Ambassador Extraordinary
and Plenipotentiary of Japan
[Signature]

DIPLOMATIC NOTE

October 19, 2012

His Excellency
Ichiro Fujisaki,
Ambassador of Japan.

Excellency,

I have the honor to acknowledge the receipt of your note of today's date, which reads as follows:

"Excellency,

I have the honor to refer to the agreement between the Government of Japan and the Government of the United States of America concerning the cooperation between the Ministry of Economy, Trade and Industry of Japan and the National Aeronautics and Space Administration of the United States of America on the Advanced Spaceborne Thermal Emission and Reflection Radiometer (ASTER) Program (hereinafter referred to as "the Program"), which was effected by the Exchange of Notes dated October 24, 1996 and extended for a period of eight years from October 24, 2004 (hereinafter referred to as "the Present Agreement").

In consideration of the continuing mutually beneficial relationship between the two Governments in the field of peaceful exploration and use of outer space; taking into account the Agreement between the Government of Japan and the Government of the United States of America on Cooperation in Research and Development in Science and Technology, signed at Toronto on June 20, 1988, as extended and amended; and reaffirming that the provisions of the Agreement between the Government of Japan and the Government of the United States of America Concerning Cross-Waiver of Liability for Cooperation in the Exploration and Use of Space for Peaceful Purposes, signed at Washington on April 24, 1995, and the Exchange of Notes of the same date between the two Governments concerning subrogated claims shall apply to the Program, I have further the honor to propose, on behalf of the Government of Japan, that the Present Agreement shall be extended for a period of seven years from October 24, 2012.

I have further the honor to propose that, if the foregoing is acceptable to the Government of the United States of America, this Note and Your Excellency's Note in reply shall constitute an agreement between the two Governments, which shall enter into force on the date of Your Excellency's reply.

Accept, Excellency, the renewed assurances of my highest consideration."

I have further the honor to confirm on behalf of the Government of the United States of America that the foregoing is acceptable to the Government of the United States of America and to agree that your note and this note in reply shall constitute an agreement between the two Governments, which shall enter into force on the date of this reply.

Accept, Excellency, the renewed assurances of my highest consideration.

For the Secretary of State:
[Signature]

State Department Document Number: 12-184

Amendment One to the Memorandum of Understanding of August 23 and September 23, 2005 Among the Department of Defence of Australia and the Department of National Defence of Canada and the Ministry of Defense of the Republic of Finland and the Ministry of Defense of the State of Kuwait and the Ministry of Defense of the Kingdom of Spain and the Federal Department of Defense, Civil Protection and Sports of the Swiss Confederation and the Department of Defense of the United States of America Concerning the Cooperative Framework for the F/A-18 Program

Signed at Arlington, Ottawa, Williamtown,
Madrid, Bern, Kuwait, Tikkakoski, and Kuala Lumpur,
June 14, 22, 24 and 28, July 8, August 19 and 24, 2010
Entered into force August 24, 2010

CTIA Document Number: 12771.001

(Short Title: F/A-18 FRAMEWORK MOU)

Certified to be a true copy.
[Signature]

PHIL WHEELER
International Agreements Negotiator
Navy International Programs Office

INTRODUCTION

The Department of Defence of Australia, the Department of National Defence of Canada, the Ministry of Defense of the Republic of Finland, the Ministry of Defense of the State of Kuwait, the Ministry of Defence of Malaysia, the.Ministry of Defense of the Kingdom of Spain, the Federal Department of Defense, Civil Protection and Sports of the Swiss Confederation, and the Department of Defense of the United States of America (U.S. DoD), hereinafter referred to as the "Participants":

Having considered the Memorandum of Understanding among the Department of Defence of Australia, the Department of National Defence of Canada, the Ministry of Defense of the Republic of Finland, the Ministry of Defense of the State of Kuwait, the Ministry of Defense of the Kingdom of Spain, the Federal Department of Defense, Civil Protection and Sports of the Swiss Confederation, and the Department of Defense of the United States of America (U.S. DoD) Concerning the Cooperative Framework for the F/A-18 Program (F/A-18 Framework MOU), which entered into effect September 23, 2005,

Have reached the following understandings:

SECTION I
PURPOSE

The purpose of Amendment One to the F/A-18 Framework MOU is to provide for the accession of the Ministry of Defence of Malaysia as a Participant in the MOU.

SECTION II
AMENDMENT

The F/A-18 Framework MOU is hereby amended as follows:

1. Replace the current Title Page with the following Title Page:

MEMORANDUM OF UNDERSTANDING
AMONG THE
DEPARTMENT OF DEFENCE
OF AUSTRALIA
AND THE
DEPARTMENT OF NATIONAL DEFENCE
OF CANADA
AND THE
MINISTRY OF DEFENSE OF THE REPUBLIC
OF FINLAND
AND THE
MINISTRY OF DEFENSE OF THE STATE
OF KUWAIT
AND THE
MINISTRY OF DEFENCE
OF MALAYSIA
AND THE
MINISTRY OF DEFENSE OF THE KINGDOM
OF SPAIN
AND THE
FEDERAL DEPARTMENT OF DEFENSE, CIVIL PROTECTION AND SPORTS OF
THE SWISS CONFEDERATION
AND THE
THE DEPARTMENT OF DEFENSE
OF THE UNITED STATES OF AMERICA
CONCERNING THE
COOPERATIVE FRAMEWORK FOR THE F/A-18 PROGRAM
(Short Title: F/A-18 FRAMEWORK MOU)

2. Revise the first paragraph of the Introduction by inserting "the Ministry of Defence of Malaysia," immediately after "the Department of the Ministry of Defense of the State of Kuwait,".

3. Revise ANNEX A (SAMPLE PROJECT ARRANGEMENT) as follows:

a. Revise the Introduction by inserting "the Ministry of Defence of Malaysia," immediately after "the Department of the Ministry of Defense of the State of Kuwait,".

SECTION III
EFFECTIVE DATE AND SIGNATURES

This Amendment One will enter into effect upon signature by all Participants and will remain in effect for the same period as the F/A-18 Framework MOU that it amends. Unless specifically amended herein, all other provisions of the MOU remain unchanged.

The foregoing represents the understandings reached among the Participants on the matters referred to herein.

Signed by the authorized representatives of the Participants:

FOR THE DEPARTMENT OF DEFENCE
OF AUSTRALIA

[Signature]

Signature

AIRCDRE R. D. R. McPHAIL

Name

DIRECTOR GENERAL
AEROSPACE COMBAT SYSTEMS

Title

24 JUNE 2010

Date

RAAF WILLIAMTOWN AUSTRALIA

Location

FOR THE DEPARTMENT OF NATIONAL
DEFENCE OF CANADA

[Signature]

Signature

D L ROSS

Name

ADM Materiel

Title

22 June 2010

Date

Ottawa

Location

FOR THE MINISTRY OF DEFENSE OF THE REPUBLIC OF FINLAND

[Signature]

Signature

Brigadier General Lauri Puranen

Name

Chief of Staff AFCOMFIN

Title

19.8.2010

Date

Tikkakoski, Finland

Location

FOR THE MINISTRY OF DEFENCE OF MALAYSIA

[Signature]

Signature

General Rodzali bin Daud RMAF

Name

Chief of Air Force
Royal Malaysian Air Force

Title

24 Aug 2010

Date

Kuala Lumpur, Malaysia

Location

FOR THE MINISTRY OF DEFENSE OF
THE STATE OF KUWAIT

[Signature]

Signature

Name
Director of Foreign Military Sales Dept. KMOD
Hamed A. Al-Tawheed

Title

Jul. 8, 2010

Date

Kuwait

Location

FOR THE MINISTRY OF DEFENSE OF
THE KINGDOM OF SPAIN

[Signature]

Signature

JUAN ANTONIO DEL CASTILLO MASETE

Name

GJMALOG

Title

28 June 2010

Date

MADRID, SPAIN

Location

FOR THE FEDERAL DEPARTMENT OF DEFENSE, CIVIL PROTECTION AND SPORTS OF THE SWISS CONFEDERATION

[Signature]

Signature

Jakob Baumann; Peter Winter

Name

Chief of Armament; Director, Aeronautical Systems

Title

28 June 2010

Date

Bern, Switzerland

Location

FOR THE DEPARTMENT OF DEFENSE OF THE UNITED STATES OF AMERICA

[Signature]

Signature

S.S. VOETSCH
Rear Admiral, U.S. Navy

Name

Deputy Assistant Secretary of the Navy (International Programs)

Title

JUN 14 2010

Date

Arlington, Virginia

Location

STATE DEPARTMENT DOCUMENT NUMBER: 12-185

ACQUISITION AND CROSS-SERVICING AGREEMENT (US-CO-2) BETWEEN THE DEPARTMENT OF DEFENSE OF THE UNITED STATES OF AMERICA AND THE MINISTRY OF NATIONAL DEFENSE OF THE REPUBLIC OF COLOMBIA, WITH ANNEXES

SIGNED AT BOGOTA AND MIAMI, JUNE 27 AND 30, 2012
ENTERED INTO FORCE JUNE 30, 2012

CTIA DOCUMENT NUMBER: 18087.000

Effective Date:

JUN 30 2012

PREAMBLE

The Department of Defense of the United States of America and the Ministry of National Defense of the Republic of Colombia, hereinafter referred to as the Parties, desiring to further the interoperability, readiness, and effectiveness of their respective military forces through increased logistic cooperation, have resolved to conclude this Acquisition and Cross-Servicing Agreement (this Agreement).

ARTICLE I
PURPOSE

This Agreement is entered into for the purpose of establishing basic terms, conditions, and procedures to facilitate the reciprocal provision of Logistic Support, Supplies, and Services (LSSS) as that term is defined in Article II of this Agreement.

ARTICLE II
DEFINITIONS

1. As used in this Agreement and in any Implementing Arrangements that provide specific procedures, the following definitions apply:

a. *Classified Information.* Official information that requires protection in the interests of national security and is so designated by the application of a security classification marking. This information may be in oral, visual, magnetic, or documentary form or in the form of equipment or technology.

b. *Equal-Value-Exchange.* Payment for a Transfer conducted under this Agreement in which it is agreed that the Receiving Party shall replace Logistic Support, Supplies, and Services that it receives with Logistic Support, Supplies, and Services of an equal monetary value.

c. *Implementing Arrangement.* A written supplementary arrangement for Logistic Support, Supplies, and Services that specifies details, terms, and conditions to implement cross-servicing agreements effectively.

d. *Invoice.* A document from the Supplying Party that requests reimbursement or payment for specific Logistic Support, Supplies, and Services rendered pursuant to this Agreement and any applicable Implementing Arrangement.

e. *Logistic Support, Supplies, and Services.* Food, water, billeting, transportation (including airlift), petroleum, oils, lubricants, clothing, communication services, medical services, ammunition, base operations support (and construction incident to base operations support), storage services, use of facilities, training services, spare parts and components, repair and maintenance services, calibration services, and port services. The term also includes the temporary use of general purpose vehicles and other nonlethal items of military equipment, where such lease or loan is permitted under the national laws and regulations of the Parties. The term "Logistic Support, Supplies, and Services" refers to support, supplies, or services from any or all of the foregoing categories.

f. *Order.* A written request, in an agreed-upon format and signed by an authorized individual, for the provision of specific Logistic Support, Supplies, and Services pursuant to this Agreement and any applicable Implementing Arrangement.

g. *Point of Contact (POC).* An office or agency that is authorized by a Party to sign an Order requesting or agreeing to supply Logistic Support, Supplies, and Services under this Agreement, or by collecting or making payments for Logistic Support, Supplies, and Services supplied or received under this Agreement. The POCs are listed in the POC Annexes to this Agreement or an associated Implementing Arrangement.

h. *Receiving Party.* The Party ordering and receiving Logistic Support, Supplies, and Services.

i. *Replacement-in-Kind.* Payment for a Transfer conducted under this Agreement in which it is agreed that the Receiving Party shall replace Logistic Support, Supplies, and Services that it receives with Logistic Support, Supplies, and Services of an identical, or substantially identical, nature under agreed conditions.

j. *Supplying Party.* The Party providing Logistic Support, Supplies, and Services.

k. *Transfer.* Selling (whether for payment in currency, Replacement-in-Kind, or exchange of supplies or services of equal value), leasing, loaning, or otherwise temporarily providing Logistic Support, Supplies, and Services under the terms of this Agreement.

ARTICLE III
APPLICABILITY

1. This Agreement is designed to facilitate reciprocal logistic support between the Parties to be used primarily during combined exercises, training, deployments, port calls, operations, or other cooperative efforts, or for unforeseen circumstances or exigencies in which one of the Parties may have a need for Logistic Support, Supplies, and Services.

2. This Agreement applies to the provision of Logistic Support, Supplies, and Services from the military forces of one Party to the military forces of the other Party in return for either cash payment or the reciprocal provision of Logistic Support, Supplies, and Services to the military forces of the Supplying Party.

3. All activities of the Parties under this Agreement and any Implementing Arrangements shall be carried out in accordance with their respective national laws and regulations. All obligations of the Parties under this Agreement and any associated Implementing Arrangements shall be subject to the availability of funds for such purposes. Unless otherwise agreed in advance, a Party shall not place an Order and receive support under this Agreement and any associated Implementing Arrangement unless it has funds (or agreed-upon in-kind support) available to pay for such support. If a Party discovers that it does not have the funds to fulfill its obligations, it shall promptly notify the other Party, which shall have the right to discontinue its provision of any support that was to be paid for with such funds. This shall not affect the obligation of a Party to pay for support already received.

4. The following items are not eligible for Transfer under this Agreement, and are specifically excluded from its coverage:

a. Weapon Systems;

b. Major end items of equipment (except for the lease or loan of general purpose vehicles and other nonlethal items of military equipment where such lease or loan is permitted under the national laws and regulations of the Parties); and

c. Initial quantities of replacement and spare parts associated with the initial order of major items of organizational equipment; however, individual replacement and spare parts needed for immediate repair and maintenance services may be transferred.

5. Also excluded from Transfer by either Party under this Agreement are any items the Transfer of which is prohibited by its national laws or regulations. In accordance with U.S. law and regulation, the United States currently may not Transfer the following items under this Agreement:

a. Guided missiles;

b. Naval mines and torpedoes;

c. Nuclear ammunition (including such items such as warheads, warhead sections, projectiles, demolition munitions, and training ammunition);

d. Guidance kits for bombs or other ammunition;

e. Chemical munitions or ammunition (which do not include riot-control agents);

f. Source, byproduct, or special nuclear materials, or any other material, article, data, or thing of value the Transfer of which is subject to the Atomic Energy Act of 1954 (Title 42, United States Code, Section 2011, et. seq.); and

g. Items of military equipment designated as Significant Military Equipment on the United States Munitions List (Part 121 of Title 22 of the U.S. Code of Federal Regulations), except as allowed under the definition of Logistic Support, Supplies, and Services under U.S. law.

ARTICLE IV
TERMS AND CONDITIONS

1. Each Party shall make its best efforts, consistent with national priorities, to satisfy requests from the other Party under this Agreement for Logistic Support, Supplies, and Services. However, when an Implementing Arrangement contains a stricter standard for satisfying such requests, the standard in the Implementing Arrangement shall apply.

2. Orders may be placed or accepted only by the Points of Contact (POCs), or designees, identified by the Parties in Annexes A through J of this Agreement. When military forces of the Ministry of National Defense of the Republic of Colombia require Logistic Support, Supplies, and Services outside the U.S. Southern Command (USSOUTHCOM) Area of Responsibility (AOR), they may place Orders with the established POC from the cognizant Command or may seek the assistance of USSOUTHCOM.

3. An Implementing Arrangement under this Agreement may be negotiated on behalf of the U.S. Department of Defense by Headquarters, USSOUTHCOM, the Headquarters of other U.S. Combatant Commands, or their designees. Implementing Arrangements may be negotiated on behalf of the Republic of Colombia's Ministry of Defense by the Chief of the Joint Chiefs of Staff. Implementing Arrangements shall identify POCs and their specific authorizations or limitations.

4. Prior to submitting a written Order, the ordering Party should initially contact the Supplying Party's POC, including by telephone, fax, or e-mail to ascertain availability, price, and desired method of repayment for required materiel or services. Orders shall include all the data elements in Annex A/Tab A, as well as any other terms and details necessary to carry out the Transfer. Instructions and a standard Order form are attached. The number of this Agreement, US-CO-02, should be annotated on all Orders and related correspondence.

5. Both Parties shall maintain records of all transactions.

6. The Receiving Party shall be responsible for:

a. Arranging pick-up and transportation of supplies acquired under this Agreement. This does not preclude the Supplying Party from assisting with loading supplies acquired under this Agreement onto the transportation conveyance; and

b. Obtaining any applicable customs clearance and arranging other official actions required by national customs regulations.

7. The individual designated by the Receiving Party to receive the Logistic Support, Supplies, and Services on behalf of the Receiving Party shall sign the standard Order form (Annex A/Tab A) in the appropriate block as evidence of receipt. If the standard Order form is not available at the Supplying Party's point of issue, the individual receiving the Logistic Support, Supplies, and Services shall sign the receipt document provided by the Supplying Party as a substitute. The number of this Agreement, US-CO-02, shall be entered on the receipt document.

8. The Supplying Party shall be responsible for:

a. Notifying the Receiving Party when and where Logistic Support, Supplies, and Services are available to be picked up; and

b. Forwarding the signed receipt document to the POC authorized to accept Orders under this Agreement. The signed receipt document shall be attached to the original Order Form.

9. Logistic Support, Supplies, and Services received through this Agreement shall not be retransferred, either temporarily or permanently, to any other country, international organization, or entity (other than the personnel, employees, or agents of the military forces of the Receiving Party) without the prior written consent of the Supplying Party obtained through applicable channels.

ARTICLE V
REIMBURSEMENT

1. For Transfers of Logistic Support, Supplies, and Services under this Agreement, the Parties shall agree on payment either by cash ("reimbursable transaction"), or by Replacement-in-Kind or an Equal-Value-Exchange (both of which are exchange transactions). The Receiving Party shall pay the Supplying Party as provided in either subparagraph 1.a. or subparagraph 1.b. of this Article.

a. *Reimbursable Transaction*. The Supplying Party shall submit Invoices to the Receiving Party after delivery or performance of the Logistic Support, Supplies, and Services. Both Parties shall provide for the payment of all transactions, and each Party shall invoice the other Party at least once every three (3) months for all transactions not previously invoiced. Invoices shall be accompanied by necessary support documentation and shall be paid within sixty (60) days of the date prepared and entered upon the invoice. Payment shall be made in the currency of the Supplying Party or as otherwise agreed in the Order. In pricing a reimbursable transaction, the Parties agree to the following reciprocal pricing principles:

(1) In the case of a specific acquisition by the Supplying Party from its contractors on behalf of a Receiving Party, the price shall be no less favorable than the price charged the military forces by the contractor of the Supplying Party for identical items or services, less any amounts excluded by Article VI of this Agreement. The price charged may take into account differentials due to delivery schedules, points of delivery, and other similar considerations.

(2) In the case of Transfer from the Supplying Party's own resources, the Supplying Party shall charge the same price charged its own military forces for identical Logistic Support, Supplies, and Services, as of the date delivery or performance occurs, less amounts excluded by Article VI of this Agreement. In any case where a price has not been established or charges are not made for one's own military forces, the Parties shall agree on a price in advance, reflecting reciprocal pricing principles, excluding charges that are precluded under these same reciprocal pricing principles.

b. *Exchange Transaction*. Exchange transactions may be by Replacement-in-Kind or Equal-Value-Exchange. The Receiving Party shall pay by transferring to the Supplying Party Logistic Support, Supplies, and Services that are agreed between the Parties to be identical (or substantially identical) or to be of equal monetary value to the Logistic Support. Supplies, and Services delivered or performed by the Supplying Party. When Equal-Value-Exchange is the agreed method of payment, prior to the provision of the requested support both Parties will agree, to the extent possible, on the goods and services that will be accepted for payment. The Receiving Party is responsible for arranging return transportation and delivery of the replacement Logistic Support, Supplies, and Services to the location mutually agreed between the Parties at the time the Order is signed. If the Receiving Party does not complete the exchange within the terms of a replacement schedule agreed to or in effect at the time of the original transaction, which may not exceed one year from the date of the original transaction, the transaction shall be deemed reimbursable and governed by subparagraph 1.a. of this Article, except that the price shall be established using actual or estimated prices in effect on the date payment otherwise would have been due.

c. *Establishment of Price or Value.* The following pricing mechanisms are provided to clarify application of the reciprocal pricing principles. The price established for inventory stock materiel shall be the Supplying Party's stock list price. The price for new procurement shall be the same price paid to the contractor or vendor by the Supplying Party. The price for services rendered will be the Supplying Party's standard price, or, if not applicable, the costs directly associated with providing the services. Prices charged shall exclude all taxes and duties that the Receiving Party is exempted from paying under other agreements that the Governments of the Parties have concluded. Upon request, the Parties agree to provide information sufficient to verify that these reciprocal pricing principles have been followed and that prices do not include waived or excluded costs.

2. When a definitive price for the Order is not agreed to in advance, the Order, pending agreement on final price, shall set forth a maximum liability to the Party ordering the Logistic Support, Supplies, and Services. Then the Parties shall enter into negotiations promptly to establish the final price.

3. POCs for payments and collections for each Party are identified in the Annexes to this Agreement.

4. The price for Logistic Support, Supplies, and Services under this Agreement shall not be higher than the price for the same Logistic Support, Supplies, and Services available under any other agreement between the Parties or their Department or Ministry of Defense.

ARTICLE VI
WAIVED OR EXCLUDED COSTS

Insofar as national laws and regulations permit, the Parties shall ensure that any readily identifiable duties, taxes, and similar charges are not imposed on activities conducted under this Agreement. The Parties shall cooperate to provide proper documentation to maximize tax and customs relief. The provisions of any applicable tax and customs relief agreements also shall apply under this Agreement. The Parties shall inform each other whether the price charged for Logistic Support, Supplies, and Services includes taxes or duties. In determining whether duties, taxes, or similar charges should be levied, the pricing principles in Article V govern the value of the Logistic Support, Supplies, and Services provided by the Supplying Party.

ARTICLE VII
SECURITY OF INFORMATION

It is the intent of the Parties that activities under this Agreement and any Implementing Arrangements be carried out at the unclassified level. Unless specifically authorized by separate written agreement or arrangement, no Classified Information or material shall be provided or generated under this Agreement or any Implementing Arrangements.

ARTICLE VIII
INTERPRETATION, AMENDMENTS, AND REVISION OF INFORMATION

1. Any disagreements regarding the interpretation or application of this Agreement, any Implementing Arrangements, or transactions executed hereunder shall be resolved through consultation between the Parties and shall not be referred to any national or international tribunal or third party for settlement.

2. Either Party may, at any time, request amendment of this Agreement by providing written notice to the other Party. In the event such a request is made, the Parties shall enter into negotiations promptly. This Agreement may be amended only by written agreement between the Parties. Replacement of Annexes A through J, which list POCs, may be done by a Party transmitting the replacement Annex to the other Party through military channels, without formal amendment of this Agreement.

ARTICLE IX
ENTRY INTO FORCE AND TERMINATION

1. This Agreement, which consists of a Preamble, Articles I-IX, and Annexes A through J, shall enter into force upon the date of the last signature. This Agreement shall remain in force unless terminated by the mutual written consent of the Parties or by either Party giving not less than 180 days notice in writing to the other Party of its intent to terminate. Notwithstanding termination of this Agreement, all reimbursement obligations incurred pursuant to its terms shall remain binding on the responsible Party until satisfied. This Agreement supersedes the Acquisition and Cross-Servicing Agreement (US-CO-01) between the Department of Defense of the United States of America and the Ministry of National Defense of the Republic of Colombia, which became effective June 27, 2002.

2. Upon entry into force, this Agreement applies to all new Orders for Logistic Support, Supplies, and Services. Any references in other U.S.–Colombia documents to the Acquisition and Cross-Servicing Agreement (US-CO-01), signed June 27, 2002, will be construed as referring to this successor Agreement for purposes of Orders issued after the effective date of this Agreement. Unless otherwise agreed by written amendment to a specific Order, the referenced June 27, 2002 Agreement shall continue to apply to all Orders issued prior to entry into force of this Agreement. Any financial obligations, transactions, Orders, or requests for Logistic Support, Supplies, or Services executed prior to the effective date of this Agreement under the authority of the June 27, 2002 Agreement will remain binding.

IN WITNESS WHEREOF, the undersigned, being duly authorized by their respective Governments, have signed this Agreement.

DONE, in duplicate, in the English and Spanish languages, each being equally authentic.

FOR THE DEPARTMENT OF DEFENSE OF THE UNITED STATES OF AMERICA

[Signature]

DOUGLAS M. FRASER
General, U.S. Air Force
Commander, U.S. Southern Command

at: U.S. Southern Command,
Miami, Florida

on: 30 June 2012

FOR THE MINISTRY OF NATIONAL DEFENSE OF THE REPUBLIC OF COLOMBIA

[Signature]

JUAN CARLOS PINZON BUENO
Minister of National Defense

at: Bogota, Republic of Colombia

on: 27 June 2012

LIST OF ANNEXES

TAB C—CDRUSFLTFORCOM (Navy)

TAB D—MARFORCOM (Marine Corps)

TAB E—FORSCOM (Army)

ANNEX G—USSOUTHCOM POCs

TAB A—HQ USSOUTHCOM

TAB B—AFSOUTH (Air Force)

TAB C—USARSO (Army)

TAB D—USNAVSOUTH (Navy)

TAB E—USMARFORSOUTH (Marine Corps)

TAB F—SOCSOUTH (Special Operations)

ANNEX H—USNORTHCOM POCs

ANNEX I—USTRANSCOM POCs

ANNEX J—USAFRICOM POCs

ANNEX A
MINIMUM ESSENTIAL DATA ELEMENTS

1) Implementing Arrangements or Support Agreement

2) Date of Order

3) Designation and address of office to be billed

4) Numerical listing of stock numbers of items, if any

5) Quantity and description of material/services requested

6) Quantity furnished

7) Unit of Measurement

8) Unit price in currency of billing country, or as otherwise agreed to in the Order

9) Quantity furnished (6) multiplied by unit price (8)

10) Currency of billing country, or as otherwise agreed to in the Order

11) Total Order amount expressed in currency of billing country, or as otherwise agreed to in the Order

12) Name (typed or printed), signature, and title of authorized ordering or requisitioning representative

13) Payee to be designated on remittance

14) Designation and address of office to receive remittance

15) Recipient's signature acknowledging service or supplies received on the Order or requisition or a separate supplementary document

16) Document number of Order or requisition

17) Receiving organization

18) Issuing organization

19) Transaction type

20) Fund citation or certification of availability of funds when applicable under Parties' procedures

21) Date and place of original Transfer; in the case of an exchange transaction, a replacement schedule including time and place of replacement Transfer

22) Name, signature, and title of authorized acceptance official

23) Additional special requirement, if any, such as transportation, packaging, etc.

24) Limitation of government liability

25) Name, signature, date, and title of Supplying Party official who actually issues supplies or services

ANNEX A/TAB A
STANDARD FORM

ACQUISITION AND CROSS-SERVICING AGREEMENT (ACSA)/
MUTUAL LOGISTICS SUPPORT (MLS)
ORDER FORM

1. Requisition No.	2. Support Agreement	3. Operation/ Theater	4. Order Date
5. Requesting Unit	6. Requesting Nation	7. Providing Unit	8. Providing Nation
9. Deliver to Unit	10. Deliver to Country	11. Deliver Place	12. Deliver Time

13. REQUESTED LINE ITEM SUMMARY (SEE ATTACHED LINE ITEM DETAIL SHEET)

No.	Sub	Attch	Stock No. & Description	Unit of Meas	Quantity Request (Less Previously Received)	Quantity Received	Unit Price	Total

14. Method of Payment ☒ Cash ☐ Replacement-in Kind (RIK) ☐ Equal-Value-Exchange (EVE)		15. Currency	16. Not to Exceed Amount	17. Line Item Cost
22. Authorized Requestor		23. Authorized Supplier		18. Trans Costs
Signature		Signature		19. Other Costs
Name (Last, First MI Rank/Title)	Date	Name (Last, First MI Rank/Title)	Date	20. Total Claimed

Unit/Office	Nation/Organization	Unit/Office	Nation/Organization	21. Agreed Return Date
24. Purchase Order No.	25. Fund Citation	26 Bill To	30. Remarks	
27. Invoice No.	28. Acct No./Finance Tracking No.	29. Pay To		
31. Receipt			32. Invoice I Certify that the amount invoiced is exclusive of all taxes to which exemption has been granted under provisions of existing agreements and that the invoice is correct.	
Signature			Signature	
Name (Last, First MI Rank/Title)	Date	Name (Last, First MI Rank/Title)	Date	20. Total Claimed
Unit/Office	Nation/Organization	Unit/Office	Nation/Organization	21. Agreed Return Date

ANNEX B
MINISTRY OF NATIONAL DEFENSE
POINTS OF CONTACT, ORDERING AND FINANCIAL RESPONSIBILITIES

TAB A—COLOMBIAN ARMY
TAB B—COLOMBIAN AIR FORCE
TAB C—COLOMBIAN NAVY

ANNEX B/TAB A
COLOMBIAN ARMY POINT OF CONTACT

The Ministry directorate for **placing or accepting orders, as well as coordinating payment and collections** under this agreement:

The Colombian Army POC for **placement and acceptance of Orders** under this Agreement, is:

a) Unit:	National Army Headquarters Foreign Commercial Directorate
b) Telephone:	571-2-22-69-79/571-3-15-85-00
c) Fax:	571-2-22-69-79
Mailing address:	Cuartel General del Ejército Nacional Ministerio de Defensa Nacional Carrera 52, Calle 26- CAN Bogotá, Colombia
a) Email:	Gilberval67@hotmail.com

ANNEX B/TAB A
COLOMBIAN AIR FORCE POINT OF CONTACT

The Colombian Air Force POC for **placement and acceptance of Orders** under this Agreement is:

a) Unit:	Colombian Air Force Headquarters Directorate of Logistic Processes
b) Telephone:	571-3-15-98-00 ext. 1670
c) Fax:	571-2-22-26-30/571-2-22-03-13-/571-2-21-12-11
d) Mailing address:	Colombian Air Force Headquarters Ministry of National Defense Highway 52, Street 26- CAN Bogota, Colombia
e) Email:	diaba.secre01@fac.mil.co

The Colombian Air Force agency in the United States responsible for **payments and collections** under this Agreement is:

a) Unit:	Colombian Air Force Purchasing Agency 702 SW 34th Street Fort Lauderdale, FL 33315
b) Telephone:	954-359-0177/954-359-0177
c) Fax:	954-359-0176
d) Email:	caf@dialisdn.com

ANNEX B/TAB A
COLOMBIAN NAVY POINT OF CONTACT

The Colombian Navy POC for **placement and acceptance of Orders** under this Agreement, is:

a) Unit:	Colombian Navy Headquarters Chief of Logistic Operations
b) Telephone:	571-2-66-10-62
c) Fax:	571-2-22-25-03
d) Mailing address:	Colombian Navy Headquarters, Second Floor Ministry of Defense Highway 52, Street 26- CAN Bogota, Colombia
e) Email:	secjola@armada.mil.co

ANNEX C
USCENTCOM
POINTS OF CONTACT, ORDERING AND FINANCIAL RESPONSIBILITIES

TAB A—HQ USCENTCOM
TAB B—USARCENT (Army)
TAB C—USNAVCENT (Navy)
TAB D—USAFCENT (Air Force)
TAB E—USMARCENT (Marine Corps)
TAB F—SOCCENT (Special Operations)

ANNEX C/TAB A
HQ U.S. CENTRAL COMMAND (USCENTCOM)

1. The USCENTCOM POC for coordinated **placement and acceptance of Orders** under this Agreement is the USCENTCOM J4, Multinational Logistics Branch (CCJ4-MNL)

a. Unit:	CCJ4-MNL
b. Telephone:	Com'l: 813-529-4085/4084 DSN: 529-4085/4084
c. Fax:	
d. Message Address:	USCENTCOM//J4/MNL//
e. Mailing Address:	USCENTCOM ATTN: CCJ4-MNL 7115 South Boundary Boulevard MacDill AFB, FL 33621-5101

2. The USCENTCOM agency responsible for **payments and collections** under this Agreement is the USCENTCOM Comptroller Office.

a. Unit:	CCJ8-FM
b. Telephone:	Com'l: 813-827-5884 DSN: 651-5884
c. Fax:	Com'l: 813-827-4218/4648 DSN: 651-4218 /4648
d. Message Address:	USCENTCOM//CCJ8//
e. Mailing Address:	USCENTCOM ATTN: CCJ8-FM 7115 South Boundary Boulevard MacDill AFB, FL 33621-5101

ANNEX C/TAB B
THIRD U.S. ARMY/U.S. ARMY FORCES CENTRAL COMMAND (USARCENT)

1. The USARCENT POC responsible for **placement and acceptance of Orders** is the G-4, Logistics Sustainment Division.

a. Unit:	Third U.S. Army, G-4
b. Telephone:	Com'l: 803-885-7504 DSN:
c. Fax:	Com'l: DSN: Com'l: DSN:
d. Mailing Address:	Third U.S. Army ATTN: G-4, AFRD-GD 1 Gabreski Drive Shaw AFB, SC 29152

2. The USARCENT agency responsible for **payments and collections** under this Agreement is the USARCENT Comptroller.

a. Unit:	Third U.S. Army, Comptroller
b. Telephone:	Com'l: 803-885-8964 DSN:
c. Fax:	Com'l: DSN:
d. Mailing Address:	Third U.S. Army ATTN: Comptroller, AFRD-CM 1 Gabreski Drive Shaw AFB, SC 29152

ANNEX C/TAB C
U.S. NAVAL FORCES CENTRAL COMMAND (USNAVCENT)

1. The USNAVCENT POC for coordinated **placement and acceptance of Orders** under this Agreement is the USNAVCENT N4.

a. Unit:	COMUSNAVCENT-BAHRAIN Code: N4/Coalition Logistics Officer
b. Telephone:	Com'l: (CC) 973-1785-3721/4183 DSN: 318-439-9432/4183
c. Fax:	Com'l: 973-1785-4350 DSN: 318-439-4350 Com'l: 973-1785-4579 (Classified) DSN: 318-439-4579 (Classified)
d. Message Address:	COMUSNAVCENT//N4//COALITION LOGISTICS OFFICER//
e. Mailing Address:	COMUSNAVCENT Code: N4/LRC/Coalition Logistics Officer/ FPO, AE 09501-6008

2. The USNAVCENT agency responsible for **payments and collections** under this Agreement is the COMUSNAVCENT COMPTROLLER.

a. Unit:	COMUSNAVCENT Comptroller, CODE NOOCF
b. Telephone:	Com'l: 973-1785-3029 DSN: 318-439-3029
c. Fax:	Com'l: 973-1785-4350 DSN: 318-439-4350
d. Message Address:	COMUSNAVCENT//N00CF//
e. Mailing Address:	COMUSNAVCENT Code: NOOCF FPO, AE 09501-6503

ANNEX C/TAB D
U.S. AIR FORCES CENTRAL COMMAND (USAFCENT)

1. The USCENTAF POC for coordinated **placement and acceptance of Orders** under this Agreement is the USAFCENT/A4, Director of Logistics.

a. Unit:	US CENTAF/ A4–LGXP
b. Telephone:	Com'l: 803-895-4457/44344 DSN: 965-4457/4344
c. Fax:	Com'l: 803-895-2932 DSN: 965-2932
d. Message Address:	COMUSCENTAF SHAW AFB SC//A4//
e. Mailing Address:	USAFCENT/ A4–A4XP 524 Shaw Drive, Suite 135 Shaw AFB, SC 29152-5029

2. The USCENTAF agency responsible for **payments and collections** under this Agreement is the 9th Air Force Financial Management Analysis Branch.

a. Unit:	9 AF/USAFCENT/FMA
b. Telephone:	Com'l: 803-895-6690 DSN: 965-6690
c. UNCLASSIFIED Fax:	Com'l: 803-895-6877 DSN: 965-6877
d. Message Address:	USAFCENT SHAW AFB SC//FMA//
e. Mailing Address:	9 AF/USAFCENT/FMA 411 Myers Street, Building 1049 Shaw AFB, SC 29152-5029

ANNEX C/TAB E
U.S. MARINE FORCES CENTRAL COMMAND (USMARCENT)

1. The USMARCENT POC for coordinated **placement and acceptance of Orders** under this Procedural Agreement is the USMARCENT G-4:

a. Unit:	USMARCENT G4
b. Telephone:	Com'l: 813-827-7098 DSN: 651-7098
c. Fax:	Com'l: 813-827-7037 DSN: 651-7037
d. Message Address:	COMUSMARCENT G4 (MC)
e. Mailing Address:	USMARCENT, G-4, MacDill AFD 7115 South Boundary Boulevard, Bldg 535 Tampa, FL 33621-5101

2. The USMARCENT agency responsible for **payments and collections** under this Agreement is the USMARCENT G-8:

a. Unit:	USMARCENT G-8
b. Telephone:	Com'l: 813-827-7319 DSN: 651-7319
c. Fax:	Com'l: 813-827-7037 DSN: 651-7037
d. Message Address:	COMUSMARCENT G8 (MC)
e. Mailing Address:	USMARCENT, G-8, MacDill AFB, 7115 South Boundary Boulevard, BLDG 535 Tampa, FL 33621-5101

ANNEX C/TAB F
SPECIAL OPERATIONS COMMAND CENTRAL (SOCCENT)

1. The Special Operations Command Central (SOCCENT) POC for coordinated **placement and acceptance of Orders** under this Agreement is the SOCCENT, J4.

a. Unit:	SOCCCENT, J4
b. Telephone:	Com'l: 813-828-0297 DSN: 968-0297
c. Fax:	Com'l: 813-828-4826 DSN: 968-4826 Com'l: 813-828-8372 (Classified) DSN: 968-8372 (Classified)
d. Message Address:	COMSOCCENT MACDILL AFB FL//J4//
e. Mailing Address:	HQ, SOCCENT ATTN: SOCCENT, J4 7115 South Boundary Boulevard MacDill AFB, FL 33621-5101

2. The Special Operations Command Central (SOCCENT) agency responsible for **payments and collections** under this Agreement is the SOCCENT Comptroller.

a. Unit:	SOCCENT, Comptroller
b. Telephone:	Com'l: (813) 828-4614//DSN: 968-4614
c. Fax:	Com'l: 813-828-8747 DSN: 968-8747 Com'l: 813-828-1894 (Classified) DSN: 968-1894 (Classified)
d. Message Address:	COMSOCCENT MACDILL AFB FL//SOCCO//
e. Mailing Address:	HQ SOCCENT ATTN: SOCCO 7115 South Boundary Boulevard MacDill AFB, FL 33621-5101

ANNEX D
USPACOM/USFJ/USFK
POINTS OF CONTACT, ORDERING AND FINANCIAL RESPONSIBILITIES

TAB A—USPACOM
TAB B—COMPACFLT (Navy)
TAB C—USARPAC (Army)
TAB D—MARFORPAC (Marines)
TAB E—PACAF (Air Force)
TAB F—SOCPAC (Special Operations Command)
TAB G—HQ USFJ
TAB H—USARJ (Army)
TAB I—MARFORJ (Marines)
TAB J—USAFJ (Air Force)
TAB K—HQ USFK
TAB L—HQ USAFK (Air Force)

ANNEX D/TAB A
COMMANDER, U.S. PACIFIC COMMAND (CDRUSPACOM)

1. The USPACOM POC for coordinated **placement and acceptance of Orders** under this Agreement is the J42, Logistics Readiness Division, International Logistics & Sustainment Branch:

a. Unit:	HQ USPACOM J4
b. Telephone:	Com'l: (808) 477-9400 or DSN: 315-477-9400
c. Fax:	Com'l: (808) 477-0936 or DSN: 315-477-0936
d. Message Address:	CDRUSPACOM HONOLULU HI//J4//
e. Mailing Address:	HQ USPACOM J42 Bldg 700, Box 64028 Camp H. M. Smith, HI 96861-4028

2. The USPACOM POC responsible for **payments and collections** under this Agreement is the Comptroller:

a. Unit:	HQ USPACOM J05
b. Telephone:	Com'l: (808) 477-1175 or DSN: 315-477-1175
c. Fax:	Com'l: (808) 477-0535 or DSN: 315-477-0535
d. Message Address:	CDRUSPACOM HONOLULU HI//J05//
e. Mailing Address:	HQ USPACOM J05 Bldg 700, Box 64037 Camp H. M. Smith, HI 96861-4037

ANNEX D/TAB B
COMMANDER, U.S. PACIFIC FLEET (COMPACFLT)

1. The COMPACFLT POC responsible for **placement and acceptance of Orders** under this Agreement is:

a. Unit:	COMPACFLT (N403)
b. Telephone:	DSN: 315-474-6915 or Com'l: (808) 474-6915
c. Fax:	DSN: 315-474-5464 or Com'l: (808) 474-5464
d. Message Address:	COMPACFLT PEARL HARBOR HI//N403//
e. Mailing Address:	Commander, U.S. Pacific Fleet Code N403 250 Makalapa Drive Pearl Harbor, HI 96860-3131

2. The COMPACFLT POC for **payments and collections** under this Agreement is:

a. Unit:	COMPACFLT (N00F)
b. Telephone:	DSN: 315-471-8215 or Com'l: (808) 471-8215
c. Fax:	DSN: 315-474-6937 or Com'l: (808) 474-6937
d. Message Address:	COMPACFLT PEARL HARBOR HI//N00F//
e. Mailing Address:	Commander, U.S. Pacific Fleet Code N00F 250 Makalapa Drive Pearl Harbor, HI 96860-3131

ANNEX D/TAB C
U.S. ARMY PACIFIC (USARPAC)

1. The USARPAC POC responsible for **placement and acceptance of Orders** under this Agreement is Headquarters USARPAC Logistics Plans and International Programs:

a. Unit:	USARPAC/APLG-PEPM
b. Telephone:	DSN: 315-438-8621 or Com'l: (808) 438-8621
c. Fax:	DSN: 315-438-3460 or Com'l: (808) 438-3460
d. Message Address:	CDRUSARPAC FT SHAFTER HI//APLG-PEPM//
e. Mailing Address:	Commander, U.S. Army, Pacific Attn: APLG-PEPM, Plans, Exercises, Policy/ Programs and Multinational Interagency Ft. Shafter, HI 96858

2. The USARPAC POC responsible for **payments and collections** under this Agreement is the Defense Finance and Accounting Service, Honolulu Operating Location:

a. Unit:	DFAS
b. Telephone:	DSN: 315-472-3760 or Com'l: (808) 472-3760
c. Fax:	DSN: 315-472-8250 or Com'l: (808) 472-8250
d. Message Address:	DFAS HONOLULU HI//
e. Mailing Address:	DFAS Box 77, Building 1392 Pearl Harbor, HI 96860-7552

ANNEX D/TAB D
MARINE FORCES PACIFIC (MARFORPAC)

1. The MARFORPAC POC responsible for **placement and acceptance of Orders** under this Agreement is:

a. Unit:	MARFORPAC, G4
b. Telephone:	Com'l: (808) 477-8341/8595 or DSN: 315-477-8341/8595
c. Fax:	Com'l: (808) 477-8710 or DSN: 315-477-8710
d. Message Address:	COMMARFORPAC//G4//
e. Mailing Address:	MARFORPAC, G4 Attn: Multinational Logistics Branch Box 64118 Camp H. M. Smith, HI 96861-4118

2. The MARFORPAC POC responsible for **payments and collections** under this Agreement is:

a. Unit:	MARFORPAC, G8
b. Telephone:	Com'l: (808) 477-8557 or DSN: 315-477-8557
c. Fax:	Com'l: (808) 477-8702 or DSN: 315-477-8702
d. Message Address:	COMMARFORPAC//G8//
e. Mailing Address:	MARFORPAC, G-8 Box 64112 Camp H. M. Smith, HI 96861-4112

ANNEX D/TAB E
PACIFIC AIR FORCES (PACAF)

1. The PACAF POC responsible for **placement and acceptance of Orders** under this Agreement is Headquarters PACAF Logistics Directorate, Resource Integration Division:

a. Unit:	PACAF/A4P
b. Telephone:	DSN: 315-449-3778 or Com'l: (808) 449-3778
c. Fax:	DSN: 315-449-4778 or Com'l: (808) 449-4778
d. Message Address:	HQ PACAF HICKAM AFB HI//A4P//
e. Mailing Address:	HQ PACAF/A4P 25 E. Street, Suite H-302 Hickam AFB, HI 96853-5427

2. The PACAF POC responsible for **payments and collections** under this Agreement:

a. Unit:	DFAS-Indianapolis
b. Telephone:	Com'l: 317-510-8548 DSN: 699-8548
c. Fax:	Com'l: 317-275-0304 DSN 510-366-0304
d. Mailing Address:	

For checks, make payable to "U.S. Treasury" and forward to:

DFAS-IN
3801 Remittances
P.O. Box 269339
Indianapolis, IN 46226-0670

For payment through wire transfer, the following info is required:

United States Treasury
New York, New York
ABA (Bank routing) number: 021 030 004
Agency Name: DFAS-ADY/DE
Agency Location Code: 00003801
Norfolk, VA 23551-2488

3. The PACAF POC responsible for **receiving supporting documentation** used to bill the recipient of Logistic Support, Supplies, and Services under this Agreement is:

a. Unit:	DFAS Limestone
b. Telephone:	DSN: 312-220-1400 or Com'l: (207) 328-1400
c. Fax:	DSN: 312-220-1414 or Com'l: (207) 220-1414
d. Message Address:	DFAS Limestone// ME//
e. Mailing Address:	DFAS Limestone Suite 207 27 Arkansas Road Limestone, ME 04751-6216

ANNEX D/TAB F
SPECIAL OPERATIONS COMMAND PACIFIC (SOCPAC)

1. The SOCPAC POC responsible for **placement and acceptance of Orders** under this Agreement is:

a. Unit:	SOCPAC/SOJ4
b. Telephone:	DSN: 315-477-0616 or Com'l: (808) 477-0616
c. Fax:	DSN: 315-477-2908 or Com'l: (808) 477-2908
d. Message Address:	COMSOCPAC HONOLULU HI//SOJ4//
e. Mailing Address:	HQ SOCPAC/SOJ4 Box 64046 Camp H. M. Smith, HI 96861-4046

2. The SOCPAC POC responsible for **payments and collections** under this Agreement is:

a. Unit:	SOCPAC/SOJ08
b. Telephone:	DSN: 315-477-2603 or Com'l: (808) 477-2603
c. Fax:	DSN: 315-477-1574 or Com'l: (808) 477-1574
d. Message Address:	COMSOCPAC HONOLULU HI//SOJO8//
e. Mailing Address:	HQ SOCPAC/SOJO8 Bldg 700, Box 64046 Camp H. M. Smith, HI 96861-4046

ANNEX D/TAB G
HQ U.S. FORCES JAPAN (HQ USFJ)

1. The HQ USFJ POC responsible for **placement and acceptance of Orders** under this Agreement is:

a. Unit:	USFJ/J43
b. Telephone:	Com'l: 0425-52-2511 ext. 5-2445 DSN: 315-225-2445
c. Fax:	Com'l: 0425-52-2511 ext. 5-4709 DSN: 315-225-4709
d. Message Address:	COMUSJAPAN YOKOTA AB JA//J4//
e. Mailing Address:	Headquarters, United States Forces, Japan Logistics Directorate/J4, Yokota Air Base Fussa-Shi, Tokyo 197

2. The HQ USFJ agency responsible for **payments and collections** under this Agreement is:

a. Unit:	DFAS-J
b. Telephone:	Com'l: 0425-52-2511, ext. 5-9838 DSN: 315-225-9838
c. Fax:	Com'l: 0425-52-2511, ext. 5-9841 DSN: 315-225-3213
d. Message Address:	DFAS JAPAN YOKOTA JA//
e. Mailing Address:	DFAS-J, Unit 5220, Bldg 206 Yokota Air Base Fussa-Shi, Tokyo 197

ANNEX D/TAB H
U.S. ARMY JAPAN (USARJ)

1. The USARJ POC responsible for **placement and acceptance of Orders** under this Agreement is:

a. Unit:	USARJ, DCS, G4
b. Telephone:	Com'l: 0462-51-1788 ext. 263-7204 DSN: 315-263-5471
c. Fax:	Com'l: 0462-51-1788 ext. 263-8372 DSN: 315-263-8372
d. Message Address:	CDRUSARJ 9th TSC CP ZAMA JA//DSCLOG//
e. Mailing Address:	HQ, USARJ/DCS, G4 ATTN: APAJ-GD-LOG, (ACSA POC) Camp Zama, Zama-Shi Kanagawa-Ken, 288-0000

2. The USARJ POC responsible for **placement and acceptance of Orders** for the **836th U.S. Army Transportation Battalion** under this Agreement is:

a. Unit:	836th U.S. Army Transportation Bn
b. Telephone:	Com'l: 0454-53-4840 ext. 269-6630 DSN: 315-269-6330
c. Fax:	Com'l: 0454-53-4840 ext. 269-6246 DSN: 315-269-6739
d. Message Address:	CDR 836TH TRANS BN YOKOHAMA JA//SDPC-YO-XO//
e. Mailing Address:	836th U.S. Army Transportation Bn ATTN: SDPC-YO-XO Mizuho Sanbashi Kanagawa-Ku Yokohama-Shi, 221-0034

3. The USARJ POC responsible for **placement and acceptance of Orders** for the **835th U.S. Army Transportation Bn** under this Agreement is:

a. Unit:	835th U.S. Army Transportation Bn
b. Telephone	Com'l: 098-857-3844 DSN: 315-648-7729
c. Fax:	Com'l: 098-892-5111 ext. 648-7731 DSN: 315-648-7731
d. Message Address:	CDR 835TH TRANS BN OKINAWA JA//MTPC-OK-XO//
e. Mailing Address:	835th U.S. Army Transportation Bn ATTN: MTPC-OK-XO Shisetsu, Bldg, 305 Nahagunko-Nai, Kakinohana-Cho Naha-Shi, Okinawa 900

4. The USARJ agency responsible for **payments and collections** under this Agreement is:

a. Unit:	DFAS-J (Army Accounting)
b. Telephone:	Com'l: 042-552-2511 ext. 5-5340 DSN: 315-225-5340
c. Fax:	Com'l: 042-552-2511 ext. 5-3523 DSN: 315-225-3523
d. Message Address:	DFAS JAPAN YOKOTA JA//
e. Mailing Address:	DFAS-J (Army Accounting) Unit 5220 ATTN: AAOA Yokota Air Base Fussa-Shi, Tokyo 197

ANNEX D/TAB I
MARINE FORCES JAPAN (MARFORJ)

1. The MARFORJ POC responsible for **placement and acceptance of Orders** for the **III MEF** under this Agreement is:

a. Unit:	III Marine Expeditionary Force (G-4/Supply)
b. Telephone:	Com'l: 0988-92-5111 ext. 622-7137 DSN: 315-622-7137
c. Fax:	Com'l: 0988-92-5111 ext. 622-9019 DSN: 315-622-9019
d. Message Address:	CG III MEF//G4//
e. Mailing Address:	Commanding General ATTN: AC/S G4/MRB/SUP Unit 35601 FPO, AP 96606-5061

2. The MARFORJ POC responsible for **placement and acceptance of Orders** for **Marine Forces Japan, Camp Butler** under this Agreement is:

a. Unit:	Marine Corps Base, Camp S.D. Butler (G-4/)
b. Telephone:	Com'l: 0988-92-5111 ext. 645-7223 DSN: 315-645-7223
c. Fax:	Com'l: 098-892-5111 ext. 645-7231 DSN: 315-645-7231
d. Message Address:	CG MCB CP BUTLER JA//G4//SUPPLY//
e. Mailing Address:	Commanding General, Marine Corps Base, Camp S.D. Butler (G4) ATTN: ACSA POC Unit 35001 FPO AP 96373-5001, Central Post Office Naha-shi, Okinawa-ken 900

3. The MARFORJ agency responsible for **payments and collections** under this Agreement is:

a. Unit:	Marine Forces Japan, Camp Butler (Comptroller)
b. Telephone:	Com'l: 098-892-5111 ext. 645-7310 DSN: 315-645-7310
c. Fax:	Com'l: 098-892-5111 ext. 645-7351 DSN: 315-645-7759
d. Message Address:	DMS CG MCBUTLER COMPT JA//COMPT//
e. Mailing Address:	Commanding General, Marine Forces Japan (Comptroller) Unit 35001 ATTN: ACSA POC FPO AP 96373-5001 or Commanding General, Marine Forces Japan (Comptroller) Unit 35001 ATTN: ACSA POC Central Post Office, Naha-shi, Okinawa-ken 900

ANNEX D/TAB J
U.S. AIR FORCES JAPAN (USAFJ)

1. The USAFJ POC responsible for **placement and acceptance of Orders** under this Agreement is:

a. Unit:	HQ 5AF/ A4A7 (Logistics and Engineering)
b. Telephone:	Com'l: 011-81-311-755-4527 Japanese phone: 0425-52-2511, ext. 5-4527 DSN: 315-225-4527
c. Fax:	None
d. Message Address:	5AF YOKOTA AB A4/A4A7//
e. Mailing Address:	HQ 5AF/A4A7, Unit 5087, Bldg 714 Logistics and Engineering Directorate ATTN: ACSA POC Yokota Air Base, Fussa-Shi, Tokyo 197
f. Email	5af.a4a7@yokota.af.mil

2. The USAFJ agency responsible for **payments and collections** under this Agreement is:

a. Unit:	DFAS-J
b. Telephone:	Com'l: 0425-52-2511, ext. 5-9838 DSN: 315-225-9838
c. Fax:	Com'l: 0425-52-2511, ext. 5-9841 DSN: 315-225-3213
d. Message Address:	DFAS JAPAN YOKOTA JA//
e. Mailing Address:	DFAS-J, Unit 5220, Bldg 206 Yokota Air Base, Fussa-Shi, Tokyo 197

ANNEX D/TAB K
U.S. FORCES KOREA (HQ USFK)

1. The HQ USFK POC for coordinated **placement and acceptance of Orders** under this Agreement is the USFK J45, Multinational Logistics Division:

a. Unit:	USFK J4
b. Telephone:	Com'l: +82 (0) 505-723-6078 or DSN: 315-723-6078
c. Fax:	Com'l: +82 (0) 505-723-8477 or DSN: 315-723-8477
d. Message Address:	
e. Mailing Address:	USFK J4 ATTN: MLD MLSA Mgr Unit 15273 APO AP 96204

2. The HQ USFK POC responsible for **payments and collections** under this Agreement is the Comptroller:

a. Unit:	175th FMC, Unit #15300
b. Telephone:	Com'l: +82 (0) 505-723-7793 or DSN: 315-723-7793
c. Fax:	Com'l: +82 (0) 505-723-3165 or DSN: 315-723-3165
d. Message Address:	
e. Mailing Address:	175th FMC, Unit #15300 ATTN: EAFC-CPA-AOG APO AP 96205-0073

ANNEX D/TAB L
U.S. AIR FORCES KOREA (HQ USAFK)

1. The HQ USAFK POC for coordinated **placement and acceptance of Orders** under this Agreement is:

a. Unit:	HQ 7AF 607 ASUS/LGP (A4P) (International Agreements—Programs Division)
b. Telephone:	Com'l: 011-82-31-661-8596/7771 DSN: 315-784-8596/7771
c. Fax:	Com'l: 011-82-31-661-1103 DSN: 315-784-1103
d. Message Address:	7AF OSAN AB ROK/LGP//
e. Mailing Address:	HQ 7AF 607 Air Support Squadron/LGP Unit 2117 (Attn: LGP Chief) APO, AP 96278-2117

2. The HQ USAFK POC for **payments and collections** under this Agreement is:

a. Unit:	DFAS Japan
b. Telephone:	Com'l: 011-81-311-755-6049
c. Fax:	None provided
d. Message Address:	None provided
e. Mailing Address:	DFAS Japan Unit 5220 APO AP 96328-5220

ANNEX E
USEUCOM
POINTS OF CONTACT, ORDERING AND FINANCIAL RESPONSIBILITIES

TAB A—USEUCOM
TAB B—USAFE (Air Force)
TAB C—USAREUR (Army)
TAB D—USNAVEUR (Navy)
TAB E—USMARFOREUR (Marine Corps)
TAB F—SOCEUR (Special Operations)
TAB G—USAREUR KFOR

ANNEX E/TAB A
HQ U.S. EUROPEAN COMMAND (HQ USEUCOM)

1. The HQ USEUCOM POC for coordinated **placement and acceptance of Orders** under this Agreement is the ECJ4 Logistics Support Division, Multinational Agreements Branch:

a. Unit:	HQ USEUCOM ECJ4-LS-MNA
b. Telephone:	Com'l: 49-711-680-7474 or 1490 DSN: 314-430-7474 or 1490
c. Fax:	Com'l: 49-711-680-7476 DSN: 314-430-7476
d. Mailing Address:	(Commercial) HQ USEUCOM-ECJ4 G.E.B. 2304 Patch Barracks 70569 Stuttgart-Vaihingen, Germany (Military) HQ USEUCOM-ECJ4 Unit 30400 APO AE 09131

2. The HQ USEUCOM agency responsible for policy issues regarding **payments and collections** under this Agreement is the Comptroller:

a. Unit:	HQ USEUCOM-ECCM
b. Telephone:	Com'l: 49-711-680-5985 DSN: 314-430-5985
c. Fax:	Com'l: 49-711-680-6350 DSN: 314-430-6350
d. Mailing Address:	(Commercial) HQ USEUCOM-ECCM G.E.B. 2304 Patch Barracks 70569 Stuttgart-Vaihingen, Germany (Military) HQ USEUCOM-ECCM Unit 30400 APO AE 09131

ANNEX E/TAB B
U.S. AIR FORCES EUROPE (USAFE)

1. The HQ USAFE POC responsible for **placement and acceptance of Orders** under this Agreement is Headquarters USAFE Logistics Readiness Division, International Logistics Branch:

a. Unit:	HQ USAFE/A4RI
b. Telephone:	Com'l: 49-(0)6371-47-6788 DSN: 314-480-6788
c. Fax:	Com'l: 49-(0)6371-47-9255 DSN: 314-480-9255
d. Email Address:	usafe.a4ri@ramstein.af.mil
e. Message Address:	HQ USAFE RAMSTEIN AB GE//A4RI//
f. Mailing Address:	(Commercial) HQ USAFE/A4RJ Gebäude 528 Zimmer 102 Flugplatz 66877 Ramstein, Germany (Military) HQ USAFE/A4RI Unit 3050 Box 105 APO AE 09094-0105

2. The HQ USAFE agency responsible for **payments and collections** under this Agreement is the Defense Finance and Accounting Service, Ramstein AB:

a. Unit:	DFAS-DJF-ARER
b. Telephone:	Com'l: 49-(0)6371-47-2068/7573 DSN: 314-480-2068/7573
c. Fax:	Com'l: 49-(0)6371-47-7582 DSN: 314-480-7582
d. Email Address:	usafe.dfas.ce@ramstein.af.mil
e. Message Address:	HQ USAFE RAMSTEIN AB GE//FM-DFAS//
f. Mailing Address:	(Commercial) HQ USAFE/FM-DFAS Gebäude 413 Zimmer 116 Flugplatz 66877 Ramstein, Germany (Military) HQ USAFE/FM-DFAS Unit 3050 Box 5 APO AE 09094-0505

ANNEX E/TAB C
U.S. ARMY EUROPE (USAREUR)

1. The USAREUR agencies responsible for **placement and acceptance of Orders** are:

For Logistics Support, Supplies, and Services in connection with training at **Grafenwoehr and Hohenfels:**

a. Unit:	Commander 7th U.S. Army JMTC
b. Telephone:	Com'l: +49-9641-83-7159 DSN: 314-475-7159
c. Fax:	Com'l: +49-9641-83-8416 DSN: 314-475-8416
d. Mailing Address:	(Commercial) Commander, 7th U.S. Army JMTC ATTN: AETT-RM-MGT Grafenwoehr Lager D-92655 Grafenwoehr, Germany
	(Military) Commander, 7th U.S. Army JMTC ATTN: AETT-RM-MGT Unit 28130 APO AE 09114-8130

For all other Logistics Support, Supplies, and Services:

a. Unit:	Commander, HQ USAREUR/7A
b. Telephone:	Com'l: +49-6221-57-6375 DSN: 314-370-6375
c. Fax:	Com'l: +49-6221-57-4002 / 6194 DSN: 314-370-4002/6194
d. Mailing Address:	(Commercial) Commander, HQ USAREUR/7A ATTN: AEAGF-IA Roemerstrasse 168 D-69126 Heidelberg, Germany
	(Military) Commander, HQ USAREUR/7A ATTN: AEAGF-IA Unit 29351 APO AE 09014

For **placing and executing Purchase Orders (contracts) over $25,000:**

a. Unit:	U.S. Army Contracting Center, Europe (USACCE)
b. Telephone:	Com'l: +49 611-816-2148 / 2153 DSN: 314-336-2148 / 2153
c. Fax:	Com'l: +49 611-816-2175 DSN: 314-336-2175
d. Mailing Address	(Civilian) U.S. Army Contracting Command, Europe Konrad Adenauer Ring 39 D-65187 Wiesbaden, Germany (Military) U.S. Army Contracting Command, Europe APO AE 09096 MR 410, Box 744

Office for **Making Payments for HQ USAREUR/7A (including payments for BALKANS AREA of OPERATIONS):**

a. Unit:	Defense Finance & Accounting Service-Europe (DFAS-EUROPE)
b. Telephone:	Com'l: +49-631-411-6443 / 6520 / 6521 / 6522 DSN: 314-483-6443 / 6520 / 6521 / 6522
c. Fax:	Com'l: +49-631-411-6362
d. Mailing Address:	(Commercial) DFAS-Europe Vendor Pay Kleber Kaserne, Gebaeude 3200 ATTN: LW Mannheimer Strasse 218/219 D-67657 Kaiserslautern, Germany (Military) DFAS-Europe Vendor Pay, ATTN: LW Unit 23122 APO AE 09227

Office for **Collecting Payments for HQ USAREUR/7A (including collections for BALKANS AREA of OPERATIONS):**

a. Unit:	Defense Finance and Accounting Service-Jacksonville/ Indianapolis
b. Telephone:	Com'l: +01 317-510-1416 DSN: 312 699-1416
c. Fax:	Com'l: +01 317 510-4181 DSN: 312 699-4181
d. Mailing Address:	(Civilian) 3801 Collections DFAS-JAX/IN PO Box 269490 Indianapolis, IN 46226-9490, USA

ANNEX E/TAB D
U.S. NAVY EUROPE (USNAVEUR)

1. The USNAVEUR agency responsible for **placement and acceptance of Orders** under this Agreement is:

a. Unit:	COMUSNAVEUR (CNE)-COM SIXTH FLEET (C6F) (N4)
b. Telephone:	Com'l: 39-081-568-1832/1840 DSN: 314-626-1832/1840
c. Fax:	Com'l: 39-081-568-1272 DSN: 314-626-1272
d. Message Address:	COMUSNAVEUR NAPLES IT//N4 ACSA//
e. Mailing Address:	(Commercial) COMUSNAVEUR-C6F N4 LOGISTICS PLANS (ACSA) Marina Militaire Americana Viale Fulco Ruffo Di Calabria Aereoporto Capodichino Napoli, Italia 80144 (Military) COMUSNAVEUR-C6F N4 LOG PLANS (ACSA) PSC 817, Box 70 FPO, AE 09622

2. The USNAVEUR agency for **payments and collections** for Logistics Support, Supplies, and Services is:

a. Unit:	COMUSNAVEUR (COMPTROLLER)
b. Telephone:	Com'l: 39-081-568-3817 DSN: 314-626-3817
c. Fax	Com'l: 39-081-568-3143 DSN: 314-626-3143
d. Message Address:	COMUSNAVEUR NAPLES IT//N02F//
e. Mailing Address:	(Commercial) COMUSNAVEUR-C6F COMPTROLLER Marina Militare Americana Viale Fulco Ruffo Di Calabria Aereoporto Capodichino Napoli, Italia 80144 (Military) COMUSNAVEUR-C6F COMPTROLLER PSC 817, Box 70 FPO, AE 09622

ANNEX E/TAB E
MARINE FORCES EUROPE (MARFOREUR)

1. The MARFOREUR agency responsible for **placement and acceptance of Orders** under this Agreement is:

a. Unit:	HQ MARFOREUR/G4
b. Telephone:	Com'l: 49-703-115-3141 DSN: 314-431-3141
c. Fax:	Com'l: 49-7031-15-519 DSN: 314-431-2519
d. Mailing Address:	Commanding Officer Headquarters Marine Forces Europe Panzer Kaserne APO AE 09046

2. The MARFOREUR agency responsible for **payments and collections** under this Agreement is:

a. Unit:	HQ MARFOREUR/G4
b. Telephone:	Com'l: 49-7031-15-438 DSN: 314-431-5438
c. Fax:	Com'l: 49-7031-15-519 DSN: 314-431-5519
d. Mailing Address:	Commanding Officer Headquarters Marine Forces Europe Panzer Kaserne APO AE 09046

ANNEX E/TAB F
SPECIAL OPERATIONS COMMAND EUROPE (SOCEUR)

1. The SOCEUR agency responsible for **placement and acceptance of Orders** under this agreement is:

a. Unit:	SOCEUR/J4
b. Telephone:	Com'l: 49-711-680-4963 DSN: 314-430-4963
c. Fax:	Com'l: 49-711-680-577 DSN: 314-430-0577
d. Mailing Address:	HQ USEUCOM SOCEUR/SOJ4 Unit 30400 APO AE 09131

2. The SOCEUR agency responsible for **payments and collections** under this Agreement is:

a. Unit:	SOCEUR/J8
b. Telephone:	Com'l: 49-711-680-7249 DSN: 314-430-7249
c. Fax:	Com'l: 49-711-5771 DSN: 314-430-5771
d. Mailing Address:	HQ USEUCOM SOCEUR/SOJ8 Unit 30400 APO AE 09131

ANNEX E/TAB G
U.S. ARMY EUROPE (USAREUR) Kosovo Forces (KFOR) (KOSOVO AO)

1. The USAREUR KFOR agency responsible for **placement and acceptance of Orders** is:

a. Unit:	Task Force Falcon / AST Balkans, Camp Bondsteel
b. Telephone:	Com'l: +49-621-730-781-3083 / 3892 / 6401 DSN: 314-781-3083 / 3892 / 6401
d. Commercial Fax:	Com'l: +49-621-730-781-3891 DSN: 314-781-3891
e. Mailing Address:	AST Balkans, Camp Bondsteel ATTN: Multi-National Support Cell APO AE 09340

2. The 266th Theater Finance Command agency responsible for **payments and collections** for Logistics Support, Supplies, and Services is:

a. Unit:	Finance Office
b. Telephone:	Com'l: +49-621-730-781-5133 / 4272 / 3721 DSN: 314-781-5133 / 4272 / 3721
c. Fax:	Com'l: +49-621-730-781-5465 DSN: 314-781-5465
d. Mailing Address:	Finance Office Camp Bondsteel, Kosovo Task Force Falcon / KFOR # APO AE 09340

ANNEX F
JOINT STAFF J4 HAMPTON ROADS
POINTS OF CONTACT, ORDERING AND FINANCIAL RESPONSIBILITIES

TAB A—JSJ4HR
TAB B—ACC (Air Force)
TAB C—CDRUSFLTFORCOM (Navy)
TAB D—MARFORCOM (Marine Corps)
TAB E—FORSCOM (Army)

ANNEX F/TAB A
JOINT STAFF J4 HAMPTON ROADS (HR)

1. The JSJ4HR POC for coordinated **placement and acceptance of Orders** under this Agreement is the J4 Readiness, Requirements and Initiatives Division:

a. Unit:	JSJ4HR
b. Telephone:	Com'l: (757) 836-5172 or 5924 DSN: 836-5197 or 8029
c. Fax:	Com'l: (757) 836-5937 DSN: 836-5937
d. Message Address:	COMUSJFCOM NORFOLK VA//J45//
e. Mailing Address:	Joint Staff J4 Hampton Roads 7927 Ingersol Street Suite 110 Norfolk, VA 23551-2531

2. The JSJ4HR agency responsible for **payments and collections** under this Agreement is the Comptroller:

a. Unit:	Joint Staff JSSE Comptroller
b. Telephone	Com'l: (757) 836-6649 DSN: 836-6649
c. Fax:	Com'l: (757) 836-5796/6648 DSN: 836-6648
d. Message Address:	COMUSJFCOM NORFOLK VA//J02F//
e. Mailing Address:	Joint Staff JSSE Comptroller 1562 Mitscher Avenue, Suite 200 Norfolk, VA 23551-2488

ANNEX F/TAB B
AIR COMBAT COMMAND (ACC)

1. The ACC POC for coordinated **placement and acceptance of Orders and for payment and collections** under this Agreement is:

a. Unit:	Command Staff HQ ACC A4XP
b. Telephone:	Com'l: (757) 764-5610 DSN: 574-5610
c. Fax:	Com'l: (757) 764-7897 DSN: 574-7897
d. Message Address:	HQ ACC LANGLEY AFB VA// A4XP //
e. Mailing Address:	Headquarters Air Combat Command/ A4X 130 Andrews Street, Ste 211 Langley AFB, VA 23665

ANNEX F/TAB C
COMMANDER, U.S. FLEET FORCES COMMAND (CDRUSFLTFORCOM)

1. The CDRUSFLTFORCOM POC for coordinated **placement and acceptance of Orders** under this Agreement is:

a. Unit:	FFC N413 Logistics Operations Plans and Policy
b. Telephone:	Com'l: (757) 836-3789 DSN: 836-3789
c. Fax:	Com'l: (757) 836-3772 DSN: 836-3772
d. Message Address:	COMUSFLTFORCOM NORFOLK VA//N413
e. Mailing Address:	Commander, U.S. Fleet Forces Command Code N413 1562 Mitscher Avenue, Suite 250 Norfolk, VA 23551-2487

2. The CDRUSFLTFORCOM POC for coordinated **payment and collections** under this Agreement is:

a. Unit:	N02F Finance and Accounting US-FFC
b. Telephone:	Com'l: (757) 836-6929 DSN: 836-6929
c. Fax:	Com'l: (757) 836-6987 DSN: 836-6987 Comptroller US-FFC (757) 836-6902 DSN: 836-6902
d. Message Address:	COMUSFLTFORCOM NORFOLK VA//N02F
e. Mailing Address:	Commander, U.S. Fleet Forces Command Code N02F 1562 Mitscher Avenue, Suite 250 Norfolk, VA 23551-2487

ANNEX F/TAB D
U.S. MARINE FORCES COMMAND (MARFORCOM)

1. The MARFORCOM POC for coordinated **placement and acceptance of Orders** under this Agreement is:

a. Unit:	G4A Logistics Plans and Operations
b. Telephone:	Com'l: (757) 836-1647 or 1582 or 1518 DSN: 836-1647 or 1582 or 1518
c. Fax:	Com'l: (757) 836-1678 DSN: 836-1678
d. Message Address:	COMMARFORCOM//G4
e. Mailing Address:	U.S. Marine Corps Forces Code G4A 1775 Forrestal Drive Norfolk, VA 23551-2400

2. The MARFORCOM POC for **payment and collections** coordinated under this Agreement is:

a. Unit:	Comptroller
b. Telephone:	Com'l: (757) 836-2091 or secondary is 2177 DSN: 565-2091 or 2177
c. Fax:	Com'l: (757) 445-4054 DSN: 565-4054
d. Message Address:	COMMARFORCOM//COMPT
e. Mailing Address:	U.S. Marine Corps Forces Code COMPT 1775 Forrestal Drive Norfolk, VA 23551-2400

ANNEX F/TAB E
ARMY FORCES COMMAND (FORSCOM)

1. The FORSCOM POC for coordinated **placement and acceptance of Orders** under this Agreement is:

a. Unit:	AFLG-POFP, G4 Plans, Ops, Force Projection
b. Telephone:	Com'l: (404) 464-6161 or 5636 DSN: 367-6161 or 5636
c. Fax:	Com'l: (404) 464-5685 DSN: 367-5685
d. Message Address:	CDRFORSCOM FT MCPHERSON GA//AFLG-POT
e. Mailing Address:	Headquarters US Army Forces Command Code AFLG-POFP 1777 Hardee Avenue S.W. Ft. McPherson, GA 30330-1062

2. The FORSCOM POC for **payment and collections** coordinated under this Agreement is:

a. Unit:	AFRM-RI-O, Resource Management
b. Telephone:	Com'l: (404) 464-5687 or 6213 DSN: 367-5687 or 6213
c. Fax:	Com'l: (404) 464-6564 DSN: 367-6564
d. Message Address:	CDRFORSCOM FT MCPHERSONGA//AFRM-RI-O//
e. Mailing Address:	Headquarters Forces Command Code AFRM-RI-O 1777 Hardee Avenue Ft. McPherson, GA 30330-1062

ANNEX G
USSOUTHCOM
POINTS OF CONTACT, ORDERING AND FINANCIAL RESPONSIBILITIES

TAB A—HQ USSOUTHCOM
TAB B—AFSOUTH (Air Force)
TAB C—USARSOUTH (Army)
TAB D—USNAVSOUTH (Navy)
TAB E—USMARFORSOUTH (Marine Corps)
TAB F—SOCSOUTH (Special Operations)

ANNEX G/TAB A
HQ U.S. SOUTHERN COMMAND (HQ USSOUTHCOM)

1. The HQ USSOUTHCOM POC for coordinated **placement and acceptance of Orders** under this Agreement is the ES-LOG Joint Logistics Operations Center:

a. Unit:	SOUTHCOM ES-Log
b. Telephone:	Com'l: (305) 437-1427 or 1400 DSN: 567-1427 or 1400
c. Fax:	Com'l: (305) 437-1443 DSN: 567-1443 Com'l: (305) 437-1444 (Classified) DSN: 567-1444 (Classified)
d. Message Address:	CDR USSOUTHCOM MIAMI FL//ES-LOG//(CM)
e. Mailing Address:	COMMANDER HQ USOUTHCOM-ES-LOG 3511 NW 91st Ave. Miami, FL 33172-1217

2. The HQ USSOUTHCOM agency responsible for coordinating **payments and collections** under this Agreement is the Comptroller:

a. Unit:	USSOUTHCOM-R&A
b. Telephone:	Com'l: (305) 437-1814 or 1811 DSN: 567-1814 or 1811
c. Fax:	Com'l: (305) 437-1840 DSN: 567-1840
d. Message Address:	CDR USSOUTHCOM MIAMI FL//R&A//(CM)
e. Mailing Address:	COMMANDER HQ USSOUTHCOM (Attn: R&A) 3511 NW 91st Ave. Miami, FL 33172-1217

ANNEX G/TAB B
AFSOUTH
AIR FORCES SOUTHERN (AFSOUTH)

1. The AFSOUTH POC for coordinated **placement and acceptance of Orders** under this Agreement is the AFSOUTH A4:

a. Unit:	AFSOUTH A4X
b. Telephone:	Com'l: 520-228-3022 DSN: 228-3022
c. Fax:	Com'l: 520-228-3015 DSN: 228-3015 Com'l: N/A (Classified) DSN: N/A (Classified)
d. Message Address:	AFSOUTH DAVIS MONTHAN AFB AZ//A4X//
e. Mailing Address:	COMMANDER 12 AF (AFSOUTH) 2915 S. 12th AF Dr., Suite 144B ATTN: A4X DMAFB, AZ 85707

2. The AFSOUTH agency responsible for coordinating **payments and collections** under this Agreement is the Financial Management Office:

a. Unit:	12 AF (AFSOUTH)/FM
b. Telephone:	Com'l: 520-228-6406 DSN: 228-6406
c. Fax:	Com'l: 520-228-7129 DSN: 228-7129
d. Message Address:	AFSOUTH DAVIS MONTHAN AFB AZ//FM//
e. Mailing Address:	12 AF (AFSOUTH) FM 2915 S. Twelfth AF Dr., Suite 233 DMAFB, AZ 85707-4100

ANNEX G/TAB C
USARSO
U.S. ARMY SOUTH (USARSO)

1. The USARSO POC for coordinated **placement and acceptance of Orders** under this Agreement is USARSO DCS G-4:

a. Unit:	USARSOUTH DCS G-4
b. Telephone:	Com'l: 10-295-6713 DSN: 421-6713
c. Fax:	Com'l: 210-295-6369 DSN: 421-6369
d. Message Address:	HQ USARSO G4 FT SAM HOUSTON TX
e. Mailing Address:	Deputy Chief of Staff, G-4, U.S. Army South Attn: ARSO-LG 2450 Stanley Road, Suite 301 Ft. Sam Houston, TX 78234-7517

2. The USARSO agency responsible for coordinating **payments and collections** under this Agreement is the USARSO DCS G-8:

a. Unit:	USARSO G-8
b. Telephone:	Com'l: 210-295-6031 DSN: 312-421-6031
c. Fax:	Com'l: 210-295-6306 DSN: 312-421-6306
d. Message Address:	HQ USARSO G8 FT SAM HOUSTON TX
e. Mailing Address:	Deputy Chief of Staff, G-8, U.S. Army South Attn: ARSO-RM-FS 2450 Stanley Road, Suite 303 Ft. Sam Houston, TX 78234-7517

ANNEX G/TAB D
USNAVSOUTH
U.S. NAVAL FORCES SOUTH (USNAVSOUTH)

1. The USNAVSOUTH POC for coordinated **placement and acceptance of Orders** under this Agreement is the USNAVSOUTH (N41A):

a. Unit:	USNAVSOUTH/COMUSNAVSO
b. Telephone:	Com'l: 904-270-4037, ext. 3207/3232 DSN: 960-1037, ext. 3207/3232
c. Fax:	Com'l: 904-270-4055 DSN: N/A Com'l: N/A (Classified) DSN: N/A (Classified)
d. Message Address:	COMUSNAVSO
e. Mailing Address:	COMMANDER HQ USNAVSOUTH (Attn: N41A) BLDG 1878 NAVAL STATION Mayport, FL 32228-0003

2. The USNAVSOUTH agency responsible for coordinating **payments and collections** under this Agreement is the Comptroller:

a. Unit:	USNAVSOUTH/COMUSNAVSO
b. Telephone:	Com'l: 904-270-4037, ext. 3207/3232 DSN: 960-1037, ext. 3207/3232
c. Fax:	Com'l: 904-270-4055 DSN: N/A
d. Message Address:	COMUSNAVSO
e. Mailing Address:	COMMANDER HQ USNAVSOUTH (Attn: N41A) BLDG 1878 NAVAL STATION Mayport, FL 32228-0003

ANNEX G/TAB E
USMARFORSOUTH
U.S. MARINE FORCES SOUTH (USMARFORSOUTH)

1. The USMARFORSOUTH POC for coordinated **placement and acceptance of Orders** under this Agreement is the USMARFORSOUTH Comptroller:

a. Unit:	USMARFORSOUTH Comptroller
b. Telephone:	Com'l: 305-437-2604 DSN: 567-2604
c. Fax:	Com'l: 305-437-2542 DSN: 567-2542 Com'l: N/A (Classified) DSN: N/A (Classified)
d. Message Address:	COMMARFORSOUTH
e. Mailing Address:	COMMANDER HQ USMARFORSOUTH/Comptroller 8420 NW 52nd St. Suite 100 Miami, FL 33166

2. The USMARFORSOUTH agency responsible for coordinating **payments and collections** under this Agreement is the USMARFORSOUTH Comptroller:

a. Unit:	USMARFORSOUTH Comptroller
b. Telephone:	Com'l: 305-437-2604 DSN: 567-2604
c. Fax:	Com'l: 305-437-2542 DSN: 567-2542
d. Message Address:	COMMARFORSOUTH
e. Mailing Address:	COMMANDER HQ USMARFORSOUTH (Attn: Comptroller) 8420 NW 52nd St. Suite 100 Miami, FL 33166

ANNEX G/TAB F
SOCSOUTH
SPECIAL OPERATIONS COMMAND SOUTH (SOCSOUTH)

1. The SOCSOUTH POC responsible for coordinated **placement and acceptance of Orders** under this Agreement is the SOCSOUTH J4:

a. Unit:	SOCSOUTH
b. Telephone:	Com'l: 305-224-6403 DSN: 791-6403
c. Fax:	Com'l: 305-224-6415 DSN: N/A Com'l: N/A (Classified) DSN: N/A (Classified)
d. Message Address:	COMSOCSOUTH //J4//
e. Mailing Address:	HQ SOCSOUTH 29350 CORAL SEA BLVD BOX 6 HOMESTEAD, FL 33035

2. The SOCSOUTH POC responsible for coordinating **payments and collections** under this Agreement is the SOCSOUTH J8:

a. Unit:	SOCSOUTH
b. Telephone:	Com'l: 305-224-6380 DSN: 791-6380
c. Fax:	Com'l: 305-224-6386 DSN: 791-6386
d. Message Address:	COMSOCSOUTH //J8//
e. Mailing Address:	HQ SOCSOUTH 29350 CORAL SEA BLVD BOX 6 HOMESTEAD, FL 33035

ANNEX H
USNORTHCOM
POINTS OF CONTACT, ORDERING AND FINANCIAL RESPONSIBILITIES
U.S. NORTHERN COMMAND (USNORTHCOM)

1. The USNORTHCOM POC for coordinated **placement and acceptance of Orders** under this Agreement is:

a. Unit:	NORAD-USNORTHCOM/J4
b. Telephone:	Com'l: (719) 554-1685 or 5585 DSN: 692-1685 or 5585
c. Fax:	Com'l: (719) 554-3062 or 0813 DSN: 692-3062 or 0813
d. Message Address:	NORAD-NORTHCOM PETERSON AFB CO//J4//
e. Mailing Address:	250 Vandenberg St. St. B016 Peterson AFB CO 80914-3816

2. The USNORTHCOM agency responsible for **payments and collections** under this Agreement is:

a. Unit:	NORAD-USNORTHCOM/J8
b. Telephone:	Com'l: (719) 556-6032 DSN: 834-6032
c. Fax:	Com'l: (719) 556-0334 DSN: 834-0334
d. Message Address:	NORAD-NORTHCOM PETERSON AFB CO//J8//
e. Mailing Address:	250 Vandenberg St. Rm 1031 Peterson AFB CO 80914-3816

ANNEX I
USTRANSCOM
POINTS OF CONTACT, ORDERING AND FINANCIAL RESPONSIBILITIES
U.S. TRANSPORTATION COMMAND (USTRANSCOM)

1. The USTRANSCOM POC for coordinated **placement and acceptance of Orders** under this Agreement is the TCJ3 Deployment and Distribution Operations Center (DDOC):

a. Unit:	USTRANSCOM-TCJ3-O
b. Telephone:	Com'l: (618) 229-1747 or 4946 DSN: 779-1747 or 4946
c. Fax:	Com'l: (618) 256-1363 DSN: 576-1363 Com'l: (618) 256-6859 (Classified) DSN: 576-6859 (Classified)
d. Message Address:	USTRANSCOM SCOTT AFB IL//TCJ3-O//
e. Mailing Address:	USTRANSCOM TCJ3-O (DDOC) 508 Scott Drive Bldg. 1900 Scott AFB IL, 62225-5357
f. E-mail Address:	USTC-DDOCCHIEF@ustranscom.mil

2. The USTRANSCOM agency responsible for **payments and collections** under this Agreement is the TCJ8 Program Analysis and Financial Management Directorate:

a. Unit:	USTRANSCOM-TCJ8
b. Telephone:	Com'l: (618) 229-5358 DSN: 779-5358
c. Fax:	Com'l: (618) 256-4477 DSN: 576-4477
d. Message Address:	USTRANSCOM SCOTT AFB IL//TCJ8//
e. Mailing Address:	HQ USTRANSCOM—TCJ8 203 West Losey Bldg. 1700 Scott AFB IL, 62225-5233
f. E-mail Address	ustcj8@ustranscom.mil

ANNEX J
USAFRICOM
POINTS OF CONTACT, ACSA ORDERING AND FINANCIAL RESPONSIBILITIES
U.S. AFRICAN COMMAND (USAFRICOM)

1. The USAFRICOM POC's responsible for **placement and acceptance of Orders** are:

a. Unit:	HQ USAFRICOM OPL-LSM-ACSA
b. Telephone:	Com'l: 49-711-729-4972 DSN: 314-421-4972
c. Fax:	Commercial: 49-711-729-2843
d. Message Address:	
e. Mailing Address:	HQ USAFRICOM OPL-LSM-ACSA Unit 29951 APO AE 09751-9951 or
a. Unit:	HQ USAFRICOM RES-FMC
b. Telephone:	Commercial: 49-711-729-4901 DSN: 314-421-4901
c. Fax:	Commercial: 49-711-729-4839
d. Message Address:	
e. Mailing Address:	HQ USAFRICOM RES-FMC Unit 29951 APO AE 09751-9951

2. The USAFRICOM POC agency responsible for **payments and collection** for Logistics Support, Supplies, and Services is:

a. Unit:	HQ USAFRICOM RES-FMB
b. Telephone:	Com'l: 49-711-729-4858 DSN: 314-421-4858
c. Fax:	Com'l: 49-711-729-4839
d. Message Address:	
e. Mailing Address:	HQ USAFRICOM RES-FMB Unit 29951 APO AE 09751-9951

CERTIFYING STATEMENT

I, THE UNDERSIGNED, hereby certify that the attached text is a true and complete copy of **TIAS 12821**—Memorandum of Understanding (MOU) between the United States and the United Kingdom of Great Britain and Northern Ireland for cooperation in the development of Combined Arms Tactical Training equipments, signed at Alexandria and Abbey Wood December 6, 1996, that no reservations or declarations or objections were made by the Signatories or Parties thereto, and that it was concluded in the English language.

I FURTHER CERTIFY that the MOU came into force on December 6, 1996, upon signature, in accordance with Section 16.6 of the MOU.

IN TESTIMONY WHEREOF, I,

Hillary Rodham Clinton

Secretary of State, have hereunto caused the Seal of the Department of State of the United States of America to be affixed and my name subscribed by the Treaty Registration Officer of the said Department, at the City of Washington, in the District of Colombia, this seventh day of November, 2012.

____

Secretary of State

By ____________________________

Treaty Registration Officer

STATE DEPARTMENT DOCUMENT NUMBER: 12-186

DEVELOPMENT AGREEMENT BETWEEN THE UNITED STATES OF AMERICA AND THE REPUBLIC OF GHANA FOR IMPROVED READING PERFORMANCE IN PRIMARY SCHOOL

SIGNED ON SEPTEMBER 26, 2012
ENTERED INTO FORCE SEPTEMBER 26, 2012

CTIA DOCUMENT NUMBER: 18088.000

USAID DEVELOPMENT AGREEMENT No. 641-004

CERTIFIED TO BE A TRUE COPY OF THE ORIGINAL SIGNED BY CHERYL ANDERSON, USAID GHANA MISSION DIRECTOR, AND DR. KWABENA DUFFUOR, MINISTER FOR FINANCE AND ECONOMIC PLANNING, GOVERNMENT OF GHANA. [Signature]

RESPONSIBLE OFFICIAL: THOMAS CRUBAUGH, SUPERVISORY PROGRAM OFFICER, USAID GHANA.

DEVELOPMENT AGREEMENT

Dated: September 26, 2012

Between

The United States of America, through the United States Agency for International Development ("USAID")

and

The Republic of Ghana (the "Grantee"), through the Ministry of Finance and Economic Planning

Article 1: Purpose.

The purpose of this Development Agreement (the "Agreement") is to set out the understanding of the Parties named above (the "Parties") in connection with the Objective described below. This Agreement replaces the Strategic Objective Grant Agreement for Strategic Objective Number Eight;

Improved Quality of and Access to Basic Education, 641-008 (SOAG No. 8), dated September 15, 2003, as amended, in its entirety.

Article 2: Functional Objective, Program Areas and Program Elements.

Section 2.1. ***Functional Objective, Program Areas***. In order to further the foreign assistance objective of Investing in People (the "Functional Objective") articulated by the Government of the United States of America under the Strategic Framework for United States Foreign Assistance, the Parties hereto agree to work together by focusing on activities in the area of Education (the "Program Area," and, together with the Functional Objective, the "Objective") and the Program Element of Basic Education.

Section 2.2. ***Program Elements***. In order to realize the Development Objective, within the Basic Education Program Element, the Parties agree to work together to support key priorities in Ghana's Education Strategic Plan, with an emphasis on improving the quality of education and learning outcomes, specifically early grade reading, the use of mother tongue instruction and the transition and exit strategy to English language. Portfolio programming will support reading performance improvement in primary school, investigate early grade math performance, provide complementary support to strengthen basic education management systems linked to reading and help to enhance institutional accountability and transparency. Specific activities will include strengthening the instructional practices of teachers, reinforcing the use of quality teaching and learning materials, improving the supervision and oversight functions of responsible basic education institutions, improving the use of monitoring, evaluation and data, and engaging parents, communities and district education oversight bodies in the participatory and transparent management of the school system.

The performance indicators by which progress toward achievement of this Program Element will be measured are described in Annex 1 to this Agreement, the Amplified Description, which is attached to and forms part of this Agreement. Within the limits of the definition of the Objective in Section 2.1, this Section 2.2 may be changed by written agreement of the authorized representatives of the Parties without formal amendment of this Agreement.

Section 2.3. ***Annex 1, Amplified Description***. Annex 1, attached, amplifies the above Objective and describes the Program Elements, Program Sub-Elements and Indicators that will be used to measure the progress and achievement in each of the Program Areas. Within the limits of the definition of the Objective set forth in Section 2.1, Annex 1 may be changed by written agreement of the authorized representatives of the Parties without formal amendment of this Agreement.

Article 3: Contributions of the Parties.

Section 3.1. ***USAID Contribution***.

(a) The Grant. To help achieve the Objective set forth in this Agreement, USAID, pursuant to the Foreign Assistance Act of 1961, hereby grants to the Grantee, under the terms of this Agreement, an amount of Twenty-Eight Million Eight Hundred Eight Thousand U.S. Dollars ($28,808,000), which is being obligated directly under this agreement. An additional Forty-Two Thousand U.S. Dollars ($42,000) is being obligated outside of the Agreement by USAID for activities that support the objectives of the Agreement.

(b) Total Estimated USAID Contribution. USAID's total estimated contribution to the achievement of the Objective will be One Hundred Sixty Million U.S. Dollars ($160,000,000), which will be provided in increments. Subsequent increments will be subject to the availability of funds to USAID for this purpose and the mutual agreement of the Parties, at the time of each subsequent increment, to proceed. Each such incremental contribution provided, if any, shall cumulatively increase the total amount of the Grant set forth in Section 3.1 and consequently may increase the Grantee's contribution under Section 3.2. This estimated total contribution includes certain other obligations that have been or will be made directly by USAID to other implementers or through other instruments in support of the objective, as specified in Section 3.1(a) above and in the Illustrative Financial Plan attached hereto.

(c) If at any time USAID determines that its contribution under Section 3.1 (a) exceeds the amount which reasonably can be committed for achieving the Objective of this Agreement during the current or next U.S. fiscal year, USAID may, upon written notice to the Grantee, withdraw the excess amount, thereby reducing the amount of the Grant as set forth in Section 3.1(a). Actions taken pursuant to this subsection will not revise USAID's total estimated contribution set forth in 3.1(b).

(d) The Parties agree that USAID's contribution may be disbursed through mechanisms including grants, cooperative agreements and contracts with non-governmental organizations and private companies in order to carry out the activities described in Annex 1 of this Agreement or described in Implementation Letters issued in accordance with Section A.2 of Annex 2 of this Agreement. USAID agrees to notify the Grantee via Implementation Letters of any recipients of such funding and the Parties further agree that any such implementing partner carrying out activities in furtherance of the Objective shall receive all of the rights, privileges and other benefits set forth in this Agreement.

Section 3.2. ***Grantee Contribution.***

(a) The Grantee agrees to provide or cause to be provided all funds, in addition to those provided by USAID and any other donor identified in Annex 1, and all other resources required to complete, on or before the Completion Date, all activities necessary to achieve the Objectives. The basis for determining the Grantee's contribution and the nature of the contribution will be further described in an Implementation Letter.

(b) The Grantee's contribution, based on USAID's contribution in Section 3.1(a), will not be less than the equivalent of one-third of the portion of the Grant that is used to support activities that directly benefit the Grantee or involves the direct and substantial involvement of the Government of Ghana in the administration, provided that such amount may be reduced with the written consent of USAID. The Grantee's contribution may include either cash or in-kind contributions or both. The dollar equivalent amount of the Grantee's contribution shall be set forth in an Implementation Letter and shall be subsequently included in the Illustrative Financial Plan included in Annex 1 of this Agreement. The amount of the Grantee's contribution shall be adjusted upon any increase in the amount of the Grant set forth in Section 3.1(a), in accordance with the formula described in the first sentence of this paragraph, and the precise amount of such adjustment shall be indicated in an Implementation Letter. The Grantee will report at least annually in a format to be agreed upon with USAID on its cash and in-kind contributions.

Article 4: Completion Date.

(a) The Completion Date, which is September 30, 2018, or such other date as the Parties may agree to in writing, is the date by which the Parties estimate that all the activities necessary to achieve the Objective will be completed.

(b) Except as USAID may otherwise agree to in writing, USAID will not issue or approve documentation that would authorize disbursement of the Grant for services performed or goods furnished after the Completion Date.

(c) Requests for disbursement, accompanied by necessary supporting documentation prescribed in Implementation Letters, are to be received by USAID no later than nine (9) months following the Completion Date, or such other period as USAID agrees to in writing before or after such period. After such period USAID, at any time or times, may give notice in writing to the Grantee and reduce the amount of the Grant by all or any part thereof for which requests for disbursement, accompanied by necessary supporting documentation prescribed in Implementation Letters, were not received before the expiration of such period.

Article 5: Conditions Precedent to Disbursement.

Section 5.1. ***First Disbursement.*** Prior to the first disbursement under the Grant, or to the issuance by USAID of documentation pursuant to which disbursement will be made, the Grantee will, except as the Parties may otherwise agree in writing, furnish to USAID in form and substance satisfactory to USAID:

(a) An opinion of counsel acceptable to USAID that (i) this Agreement has been duly authorized or ratified by, and executed on behalf of the Grantee, (ii) this Agreement constitutes a valid and legally binding obligation of the Grantee in accordance with all of its terms, and (iii) all internal actions and approvals necessary to give effect to this Agreement have been obtained by or on behalf of the Grantee; and

(b) A signed statement in the name of the person holding or acting in the office of the Grantee specified in Section 7.2, which designates by name and title any additional representatives each of whom may act pursuant to Section 7.2.

Section 5.2. ***Notification.*** USAID will promptly notify the Grantee when USAID has determined that a condition precedent has been met.

Section 5.3. ***Terminal Dates for Conditions Precedent.***

(a) The terminal date for meeting the conditions specified in Section 5.1 is sixty (60) days from the date of this Agreement or such later date as USAID may agree to in writing before or after the above terminal date. If the conditions precedent in Section 5.1 have not been met by the above terminal date, USAID, at any time, may terminate this Agreement by written notice to the Grantee.

Article 6: Special Covenants.

The Parties agree to carry out the terms of the following special covenants:

Section 6.1. ***Permits and Other Approvals and Authorizations.***

The Grantee, in conjunction with the appropriate Government of Ghana ministries and offices, hereby covenants and agrees to issue, renew and/or extend free of charge and in a timely manner all official permits, visas, exemptions and any other permissions (including all approvals as may be required from time to time to ensure full access to information, project sites and relevant offices) for the Applicable Persons (as defined below) carrying out activities financed by USAID under this Agreement (collectively, the "Required Documents"). For purposes of this provision, Applicable Persons is defined as: (1) employees and consultants of any contractors, grantees and other organizations carrying out activities financed by USAID under this Agreement and (b) members of such employees' and consultants' households. Any renewals or extensions of such Required Documents that are required, or become required, in order for such employees, consultants and dependent family members to legally reside in Ghana and undertake the activities contemplated by and financed under this Agreement shall also be issued free of charge.

Section 6.2. ***Monitoring and Evaluation.***

Except as the Parties otherwise stipulate in writing, the Parties agree that:

(a) USAID and its implementing partners will systematically monitor and report progress on performance indicators during the Agreement period (illustrative indicators are described in Annex 1);

(b) The strategy baseline survey conducted by USAID at the beginning of this Agreement will serve as a baseline for measuring progress under this Agreement;

(c) Funds available under this Agreement may be used for monitoring and evaluation purposes (such costs are part of the "USAID/Ghana Program Support Costs" indicated in the Illustrative Financial Plan); and

(d) The Grantee, through the Ministry of Education, will ensure that public sector agencies associated with the Agreement undertake reasonable efforts to produce and/or obtain and provide to USAID all data needed to measure performance of activities under this Agreement.

Article 7: Miscellaneous.

Section 7.1. ***Communications***. Any notice, request, document, or other communication submitted by either Party to the other under this Agreement will be in writing or by telegram, telefax, cable or electronic mail ("e-mail"), and will be deemed duly given or sent when delivered to such Party at the following address:

To USAID:
Mail Address:
Mission Director
United States Agency for International Development
No. 24 Fourth Circular Rd.
P.O. Box GP 194 ACCRA
Cantonments, Accra, Ghana

Email: canderson@usaid.gov
Alternate address for cables:
Telefax: (233) 302-741-365

To the Grantee:
Mail Address:
Minister
Ministry of Finance and Economic Planning
P.O. Box M.40
Accra, Ghana

Email:
Alternate address for cables:
Telefax: (233)21-666556

All such communications will be in English, unless the Parties otherwise agree in writing. Other addresses may be substituted for the above upon the giving of notice.

Section 7.2. ***Representatives.*** For all purposes relevant to this Agreement, the Grantee will be represented by the individual holding or acting in the Ministry of Finance and Economic Planning, and USAID will be represented by the individual holding or acting in the Office of the Director of USAID/Ghana, each of whom, by written notice, may designate additional representatives for all implementation actions as specified under Annex 1. The names and titles of the additional representatives of the Grantee, with specimen signatures, will be provided pursuant to Section 5.1(b) to USAID, which may accept as duly authorized any instrument signed by such additional representatives (or any individuals subsequent holding or acting in the office of such representatives) in accordance with this Section 7.2, until receipt of written notice of revocation of their authority.

Section 7.3. ***Standard Provisions Annex***. A "Standard Provisions Annex" (Annex 2) is attached to and forms part of this Agreement.

Section 7.4. ***Language of Agreement.*** This Agreement was prepared only in English.

IN WITNESS WHEREOF, the United States of America and the Grantee, each acting through its duly authorized representatives, have caused this Agreement to be signed in their names and delivered as of the day and year first above written.

UNITED STATES OF AMERICA

[Signature]

Cheryl Anderson
Mission Director
United States Agency for International Development

Date: 9/26/12

REPUBLIC OF GHANA

[Signature]

Minister
Ministry of Finance and Economic Planning

DR. KWABENA DUFFUOR
MIN. OF FIN. & ECON. PLANNING
P. O. BOX MB 40
ACCRA

Date: ____________

STATE DEPARTMENT DOCUMENT NUMBER: 12-187

DEVELOPMENT AGREEMENT BETWEEN THE UNITED STATES OF AMERICA AND THE REPUBLIC OF GHANA FOR EQUITABLE IMPROVEMENTS IN HEALTH STATUS

SIGNED ON SEPTEMBER 26, 2012
ENTERED INTO FORCE SEPTEMBER 26, 2012

CTIA DOCUMENT NUMBER: 18089.000

USAID DEVELOPMENT AGREEMENT No. 641-003

CERTIFIEDTO [*sic*] BE A TRUE COPY OF THE ORIGINAL SIGNED BY CHERYL ANDERSON, USAID GHANA MISSION DIRECTOR, AND DR. KWABENA DUFFUOR, MINISTER OF FINANCE AND ECONOMIC PLANNING, GOVERNMENT OF GHANA. [Signature]

RESPONSIBLE OFFICER: THOMAS CRUBAUGH, SUPERVISORY PROGRAM OFFICER, USAID GHANA.

DEVELOPMENT AGREEMENT

Dated: September 26, 2012

Between

The United States of America, through the United States Agency for International Development ("USAID")

and

The Republic of Ghana (the "Grantee"), through the Ministry of Finance and Economic Planning

Article 1: Purpose.

The purpose of this Development Agreement (the "Agreement") is to set out the understanding of the Parties named above (the "Parties") in connection with the Objective described below. This Agreement replaces Strategic Objective Agreement for Strategic Objective Number 7, Improved Health Status (SOAG No. 7) 641-007, dated September 15, 2003, as amended, in its entirety.

Article 2: Functional Objective, Program Areas and Program Elements.

Section 2.1. ***Functional Objective, Program Areas.*** In order to further the foreign assistance objective of Investing in People (the "Functional Objective") articulated by the Government of the

United States of America under the Strategic Framework for United States Foreign Assistance, the Parties hereto agree to work together by focusing on activities in the area of Health and Education (collectively, the "Program Areas," and, together with the Functional Objective, the "Objective").

Section 2.2. ***Program Elements.*** In order to achieve the Objective, the Parties agree to work together to: improve delivery of health service at the community, district, and regional levels, including interventions to encourage positive behavior change, improve the quality of service delivery and strengthen health systems within each of the eight following Program Elements: HIV/AIDS, Tuberculosis (TB), Malaria, Maternal and Child Health, Family Planning and Reproductive Health, Water Supply and Sanitation, and Nutrition, and Higher Education (collectively, the "Program Elements.") The performance indicators by which progress toward achievement of these Program Elements will be measured are described in Annex 1 to this Agreement, the Amplified Description, which is attached to and forms part of this Agreement. Within the limits of the definition of the Functional Objective and Program Areas in Section 2.1, this Section 2.2 may be changed by written agreement of the authorized representatives of the Parties without formal amendment of this Agreement.

Section 2.3. ***Annex 1, Amplified Description.*** Annex 1, attached, amplifies the above Objective and describes the Program Elements, Program Sub-Elements and Indicators that will be used to measure the progress and achievement in each of the Program Areas. Within the limits of the definition of the Functional Objective set forth in Section 2.1, Annex 1 may be changed by written agreement of the authorized representatives of the Parties without formal amendment of this Agreement.

Article 3: Contributions of the Parties.

Section 3.1. ***USAID Contribution.***

(a) The Grant. To help achieve the Objective set forth in this Agreement, USAID pursuant to the Foreign Assistance Act of 1961, hereby grants to the Grantee under the terms of this Agreement an amount of Thirty-Nine Million Three Hundred Thirty-Four Thousand Six Hundred Seventy-Nine U.S. Dollars ($39,334,679). An additional amount of Thirty-Two Million Forty-Five Thousand Three Hundred Twenty-One U.S. Dollars ($32,045,321) will be obligated through USAID/Washington mechanisms in support of the Objective.

(b) Total Estimated USAID Contribution. USAID's total estimated contribution to the achievement of the Objective will be Four Hundred Ten Million U.S. Dollars ($410,000,000), which will be provided in increments. Subsequent increments will be subject to the availability of funds to USAID for this purpose and the mutual agreement of the Parties, at the time of each subsequent increment, to proceed. Each such incremental contribution provided, if any, shall cumulatively increase the total amount of the Grant set forth in Section 3.1 and consequently may increase the Grantee's contribution under Section 3.2. This estimated total contribution includes certain other obligations that have been or will be made directly by USAID to other implementers or through other instruments in support of the objective, as specified in Section 3.1(a) above and in the Illustrative Financial Plan attached hereto.

(c) If, at any time, USAID determines that its contribution under Section 3.1(a) exceeds the amount which reasonably can be committed for achieving the Objective of this Agreement during the current or next U.S. fiscal year, USAID may, upon written notice to the Grantee, withdraw the excess amount, thereby reducing the amount of the Grant as set forth in Section 3.1(a).

Actions taken pursuant to this subsection will not revise USAID's total estimated contribution set forth in 3.1(b).

(d) The Parties agree that USAID's contribution may be disbursed through mechanisms including grants, cooperative agreements and contracts with non-governmental organizations and private companies in order to carry out the activities described in Annex 1 of this Agreement or described in Implementation Letters issued in accordance with Section A.2 of Annex 2 of this Agreement. USAID agrees to notify the Grantee via Implementation Letters of any recipients of such funding and the Parties further agree that any such implementing partner carrying out activities in furtherance of the Objective shall receive all of the rights, privileges and other benefits set forth in this Agreement.

Section 3.2. ***Grantee Contribution.***

(a) The Grantee agrees to provide or cause to be provided all funds, in addition to those provided by USAID and any other donor identified in Annex 1, and all other resources required to complete, on or before the Completion Date, all activities necessary to achieve the Objectives. The basis for determining the Grantee's contribution and the nature of the contribution will be further described in an Implementation Letter.

(b) The Grantee's contribution, based on USAID's contribution in Section 3.1(a), will not be less than the equivalent of one-third of the portion of the Grant that is used to support activities that directly benefit the Grantee or involves the direct and substantial involvement of the Government of Ghana in the administration, provided that such amount may be reduced with the written consent of USAID. The Grantee's contribution may include either cash or in-kind contributions or both. The dollar equivalent amount of the Grantee's contribution shall be set forth in an Implementation Letter and shall be subsequently included in the Illustrative Financial Plan included in Annex 1 of this Agreement. The amount of the Grantee's contribution shall be adjusted upon any increase in the amount of the Grant set forth in Section 3.1(a), in accordance with the formula described in the first sentence of this paragraph, and the precise amount of such adjustment shall be indicated in an Implementation Letter. The Grantee will report at least annually in a format to be agreed upon with USAID on its cash and in-kind contributions.

Article 4: Completion Date.

(a) The Completion Date, which is September 30, 2018, or such other date as the Parties may agree to in writing, is the date by which the Parties estimate that all the activities necessary to achieve the Objective will be completed.

(b) Except as USAID may otherwise agree to in writing, USAID will not issue or approve documentation that would authorize disbursement of the Grant for services performed or goods furnished after the Completion Date.

(c) Requests for disbursement, accompanied by necessary supporting documentation prescribed in Implementation Letters, are to be received by USAID no later than nine (9) months following the Completion Date, or such other period as USAID agrees to in writing before or after such period. After such period USAID, at any time or times, may give notice in writing to the Grantee and reduce the amount of the Grant by all or any part thereof for which requests for disbursement, accompanied by necessary supporting documentation prescribed in Implementation Letters, were not received before the expiration of such period.

Article 5: Conditions Precedent to Disbursement.

Section 5.1. ***Disbursement.*** Prior to the disbursement under the Grant, or to the issuance by USAID of documentation pursuant to which disbursement will be made, the Grantee will, except as the Parties may otherwise agree in writing, furnish to USAID in form and substance satisfactory to USAID:

(a) An opinion of counsel acceptable to USAID that (i) this Agreement has been duly authorized or ratified by, and executed on behalf of the Grantee, (ii) this Agreement constitutes a valid and legally binding obligation of the Grantee in accordance with all of its terms, and (iii) all internal actions and approvals necessary to give effect to this Agreement have been obtained by or on behalf of the Grantee; and

(b) A signed statement in the name of the person holding or acting in the office of the Grantee specified in Section 7.2, which designates by name and title any additional representatives each of whom may act pursuant to Section 7.2.

Section 5.2. ***Notification.*** USAID will promptly notify the Grantee when USAID has determined that a condition precedent has been met.

Section 5.3. ***Terminal Dates for Conditions Precedent.*** The terminal date for meeting the conditions specified in Section 5.1 is sixty (60) days from the date of this Agreement or such later date as USAID may agree to in writing before or after the above terminal date. If the conditions precedent in Section 5.1 have not been met by the above terminal date, USAID, at any time, may terminate this Agreement by written notice to the Grantee.

Article 6: Special Covenants.

The Parties agree to carry out the terms of the following special covenants:

Section 6.1. ***Permits and Other Approvals and Authorizations.***

The Grantee, in conjunction with the appropriate Government of Ghana ministries and offices, hereby covenants and agrees to issue, renew and/or extend free of charge and in a timely manner all official permits, visas, exemptions and any other permissions (including all approvals as may be required from time to time to ensure full access to information, project sites and relevant offices) for the Applicable Persons (as defined below) carrying out activities financed by USAID under this Agreement (collectively, the "Required Documents"). For purposes of this provision, Applicable Persons is defined as: (1) employees and consultants of any contractors, grantees and other organizations carrying out activities financed by USAID under this Agreement and (b) members of such employees' and consultants' households. Any renewals or extensions of such Required Documents that are required, or become required, in order for such employees, consultants and dependent family members to legally reside in Ghana and undertake the activities contemplated by and financed under this Agreement shall also be issued free of charge.

Section 6.2. ***Monitoring and Evaluation.***

Except as the Parties otherwise stipulate in writing, the Parties agree that:

(a) USAID and its implementing partners will systematically monitor and report progress on performance indicators during the Agreement period (illustrative indicators are described in Annex 1);

(b) The strategy baseline survey conducted by USAID at the beginning of this Agreement will serve as a baseline for measuring progress under this Agreement;

(c) Funds available under this Agreement may be used for monitoring and evaluation purposes (such costs are part of the "Management Support Costs" indicated in the Illustrative Financial Plan); and

(d) The Grantee, through the Ministry of Health, will ensure that public sector agencies associated with the Agreement undertake reasonable efforts to produce and/or obtain and provide to USAID all data needed to measure performance of activities under this Agreement.

Article 7: Miscellaneous.

Section 7.1. ***Communications***. Any notice, request, document, or other communication submitted by either Party to the other under this Agreement will be in writing or by telegram, telefax, cable or electronic mail ("e-mail"), and will be deemed duly given or sent when delivered to such Party at the following address:

To USAID:
Mail Address:
Mission Director
United States Agency for International Development
No. 24 Fourth Circular Rd.
P.O. Box GP 194 ACCRA
Cantonments, Accra, Ghana

E-mail: chanderson@usaid.gov
Alternate address for cables:
Telefax: (233)302 741-365

To the Grantee:
Mail Address:
Minister
Ministry of Finance and Economic Planning
P.O. Box M.40
Accra, Ghana

E-mail:
Alternate address for cables:
Telefax: (233)21-666556

All such communications will be in English, unless the Parties otherwise agree in writing. Other addresses may be substituted for the above upon the giving of notice.

Section 7.2. ***Representatives***. For all purposes relevant to this Agreement, the Grantee will be represented by the individual holding or acting in the Ministry of Finance and Economic Planning, and USAID will be represented by the individual holding or acting in the Office of the Director at USAID/Ghana, each of whom, by written notice, may designate additional representatives for all implementation actions as specified under Annex 1. The names and titles of the additional representatives of the Grantee, with specimen signatures, will be provided pursuant to Section 5.1(b) to USAID, which may accept as duly authorized any instrument signed by such additional representatives (or any individuals subsequent holding or acting in the office of such representatives) in accordance with this Section 7.2, until receipt of written notice of revocation of their authority.

Section 7.3. ***Standard Provisions Annex***. A "Standard Provisions Annex" (Annex 2) is attached to and forms part of this Agreement.

Section 7.4. ***Language of Agreement.*** This Agreement was prepared only in English.

IN WITNESS WHEREOF, the United States of America and the Grantee, each acting through its duly authorized representatives, have caused this Agreement to be signed in their names and delivered as of the day and year first above written.

UNITED STATES OF AMERICA

[Signature]

Cheryl Anderson
Mission Director
United States Agency for International Development

Date: 9/26/12

REPUBLIC OF GHANA

[Signature]

Minister
Ministry of Finance and Economic Planning

DR. KWABENA DUFFUOR
MIN. OF FIN. & ECON. PLANNING
P. O. BOX MB 40
ACCRA

Date: 9/26/12

STATE DEPARTMENT DOCUMENT NUMBER: 12-188

DEVELOPMENT AGREEMENT BETWEEN THE UNITED STATES OF AMERICA AND THE REPUBLIC OF GHANA FOR SUSTAINABLE AND BROADLY SHARED ECONOMIC GROWTH

SIGNED ON SEPTEMBER 26, 2012
ENTERED INTO FORCE SEPTEMBER 26, 2012

CTIA DOCUMENT NUMBER: 18090.000

USAID DEVELOPMENT AGREEMENT No.641-002

CERTIFIED TO BE A TRUE COPY OF THE ORIGINAL SIGNED BY CHERYL ANDERSON, USAID GHANA MISSION DIRECTOR, AND DR. KWABENA DUFFUOR, MINISTER OF FINANCE AND ECONOMIC PLANNING, GOVERNMENT OF GHANA. [Signature]

RESPONSIBLE OFFICER: THOMAS CRUBAUGH, SUPERVISORY PROGRAM OFFICER, USAID GHANA.

DEVELOPMENT AGREEMENT

Dated: September 26, 2012

Between

The United States of America, through the United States Agency for International Development ("USAID")

and

The Republic of Ghana (the "Grantee"), through the Ministry of Finance and Economic Planning

Article 1: Purpose.

The purpose of this Development Agreement (the "Agreement") is to set out the understanding of the Parties named above (the "Parties") in connection with the Objective described below. This Agreement replaces the Strategic Objective Grant Agreement for Strategic Objective No. 6: Economic Growth, 641-006 ("SOAG No. 6"), dated September 15, 2003, as amended, in its entirety.

Article 2: Functional Objective, Program Areas and Program Elements.

Section 2.1. ***Functional Objective, Program Areas.*** In order to further the foreign assistance objective of Economic Growth (the "Functional Objective") articulated by the Government of the

United States of America under the Strategic Framework for United States Foreign Assistance, the Parties hereto agree to work together by focusing on activities in the areas of: Infrastructure, Agriculture, Economic Opportunity, and Environment (collectively, the "Program Areas," and, together with the Functional Objective, the "Objective").

Section 2.2. ***Program Elements***. In order to achieve the Objective, the Parties agree to work together to provide technical assistance for key staff in ministries, departments, agencies, and Ghanaian public and private companies and to provide support to small and medium enterprises (SMEs) in the Western Region, within the Modern Energy Services Program Element. Within the Agricultural Enabling Environment and Agricultural Sector Capacity Program Elements, the Parties agree to assist agricultural enterprises and farmer-based organizations to acquire the technical and managerial skills necessary to increase productivity, market share, and improve markets for staple crops. Activities will also build the capacity of the Ministry of Food and Agriculture and support the Comprehensive Africa Agriculture Development Program. Within the Natural Resources and Biodiversity Program Element, the Parties agree to strengthen local government and community-level capacity to address management of coastal resources and fisheries. Activities will also engage the oil industry to leverage additional resources for coastal ecosystem protection and create a local government structure that can effectively interact with oil companies. The performance indicators by which progress toward achievement of these Program Elements will be measured are described in Annex 1 to this Agreement, the Amplified Description, which is attached to and forms part of this Agreement. Within the limits of the definition of the Functional Objective in Section 2.1, this Section 2.2 may be changed by written agreement of the authorized representatives of the Parties without formal amendment of this Agreement.

Section 2.3. ***Annex 1, Amplified Description***. Annex 1, attached, amplifies the above Objective and describes the Program Elements, Program Sub-Elements and Indicators that will be used to measure the progress and achievement in each of the Program Areas. Within the limits of the definition of the Functional Objective set forth in Section 2.1, Annex 1 may be changed by written agreement of the authorized representatives of the Parties without formal amendment of this Agreement.

Article 3: Contributions of the Parties.

Section 3.1. ***USAID Contribution.***

(a) The Grant. To help achieve the Objective set forth in this Agreement, USAID pursuant to the Foreign Assistance Act of 1961, hereby grants to the Grantee, under the terms of this Agreement, an amount of Forty Six Million Three Hundred Ninety-Seven Four Hundred Two U.S. Dollars ($46,397,402), which is being obligated directly under this Agreement. An additional sum of One Hundred Seventy-Seven Thousand Five Hundred Ninety-Eight U.S. Dollars ($177,598) will be transferred to Washington and obligated outside the scope of this Agreement into various instruments that will contribute to the achievement of the Objective.

(b) Total Estimated USAID Contribution. USAID's total estimated contribution to the achievement of the Objective will be Two Hundred and Seventy Million U.S. Dollars ($ 270,000,000). Subsequent increments will be subject to the availability of funds to USAID for this purpose and the mutual agreement of the Parties, at the time of each subsequent increment, to proceed. Each such incremental contribution provided, if any, shall cumulatively increase the total amount of the Grant set forth in Section 3.1 and consequently may increase the Grantee's contribution under Section 3.2. This estimated total contribution includes certain other obligations that have been or will be made directly by USAID to implementing partners or through other instruments in support of the Objective , as specified in Section 3.1 (a) above and in the Illustrative Financial Plan attached hereto.

(c) If at any time USAID determines that its contribution under Section 3.1(a) exceeds the amount which reasonably can be committed for achieving the Objective of this Agreement during the current or next U.S. fiscal year, USAID may, upon written notice to the Grantee, withdraw the excess amount, thereby reducing the amount of the Grant as set forth in Section 3.1(a). Actions taken pursuant to this subsection will not revise USAID's total estimated contribution set forth in 3.1(b).

(d) The Parties agree that USAID's contribution may be disbursed through mechanisms including grants, cooperative agreements and contracts with non-governmental organizations and private companies in order to carry out the activities described in Annex 1 of this Agreement or described in Implementation Letters issued in accordance with Section A.2 of Annex 2 of this Agreement. USAID agrees to notify the Grantee via Implementation Letters of any recipients of such funding and the Parties further agree that any such implementing partner carrying out activities in furtherance of the Objective shall receive all of the rights, privileges and other benefits set forth in this Agreement.

Section 3.2. ***Grantee Contribution.***

(a) The Grantee agrees to provide or cause to be provided all funds, in addition to those provided by USAID and any other donor identified in Annex 1, and all other resources required to complete, on or before the Completion Date, all activities necessary to achieve the Objectives. The basis for determining the Grantee's contribution and the nature of the contribution will be further described in an Implementation Letter.

(b) The Grantee's contribution, based on USAID's contribution in Section 3.1(a), will not be less than the equivalent of one-third of the portion of the Grant that is used to support activities that directly benefit the Grantee or involves the direct and substantial involvement of the Government of Ghana in the administration, provided that such amount may be reduced with the written consent of USAID. The Grantee's contribution may include either cash or in-kind contributions or both. The dollar equivalent amount of the Grantee's contribution shall be set forth in an Implementation Letter and shall be subsequently included in the Illustrative Financial Plan included in Annex 1 of this Agreement. The amount of the Grantee's contribution shall be adjusted upon any increase in the amount of the Grant set forth in Section 3.1(a), in accordance with the formula described in the first sentence of this paragraph, and the precise amount of such adjustment shall be indicated in an Implementation Letter. The Grantee will report at least annually in a format to be agreed upon with USAID on its cash and in-kind contributions.

Article 4: Completion Date.

(a) The Completion Date, which is September 30, 2018 or such other date as the Parties may agree to in writing, is the date by which the Parties estimate that all the activities necessary to achieve the Objective will be completed.

(b) Except as USAID may otherwise agree to in writing, USAID will not issue or approve documentation that would authorize disbursement of the Grant for services performed or goods furnished after the Completion Date.

(c) Requests for disbursement, accompanied by necessary supporting documentation prescribed in Implementation Letters, are to be received by USAID no later than nine (9) months following the Completion Date, or such other period as USAID agrees to in writing before or after such period. After such period USAID, at any time or times, may give notice in writing to the Grantee and reduce the amount of the Grant by all or any part thereof for which requests for disbursement, accompanied by necessary supporting documentation prescribed in Implementation Letters, were not received before the expiration of such period.

Article 5: Conditions Precedent to Disbursement.

Section 5.1. ***Disbursement.*** Prior to the disbursement under the Grant, or to the issuance by USAID of documentation pursuant to which disbursement will be made, the Grantee will, except as the Parties may otherwise agree in writing, furnish to USAID in form and substance satisfactory to USAID:

(a) An opinion of counsel acceptable to USAID that (i) this Agreement has been duly authorized or ratified by, and executed on behalf of the Grantee, (ii) this Agreement constitutes a valid and legally binding obligation of the Grantee in accordance with all of its terms, and (iii) all internal actions and approvals necessary to give effect to this Agreement have been obtained by or on behalf of the Grantee; and

(b) A signed statement in the name of the person holding or acting in the office of the Grantee specified in Section 7.2, which designates by name and title any additional representatives each of whom may act pursuant to Section 7.2.

Section 5.2. Notification. USAID will promptly notify the Grantee when USAID has determined that a condition precedent has been met.

Section 5.3. Terminal Dates for Conditions Precedent.

(a) The terminal date for meeting the conditions specified in Section 5.1 is sixty (60) days from the date of this Agreement or such later date as USAID may agree to in writing before or after the above terminal date. If the conditions precedent in Section 5.1 have not been met by the above terminal date, USAID, at any time, may terminate this Agreement by written notice to the Grantee.

Article 6: Special Covenants.

The parties agree to carry out the terms of the following special covenants:

Section 6.1 ***Permits and Other Approvals and Authorizations.***

The Grantee, in conjunction with the appropriate Government of Ghana ministries and offices, hereby covenants and agrees to issue, renew and/or extend free of charge and in a timely manner all official permits, visas, exemptions and any other permissions (including all approvals as may be required from time to time to ensure full access to information, project sites and relevant offices) for the Applicable Persons (as defined below) carrying out activities financed by USAID under this Agreement (collectively, the "Required Documents"). For purposes of this provision, Applicable Persons is defined as: (1) employees and consultants of any contractors, grantees and other organizations carrying out activities financed by USAID under this Agreement and (b) members of such employees' and consultants' households. Any renewals or extensions of such Required Documents that are required, or become required, in order for such employees, consultants and dependent family members to legally reside in Ghana and undertake the activities contemplated by and financed under this Agreement shall also be issued free of charge.

Section 6.2 ***Monitoring and Evaluation***.

Except as the Parties otherwise stipulate in writing, the Parties agree that:

(a) USAID and its implementing partners will systematically monitor and report progress on performance indicators during the Agreement period (illustrative indicators are described in Annex 1);

(b) The strategy baseline survey conducted by USAID at the beginning of this Agreement will serve as a baseline for measuring progress under this Agreement:

(c) Funds available under this Agreement may be used for monitoring and evaluation purposes (such costs are part of the "Management Support Costs" indicated in the Illustrative Financial Plan); and

(d) The Grantee, through the Ministry of Food and Agriculture, the Ministry of Trade and Industry, and the Ministry of Energy will ensure that public sector agencies associated with the Agreement undertake reasonable efforts to produce and/or obtain and provide to USAID all data needed to measure performance of activities under this Agreement.

Article 7: Miscellaneous.

Section 7.1. ***Communications***. Any notice, request, document, or other communication submitted by either Party to the other under this Agreement will be in writing or by telegram, telefax, cable or electronic mail ("e-mail"), and will be deemed duly given or sent when delivered to such Party at the following address:

To USAID:
Mail Address:
Mission Director
United States Agency for International Development
No. 24 Fourth Circular Rd.
P.O. Box GP 194 ACCRA
Cantonments, Accra, Ghana

Email: canderson@usaid.gov
Alternate address for cables:
Telefax: (233) 302-741-365

To the Grantee:
Mail Address:
Minister
Ministry of Finance and Economic Planning
P.O. Box M.40
Accra, Ghana

Email:
Alternate address for cables:
Telefax: (233)21-666556

All such communications will be in English, unless the Parties otherwise agree in writing. Other addresses may be substituted for the above upon the giving of notice.

Section 7.2. ***Representatives.*** For all purposes relevant to this Agreement, the Grantee will be represented by the individual holding or acting in the Ministry of Finance and Economic Planning, and USAID will be represented by the individual holding or acting in the Office of the Director of USAID/Ghana, each of whom, by written notice, may designate additional representatives for all implementation actions as specified under Annex 1. The names and titles of the additional representatives of the Grantee, with specimen signatures, will be provided pursuant to Section 5.1(b) to USAID, which may accept as duly authorized any instrument signed by such additional representatives (or any individuals subsequent holding or acting in the office of such representatives) in accordance with this Section 7.2, until receipt of written notice of revocation of their authority.

Section 7.3. ***Standard Provisions Annex.*** A "Standard Provisions Annex" (Annex 2) is attached to and forms part of this Agreement.

Section 7.4. ***Language of Agreement.*** This Agreement was prepared only in English.

IN WITNESS WHEREOF, the United States of America and the Grantee, each acting through its duly authorized representatives, have caused this Agreement to be signed in their names and delivered as of the day and year first above written.

UNITED STATES OF AMERICA

[Signature]

Cheryl Anderson
Mission Director
United States Agency for International Development

Date: 9/26/12

REPUBLIC OF GHANA

[Signature]

Minister
Ministry of Finance and Economic Planning

DR. KWABENA DUFFUOR
MIN. OF FIN. & ECON. PLANNING
P. O. BOX MB 40
ACCRA

Date: 9/26/12

STATE DEPARTMENT DOCUMENT NUMBER: 12-189

AMENDMENT NUMBER THIRTEEN TO THE STRATEGIC OBJECTIVE GRANT AGREEMENT OF AUGUST 23, 2005, AS AMENDED, BETWEEN THE UNITED STATES OF AMERICA AND THE UNITED REPUBLIC OF TANZANIA FOR STRATEGIC OBJECTIVE NO. 11, HEALTH STATUS OF TANZANIAN FAMILIES IMPROVED, WITH ANNEX

SIGNED ON SEPTEMBER 24 AND 26, 2012
ENTERED INTO FORCE SEPTEMBER 26, 2012

CTIA DOCUMENT NUMBER: 13650.004

R. M. Khijjah The Permanent Secretary, Ministry of Finance and Economic Affairs and Robert F. Cunnane, USAID Mission Director, Tanzania

Signed By: [Signature]

Robert F. Cunnane
Mission Director

Dated: Nov 13, 2012

Agreement Number 621-0011.01-13

Date: SEPTEMBER 26, 2012

AMENDMENT NUMBER THIRTEEN TO THE STRATEGIC OBJECTIVE GRANT AGREEMENT BETWEEN

The United Republic of Tanzania, represented by the Ministry of Finance ("GOT")

AND

The United States of America, acting through The United States Agency for International Development ("USAID")

This is Amendment Number Thirteen to the Strategic Objective Grant Agreement for Strategic Objective 11, Health Status of Tanzanian Families Improved dated August 23, 2005 (as amended, the "Agreement"), between USAID and the GOT ("the Parties") as amended by the Parties through Amendment Number One on May 23, 2006, Amendment Number Two on August 2, 2006, Amendment Number Three of August 24, 2007, Amendment Number Four on September 11, 2007, Amendment Number Five on March 27, 2008, Amendment Number Six on April 30, 2008, Amendment Number Seven on August 15, 2008, Amendment Number Eight on December 22, 2008, Amendment Number Nine on April 8, 2009, Amendment Number Ten on September 10, 2009, Amendment Number Eleven on August 23, 2010 and Amendment Number Twelve on September 29, 2011.

WHEREAS, the Parties hereto desire to make an amendment to the Agreement by: (1) funding the USAID grant by an additional increment of Seventy-Eight Million, Fifty Five Thousand, Six Hundred Forty Nine United States ('U.S') Dollars ($78,055,649) (2) funding Twenty-Six Million, One Hundred Sixty-Four Thousand, Nine Hundred Six U.S. Dollars ($26,164,906) in additional support, which has been obligated outside of this Agreement by USAID/Tanzania and through field support by USAID/Washington into grants or contracts to carry out activities in Tanzania in furtherance of the objectives under this Agreement; (3) increasing the Estimated Life of Agreement Funding by One Hundred Four Million, Two Hundred Twenty Thousand, Five Hundred Fifty Five U.S. Dollars ($104,220,555) to Four Hundred Seventy-One Million, Five Hundred Seventy Six Thousand, Six Hundred Seventy Six U.S. Dollars ($471,576,676); and (4) amending the Illustrative Financial Plan for the purposes of supporting malaria control activities, family planning and reproductive health activities, maternal and child health activities, and infectious disease activities.

NOW THEREFORE, the Agreement is hereby amended as follows:

1. Article 3, Section 3.1, paragraph (a), "The Grant" is hereby deleted in its entirety and replaced by the following:

> "(a) The Grant. To help achieve the Objective and Results set forth in this Agreement, USAID, pursuant to the Foreign Assistance Act of 1961, as amended, hereby grants to the GOT under the terms of this agreement, as amended, an amount not to exceed Four Hundred Seventy-One Million, Five Hundred Seventy Six Thousand, Six Hundred Seventy Six U.S. Dollars ($471,576,676); (the "Grant").

2. Article 3, Section 3.1 paragraph (b), "Total Estimated Contribution" is hereby deleted in its entirety and replaced by the following:

> "(b) Total Estimated USAID Contribution. USAID's total estimated contribution to achievement of the Objective shall be Four Hundred Seventy-One Million, Five Hundred Seventy Six Thousand, Six Hundred Seventy Six U.S. Dollars ($471,576,676); all of which has been obligated to date and is to be provided in increments. Of this amount, Three Hundred Nineteen Million, Four Hundred Twenty One Thousand, Three Hundred Ninety U.S. Dollars ($319,421,390) has been granted directly under this Agreement; Twenty-Five Million, Eight Hundred Twenty- Four Thousand, Seven Hundred Twenty-Nine U.S. Dollars ($25,824,729) has been obligated by USAID/Tanzania directly into grants or contracts to provide early funding for inside residual spraying and other activities for malaria control program under the US Presidential Malaria Initiative (PMI) in Tanzania; and One Hundred Twenty-Six Million, Three Hundred Thirty Thousand, Five Hundred Fifty-Seven U.S. Dollars ($126,330,557) has been obligated by USAID/Washington directly into grants or contracts to carry out activities in Tanzania in furtherance of the objectives under this Agreement. Subsequent increments are subject to the availability of funds to USAID for this purpose and the mutual agreement of the Parties, at the time of each subsequent increment, to proceed."

2. The Strategic Objective Grant Agreement 621-0011.01-13 Illustrative Budget contained in Annex 1 is hereby deleted in its entirety and replaced with a new "Annex 1 Illustrative Budget," which is attached hereto.

3. Except as amended herein, all other terms and conditions of the Strategic Objective Grant Agreement, as amended, remain in full force and effect in accordance with its terms.

IN WITNESS WHEREOF, THE Government of the United Republic of Tanzania and the Government of the United States of America, each acting through its duly authorized representative, have caused this Amendment Number Thirteen to the Strategic Objective Grant Agreement for Strategic Objective 11, Health Status of Tanzania Families Improved to be made effective as of the day and year above written.

ON BEHALF OF THE GOVERNMENT OF THE UNITED REPUBLIC OF TANZANIA

By: [Signature]

PERMANENT SECRETARY
MINISTRY OF FINANCE
P.O. Box 9111
DAR ES SALAAM

Name: R. M. KHIJJAH

Title: PERMAMENT SECRETARY

Date: 24.09.2012

ON BEHALF OF THE GOVERNMENT OF THE UNITED STATES OF AMERICA

By: [Signature]

Name: Robert F. Cunnane

Title: Mission Director

Date: Sept 26, 2012

Annex 1 to the 13th Amendment to SOAG 621-0011.01

Annex 1 to the Amplified Description Financial Plan
Strategic Objective Grant Agreement Illustrative Budget (U.S. $)

	Direct Obligations Under SOAG *Amendment #13*[1]			Obligated by USAID/Tanzania Outside of the Agreement[2]			Indirect Obligations via USAID/ Washington ("Field Support") Under this Agreement[3]				
	Previous Obligations	**New Obligations[5][6]**	**Obligations to Date**	**Previous Obligations**	**New Obligations**	**Obligations to Date**	**Previous Obligations**	**New Obligations**	**Obligations to Date**	**Total Agreement Funding to Date**	**Estimated Life of Agreement Funding**
Public Sector Program Support	$216,929,456	$74,124,969	$291,054,425	$25,422,073	$0	$25,422,073	$93,132,763	$26,164,906	$119,297,669	$435,774,167	
Social Marketing / Voluntary Sector	$13,174,068	0	$13,174,068	$0	$0	$0	$4,397,000	$0	$4,397,000	$17,571,068	
Administration[4]	$11,262,217	$3,930,680	$15,192,897	$402,656	$0	$402,656	$2,635,888	0	$2,635,888	$18,231,441	
Total Budget	$241,365,741	$78,055,649	$319,421,390	$25,824,729	$0	$25,824,729	$100,165,651	$26,164,906	$126,330,557	$471,576,676	$471,576,676

[1] FY 2012 funds obligated bilaterally through this amendment.

[2] FY 2012 funds obligated by USAID/Tanzania outside of this agreement but in support of Strategic Objective 11.

[3] Resources under "Field Support" are for commodities and activities in the Public Sector, Social Marketing, Voluntary Health Services and Administrative areas contracted by USAID/Washington for activities directly implemented in Tanzania.

[4] The Line Item "Administration" is for personnel, monitoring and evaluation, audit, procurement of commodities, and other costs related to administration of the SO11 program.

[5] Includes $153,568 which are 2012-GH-H-X(PEPFAR) funds under "Public Sector Program Support"

[6] Includes $196,761 which are 2011/2012 DV funds under "Administration" for evaluation of an HIV/AIDS project (Engender Health)

STATE DEPARTMENT DOCUMENT NUMBER: 12-190

AMENDMENT NUMBER THIRTEEN TO THE STRATEGIC OBJECTIVE GRANT AGREEMENT OF JULY 26, 2005, AS AMENDED, BETWEEN THE UNITED STATES OF AMERICA AND THE UNITED REPUBLIC OF TANZANIA FOR STRATEGIC OBJECTIVE NO. 12: INCOMES OF SMALL FARMERS INCREASED IN SELECTED AGRICULTURAL COMMODITY SUB-SECTORS, WITH ANNEX

SIGNED ON SEPTEMBER 22 AND 26, 2012
ENTERED INTO FORCE SEPTEMBER 26, 2012

CTIA DOCUMENT NUMBER: 13784.003

Certified to be a true copy of the original signed by R. M. Khijjah The Permanent Secretary, Ministry of Finance and Economic Affairs and Robert F. Cunnane, USAID Mission Director, Tanzania.

Signed By: [Signature]
Robert F. Cunnane
Mission Director

Dated: Nov 13, 2012

Agreement Number 621-0012.13

Date: SEPTEMBER 26, 2012

Amendment Number Thirteen to the Strategic Objective Grant Agreement

between

The United Republic of Tanzania, represented by The Ministry of Finance ("GOT")

and

The United States of America, acting through The United States Agency for International Development ("USAID")

1. *Purpose of the Amendment*

This is Amendment Number Thirteen to the Strategic Objective Agreement for SO-12, Incomes of Small Farmers Increased in Selected Commodity Sub-sectors, dated July 26, 2005 (the "Agreement") between USAID and the GOT (the "Parties"), as amended by the Parties through Amendment Number One on September 2, 2005, Amendment Number Two on September 26, 2005, Amendment Number Three on September 13, 2006, Amendment Number Four on August 3, 2007, Amendment Number Five on August 28, 2008, Amendment Number Six on September 28, 2009, Amendment Number Seven on November 16, 2009, Amendment Number Eight on January 5, 2010, Amendment Number Nine on September 16, 2010, Amendment Number Ten on July 13, 2011, Amendment Number Eleven on September 19, 2011, and Amendment Number Twelve on February 22, 2012.

WHEREAS, the Parties hereto desire to amend the Agreement by: (1) funding the USAID grant by an increment of Seventy-Seven Million, Two Hundred Thousand United States ('U.S') Dollars ($77,200,000) to support existing agriculture-related activities as part of the Feed the Future initiative; and (2) amending the Illustrative Financial Plan contained in Annex 1 of the Agreement.

2. *Financing*

Article 3, Section 3.1, paragraph (a), "The Grant," is hereby deleted in its entirety and replaced by the following:

> "(a) The Grant. To help achieve the Objective and Results set forth in this Agreement, USAID, pursuant to the Foreign Assistance Act of 1961, as amended, hereby grants to the GOT under the terms of this Agreement, as amended, an amount not to exceed Two Hundred Eleven Million, Seven Hundred Ninety-Five Thousand, Five Hundred Forty-Six U.S Dollars ($211,795,546) (the "Grant")".

Article 3, Section 3.1 paragraph (b), "Total Estimated Contribution", is hereby deleted in its entirety and replaced by the following:

> "(b)(i) Total Estimated USAID Contribution. USAID's total estimated contribution to achievement of the Objective will be Two Hundred and Nine Million, Two Hundred Seventy-Three Thousand, Nine Hundred Sixty-Four U.S Dollars ($209,273,964) (the entirety of which has been directly obligated under this Agreement.
>
> (b)(ii) An additional amount of Two Million Five Hundred Twenty-One Thousand, Five Hundred Eighty-Two U.S. Dollars ($2,521,582) has been obligated outside of this Agreement by USAID/Tanzania and USAID/Washington directly into grants and/or contracts, to carry out activities in Tanzania in furtherance of the objectives of this Agreement."

3. *Illustrative Financial Plan*

The Illustrative Financial Plan contained in Annex 1 of Strategic Objective Agreement number 621-0012.12 is hereby replaced in its entirety and a new Illustrative Financial Plan, which is attached hereto, is hereby substituted.

4. *Other Terms and Conditions*

Except as amended herein, all other terms and conditions of the Agreement remain in full force and effect.

IN WITNESS WHEREOF, the United States of America and the Government of the United Republic of Tanzania, each acting through its respective duly authorized representatives, have caused this Thirteenth Amendment to be made effective as of the day and year first written above.

ON BEHALF OF THE GOVERNMENT OF THE UNITED REPUBLIC OF TANZANIA

BY: [Signature]

NAME: R. M. KHIJJAH

TITLE: PERMANENT SECRETARY

DATE: 22.09.2012

ON BEHALF OF THE GOVERNMENT OF THE UNITED STATES OF AMERICA

BY: [Signature]

NAME: Robert F. Cunnane

TITLE: Mission Director

DATE: Sept 26, 2012

Annex 1 to the 13th Amendment to SOAG 621-0012.13

Amplified Description Financial Plan
Strategic Objective Grant Agreement Illustrative Budget (U.S $)
7/6/2012

BUDGET LINES	PRIOR OBLIGATIONS			AMENDMENT #13 OBLIGATIONS						OBLIGATIONS TO DATE			
				Feed the Future (Agriculture & Nutrition)			Social Assistance Program						
	Directly thru this Agreement	By Mission outside this Agreement	Indirectly thru USAID Washington	Directly thru this Agreement[1]	By Mission outside this Agreement[2]	Indirectly thru USAID Washington[3]	Directly thru this Agreement[1]	By Mission outside this Agreement[2]	Indirectly thru USAID Washington[3]	Directly thru this Agreement	By Mission outside this Agreement	Indirectly thru USAID Washington	Total
IR 12.1 Increased Productivity of Selected Agricultural Commodities	$104,182,541	$0	$858,000	$73,100,000	$0	$1,207,000	$0	$0	$0	$177,282,541	$0	$2,065,000	$179,347,541
IR 12.2 Increased Trade of Selected Agricultural Commodities	$16,386,184	$0	$0	$0	$0	$0	$0	$0	$0	$16,386,184	$0	$0	$16,386,184
Administration[4]	$12,712,239	$306,582	$150,000	$2,893,000	$0	$0	$0	$0	$0	$15,605,239	$306,582	$150,000	$16,061,821
Total	***$133,280,964***	***$306,582***	***$1,008,000***	***$75,993,000***	***$0***	***$1,207,000***	***$0***	***$0***	***$0***	***$209,273,964***	***$306,582***	***$2,215,000***	***$211,795,546***

[1] FY 2012 funds obligated bilaterally through this amendment.

[2] FY 2012 funds obligated by USAID/Tanzania outside of this agreement but in support of Strategic Objective 12.

[3] FY 2012 funds obligated through USAID/Washington Global Field Support mechanisms in support of Strategic Objective 12.

[4] The line item "Administration" will be used to finance personnel; monitoring and evaluation; audits; procurement of commodities and services; training; and other costs related to the administration of the Strategic Objective 12 Program.

STATE DEPARTMENT DOCUMENT NUMBER: 12-191

AGREEMENT BETWEEN THE DEPARTMENT OF DEFENSE OF THE UNITED STATES OF AMERICA AND THE MINISTRY OF DEFENSE OF THE REPUBLIC OF ECUADOR CONCERNING HEALTH CARE FOR MILITARY MEMBERS AND THEIR DEPENDENTS

SIGNED AT QUITO AND WASHINGTON D.C.,
SEPTEMBER 27 AND OCTOBER 5, 2012
ENTERED INTO FORCE OCTOBER 5, 2012

CTIA DOCUMENT NUMBER: 18091.000

The Department of Defense of the United States of America and the Ministry of Defense of the Republic of Ecuador, hereinafter referred to as "the Parties," desire effective cooperation in an exchange of health care;

Whereas, the laws and regulations of the United States provide that inpatient medical care in Department of Defense military medical treatment facilities in the United States may be furnished on a space-available basis without cost to foreign force members and their accompanying dependents in the United States, if comparable care is made available to a comparable number of United States force members and their dependents in the country of the foreign force member;

Whereas the Parties have determined that appropriate conditions exist to assure that comparable care for comparable numbers of persons may be made available by each Party; and

Considering the importance of establishing cooperative actions for the availability of medical care under the principle of reciprocity;

The Parties agree as follows:

ARTICLE I
Objective

This Agreement establishes an understanding between the Parties that reciprocal inpatient medical treatment and other medical treatment may be made available at military treatment facilities for the military members and their dependents of the Armed Forces of the United States of America and the Ministry of Defense of the Republic of Ecuador on a space-available basis. Medical care that may be provided at the military medical facilities in the respective territory of each Party shall be without charge.

ARTICLE II
Definitions

1. Dependents: The term "dependents" is defined as follows:

a. Spouse: A person who, based on the laws and military regulations of the military member's country, is considered to be the lawful wife or husband of the military member.

b. Dependent child: A military member's child who depends on the military member for support, and who has not attained the age of 21, or if enrolled in a full-time course of study at an institution of higher learning, the age of 23.

2. Subsistence surcharge: A charge for meals consumed in the military treatment facilities of the Parties.

ARTICLE III
Scope

This Agreement applies to military members, and their dependents, of the United States of America and Ecuadorian military members, and their dependents, who are in each other's country at the official invitation of the receiving Government, or who are in each other's country as crew of a visiting military aircraft or military vessel that lands at each other's airfields or visits each other's ports on official military business.

In addition to the dependents of the Ecuadorian military members covered in the preceding paragraph, the accompanying dependents of a military student in the International Military Education & Training (IMET) Program shall be covered (understanding that the IMET Program covers the IMET students).

No more than six Ecuadorian officers and their dependents assigned to the Inter-American Defense Board and the Inter-American Defense College are covered by this Agreement. The senior defense military attaché of Ecuador will select those eligible for care.

Requirements for identification and proof of eligibility by persons requesting health care under this Agreement shall be as prescribed by the Party furnishing the care.

ARTICLE IV
Representatives

In the implementation and administration of this Agreement, the Representative of the Department of Defense of the United States shall be the Assistant Secretary of Defense for Health Affairs, and the Representative of the Ministry of Defense of the Republic of Ecuador shall be the Minister of Defense.

ARTICLE V
Medical Attention Available

1. The Department of Defense of the United States may make available in its military treatment facilities in the United States of America:

a. for Ecuadorian military members covered by this agreement, outpatient and inpatient care in Department of Defense medical and dental treatment facilities, without charge (except for a subsistence surcharge, if applicable). Medications available at the military treatment facilities are available without charge.

b. for dependents accompanying those military members:

i. outpatient and inpatient medical care in Department of Defense medical treatment facilities, without charge (except for a subsistence surcharge, if applicable); and

ii. dental care in Department of Defense medical and dental facilities, without charge, to the same extent that such care may be made available in military medical treatment facilities within the United States to dependents of United States military members.

2. If care is provided pursuant to paragraph 1 of this Article, Ecuadorian military members and their dependents receiving care in a Department of Defense military medical treatment facility shall receive a copy of the medical records regarding the care provided and any follow-on treatment plan for their personal medical records.

3. The Ministry of Defense of the Republic of Ecuador may make available in their military medical treatment facilities in Ecuador:

a. for United States military members covered by this Agreement, outpatient and inpatient care in Ministry of Defense medical and dental treatment facilities, without charge (except for a subsistence surcharge, if applicable). Medications available at the military treatment facilities are available without charge.

b. for dependents accompanying those military members:

i. outpatient and inpatient medical care in Ministry of Defense of the Republic of Ecuador medical treatment facilities, without charge (except for a subsistence surcharge, if applicable); and

ii. dental care in Ministry of Defense medical and dental treatment facilities, without charge, to the same extent that such care is made available in military medical treatment facilities within the Ministry of Defense of the Republic of Ecuador to dependents of Ecuadorian military members.

4. If care is provided pursuant to paragraph 3 of this Article, United States military members and their dependents receiving care in a Ministry of Defense of the Republic of Ecuador military medical treatment facility shall receive a copy of the medical records regarding the care provided and any follow-on treatment plan for their personal medical records.

ARTICLE VI
Expenses

Each party shall pay the expenses resulting from treatment it provides pursuant to this Agreement, in accordance with its applicable laws and regulations, and subject to the availability of funds appropriated for these purposes.

ARTICLE VII
Dispute Resolution

Questions relating to interpretation of the provisions of this Agreement, or implementation of this Agreement, shall be resolved through consultations between the Representatives of the Parties.

ARTICLE VIII
Final Dispositions

This Agreement shall enter into force on the date of the final signature and shall remain in force for three years, unless terminated by either Party by giving at least ninety days written notice to the other Party. It may be extended by mutual written agreement of the Parties.

This Agreement may be amended by mutual written agreement of the Parties.

This Agreement is in two originals in the English and Spanish languages, both texts being equally authentic.

For the Department of Defense
of the United States of America

[Signature]

ERIN C. CONATON
Under Secretary of Defense
(Personnel and Readiness)

Date: 27 September 2012

For the Ministry of Defense of the
Republic of Ecuador

[Signature]

MIGUEL CARVAJAL
Minister of Defense

Date: 5 October 2012

Certified True Copy
[Signature]
Col Edwin A. Hurston

STATE DEPARTMENT DOCUMENT NUMBER: 12-192

FRAMEWORK AGREEMENT ON INTEGRATED CROSS-BORDER MARITIME LAW ENFORCEMENT OPERATIONS BETWEEN THE UNITED STATES OF AMERICA AND CANADA

SIGNED AT DETROIT, MAY 26, 2009
ENTERED INTO FORCE OCTOBER 11, 2012

CTIA DOCUMENT NUMBER: 18092.000

PREAMBLE

THE GOVERNMENT OF THE UNITED STATES OF AMERICA and **THE GOVERNMENT OF CANADA** (hereinafter "the Parties");

CONSIDERING that it is in the common interest of both countries to enhance their border co-operation;

RECOGNISING the principle of sovereignty of states;

RECOGNISING the importance of respecting fundamental rights and freedoms notably privacy;

COMMITTED to the prevention, detection, suppression, investigation, and prosecution of any criminal offence or violation of law related to border enforcement including, but not limited to, the illicit drug trade, migrant smuggling, trafficking of firearms, the smuggling of counterfeit goods and money, and terrorism;

DESIRING Integrated Cross-Border Maritime Law Enforcement operations to be intelligence-driven, based on joint United States-Canada threat and risk assessment and coordinated with existing cooperative cross-border policing programs and activities;

RECALLING their continuing cooperation and record of successful partnership in pursuing seamless law enforcement operations at their shared border; and

COGNISANT of the reciprocal nature of this Agreement;

HAVE AGREED as follows:

ARTICLE 1
Purpose of the Agreement

The purpose of this Agreement is to provide the Parties additional means in shared waterways to prevent, detect, suppress, investigate, and prosecute criminal offences or violations of law including, but not limited to, illicit drug trade, migrant smuggling, trafficking of firearms, the smuggling of counterfeit goods and money, and terrorism.

ARTICLE 2
Definitions

1. **"Designated cross-border maritime law enforcement officer"** means: an individual designated or appointed pursuant to Article 6.

2. **"Host country"** means: the Party in whose territory an activity in the context of integrated cross-border maritime law enforcement operations is taking place.

3. **"Integrated cross-border maritime law enforcement operation"** means: the deployment of a vessel crewed jointly by designated cross-border maritime law enforcement officers from the United States and Canada for law enforcement or related purposes in shared waterways.

4. **"Participating agency"** means: an agency directly participating in integrated cross-border maritime law enforcement operations.

5. **"Shared waterways"** means: undisputed areas of the sea or internal waters along the international boundary between the United States and Canada.

ARTICLE 3
Scope of Integrated Cross-Border Maritime Law Enforcement Operations

1. Integrated cross-border maritime law enforcement operations shall only take place in shared waterways except as otherwise provided by this Article.

2. Designated cross-border maritime law enforcement officers shall only enforce the domestic laws of the host country within which they find themselves as directed by a designated cross-border maritime law enforcement officer of the host country.

3. In urgent and exceptional circumstances designated cross-border maritime law enforcement officers may continue activities undertaken in the course of an integrated cross-border maritime law enforcement operation on land adjacent to shared waterways.

4. For the purposes of this Article, urgent and exceptional circumstances include circumstances in which a designated cross-border maritime law enforcement officer has reasonable grounds to suspect that the continuation of the activities undertaken in the course of integrated cross-border maritime law enforcement operations on land adjacent to shared waterways is necessary to prevent:

(a) imminent bodily harm or death to any person;

(b) the immediate and unlawful flight of persons liable to detention or arrest; or

(c) the imminent loss or imminent destruction of evidence.

5. In all instances where designated cross-border maritime law enforcement officers continue activities on land adjacent to shared waterways they shall notify the appropriate host country law enforcement authorities as soon as operationally practicable.

ARTICLE 4
Direction of Integrated Cross-Border Maritime Law Enforcement Operations

Integrated cross-border maritime law enforcement operations shall only be carried out as directed by a designated cross-border maritime law enforcement officer of the host country.

ARTICLE 5
Central Authorities

1. The Parties designate the following central authorities to co-ordinate the implementation of this Agreement:

(a) The Government of Canada designates the Commissioner of the Royal Canadian Mounted Police or his or her designate as its Central Authority.

(b) The Government of the United States designates the Commandant of the United States Coast Guard or his or her designate as its Central Authority.

2. A Party may change the designated Central Authority upon written notification thereof to the other Party.

ARTICLE 6
Designation

1. The Central Authority for the United States may appoint or arrange for the appointment of an individual as a designated cross-border maritime law enforcement officer who is a:

(a) member of the Royal Canadian Mounted Police; or

(b) police officer appointed or employed under the law of a province of Canada and who has:

(i) been recommended for appointment by the Central Authority for Canada; and

(ii) satisfactorily completed all the required training for appointment as a designated cross-border maritime law enforcement officer in accordance with Article 7(1)(a).

2. The Central Authority for the United States may appoint or arrange for the appointment of an individual as a designated cross-border maritime law enforcement officer who is a pilot, co-pilot, observer or other member of the crew of an aircraft operated by the Royal Canadian Mounted Police or a police service established under the law of a province of Canada providing aerial support to an integrated cross-border maritime law enforcement operation who has:

(a) been recommended for appointment by the Central Authority for Canada; and

(b) satisfactorily completed all the required training for appointment as a designated cross-border maritime law enforcement officer in accordance with Article 7(1)(b).

3. The Central Authority for Canada may appoint an individual as a designated cross-border maritime law enforcement officer who is:

(a) a commissioned, warrant, or petty officer of the United States Coast Guard; or

(b) a police officer or other law enforcement officer appointed or employed under the law of the United States of America or of a State of the United States of America and who has:

(i) been recommended for appointment by the Central Authority for the United States; and

(ii) satisfactorily completed all the required training for appointment as a designated cross-border maritime law enforcement officer in accordance with Article 7(1)(a).

4. The Central Authority for Canada may appoint an individual as a designated cross-border maritime law enforcement officer who is a pilot, co-pilot, observer or other member of the crew of an aircraft operated by the United States Coast Guard or a police service or other law enforcement agency of the United States of America or of a State of the United States of America providing aerial support to an integrated cross-border maritime law enforcement operation who has:

(a) been recommended for appointment by the Central Authority for the United States; and

(b) satisfactorily completed all the required training for appointment as a designated cross-border maritime law enforcement officer in accordance with Article 7(1)(b).

5. A designation under this Article shall remain in force until it is suspended, revoked or withdrawn.

6. A cross-border maritime law enforcement officer designated under paragraphs 1 and 2 of this Article shall have the powers of a Customs Officer (excepted) in accordance with United States law while operating in the United States.

7. A cross-border maritime law enforcement officer designated under paragraphs 3 and 4 of this Article shall have the powers of a peace officer in accordance with Canadian law while operating in Canada.

8. Each Party shall establish and promulgate a single document setting out the policies that apply to integrated cross-border maritime law enforcement operations and training for and in their respective territories.

ARTICLE 7
Training

1. The Central Authorities shall coordinate the development of and approve a joint training program for designated cross-border maritime law enforcement officers that includes training on the applicable laws, regulations, constitutional considerations and policies of both Parties, and in particular, depending on the anticipated role of the integrated cross-border maritime law enforcement officer, those pertaining to:

(a) the use of force, marine safety, operational procedures and protection of informants and other sensitive information; and

(b) aviation regulations and flight safety procedures.

2. The Central Authorities shall, from time to time, review the joint training program.

ARTICLE 8
Customs and Immigration Reporting

To facilitate integrated cross-border maritime law enforcement operations, the Parties shall provide designated cross-border maritime law enforcement officers alternative mechanisms to meet customs and immigration reporting requirements between ports of entry.

ARTICLE 9
Work Permits

To facilitate integrated cross-border maritime law enforcement operations, each Party shall, to the extent required by its domestic law, provide exemptions from work permit requirements to designated cross-border maritime law enforcement officers.

ARTICLE 10
Custody of Persons, Vessels, or Things Detained or Seized

1. In all cases where a person, vessel, or thing is detained or seized, during the course of an integrated cross-border maritime law enforcement operation, such person, vessel, or thing shall be dealt with in accordance with the laws of the host country.

2. In no case shall any person, vessel, or thing detained or seized in the host country be removed from the host country except in accordance with the laws of the host country.

3. Paragraph 2 shall not apply in respect of any vessel or thing detained or seized in the host country in situations of operational or geographical necessity including when:

(a) before delivering the vessel or thing that was lawfully seized to the place where the vessel or thing is to be delivered in the host country, designated integrated cross-border maritime law enforcement officers are required to participate in continuing integrated cross-border maritime law enforcement activities or respond to an emergency in the waters of the other Party;

(b) due to poor weather or mechanical difficulties with a vessel operated by designated integrated cross-border maritime law enforcement officers it is necessary to transit through the waters of the other Party in order to reach the nearest port; or,

(c) the navigable shipping channels between the location in the host country where the vessel or thing was lawfully seized and the place where the vessel or thing is to be delivered in the host country pass through the waters of the other Party.

4. In situations of operational or geographical necessity described in paragraph 3 when a vessel or thing lawfully seized in the host country is transported through the waters of the other Party, that vessel or thing remains under the physical custody and control of the designated cross-border law enforcement officer of the host country.

ARTICLE 11
Accountability

1. While engaging in integrated cross-border maritime law enforcement operations a designated cross-border maritime law enforcement officer shall be subject to the domestic laws of the Party in whose territory any criminal misconduct is alleged to have occurred and be subject to the jurisdiction of the courts of that Party subject to the rights and privileges that a law enforcement officer

from the host country would be able to assert in the same situation and subject to the rights and privileges that the host country would be able to assert in the same situation.

2. Any claim submitted for damage, harm, injury, death or loss resulting from an integrated cross-border maritime law enforcement operation carried out by a Party under this Agreement shall be resolved in accordance with the domestic law of the Party to which the claim is brought and with international law. The Parties shall consult at the request of either Party with a view to resolving the matter and deciding any questions relating to compensation or payment.

3. Each Party shall make best efforts to ensure the cooperation of designated cross-border maritime law enforcement officers with any investigation, inquest or hearing that relates to an internal investigation or is held by a civilian oversight body into the exercise of enforcement powers by such officers, subject to the rights and privileges that a law enforcement officer from the country in which the investigation or proceeding takes place would be able to assert in the same situation and subject to the rights and privileges that country would be able to assert in the same situation. Upon request, each Party shall make best efforts to provide all unclassified documents and other unclassified information relating to a designated cross-border maritime law enforcement operation that is the subject of an investigation, inquest or hearing that relates to an internal investigation or is held by a civilian oversight body.

4. The participating agency that employs a designated cross-border maritime law enforcement officer shall be solely responsible for the professional review of and discipline procedures for its participating officers. If a participating agency undertakes any professional review and discipline procedure arising from cross-border maritime law enforcement activity, then the Central Authority shall ensure that any results from such a procedure are communicated to the other Central Authority.

5. A Party may decline to cooperate under paragraphs 3 and 4 of this Article only where such cooperation would be contrary to or inconsistent with its public policy, substantive national interests, domestic law and regulations, or interferes with an ongoing investigation or prosecution.

6. Before denying or postponing cooperation the Party, through its Central Authority, shall:

(a) promptly inform the other Party of the reason for considering denial or postponement; and

(b) consult with the other Party to determine whether assistance may be given subject to such terms and conditions as the Party whose cooperation is at issue deems necessary.

ARTICLE 12
Firearms, Ammunitions and Other Standard Law Enforcement Weapons

While engaging in integrated cross-border maritime law enforcement operations in shared waterways a designated cross-border maritime law enforcement officer may carry firearms, ammunition, and other standard law enforcement weapons jointly approved by the Central Authorities for the United States and Canada.

ARTICLE 13
Use of force

The designated cross-border maritime law enforcement officers shall use force only in strict accordance with the applicable laws and policies of the host country where the use of force occurs. In all cases only force that is reasonably necessary under the circumstances shall be used.

ARTICLE 14
Information sharing

1. Subject to their domestic laws, the Parties shall assist each other in the course of integrated cross-border maritime law enforcement operations and may, for that purpose, share such information as may be necessary.

2. For the purposes of Article 14, "further sharing" means: the subsequent sharing of shared information by the receiving participating agency with, among others, a non-participating government agency or a foreign country.

3. Appropriate written arrangements shall be executed by the participating agencies regarding issues of use, further sharing, and correction of shared information, and regarding issues of storage and destruction of recorded shared information in accordance with the domestic laws of the Parties.

4. Unless required by its domestic laws or otherwise permitted by an arrangement executed pursuant to paragraph 3 of this Article, a participating agency shall not use or further share information shared pursuant to this Article for purposes other than United States-Canada integrated cross-border law enforcement operations without the consent of the participating agency sharing the information. If a participating agency uses or shares information shared pursuant to this Article according to its domestic laws, it shall, subject to exigent circumstances, provide notice to the sharing participating agency prior to such use or sharing. In case of exigent circumstances, the participating agency using or sharing the information shall provide notice to the sharing participating agency as soon as reasonably possible.

5. Designated cross-border maritime law enforcement officers shall collect information in strict accordance with the laws of the host country. A participating agency shall not use or further share information collected exclusively in the other Party's territory or waters by its officers for purposes other than Canada-United States integrated cross-border law enforcement operations without the consent of the Party in whose territory or waters the information was collected, unless the use or further sharing is required by its domestic laws, in which case the participating agency shall, subject to exigent circumstances, provide notice to the Party in whose territory or waters the information was collected prior to such use or sharing. In case of exigent circumstances, the participating agency using or sharing the information shall provide notice to the Party in whose territory or waters the information was collected as soon as reasonably possible. Nothing in this paragraph is intended to inhibit the Party in whose territory or waters the information was collected from sharing such information with the other Party pursuant to paragraph 1 of this Article or any other existing arrangements available to the Parties for the sharing of information.

6. Notwithstanding paragraphs 3, 4 and 5, the participating agency sharing the information or in whose territory or waters the information was collected may, in a particular instance, place additional restrictions on the use, sharing and further sharing of this information. Subject to its domestic laws, the participating agency which received or collected the information may accept and comply with any such restrictions or decline to receive or collect the information.

7. Information sharing related to evidence and testimony that may be needed in any criminal investigation and subsequent prosecution or other proceeding resulting from integrated cross-border maritime law enforcement operations shall be conducted pursuant to Article 15 of this Agreement.

8. (a) Nothing in this Agreement is intended to alter or supersede any law enforcement information exchange agreement in effect between the Parties.

(b) Nothing in this Article is intended to preclude a Party from sharing information related to terrorism or weapons of mass destruction with non-participating agencies within its government according to its domestic laws.

ARTICLE 15
Cooperation in Proceedings

1. The participating agencies of the Parties shall fully cooperate in providing information, evidence and testimony that may be needed in any investigation and subsequent prosecution or other proceeding resulting from integrated cross-border maritime law enforcement operations.

2. Cooperation shall include:

(a) using best efforts to facilitate a request by the other Party to provide any relevant information or evidence in the possession or control of the participating agencies; and

(b) using best efforts to facilitate the availability and appearance of any designated cross-border maritime law enforcement officer or other employee of a participating agency in order to give testimony relevant to any prosecution or proceeding resulting from integrated cross-border maritime law enforcement operations.

3. The Central Authority of each Party, or officials designated by the Central Authority, shall have the authority to make, receive and respond to requests for information, evidence and testimony under this Article.

4. If a competent judicial authority of a Party, in relation to a prosecution or other proceeding, issues a subpoena or order relating to the production of information or evidence referenced in paragraph 2(a), or the appearance of a witness referenced in paragraph 2(b), that Party may make a request for such information, evidence or appearance pursuant to paragraph 3, and the relevant participating agency shall use best efforts to facilitate such request.

5. When the Party receiving a request believes that information, evidence or testimony sought pursuant to this Article may include, or give rise to the disclosure of, information that it views as privileged or otherwise sensitive, it shall so advise the requesting Party. Either Party may request consultations to determine whether there are limitations on disclosure, assertions of privilege, restrictions on a potential witness's testimony or other conditions that may be sufficient to address the concerns of the Party receiving a request.

6. Before denying or postponing the provision or facilitation of information, evidence or testimony pursuant to this Article, the Party receiving a request shall, through its Central Authority and in consultation with its relevant prosecution authorities, promptly inform the Central Authority of the requesting Party of the reason for considering denial or postponement. The Central Authority of the requesting Party shall consult with its relevant prosecution authorities to determine whether it may accept the information, evidence or testimony subject to such terms and conditions as the other Party may deem necessary. If the requesting Party accepts assistance subject to such terms and conditions, then it shall comply with said terms and conditions.

7. Unless required by domestic law, a requesting Party shall not use or disclose information, evidence or testimony provided by the other Party other than for the purposes for which it was requested without the prior consent of the Central Authority of the other Party. However,

information, evidence or testimony made public in such prosecution or proceeding may thereafter be used for any purpose.

8. Nothing in this Article shall limit or otherwise affect the rights and obligations of the Parties under other agreements or treaties governing cooperation and mutual assistance in the investigation, prosecution and suppression of crime.

ARTICLE 16
Dispute Resolution

1. The Parties shall seek to resolve the disputes between them that may arise in interpreting or applying this Agreement through consultations between Central Authorities.

2. The Parties shall consult promptly at the request of either Party concerning any dispute which has not been resolved by the Central Authorities.

ARTICLE 17
Expenses and Operational Costs

1. Subject to availability of funds, the Parties shall assume the expenses and operational costs of their respective human and material resources.

2. Costs arising from the implementation of Article 15 of this Agreement shall be dealt with as follows:

(a) The Requested Party shall assume all ordinary expenses of executing a request for cooperation within its boundaries, except:

(i) fees of experts;

(ii) expenses of translation, interpretation and transcription; and

(iii) travel and incidental expenses of persons travelling to the Requested Party's territory to attend the execution of a request for cooperation.

(b) A Requesting Party shall assume all ordinary expenses required to present evidence from the Requested Party in the Requesting Party's territory, including:

(i) travel and incidental expenses of witnesses travelling to the Requesting Party's territory, including those of accompanying officials; and

(ii) fees of experts.

(c) If it becomes apparent that expenses of an extraordinary nature are required to fulfill a request for cooperation, the Parties shall consult to determine the terms and conditions under which the cooperation will continue.

(d) The Parties shall agree on practical measures as appropriate for the reporting and payment of costs in conformity with this Article.

ARTICLE 18
Effect on Rights and Privileges

1. This Agreement creates rights and obligations between the Parties.

2. Nothing in this Agreement:

(a) creates, alters or confers the rights, privileges and benefits due to any person or entity in any administrative or judicial proceeding conducted under the jurisdiction of either Party;

(b) shall give rise to a right on the part of a private party or entity to obtain, suppress or exclude any evidence or to impede the execution of a request for evidence;

(c) shall in any way limit the rights and authority of any designated cross-border maritime law enforcement officer while operating in his or her country;

(d) shall be construed to alter existing international agreements or other arrangements pertaining to Mutual Legal Assistance between the Parties; and

(e) shall constitute a precedent for any future discussions or negotiations between the Parties.

ARTICLE 19
Entry into force, Amendment and Termination of the Agreement

1. This Agreement shall enter into force upon an exchange of diplomatic notes confirming that the necessary internal procedures of each Party therefor have been completed.

2. Any amendment of this Agreement must be agreed in writing by the Parties and shall enter into force upon an exchange of diplomatic notes confirming that the necessary internal procedures of each Party therefor have been completed.

3. This Agreement may be terminated by either Party by written notification to the other Party. The termination shall take effect six months from the date of such notification.

4. Notwithstanding paragraph 3 of this Article, the obligations contained in Article 15 shall continue for prosecutions that have been commenced prior to the time of termination until such prosecutions are over.

5. In case of termination, the Government of the United States of America and the Government of Canada shall reach agreement on the return or destruction, or continued use and storage, of the information that has already been communicated between them.

6. The Parties agree to meet in order to review this Agreement at the end of five years from the date of its entry into force.

IN WITNESS WHEREOF, the undersigned, duly authorised by their respective Government, have signed this Agreement.

DONE at Detroit, this twenty-sixth day of May 2009, in duplicate, in the English and French languages, both versions being equally authentic.

[Signature]

FOR THE GOVERNMENT OF THE UNITED STATES OF AMERICA:

FOR THE GOVERNMENT OF CANADA:

[Signature]

STATE DEPARTMENT DOCUMENT NUMBER: 12-193

AGREEMENT BETWEEN THE UNITED STATES OF AMERICA AND THE REPUBLIC OF THE PHILIPPINES ON SCIENTIFIC AND TECHNOLOGICAL COOPERATION, WITH ANNEX

SIGNED AT WASHINGTON D.C., JUNE 8, 2012
ENTERED INTO FORCE OCTOBER 15, 2012

CTIA DOCUMENT NUMBER: 18093.000

The Government of the United States of America and the Government of the Republic of the Philippines, hereinafter referred to as the "Parties,"

Noting the mutual desire to strengthen the traditional ties of friendship existing between the two countries; and

Recognizing the advantages to be derived by their respective peoples in promoting and developing scientific and technological cooperation within the limits of their capacities,

Have agreed as follows:

Article I

1. The purposes of this Agreement are to strengthen scientific, technological, and institutional capabilities of the Parties, to broaden and expand relations between the scientific and technological communities in both countries, and to promote scientific and technological cooperation in areas of mutual benefit.

2. The principal objectives of this cooperation are to provide opportunities to exchange ideas, information, skills, and techniques and to collaborate on scientific and technological endeavors of mutual interest, including but not limited to:

a. Information and communication technologies;

b. Research and education exchanges;

c. Science-based decision making;

d. Environmental and biodiversity protection;

e. Natural and physical sciences;

f. Agriculture, food, and nutrition;

g. Marine sciences;

h. Health sciences, and allied health services including biomedical, behavioral and social science research;

i. Public health and public health emergencies of international concern;

j. Prevention and control of non-communicable and communicable/infectious diseases;

k. Human resources for health;

l. Emergency medical services;

m. Climate change and global warming, including support for adaption and mitigation measures;

n. Meteorology and severe weather forecasting, including typhoons;

o. Energy;

p. Nuclear science including nuclear safety;

q. Biological sciences, including improving capacity building to strengthen biological laboratory safety and pathogen security;

r. Science, technology and engineering for sustainable development;

s. Other such forms of scientific and technological cooperation as may be mutually agreed upon.

Article II

1. The Parties shall encourage cooperation through appropriate means including: exchanges of scientific and technical information; exchanges, training and education of scientists and technical experts; the convening of joint seminars and meetings; the conduct of joint research projects; access to scientific and technical facilities; and other such forms of scientific and technological cooperation as may be mutually agreed upon.

2. Cooperation under this Agreement shall be based on shared responsibilities and equitable contributions and benefits, commensurate with the Parties' respective scientific and technological strengths and resources.

Article III

Each Party will designate a point of contact for the notification and approval of requests for authorization for access to the waters and terrestrial airspace under national jurisdiction for the purpose of scientific research within the context of agreed upon cooperative activities and in accordance with each Party's relevant laws, rules and regulations, and will treat those requests with diligence, taking into account the significance of these activities to the advancement of scientific knowledge.

Article IV

1. The Parties shall encourage and facilitate, where appropriate, the development of direct contacts and cooperation between government agencies, universities, research centers, institutions, private firms and other entities of the two countries.

2. Government agencies and designated entities of the two Parties may conclude under this Agreement implementing arrangements in specific areas of science and technology. These implementing arrangements shall cover, as appropriate, topics of cooperation, procedures for transfer

and use of equipment and funds, and other relevant issues. Unless the Parties or their designees agree otherwise, the terms of this Agreement shall apply to any implementing arrangements or agreements.

Article V

1. Cooperative activities under this Agreement shall be conducted in accordance with the applicable laws, regulations and procedures in both countries and shall be subject to the availability of funds and personnel.

2. Priority will be given to collaboration that can advance common goals in science and technology, as well as supporting partnerships between public and private research institutions and industry.

Article VI

Scientists, technical experts, governmental agencies and institutions of third countries or international organizations may, in appropriate cases, be invited by agreement of both Parties to participate, at their own expense unless otherwise agreed, in projects and programs being carried out under this Agreement.

Article VII

1. The Parties shall establish a Joint Committee composed of representatives designated by the Parties for coordinating and facilitating cooperative activities under this Agreement. The Committee shall conduct a joint review of activities, joint research projects, matters of importance in the fields of science and technology research, and policies related to the overall scientific and technological research relationship between the Parties under this agreement periodically in a meeting that shall take place alternately in the United States and in the Republic of the Philippines.

2. In the intervals between the sessions of the Committee, representatives of the two Parties shall meet, as necessary, to discuss and further the implementation of this Agreement and to exchange information on the progress of programs, projects and activities of common interest.

Article VIII

1. Scientific and technological information of a non-proprietary nature resulting from cooperation under this Agreement (other than information which is not disclosed for commercial or industrial reasons) shall be made available, unless otherwise agreed, to the world scientific community through customary channels and in accordance with normal procedures of the participating agencies and entities.

2. The treatment of intellectual property created or furnished in the course of cooperative activities under this Agreement is provided for in Annex I, which shall form an integral part of this Agreement and shall apply to all activities conducted under this Agreement, unless agreed otherwise by the Parties or their designees in writing.

Article IX

1. Each Party shall facilitate entry into and exit from its territory of appropriate personnel and equipment of the other Party, engaged in or used in projects and programs under this Agreement.

2. Each Party shall facilitate prompt and efficient access of persons of the other Party, participating in cooperative activities under this Agreement, to its relevant geographic areas, institutions, data, materials, and individual scientists, specialists and researchers as needed to carry out those activities. .

3. Each Party shall use its best efforts to provide duty free entry for materials and equipment provided pursuant to science and technology cooperation undertaken pursuant to this Agreement.

4. The Parties do not foresee the provision of foreign assistance under this Agreement. If they decide otherwise with respect to a particular activity, the relevant implementing arrangement would need to be consistent with the requirements of the laws of the respective countries that regulate activities related to foreign assistance.

Article X

In the event that differences arise between the Parties with regard to the interpretation or application of the provisions of this Agreement, the Parties shall resolve them by means of negotiations and consultations, through diplomatic channels.

Article XI

1. This agreement shall enter into force on the date of the later written notification by the Parties through diplomatic channels, indicating compliance with the domestic procedures for its entry into force. It shall remain in force for three (3) years and may be extended for further three-year periods by written agreement of the Parties.

2. This Agreement may be terminated at any time by either Party upon six (6) months' written notice to the other Party.

3. Unless otherwise agreed by the Parties, termination of this Agreement shall not affect the implementation of any cooperative activity carried out under this Agreement and not completed upon termination of this Agreement.

4. This Agreement may be amended at any time by mutual agreement of the Parties. Such amendments shall enter into force in accordance with the procedure described in paragraph 1 of this Article.

IN WITNESS WHEREOF the undersigned, being duly authorized by their respective Governments, have signed this Agreement.

Done at Washington, D.C. in duplicate, this 8th day of June, 2012, in the English language.

FOR THE GOVERNMENT OF THE
UNITED STATES OF AMERICA:

[Signature]

FOR THE GOVERNMENT OF THE
REPUBLIC OF THE PHILIPPINES:

[Signature]

ANNEX I
Intellectual Property Rights

I. General Obligation

The Parties shall ensure adequate and effective protection of intellectual property created or furnished under this Agreement and relevant implementing arrangements. Rights to such intellectual property shall be allocated as provided in this Annex.

II. Scope

A. This Annex is applicable to all cooperative activities undertaken pursuant to this Agreement, except as otherwise specifically agreed by the Parties or their designees.

B. For purposes of this Agreement, "intellectual property" shall mean the subject matter listed in Article 2 of the Convention Establishing the World Intellectual Property Organization, done at Stockholm, July 14, 1967 and may include other subject matter as agreed by the Parties.

C. Each Party shall ensure, through contracts or other legal means with its own participants, if necessary, that the other Party can obtain the rights to intellectual property allocated in accordance with this Annex. This Annex does not otherwise alter or prejudice the allocation between a Party and its nationals, which shall be determined by that Party's laws and practices.

D. Except as otherwise provided in this Agreement, disputes concerning intellectual property arising under this Agreement shall be resolved through discussions between the concerned participating institutions or, if necessary, the Parties or their designees. Upon mutual agreement of the Parties, a dispute shall be submitted to an arbitral tribunal for binding arbitration in accordance with the applicable rules of international law. Unless the Parties or their designees agree otherwise in writing, the arbitration rules of the United Nations Commission on International Trade Law (UNCITRAL) shall govern.

E. Termination or expiration of this Agreement shall not affect rights or obligations under this Annex.

III. Allocation of Rights

A. Each Party shall be entitled to a non-exclusive, irrevocable, royalty-free license in all countries to translate, reproduce, and publicly distribute scientific and technical journal articles, reports and books directly arising from cooperation under this Agreement. All publicly distributed copies of a copyrighted work prepared under this provision shall indicate the names of the authors of the work unless an author explicitly declines to be named.

B. Rights to all forms of intellectual property, other than those rights described in paragraph IIIA above, shall be allocated as follows:

(1) Visiting researchers shall receive rights, awards, bonuses and royalties in accordance with the policies of the host institution.

(2)(a) Any intellectual property created by persons employed or sponsored by one Party under cooperative activities other than those covered by paragraph III B (1) shall be owned by that Party. Intellectual property created by persons employed or sponsored by both Parties shall be jointly owned by the Parties. In addition, each creator shall be entitled to awards, bonuses and royalties in accordance with the policies of the institution employing or sponsoring that person.

(b) Unless otherwise agreed in an implementing or other arrangement, each Party shall have within its territory all rights to exploit or license intellectual property created in the course of the cooperative activities.

(c) The rights of a Party outside its territory shall be determined by mutual agreement considering the relative contributions of the Parties and their participants to the cooperative activities, the degree of commitment in obtaining legal protection and licensing of the intellectual property and such other factors deemed appropriate.

(d) Notwithstanding paragraphs III, B(2)(a) and (b) above, if a particular project has led to the creation of intellectual property protected by the laws of one Party but not the other, the Party whose laws provide for this type of protection shall be entitled to all rights to exploit or license intellectual property worldwide although creators of intellectual property shall nonetheless be entitled to awards, bonuses and royalties as provided in paragraph III B(2)(a).

(e) For each invention made under any cooperative activity, the Party employing or sponsoring the inventor(s) shall disclose the inventions promptly to the other Party together with any documentation and information necessary to enable the other Party to establish any rights to which it may be entitled. Either Party may ask the other Party in writing to delay publication or public disclosure of such documentation or information for the purpose of protecting its rights in the invention. Unless otherwise agreed in writing, the delay shall not exceed a period of six months from the date of disclosure by the inventing Party to the other Party.

IV. Business Confidential Information

In the event that information identified in a timely fashion as business-confidential is furnished or created under this Agreement, each Party and its participants shall protect such information in accordance with applicable laws, regulations, and administrative practices. Information may be identified as "business-confidential" if a person having the information may derive an economic benefit from it or may obtain a competitive advantage over those who do not have it, and the information is not generally known or publicly available from other sources, and the owner has not previously made the information available without imposing in a timely manner an obligation to keep it confidential.

State Department Document Number: 12-194

Agreement Between the United States of America and the Republic of Panama Regarding the Status of United States Personnel Who May Be Temporarily Present in Panama in Connection with a Visit by Thirty-one Officials from the U.S. Navy Mobile Security Detachment

Effected by Exchange of Notes at Panama City,
October 1 and 16, 2012
Entered into force October 16, 2012

CTIA DOCUMENT NUMBER: 18094.000

DIPLOMATIC NOTE

No. 1743

The Embassy of the United States of America presents its compliments to the Ministry of Foreign Relations of the Republic of Panama and has the honor to refer to recent discussions between representatives of the two Governments regarding the status of United States personnel, as defined in the Embassy's Note No. 834, dated July 3, 2001, and the Ministry's Note DM No. 0301/2001, dated July 10, 2001, who may be temporarily present in Panama in connection with a visit by thirty-one officials from the U.S. Navy Mobile Security Detachment, who will be in uniform and who will carry their authorized weapons. The officials will stay in Panama from January 1 through June 30, 2013. The purpose of the visit is to facilitate the transit of the Panama Canal by U.S. vessels. The Panamanian counterpart is Manager Antonio Michel at the Panama Canal Authority (ACP).

As a result of these discussions, the Embassy proposes that such personnel shall be accorded a status equivalent to that accorded to the administrative and technical staff of the Embassy of the United States of America under the Vienna Convention of Diplomatic Relations of April 18, 1961 (Vienna Convention). The understanding contained in the Embassy's Note. 835 dated July 3, 2001 and the Ministry's reply in Note No. D.M. 0300/2001 dated July 10, 2001, shall apply.

United States personnel shall be permitted to enter and exit Panama with United States identification and with collective movement or individual travel orders, in accordance with an agreement on non-immigrant visas between the United States and Panama, which has been in force since June 1, 1956, as amended, except that the Government of Panama will waive the requirement for tourist cards and related fees.

Panamanian authorities shall accept as valid driving licenses or permits issued by the appropriate U.S. authorities to U.S. personnel for operation of vehicles; and such personnel shall be authorized to wear U.S. Government attire (uniforms) and to carry authorized equipment when required for their mission while performing official duties.

The Embassy of the United States further proposes that the Government of Panama accord duty-free importation and exportation, as well as exemption from inspection and taxation of products, services, property, materials, equipment, vehicles, vessels, and aircraft introduced and/or imported into, acquired in or exported from Panama by or on behalf of the U.S. Government or its personnel, in connection with their mission in Panama; except that United States personnel shall not be exempt from Panamanian taxes on items purchased in Panama for their personal use.

The two Governments shall cooperate in taking the necessary steps to ensure the security of United States personnel and property in Panama.

Vehicles, vessels, and aircraft owned or operated by or for United States Armed Forces shall not be subject to payment of landing or port fees, pilotage charges, navigation, overflight or parking charges or lighterage or harbor dues while in Panama, except for the charges related to the normal transit of the Panama Canal, previously agreed to; however, United States Armed Forces shall pay reasonable charges for services requested and received.

It shall be the responsibility of United States personnel to respect the laws of Panama and to abstain from any activity inconsistent with the spirit of their mission. Authorities of the Government of the United States shall take the necessary steps to that end.

Appropriate Panamanian and U.S. military or civilian police authorities shall cooperate in the investigation of any crime believed to have been committed by or against United States personnel.

The Government of Panama shall accept full responsibility for, and shall hold the United States Government harmless from, any and all claims arising from the use of projects constructed, or in the process of being constructed in whole or in part, by United States personnel in connection with their mission in Panama.

Finally, both governments shall waive any and all claims (other than contractual claims) against each other for personal injury to or death of their military or civilian personnel, or for damage, loss, or destruction of the other's property arising out of activities covered by this agreement. The United States shall pay, in accordance with United States law, fair and reasonable compensation in settlement of meritorious claims by third parties arising out of acts or omissions of United States personnel, or which are otherwise incident to agreed activities by United States personnel in connection with their mission in Panama.

Additional arrangements as may be necessary may be entered into by the appropriate authorities of the two Governments.

The Embassy of the United States of America proposes that this note and the Ministry's reply thereto shall constitute an agreement between the two Governments on this subject and that its provisions shall be in effect as of the date of the Ministry's reply.

The Embassy of the United States of America avails itself of this opportunity to reiterate to the Ministry of Foreign Relations of the Republic of Panama the assurances of its highest consideration.

Embassy of the United States of America,
Panama, October 1, 2012.

U.S. Department of State
Office of Language Services
Translating Division

LS No. 11-2013-0240
Spanish/English
GPG/BBM

TRANSLATION

Republic of Panama
Ministry of Foreign Relations
Panama 4, Panama

Embassy of the United States of America,
Panama City.

AJ/DT No. 406

The Ministry of Foreign Relations presents its compliments to the Embassy of the United States of America and has the honor to acknowledge receipt of its Note Verbale No. 1743 of October 1, 2012, which reads as follows:

[See U.S. Text.]

In this regard, the Ministry of Foreign Relations has the honor to inform the Embassy of the United States of America that the above proposal is acceptable to the Government of the Republic of Panama and that the Embassy's note and this note shall constitute an agreement between our two governments which shall enter into force on the date of this note.

[Complimentary close]

Panama City, October 16, 2012
[Initialed]
[Ministry stamp]

STATE DEPARTMENT DOCUMENT NUMBER: 12-195

MEMORANDUM OF UNDERSTANDING BETWEEN THE UNITED STATES GEOLOGICAL SURVEY OF THE DEPARTMENT OF THE INTERIOR AND THE CENTER FOR EARTH OBSERVATION AND DIGITAL EARTH (CEODE) OF THE CHINESE ACADEMY OF SCIENCES (CAS) FOR COOPERATION IN THE USE OF U.S. LAND REMOTE SENSING SATELLITE DATA, WITH ANNEXES

SIGNED AT RESTON AND BEIJING, OCTOBER 10 AND 20, 2012
ENTERED INTO FORCE OCTOBER 20, 2012

CTIA DOCUMENT NUMBER: 18095.000

CH-20.0000
ACIS Ref ID: 10456

PREAMBLE

The United States Geological Survey of the United States Department of the Interior and the **Center for Earth Observation and Digital Earth (CEODE),** (hereinafter referred to as "the Parties"),

RECOGNIZING their mutual interest in the use of space technology for peaceful purposes;

NOTING the value of the United States Landsat satellite missions to cooperation among governments in space-based remote sensing of the Earth's surface;

DESIRING to establish an overall legal framework for cooperation in future land remote sensing satellite missions;

HAVE AGREED as follows:

ARTICLE 1—PURPOSE AND SCOPE OF COOPERATION

This Memorandum of Understanding (MOU) establishes the terms and conditions under which the United States Geological Survey (USGS) will provide United States-owned land remote sensing satellite data and **CEODE** will receive, process, archive, distribute, and exchange such data in cooperation with the USGS. This MOU consists of a main text, a definition of terms annex, and mission-specific annexes. The annexes integral part of this MOU.

ARTICLE 2—RESPONSIBILITIES OF THE PARTIES

A. The USGS shall endeavor to provide operational land remote sensing satellite service under the terms of this MOU and shall:

1. Program land remote sensing satellites to collect and provide remote sensing data of areas within the acquisition radius of **CEODE's** ground station(s) to the extent that such requests can be accommodated by the spacecraft. The USGS will endeavor to schedule satellite downlink resources to meet requests from all participating ICs in an equitable and balanced manner, subject to conflict-resolution guidelines to be provided to all stations. Programming details to meet such requests will be arranged by mutual decision of the Parties' technical representatives.

2. Provide **CEODE** with orbital elements for calculating the antenna pointing angles necessary to acquire the satellite-transmitted signals and with the necessary ancillary and calibration information for processing the data acquired.

3. Reserve the right to curtail or terminate transmission of satellite data to **CEODE** for reasons of (1) spacecraft or USGS ground equipment limitations, or (2) non-payment of annual access fee as agreed in any mission-specific Annex to this MOU. In these cases, the USGS will notify **CEODE** and discuss the planned action in the most expeditious manner possible.

4. Provide to **CEODE,** upon request by **CEODE,** reasonable quantities of raw USGS land remote sensing satellite data extracted from the USGS archive in an agreed-upon format and delivered electronically or on media at a price to be negotiated.

5. Provide support for anomaly resolution for USGS land remote sensing satellite missions.

6. Endeavour to ensure that any radio frequency problem occurring in relation to data reception by **CEODE's** ground station(s) is resolved to the satisfaction of the Parties.

B. **CEODE** shall:

1. Operate (a) ground station(s) for the reception, processing, archiving, distribution, and exchange of USGS land remote sensing satellite data at its own expense, including the cost of establishing and operating the necessary communication links with the USGS's Mission Operations Center (MOC) and the USGS's data center located at the Earth Resources Observation and Science (EROS) Center.

2. Produce land remote sensing satellite data products in accordance with agreed-upon USGS-sponsored distribution formats.

3. Ensure that all USGS land remote sensing satellite data acquired by **CEODE** are available for sale or distribution on a public, nondiscriminatory basis. This applies to all USGS land remote sensing satellite data acquired under this and previous Landsat MOUs signed with U.S. Government agencies.

4. Make available to the USGS, upon request, English-language copies of any arrangements signed by **CEODE** concerning the distribution of USGS land remote sensing satellite data from **CEODE.** Such arrangements shall be consistent with this MOU.

5. Maintain a current inventory of its USGS land remote sensing satellite data holdings and provide at least monthly updates of its metadata to the USGS in an agreed-upon format, electronically or on agreed-upon media, once the ground station(s) is (are) operational. These metadata may be made available publicly through USGS data facilities.

6. Establish and maintain a computer-accessible electronic system, with external public access, of browse imagery for its USGS land remote sensing satellite data holdings, or provide browse data at least monthly to the USGS in an agreed-upon format and on agreed-upon media, once the ground station(s) is (are) operational. **CEODE** browse imagery may be made available publicly through USGS data facilities.

7. Maintain USGS land remote sensing satellite data that have met **CEODE** quality standards in **CEODE's** archive for at least 10 years following data acquisition, using accepted archive management practices. If **CEODE** plans to discard data, it will issue a purge alert to the USGS, which will be given first right of refusal to acquire the data at a price to be negotiated.

8. Endeavor to ensure that any radio frequency problem occurring in relation to data reception by **CEODE's** ground station(s) is resolved to the satisfaction of the Parties. Questions concerning radio frequency interference by the USGS land remote sensing spacecraft raised by entities in third countries will be referred to the USGS.

9. When requested by the USGS in support of key U. S. Government programs, provide reasonable quantities of **CEODE**-held USGS land remote sensing satellite data, in an agreed-upon format, electronically or on media, and at a price to be negotiated.

10. Repatriate to the USGS, within 30 days of downlink, any USGS land remote sensing satellite data received which is unique to **CEODE's** archive.

11. For purposes of validating data quality, exchange limited amounts of **CEODE**-held USGS land remote sensing satellite data, in an agreed-upon format, electronically or on media, when requested by the USGS. Data for this purpose shall be exchanged annually, at no cost to the USGS.

12. When requested by the USGS in response to a significant loss of spacecraft capability to record data for the USGS archive, routinely provide sufficient quantities of newly acquired USGS land remote sensing satellite data to meet U.S. Government mission requirements, in an agreed-upon format, electronically or on media, at a cost to be negotiated. For any support necessary to **CEODE** beyond providing USGS land remote sensing satellite data to the USGS as described above, the Parties will negotiate specific financial terms.

13. Communicate with the MOC on spacecraft information, in order to maximize data collection and efficiency of spacecraft operations.

14. Provide support for anomaly resolution of USGS land remote sensing satellite missions.

ARTICLE 3—INTERNATIONAL MISSION COORDINATION

A. Each Party shall designate program representatives to be responsible for the implementation of this MOU. Supplemental meetings between the Parties will be held by mutual agreement.

B. Program management representatives from the Parties will participate in annual meetings of the Landsat Ground Station Operations Working Group (LGSOWG). This group, chaired by the USGS, will serve as a forum for the exchange of policy, programmatic and management information among station operators and the USGS.

C. Technical representatives from the Parties will participate in annual meetings of the Landsat Technical Working Group (LTWG). This group, also chaired by the USGS, will review and coordinate technical and operational aspects of USGS international mission support.

ARTICLE 4—SCIENCE AND APPLICATIONS DEVELOPMENT

1. The Parties will seek to identify opportunities for cooperation in improved land remote sensing satellite data collection, user accessibility, and data distribution.

2. The Parties will seek to identify opportunities to support new research in the use of land remote sensing satellite data, and the development of related applications to enhance land use practices, ecosystems management, climate change research, and other areas of Earth systems science.

3. The Parties will seek to cooperate in the support of global observation and science programs involving the use of land remote sensing satellite data.

4. The Parties will consult with one another on best practices and improved means of cooperation in the long-term archiving and preservation of land remote sensing satellite data.

5. The Parties will share information and consider opportunities for training and capacity building in the use of land remote sensing satellite data.

6. Subject to the provisions of Article 10, the Parties will share information on their respective development and potential for cooperation in their respective land remote sensing satellite missions.

ARTICLE 5—USER SERVICE ARRANGEMENTS

The USGS reserves the right to service the land remote sensing satellite data requests of all users affiliated with U.S. Government programs.

ARTICLE 6—FINANCIAL ARRANGEMENTS AND LEGAL AUTHORIZATION

1. The Parties shall be responsible for funding their respective activities under this MOU. Additionally, **CEODE,** or its designated agent, shall pay to the USGS, or ensure the appropriate authorities of **CEODE's** government pay to the USGS, in a timely manner, any access fees described in any mission-specific Annex(es). These fees are required to enable the USGS to administer all operations in support of a global network of cooperating ground receiving stations.

2. Obligations under this Agreement and any Implementing Annexes shall be subject to the availability of funding obtained through each Party's funding procedures.

3. Should either Party encounter budgetary problems that may affect the activities carried out under this MOU, that Party shall notify and consult with the other Party in a timely manner in order to minimize the negative impact of such problems on the cooperation.

ARTICLE 7—DUTIES, FEES, AND TAXES

In accordance with its national laws and regulations, each Party shall seek to ensure free customs clearance and waiver of all applicable duties, fees, and taxes for the import or export of goods necessary for the implementation of this MOU. In the event that any duties, fees, or taxes of any kind are nonetheless levied on such goods, such duties, fees, or taxes shall be borne by the Party of the country levying them.

ARTICLE 8—ENTRY AND EXIT OF PERSONNEL

On a reciprocal basis, each Party shall use reasonable efforts to facilitate, in accordance with its laws and regulations, the entry to and exit from its territory of personnel engaged in joint activities pursuant to this MOU.

ARTICLE 9—LAWS, WARRANTIES, RIGHTS, AND LIABILITY

1. The activities under this MOU will be conducted in accordance with the applicable laws and regulations of the Parties' countries, respectively, and shall be subject to the availability of appropriate funds.

2. The USGS does not warrant the suitability of its land remote sensing data for any purpose and shall not be liable for any damage or injury brought about by use of USGS land remote sensing satellite systems and their data.

3. The USGS retains the ownership right to all raw land remote sensing data acquired by its satellites. Beyond the provisions of Article 2.B.3, the USGS places no restrictions on **CEODE** to disclose, use, manipulate, generate products from, distribute, or sell USGS land remote sensing satellite data.

ARTICLE 10—EXCHANGE OF TECHNICAL INFORMATION

1. Technical information exchanged between the Parties will be subject to the applicable laws, regulations, and policies of the Parties' countries, respectively. In the event it is necessary to exchange technical information and the furnishing Party considers that such technical information is to be protected for proprietary or export control purposes, such information must be clearly marked with a legend indicating the country of origin, the conditions of release, that the information relates to this MOU, and that it is furnished in confidence.

2. The Parties USGS and **CEODE** will take all lawful steps available to prevent disclosure of such protected or proprietary technical information without the consent of the other Party and to ensure that it is used only for the purposes of this MOU.

3. The USGS and **CEODE** may release to the public other general, nontechnical information regarding each other's programs or operations after ensuring, through consultation with each other when necessary, that this information is fairly and accurately represented.

4. The USGS and **CEODE** may exchange appropriate technical information and documentation for the purposes of downlinking, processing, and archiving USGS land remote sensing satellite data as well as for generating and distributing products from that data.

ARTICLE 11—CONSULTATIONS AND SETTLEMENT OF DISPUTES

1. The Parties shall consult, as appropriate, to review the implementation of activities undertaken pursuant to this MOU, and to exchange views on potential areas of future cooperation.

2. In the event questions arise regarding the interpretation, application, or implementation of activities under this MOU, the Program Managers of the Parties shall endeavor to resolve the questions. If the Program Managers are unable to reach an agreement, then the matter will be referred to a more senior level of the Parties for joint resolution.

ARTICLE 12—ENTRY INTO FORCE, DURATION, AND TERMINATION

1. This MOU shall enter into force upon signature by both Parties and remain in force through the operational lifetime of the USGS land remote sensing spacecraft(s) from which **CEODE** receives USGS land remote sensing data. This MOU may be amended by mutual agreement of the Parties.

2. In the event that either of the Parties is unable to comply with any provision of this MOU, either Party, after consultation with the other, shall have the option of terminating this MOU, providing at least 30 days' notice of such action, forwarded in writing by one Party to the other.

3. Notwithstanding termination or expiration of this MOU, the obligations of the Parties set forth in Article 2.B.3, Article 2.B.7, Article 9.2, Article 9.3, and Article 10 of this MOU shall continue to apply.

ARTICLE 13—SIGNATURE

IN WITNESS THEREOF, respective representatives of the Parties have signed this Memorandum of Understanding.

For the United States Geological Survey
of the Department of the Interior:

[Signature]

Marcia McNutt
Director
U.S. Geological Survey
Reston, Virginia

OCT 10 2012

Date

Place

For CEODE:

[Signature]

Jianbo LIU
Deputy Director General
CEODE
Beijing, China

OCT 20, 2012

Date

Place

CH-20.0000
ACIS Ref ID: 10457

ANNEX I

TO THE

MEMORANDUM OF UNDERSTANDING

BETWEEN THE

UNITED STATES GEOLOGICAL SURVEY
OF THE DEPARTMENT OF THE INTERIOR

AND THE

CENTER FOR EARTH OBSERVATION AND DIGITAL EARTH (CEODE)
OF THE CHINESE ACADEMY OF SCIENCES (CAS)

FOR COOPERATION IN THE USE OF
U.S. LAND REMOTE SENSING SATELLITE DATA

DEFINITION OF TERMS

Acquisition Radius:

An International Cooperator's (IC's) acquisition radius is that portion of the Earth over which the satellite can communicate with an IC's ground station.

Browse:

Browse is a full resolution or sub-sampled Level OR or Level 1 digital image of the Earth that can be viewed on a scene basis to quickly assess general ground area coverage, data quality, and the spatial relationships between ground area coverage and cloud coverage. A browse is an image with a reduced data volume to facilitate screening of archived Land Remote Sensing Satellite Data. Specifications regarding browse images are documented in the appropriate mission Data Format Control Book (DFCB) and made available by the USGS.

Data Format:

The Landsat Technical Working Group (LTWG) recommends the archive data format for exchanging data between an International Cooperator and USGS archives. The archive data exchange format for purposes of quality assessment and key government programs is typically the lowest level of processed data available (i.e. Mission or Raw Computer Compatible [RCC] Data) and is transferred electronically or on media. The archive data exchange format is documented in the appropriate mission Data Validation and Exchange Plan and associated Data Format Control Book (DFCB) and made available by the USGS.

Data Products Distribution Format:

The USGS Land Remote Sensing Satellite Data products are Level-ORp (Level Zero Reformatted Product) in HDF format and Level-1T (terrain corrected) in Geo-TIFF format. International Cooperators may produce data products of their choice. ICs are encouraged, but not required to produce Level ORp data products in HDF format, but are required to distribute Level-1T data products in Geo-TIFF format. Specifications regarding Level-ORp and Level-1T data products are documented in the appropriate mission Data Format Control Book (DFCB) and made available by the USGS.

International Cooperator (IC):

An International Cooperator (IC) is any non-U.S. Government agency or commercial organization acting on behalf of or in cooperation with a foreign government or international organization, which enters into an agreement with the USGS for purposes of receiving or exchanging Land Remote Sensing Satellite Data.

Key U.S. Government Programs:

Key U.S. Government Programs are any U.S. Government agencies and U.S. Government contractors, other U.S. and foreign researchers and entities involved in the United States Global Change Research Program, and U.S. and foreign researchers and foreign and international entities having signed a cooperative agreement with the United States Government involving the use of USGS Land Remote Sensing Satellite Data for non-commercial purposes.

The United States Global Change Research Program is the Executive Branch program responding to Public Law 101-606, the Global Change Research Act of 1990, and most recently described in the annual report accompanying the President's budget entitled "Our Changing Planet: The U.S. Climate Change Science Program for Fiscal Year 2012."

International counterpart programs of the U.S. Global Change Research Program are discussed in Section V of "Our Changing Planet." These include the Intergovernmental Panel on Climate Change, the World Climate Research Program, the International Council on Science, and the Group on Earth Observations.

Mission Operations Center (MOC):

The Mission Operations Center (MOC) consists of the people, procedures, and hardware/software systems used for the successful execution of real-time spacecraft operations and off-line scheduling and analysis activities. All command and control functions of the spacecraft performed by the Flight Operations Team (FOT) will take place from the MOC.

Metadata:

Metadata is descriptive information pertaining to the USGS Land Remote Sensing Satellite Data, including such information as location and acquisition date, compiled for Level OR and Level-1 data, and made available through the USGS user interface. Specifications regarding the metadata are documented in the Landsat Metadata Description Document (LMDD) and made available by the USGS.

Raw Data:

Raw Data is the USGS Land Remote Sensing Satellite Data in the form of wideband telemetry transmitted by the satellite.

U.S. Government and Affiliated Users:

U.S. Government and Affiliated Users are any Federal, State or local government agency personnel and personnel from any organization performing cooperative work with or for these government agencies.

USGS Land Remote Sensing Satellites:

USGS Land Remote Sensing Satellites are any satellites owned and operated by the USGS for the purposes of this agreement. These satellites may include, but are not limited to, the Landsat missions.

CH-20.0000
ACIS Ref ID: 10458

ANNEX II

TO THE

MEMORANDUM OF UNDERSTANDING

BETWEEN THE

**UNITED STATES GEOLOGICAL SURVEY
OF THE DEPARTMENT OF THE INTERIOR**

AND THE

**CENTER FOR EARTH OBSERVATION AND DIGITAL EARTH (CEODE)
OF THE CHINESE ACADEMY OF SCIENCES (CAS)**

**FOR COOPERATION IN THE USE OF
U.S. LAND REMOTE SENSING SATELLITE DATA**

**LANDSAT 8
ANNUAL ACCESS FEE AGREEMENT**

ARTICLE 1—INTRODUCTION

Pursuant to Article 6 of the Memorandum of Understanding (MOU) between the United States Geological Survey of the Department of the Interior and **Center for Earth Observation and Digital Earth (CEODE)** for the Direct Reception, Distribution, and Exchange of Land Remote Sensing Satellite Data; U.S. Presidential Decision Directive/National Science and Technology Council-3, as amended on October 16, 2000; and the Land Remote Sensing Policy Act of 1992, the USGS has established a fee structure to enable it to administer all operations in support of a global network of cooperating ground receiving stations for direct reception of data from the Landsat 8 mission. This Annex sets forth the related financial and administrative terms and conditions for Landsat 8 cooperation between the USGS and **CEODE.**

ARTICLE 2—FEE STRUCTURE

The fee structure comprises a one-time *initialization fee* and an *annual access fee.* If **CEODE** moves a receiving antenna to a new location greater than 50 kilometers from its original location, an *antenna move fee* will be assessed. The *annual access fee* will be payable for the United States Government (USG) Fiscal Year, which begins on October 1 and ends on September 30, and may be prorated to the remaining portion of the USG Fiscal Year, from the start date for direct transmission of Landsat 8 data to September 30.

The *initialization fee* for a new IC or a new IC station is U.S. $35,000 for each receiving site. The total *initialization fee* for **CEODE** will be U.S. $0 for the receiving site(s) located at Kashi and Miyun.

The *antenna move fee* is U.S. $15,000 and will be billed each time a station is moved a distance greater than 50 kilometers.

The *annual access fee* is U.S. $100,000 for a single station operation. Each additional ground station has an *annual access fee* of U.S. $50,000. The total *annual access fee* for **CEODE** will be U.S. $150,000 for the receiving site(s) located at Kashi and Miyun.

USG Fiscal Year 2013 is the base year for each of these fees.

ARTICLE 3—PAYMENT SCHEDULE

The one-time *initialization fee* and *antenna move fee*, if applicable, are due and payable 30 days prior to **CEODE** reception of Landsat 8 data.

The *annual access fee* will be payable annually by **CEODE**. **CEODE** will receive an annual bill 30 days prior to the start of the USG Fiscal Year (billing date of September 1).

Annual payments by **CEODE** will be due at the start of the USG Fiscal Year (October 1).

The USGS reserves the right to terminate transmission of Landsat 8 data to **CEODE** at any time that **CEODE** is in arrears in its payments to the USGS or is delinquent in regularly scheduled delivery of raw telemetry data to the USGS in accordance with MOU Article 2.A.3. The USGS will notify **CEODE** 30 days in advance of its intention to terminate transmission for these reasons. Payments may be by check or wire transfer in U.S. dollars. Payments by check shall be in U.S. dollars and shall be payable to:

Department of the Interior/USGS

Payments by check shall be mailed to

USGS Office of Financial Management
271 National Center
12201 Sunrise Valley Drive
Reston, Virginia, 20192 USA

Payments by wire transfer shall be in U.S. dollars and transferred to the USGS's bank account. The USGS will provide exact wire transfer information with each billing.

All payments must be received within 30 days from the date of invoice. Charges for late payment will be at the U. S. Treasury Department prevailing rate on the overdue balance for each 30-day period or portion thereof that payment is delayed.

ARTICLE 4—FEE CHANGES

While USGS reserves the right to make modifications to the *annual access fee* used in this fee structure, it is the USGS's intent to minimize the changes to the fee structure during the life of the Landsat 8 mission. For the Landsat 8 mission, a 3% annual increase is planned to account for average annual rates of inflation. Reasonable notification of any proposed change to these fees (*initialization, antenna move*, and *annual access fees*), taking into account the budget cycles of the parties, shall be provided in writing by the USGS to **CEODE** 60 days prior to the implementation of the proposed change. Any proposed fee change would not exceed 10% of the current *annual access fee.*

For budget planning purposes the anticipated *annual access fee* structure is as follows:

	Year 1	Year 2 (+3%)	Year 3 (+3%)	Year 4 (+3%)
Two Sites	U.S. $150,000	U.S. $154,500	U.S. $159,135	U.S. $163,909

ARTICLE 5—CONTINGENCIES

The USGS, in consultation with **CEODE,** may curtail or terminate the transmission of data and adjust the *annual access fees* if the USGS is unable to satisfy data requests due to spacecraft system capability limitations or ground receiving stations conflicts.

ARTICLE 6—DURATION AND AMENDMENT

This Annex will remain in effect as long as the MOU remains in force, and it may be amended by mutual consent of USGS and **CEODE** through an Exchange of Letters.

At the beginning of each new USG Fiscal Year, the USGS and **CEODE** will review this Annex and revise it if necessary.

ARTICLE 7—AUTHORIZING SIGNATURES

The signatures of the authorized officials below signify the agreement by the Parties to the terms of this annex.

For the United States Geological Survey
of the Department of the Interior:

[Signature]

Marcia McNutt
Director
U.S. Geological Survey
Reston, Virginia

OCT 10 2012
Date

For CEODE:

[Signature]

Jianbo LIU
Deputy Director General
CEODE
Beijing, China

OCT 20, 2012
Date

STATE DEPARTMENT DOCUMENT NUMBER: 12-196

EXTENSION OF THE AGREEMENT OF MAY 3, 2005, AS EXTENDED, BETWEEN THE UNITED STATES OF AMERICA AND THE KINGDOM OF THE NETHERLANDS CONCERNING THE STATUS OF MILITARY AND CIVILIAN PERSONNEL OF THE UNITED STATES DEPARTMENT OF DEFENSE TEMPORARILY PRESENT IN THE NETHERLANDS ANTILLES AND ARUBA IN CONNECTION WITH MILITARY EXERCISES AND TRAINING

EFFECTED BY EXCHANGE OF NOTES AT THE HAGUE,
OCTOBER 17 AND 29, 2012
ENTERED INTO FORCE OCTOBER 29, 2012

CTIA DOCUMENT NUMBER: 12107.006

Embassy of the United States of America

DAO No. 042-12

The Embassy of the United States of America presents its compliments to the Ministry of Foreign Affairs of the Kingdom of the Netherlands, and has the honor to refer to the Agreement between the United States Department of Defense temporarily present in Curacao, Sint Maarten, BES Islands and Aruba in connection with military exercises and training constituted by exchange of notes at The Hague on May 3, 2005 (the Agreement), which would have terminated, in accordance with its terms, on May 3, 2006, and was extended six times, each time for a period of one year, and terminated, in accordance with its terms, on May 3, 2012.

Desiring to continue military cooperation between our military forces in Aruba, Curacao, Sint Maarten and the BES Islands, and in view of upcoming military training and exercises and any other agreed activities, including scheduled port calls, the Government of the United States proposes that the Agreement shall again be extended for an additional period of one year, so that the Agreement will remain in force until May 3, 2013.

If the foregoing is acceptable to the Government of the Kingdom of the Netherlands, the Government of the United States proposes that this note, together with a response from the Government of the Kingdom of the Netherlands, shall constitute an Agreement between our two Governments which shall enter into force on the date of the Ministry's reply, with retroactive effect as of May 3, 2012, and shall remain in force until May 3, 2013.

The Embassy of the United States of America avails itself of this opportunity to renew to the Ministry of Foreign Affairs of the Kingdom of the Netherlands the assurances of its highest consideration.

Embassy of the United States of America
The Hague, October 17, 2012

THIS ORIGINAL/CERTIFIED COPY DOCUMENT
OF WHICH THIS IS A PHOTOCOPY, APPEARS
TO BE GENUINE AND UNALTERED AND
TO HAVE BEEN MADE AT THE TIME PURPORTED.

SIGNATURE [Signature]

DATE [Illegible] NAME & TITLE Virsa Y. Perkins
AMERICAN EMBASSY Vice Consul of the
THE HAGUE, THE NETHERLANDS United States of America

Ministry of Foreign Affairs

Treaties Division
MINBUZA-2012.28754

To the Embassy of the
United States of America
at
The Hague

The Ministry of Foreign Affairs of the Kingdom of the Netherlands presents its compliments to the Embassy of the United States of America and has the honor to refer to the Agreement between the United States of America and the Kingdom of the Netherlands concerning the status of military and civilian personnel of the United States Department of Defense temporarily present in the Netherlands Antilles and Aruba in connection with military exercises and training constituted by exchange of notes at The Hague on May 3, 2005, and to the Embassy's Note No. 042-12 of 17 October 2012 on this Agreement which reads as follows:

> "The Embassy of the United States of America presents its compliments to the Ministry of Foreign Affairs of the Kingdom of the Netherlands, and has the honor to refer to the Agreement between the United States Department of Defense temporarily present in Curacao, Sint Maarten, BES Islands and Aruba in connection with military exercises and training constituted by exchange of notes at The Hague on May 3, 2005 (the Agreement), which would have terminated, in accordance with its terms, on May 3, 2006, and was extended six times, each time for a period of one year, and terminated, in accordance with its terms, on May 3, 2012.
>
> Desiring to continue military cooperation between our military forces in Aruba, Curacao, Sint Maarten and the BES Islands, and in view of upcoming military training and exercises and any other agreed activities, including scheduled port calls, the Government of the United States proposes that the Agreement shall again be extended for an additional period of one year, so that the Agreement will remain in force until May 3, 2013.
>
> If the foregoing is acceptable to the Government of the Kingdom of the Netherlands, the Government of the United States proposes that this note, together with a response from the Government of the Kingdom of the Netherlands, shall constitute an Agreement between our two Governments which shall enter into force on the date of the Ministry's reply, with retroactive effect as of May 3, 2012, and shall remain in force until May 3, 2013.
>
> The Embassy of the Unites States of America avails itself of this opportunity to renew to the Ministry of Foreign Affairs of the Kingdom of the Netherlands the assurances of its highest consideration.".

The Ministry further has the honor to inform the Embassy of the United States of America that the proposals set forth in the Embassy's note are acceptable to the Government of the Kingdom of the Netherlands and to confirm that the Embassy's note and this note shall constitute an Agreement between the two Governments, which shall be applicable to Aruba, Curaçao, Sint Maarten and the Caribbean part of the Netherlands, and shall enter into force on the date of this reply with retroactive effect as of May 3, 2012, and shall remain in force until May 3, 2013.

The Ministry of Foreign Affairs of the Kingdom of the Netherlands avails itself of this opportunity to renew to the Embassy of the United States of America the assurances of its highest consideration.

The Hague, 29 October 2012

STATE DEPARTMENT DOCUMENT NUMBER: 12-197

IMPLEMENTING ARRANGEMENT BETWEEN THE UNITED STATES GEOLOGICAL SURVEY OF THE DEPARTMENT OF THE INTERIOR AND THE NATIONAL INSTITUTE OF AERONAUTICS AND SPACE (LAPAN) OF THE REPUBLIC OF INDONESIA FOR COOPERATION IN THE USE OF U.S. LAND REMOTE SENSING SATELLITE DATA, WITH ANNEXES

SIGNED AT RESTON AND JAKARTA,
OCTOBER 10 AND NOVEMBER 2, 2012
ENTERED INTO FORCE NOVEMBER 2, 2012

CTIA DOCUMENT NUMBER: 18096.000

ID-13.0000
ACIS Ref. ID: *10465*

PREAMBLE

The United States Geological Survey of the United States Department of the Interior and the National Institute of Aeronautics and Space (LAPAN) of the Republic of Indonesia, (hereinafter referred to as "the Parties"),

RECOGNIZING their mutual interest in the use of space technology for peaceful purposes;

NOTING the value of the United States Landsat satellite missions to cooperation among governments in space-based remote sensing of the Earth's surface;

REFERRING to the Agreement between the Government of the Republic Indonesia and the Government of the United States of America on Scientific and Technological Cooperation, signed in Jakarta on March 29th, 2010.

DESIRING to establish an overall legal framework for cooperation in future land remote sensing satellite missions;

HAVE AGREED as follows:

ARTICLE 1—PURPOSE AND SCOPE OF COOPERATION

This Implementing Arrangement (IA) establishes the terms and conditions under which the United States Geological Survey (USGS) will provide United States-owned land remote sensing satellite data and LAPAN will receive, process, archive, distribute, and exchange such data in cooperation with the USGS. This IA consists of a main text, a definition of terms annex, and mission-specific annexes. The annexes are an integral part of this IA.

ARTICLE 2—RESPONSIBILITIES OF THE PARTIES

A. The USGS shall endeavor to provide operational land remote sensing satellite service under the terms of this IA and shall:

1. Program land remote sensing satellites to collect and provide remote sensing data of areas within the acquisition radius of LAPAN's ground station(s) to the extent that such requests can be accommodated by the spacecraft. The USGS will endeavor to schedule satellite downlink resources to meet requests from all participating ICs in an equitable and balanced manner, subject to conflict-resolution guidelines to be provided to all stations. Programming details to meet such requests will be arranged by mutual decision of the Parties' technical representatives.

2. Provide LAPAN with orbital elements for calculating the antenna pointing angles necessary to acquire the satellite-transmitted signals and with the necessary ancillary and calibration information for processing the data acquired.

3. Reserve the right to curtail or terminate transmission of satellite data to LAPAN for reasons of (1) spacecraft or USGS ground equipment limitations, or (2) non-payment of annual access fee as agreed in any mission-specific Annex to this IA. In these cases, the USGS will notify LAPAN and discuss the planned action in the most expeditious manner possible.

4. Provide to LAPAN, upon request by LAPAN, reasonable quantities of raw USGS land remote sensing satellite data extracted from the USGS archive in an agreed-upon format and delivered electronically or on media at a price to be negotiated.

5. Provide support for anomaly resolution for USGS land remote sensing satellite missions.

6. Endeavour to ensure that any radio frequency problem occurring in relation to data reception by LAPAN's ground station(s) is resolved to the satisfaction of the Parties.

B. LAPAN shall:

1. Operate (a) ground station(s) for the reception, processing, archiving, distribution, and exchange of USGS land remote sensing satellite data at its own expense, including the cost of establishing and operating the necessary communication links with the USGS's Mission Operations Center (MOC) and the USGS's data center located at the Earth Resources Observation and Science (EROS) Center.

2. Produce land remote sensing satellite data products in accordance with agreed-upon USGS-sponsored distribution formats.

3. Ensure that all USGS land remote sensing satellite data acquired by LAPAN are available for sale or distribution on a public, nondiscriminatory basis. This applies to all USGS land

remote sensing satellite data acquired under this and previous Landsat IAs signed with U.S. Government agencies.

4. Make available to the USGS, upon request, English-language copies of any arrangements signed by LAPAN concerning the distribution of USGS land remote sensing satellite data from LAPAN. Such arrangements shall be consistent with this IA.

5. Maintain a current inventory of its USGS land remote sensing satellite data holdings and provide at least monthly updates of its metadata to the USGS in an agreed-upon format, electronically or on agreed-upon media, once the ground station(s) is (are) operational. These metadata may be made available publicly through USGS data facilities.

6. Establish and maintain a computer-accessible electronic system, with external public access, of browse imagery for its USGS land remote sensing satellite data holdings, or provide browse data at least monthly to the USGS in an agreed-upon format and on agreed-upon media, once the ground station(s) is (are) operational. LAPAN browse imagery may be made available publicly through USGS data facilities.

7. Maintain USGS land remote sensing satellite data that have met LAPAN quality standards in LAPAN's archive for at least 10 years following data acquisition, using accepted archive management practices. If LAPAN plans to discard data, it will issue a purge alert to the USGS, which will be given first right of refusal to acquire the data at a price to be negotiated.

8. Endeavor to ensure that any radio frequency problem occurring in relation to data reception by LAPAN's ground station(s) is resolved to the satisfaction of the Parties. Questions concerning radio frequency interference by the USGS land remote sensing spacecraft raised by entities in third countries will be referred to the USGS.

9. When requested by the USGS in support of key U. S. Government programs, provide reasonable quantities of LAPAN-held USGS land remote sensing satellite data, in an agreed-upon format, electronically or on media, and at a price to be negotiated.

10. Repatriate to the USGS, within 30 days of downlink, any USGS land remote sensing satellite data received which is unique to LAPAN's archive.

11. For purposes of validating data quality, exchange limited amounts of LAPAN-held USGS land remote sensing satellite data, in an agreed-upon format, electronically or on media, when requested by the USGS. Data for this purpose shall be exchanged annually, at no cost to the USGS.

12. When requested by the USGS in response to a significant loss of spacecraft capability to record data for the USGS archive, routinely provide sufficient quantities of newly acquired USGS land remote sensing satellite data to meet U.S. Government mission requirements, in an agreed-upon format, electronically or on media, at a cost to be negotiated. For any support necessary to LAPAN beyond providing USGS land remote sensing satellite data to the USGS as described above, the Parties will negotiate specific financial terms.

13. Communicate with the MOC on spacecraft information, in order to maximize data collection and efficiency of spacecraft operations.

14. Provide support for anomaly resolution of USGS land remote sensing satellite missions.

ARTICLE 3—INTERNATIONAL MISSION COORDINATION

A. Each Party shall designate program representatives to be responsible for the implementation of this IA. Supplemental meetings between the Parties will be held by mutual agreement.

B. Program management representatives from the Parties will participate in annual meetings of the Landsat Ground Station Operations Working Group (LGSOWG). This group, chaired by the USGS, will serve as a forum for the exchange of policy, programmatic and management information among station operators and the USGS.

C. Technical representatives from the Parties will participate in annual meetings of the Landsat Technical Working Group (LTWG). This group, also chaired by the USGS, will review and coordinate technical and operational aspects of USGS international mission support.

ARTICLE 4—SCIENCE AND APPLICATIONS DEVELOPMENT

1. The Parties will seek to identify opportunities for cooperation in improved land remote sensing satellite data collection, user accessibility, and data distribution.

2. The Parties will seek to identify opportunities to support new research in the use of land remote sensing satellite data, and the development of related applications to enhance land use practices, ecosystems management, climate change research, and other areas of Earth systems science.

3. The Parties will seek to cooperate in the support of global observation and science programs involving the use of land remote sensing satellite data.

4. The Parties will consult with one another on best practices and improved means of cooperation in the long-term archiving and preservation of land remote sensing satellite data.

5. The Parties will share information and consider opportunities for training and capacity building in the use of land remote sensing satellite data.

6. Subject to the provisions of Article 10, the Parties will share information on their respective development and potential for cooperation in their respective land remote sensing satellite missions.

ARTICLE 5—USER SERVICE ARRANGEMENTS

The USGS reserves the right to service the land remote sensing satellite data requests of all users affiliated with U.S. Government programs.

ARTICLE 6—FINANCIAL ARRANGEMENTS AND LEGAL AUTHORIZATION

1. The Parties shall be responsible for funding their respective activities under this IA. Additionally, LAPAN, or its designated agent, shall pay to the USGS, or ensure the appropriate authorities of LAPAN's government pay to the USGS, in a timely manner, any access fees described in any mission-specific Annex(es). These fees are required to enable the USGS to administer all operations in support of a global network of cooperating ground receiving stations.

2. Obligations under this Agreement and any Implementing Annexes shall be subject to the availability of funding obtained through each Party's funding procedures.

3. Should either Party encounter budgetary problems that may affect the activities carried out under this IA that Party shall notify and consult with the other Party in a timely manner in order to minimize the negative impact of such problems on the cooperation.

ARTICLE 7—DUTIES, FEES, AND TAXES

In accordance with its national laws and regulations, each Party shall seek to ensure free customs clearance and waiver of all applicable duties, fees, and taxes for the import or export of goods necessary for the implementation of this IA. In the event that any duties, fees, or taxes of any kind are nonetheless levied on such goods, such duties, fees, or taxes shall be borne by the Party of the country levying them.

ARTICLE 8—ENTRY AND EXIT OF PERSONNEL

On a reciprocal basis, each Party shall use reasonable efforts to facilitate, in accordance with its laws and regulations, the entry to and exit from its territory of personnel engaged in joint activities pursuant to this IA.

ARTICLE 9—LAWS, WARRANTIES, RIGHTS, AND LIABILITY

1. The activities under this IA will be conducted in accordance with the applicable laws and regulations of the Parties' countries, respectively, and shall be subject to the availability of appropriate funds.

2. The USGS does not warrant the suitability of its land remote sensing data for any purpose and shall not be liable for any damage or injury brought about by use of USGS land remote sensing satellite systems and their data.

3. The USGS retains the ownership right to all raw land remote sensing data acquired by its satellites. Beyond the provisions of Article 3.B.3, the USGS places no restrictions on LAPAN to disclose, use, manipulate, generate products from, distribute, or sell USGS land remote sensing satellite data.

ARTICLE 10—EXCHANGE OF TECHNICAL INFORMATION

1. Technical information exchanged between the Parties will be subject to the applicable laws, regulations, and policies of the Parties' countries, respectively. In the event it is necessary to exchange technical information and the furnishing Party considers that such technical information is to be protected for proprietary or export control purposes, such information must be clearly marked with a legend indicating the country of origin, the conditions of release, that the information relates to this IA, and that it is furnished in confidence.

2. The Parties USGS and LAPAN will take all lawful steps available to prevent disclosure of such protected or proprietary technical information without the consent of the other Party and to ensure that it is used only for the purposes of this IA.

3. The USGS and LAPAN may release to the public other general, non-technical information regarding each other's programs or operations after ensuring, through consultation with each other when necessary, that this information is fairly and accurately represented.

4. The USGS and LAPAN may exchange appropriate technical information and documentation for the purposes of downlinking, processing, and archiving USGS land remote sensing satellite data as well as for generating and distributing products from that data.

ARTICLE 11—CONSULTATIONS AND SETTLEMENT OF DISPUTES

1. The Parties shall consult, as appropriate, to review the implementation of activities undertaken pursuant to this IA, and to exchange views on potential areas of future cooperation.

2. In the event questions arise regarding the interpretation, application, or implementation of activities under this IA, the Program Managers of the Parties shall endeavor to resolve the questions. If the Program Managers are unable to reach an agreement, then the matter will be referred to a more senior level of the Parties for joint resolution.

ARTICLE 12—ENTRY INTO FORCE, DURATION, AND TERMINATION

1. This IA shall enter into force upon signature by both Parties and remain in force through the operational lifetime of the USGS land remote sensing spacecraft(s) from which LAPAN receives USGS land remote sensing data. This IA may be amended by mutual agreement of the Parties.

2. In the event that either of the Parties is unable to comply with any provision of this IA, either Party, after consultation with the other, shall have the option of terminating this IA, providing at least 30 days' notice of such action, forwarded in writing by one Party to the other.

3. Notwithstanding termination or expiration of this IA, the obligations of the Parties set forth in Article 2.B.3, Article 2.B.7, Article 9.2, Article 9.3, and Article 10 of this IA shall continue to apply.

ARTICLE 13—SIGNATURE

IN WITNESS THEREOF, respective representatives of the Parties have signed this Implementing Agreement.

For the United States Geological Survey of the Department of the Interior:

[Signature]

Marcia McNutt
Director
U.S. Geological Survey
Reston, Virginia

OCT 10 2012

Date

Place

For LAPAN:

[Signature]

Sri Kaloka Prabotosari
Prime Secretary
LAPAN
Jakarta, Indonesia

NOV 02, 2012

Date

Jakarta, Indonesia

Place

ID-13.0000
ACIS Ref. ID: 10466

ANNEX I

TO THE

IMPLEMENTING ARRANGEMENT

BETWEEN THE

UNITED STATES GEOLOGICAL SURVEY OF THE DEPARTMENT OF THE INTERIOR

AND THE

NATIONAL INSTITUTE OF AERONAUTICS AND SPACE (LAPAN) OF THE REPUBLIC OF INDONESIA

FOR COOPERATION IN THE USE OF U.S. LAND REMOTE SENSING SATELLITE DATA

DEFINITION OF TERMS

Acquisition Radius:

An International Cooperator's (IC's) acquisition radius is that portion of the Earth over which the satellite can communicate with an IC's ground station.

Browse:

Browse is a full resolution or sub-sampled Level OR or Level 1 digital image of the Earth that can be viewed on a scene basis to quickly assess general ground area coverage, data quality, and the spatial relationships between ground area coverage and cloud coverage. A browse is an image with a reduced data volume to facilitate screening of archived Land Remote Sensing Satellite Data. Specifications regarding browse images are documented in the appropriate mission Data Format Control Book (DFCB) and made available by the USGS.

Data Format:

The Landsat Technical Working Group (LTWG) recommends the archive data format for exchanging data between an International Cooperator and USGS archives. The archive data exchange format for purposes of quality assessment and key government programs is typically the lowest level of processed data available (i.e. Mission or Raw Computer Compatible [RCC] Data) and is transferred electronically or on media. The archive data exchange format is documented in the appropriate mission Data Validation and Exchange Plan and associated Data Format Control Book (DFCB) and made available by the USGS.

Data Products Distribution Format:

The USGS Land Remote Sensing Satellite Data products are Level-ORp (Level Zero Reformatted Product) in HDF format and Level-IT (terrain corrected) in Geo-TIFF format. International Cooperators may produce data products of their choice. ICs are encouraged, but not required to produce Level ORp data products in HDF format, but are required to distribute Level-IT data products in Geo-TIFF format. Specifications regarding Level-ORp and Level-IT data products are documented in the appropriate mission Data Format Control Book (DFCB) and made available by the USGS.

International Cooperator (IC):

An International Cooperator (IC) is any non-U.S. Government agency or commercial organization acting on behalf of or in cooperation with a foreign government or international organization, which enters into an agreement with the USGS for purposes of receiving or exchanging Land Remote Sensing Satellite Data.

Key U.S. Government Programs:

Key U.S. Government Programs are any U.S. Government agencies and U.S. Government contractors, other U.S. and foreign researchers and entities involved in the United States Global Change Research Program, and U.S. and foreign researchers and foreign and international entities having signed a cooperative agreement with the United States Government involving the use of USGS Land Remote Sensing Satellite Data for non-commercial purposes.

The United States Global Change Research Program is the Executive Branch program responding to Public Law 101-606, the Global Change Research Act of 1990, and most recently described in the annual report accompanying the President's budget entitled "Our Changing Planet: The U.S. Climate Change Science Program for Fiscal Year 2012."

International counterpart programs of the U.S. Global Change Research Program are discussed in Section V of "Our Changing Planet." These include the Intergovernmental Panel on Climate Change, the World Climate Research Program, the International Council on Science, and the Group on Earth Observations.

Mission Operations Center (MOC):

The Mission Operations Center (MOC) consists of the people, procedures, and hardware/software systems used for the successful execution of real-time spacecraft operations and off-line scheduling and analysis activities. All command and control functions of the spacecraft performed by the Flight Operations Team (FOT) will take place from the MOC.

Metadata:

Metadata is descriptive information pertaining to the USGS Land Remote Sensing Satellite Data, including such information as location and acquisition date, compiled for Level OR and Level-1 data, and made available through the USGS user interface. Specifications regarding the metadata are documented in the Landsat Metadata Description Document (LMDD) and made available by the USGS.

Raw Data:

Raw Data is the USGS Land Remote Sensing Satellite Data in the form of wideband telemetry transmitted by the satellite.

U.S. Government and Affiliated Users:

U.S. Government and Affiliated Users are any Federal, State or local government agency personnel and personnel from any organization performing cooperative work with or for these government agencies.

USGS Land Remote Sensing Satellites:

USGS Land Remote Sensing Satellites are any satellites owned and operated by the USGS for the purposes of this agreement. These satellites may include, but are not limited to, the Landsat missions.

ID-13.0000
ACIS Ref. ID: 10467

ANNEX II

TO THE

IMPLEMENTING ARRANGEMENT

BETWEEN THE

UNITED STATES GEOLOGICAL SURVEY
OF THE DEPARTMENT OF THE INTERIOR

AND THE

NATIONAL INSTITUTE OF AERONAUTICS AND SPACE (LAPAN)
OF THE REPUBLIC OF INDONESIA

FOR COOPERATION IN THE USE OF
U.S. LAND REMOTE SENSING SATELLITE DATA

LANDSAT 8
ANNUAL ACCESS FEE AGREEMENT

ARTICLE 1—INTRODUCTION

Pursuant to Article 6 of the Implementing Arrangement (IA) between the United States Geological Survey of the Department of the Interior and National Institute of Aeronautics and Space (LAPAN) of the Republic of Indonesia for the Direct Reception, Distribution, and Exchange of Land Remote Sensing Satellite Data; U.S. Presidential Decision Directive/National Science and Technology Council-3, as amended on October 16, 2000; and the Land Remote Sensing Policy Act of 1992, the USGS has established a fee structure to enable it to administer all operations in support of a global network of cooperating ground receiving stations for direct reception of data from the Landsat 8 mission. This Annex sets forth the related financial and administrative terms and conditions for Landsat 8 cooperation between the USGS and LAPAN.

ARTICLE 2 —FEE STRUCTURE

The fee structure comprises a one-time *initialization fee* and an *annual access fee.* If LAPAN moves a receiving antenna to a new location greater than 50 kilometers from its original location, an *antenna move fee* will be assessed. The *annual access fee* will be payable for the United States Government (USG) Fiscal Year, which begins on October 1 and ends on September 30, and may be prorated to the remaining portion of the USG Fiscal Year, from the start date for direct transmission of Landsat 8 data to September 30.

The *initialization fee* for a new IC or a new IC station is U.S. $35,000 for each receiving site. The total *initialization fee* for LAPAN will be U.S. $35,000 for the new receiving site at Rumpin and U.S. $0 for the existing receiving site(s) located at Parepare.

The *antenna move fee* is U.S. $15,000 and will be billed each time a station is moved a distance greater than 50 kilometers.

The *annual access fee* is U.S. $100,000 for a single station operation. Each additional ground station has an *annual access fee* of U.S. $50,000. The total *annual access fee* for LAPAN will be U.S. $150,000 for the receiving site(s) located at Rumpin and Parepare.

USG Fiscal Year 2013 is the base year for each of these fees.

ARTICLE 3—PAYMENT SCHEDULE

The one-time *initialization fee* and *antenna move fee*, if applicable, are due and payable 30 days prior to LAPAN reception of Landsat 8 data.

The *annual access fee* will be payable annually by LAPAN. LAPAN will receive an annual bill 30 days prior to the start of the USG Fiscal Year (billing date of September 1). Annual payments by LAPAN will be due at the start of the USG Fiscal Year (October 1).

The USGS reserves the right to terminate transmission of Landsat 8 data to LAPAN at any time that LAPAN is in arrears in its payments to the USGS or is delinquent in regularly scheduled delivery of raw telemetry data to the USGS in accordance with IA Article 2.A.3. The USGS will notify LAPAN 30 days in advance of its intention to terminate transmission for these reasons. Payments may be by check or wire transfer in U.S. dollars. Payments by check shall be in U.S. dollars and shall be payable to:

Department of the Interior/USGS

Payments by check shall be mailed to

USGS Office of Financial Management
271 National Center
12201 Sunrise Valley Drive
Reston, Virginia, 20192 USA

Payments by wire transfer shall be in U.S. dollars and transferred to the USGS's bank account. The USGS will provide exact wire transfer information with each billing.

All payments must be received within 30 days from the date of invoice. Charges for late payment will be at the U. S. Treasury Department prevailing rate on the overdue balance for each 30-day period or portion thereof that payment is delayed.

ARTICLE 4—FEE CHANGES

While USGS reserves the right to make modifications to the *annual access fee* used in this fee structure, it is the USGS's intent to minimize the changes to the fee structure during the life of the Landsat 8 mission. For the Landsat 8 mission, a 3% annual increase is planned to account for average annual rates of inflation. Reasonable notification of any proposed change to these fees (*initialization, antenna move*, and *annual access fees*), taking into account the budget cycles of the parties, shall be provided in writing by the USGS to LAPAN 60 days prior to the implementation of the proposed change. Any proposed fee change would not exceed 10% of the current *annual access fee*.

For budget planning purposes the anticipated *annual access fee* structure is as follows:

	Year 1	Year 2 (+3%)	Year 3 (+3%)	Year 4 (+3%)
One Site	U.S. $100,000	U.S. $103,000	U.S. $106,090	U.S. $109,273
Two Sites	U.S. $150,000	U.S. $154,500	U.S. $159,135	U.S. $163,909

ARTICLE 5—CONTINGENCIES

The USGS, in consultation with LAPAN, may curtail or terminate the transmission of data and adjust the *annual access fees* if the USGS is unable to satisfy data requests due to spacecraft system capability limitations or ground receiving stations conflicts.

ARTICLE 6—DURATION AND AMENDMENT

This Annex will remain in effect as long as the IA remains in force, and it may be amended by mutual consent of USGS and LAPAN through an Exchange of Letters.

At the beginning of each new USG Fiscal Year, the USGS and LAPAN will review this Annex and revise it if necessary.

ARTICLE 7—AUTHORIZING SIGNATURES

The signatures of the authorized officials below signify the agreement by the Parties to the terms of this annex.

For the United States Geological Survey of the Department of the Interior:	For LAPAN:
[Signature]	[Signature]
Marcia McNutt Director U.S. Geological Survey Reston, Virginia	Taufik Malana Deputy Chairman for Remote Sensing Affairs LAPAN Jakarta, Indonesia
OCT 10 2012	NOV 02, 2012
Date	Date

STATE DEPARTMENT DOCUMENT NUMBER: 12-198

AGREEMENT BETWEEN THE UNITED STATES OF AMERICA AND JAPAN CONCERNING A PROGRAM FOR COOPERATIVE RESEARCH ON HYBRID ELECTRIC PROPULSION

EFFECTED BY EXCHANGE OF NOTES AT TOKYO, NOVEMBER 2, 2012
ENTERED INTO FORCE NOVEMBER 2, 2012

CTIA DOCUMENT NUMBER: 18097.000

DIPLOMATIC NOTE

No. 0961

His Excellency
Koichiro Gemba,
Minister for Foreign Affairs of Japan

Excellency,

I have the honor to acknowledge the receipt of Your Excellency's Note of today's date, which reads as follows:

"Excellency,

I have the honor to refer to the Mutual Defense Assistance Agreement between Japan and the United States of America signed at Tokyo on March 8, 1954 (hereinafter referred to as "the MDA Agreement"), which provides, *inter alia,* that each Government, consistently with the principle that economic stability is essential to international peace and security, will make available to the other such equipment, materials, services, or other assistance as the Government furnishing such assistance may authorize, in accordance with such detailed arrangements as may be made between them.

The representatives of the Government of Japan and the Government of the United States of America have recently held discussions for the purpose of making such detailed arrangements as mentioned above concerning a program for the cooperative research on Hybrid Electric Propulsion (hereinafter referred to as "the Program"), taking into account the exchange of information undertaken in accordance with the Memorandum of Understanding between the Ministry of Defense of Japan and the Department of Defense of the United States of America concerning projects for cooperative research, signed on February 17, 2010 (hereinafter referred to as "the Memorandum of Understanding of 2010"), made under the Exchange of Notes of the same date between the Government of Japan and the Government of the United States of America concerning a program for the cooperative research on Image Gyro for Airborne Applications and concerning the formulation of additional programs for cooperation research under the MDA Agreement. The following is the understanding of the Government of Japan regarding the results of the above-mentioned discussions:

1. In accordance with the detailed implementing arrangements to be made under paragraph 4, the Government of Japan and the Government of the United States of America will mutually provide information, equipment, and materials which are necessary to implement the Program, subject to the laws and regulations of each country. The two Governments will jointly bear the cost necessary for the execution of the Program.

2. The Program will be undertaken through contracts with industries of Japan and industries of the United States of America to the extent necessary.

3. The present understanding will be implemented in accordance with the MDA Agreement and arrangements made thereunder, including the Agreement between the Government of Japan and the Government of the United States of America to Facilitate Interchange of Patent Rights and Technical Information for Purposes of Defense, signed at Tokyo on March 22, 1956.

4. In order to implement the present understanding, representatives of the competent authorities of the two Governments will make detailed implementing arrangements that will be applied to the Program. The detailed implementing arrangements will consist of the Memorandum of Understanding of 2010 and a project arrangement. For such arrangements, the competent authority of the Government of Japan will be the Ministry of Defense, and the competent authority of the Government of the United States of America will be the Department of Defense.

5. The financial obligations and expenditures incurred by the Government of Japan and the Government of the United States of America under the present understanding and all arrangements to be made hereunder will be subject to budget authorization pursuant to the constitutional and legislative provisions of the respective countries.

I have the honor to propose that, if the above understanding is acceptable to the Government of the United States of America, the present Note and Your Excellency's reply of acceptance shall be regarded as constituting an agreement between the two Governments which shall enter into force on the date of Your Excellency's reply and shall remain in force until six months after the date of the receipt of notice of termination by either Government.

I avail myself of this opportunity to renew to Your Excellency the assurance of my highest consideration."

I have the honor to confirm on behalf of the Government of the United States of America that the foregoing understanding is acceptable to the Government of the United States of America and to agree that Your Excellency's Note and this reply shall be regarded as constituting an agreement between the two Governments which shall enter into force on the date of this reply and shall remain in force until six months after the date of the receipt of notice of termination by either Government.

I avail myself of this opportunity to renew to Your Excellency the assurance of my highest consideration.

[Signature]

Embassy of the United States of America
Tokyo, November 2, 2012

JAPAN	)	
CITY OF TOKYO	)	**SS:**
EMBASSY OF THE UNITED STATES OF AMERICA	)	

I, Hugues P. Ogier, American Consul, Consul of the United States of America, in and for Tokyo, Japan, duly commissioned and qualified, do hereby certify that this document is a true and correct copy of the original this day exhibited to me and compared by me with the said original and found to agree therewith word for word and figure for figure.

IN WITNESS WHEREOF

I have hereunto set my hand and the official seal of the Consular Service of the United States of America at Tokyo, Japan on NOV-1 2012.

[Signature]

Hugues P. Ogier
American Consul
Consul of the United States of America
duly commissioned and qualified.

Translation

Tokyo, November 2, 2012

His Excellency
Mr. John V. Roos
Ambassador Extraordinary
and Plenipotentiary
of the United States of America

Excellency,

I have the honor to refer to the Mutual Defense Assistance Agreement between Japan and the United States of America signed at Tokyo on March 8, 1954 (hereinafter referred to as "the MDA Agreement"), which provides, *inter alia,* that each Government, consistently with the principle that economic stability is essential to international peace and security, will make available to the other such equipment, materials, services, or other assistance as the Government furnishing such assistance may authorize, in accordance with such detailed arrangements as may be made between them.

The representatives of the Government of Japan and the Government of the United States of America have recently held discussions for the purpose of making such detailed arrangements as mentioned above concerning a program for the cooperative research on Hybrid Electric Propulsion (hereinafter referred to as "the Program"), taking into account the exchange of information undertaken in accordance with the Memorandum of Understanding between the Ministry of Defense of Japan and the Department of Defense of the United States of America concerning projects for cooperative research, signed on February 17, 2010 (hereinafter referred to as "the Memorandum of Understanding of 2010"), made under the Exchange of Notes of the same date between the Government of Japan and the Government of the United States of America concerning a program for the cooperative research on Image Gyro for Airborne Applications and concerning the formulation of additional programs for cooperation research under the MDA Agreement. The following is the understanding of the Government of Japan regarding the results of the abovementioned discussions:

1. In accordance with the detailed implementing arrangements to be made under paragraph 4, the Government of Japan and the Government of the United States of America will mutually provide information, equipment, and materials which are necessary to implement the Program, subject to the laws and regulations of each country. The two Governments will jointly bear the cost necessary for the execution of the Program.

2. The Program will be undertaken through contracts with industries of Japan and industries of the United States of America to the extent necessary.

3. The present understanding will be implemented in accordance with the MDA Agreement and arrangements made thereunder, including the Agreement between the Government of Japan and the Government of the United States of America to Facilitate Interchange of Patent Rights and Technical Information for Purposes of Defense, signed at Tokyo on March 22, 1956.

4. In order to implement the present understanding, representatives of the competent authorities of the two Governments will make detailed implementing arrangements that will be applied to the Program. The detailed implementing arrangements will consist of the Memorandum of Understanding of 2010 and a project arrangement. For such arrangements, the competent

authority of the Government of Japan will be the Ministry of Defense, and the competent authority of the Government of the United States of America will be the Department of Defense.

5. The financial obligations and expenditures incurred by the Government of Japan and the Government of the United States of America under the present understanding and all arrangements to be made hereunder will be subject to budget authorization pursuant to the constitutional and legislative provisions of the respective countries.

I have the honor to propose that, if the above understanding is acceptable to the Government of the United States of America, the present Note and Your Excellency's reply of acceptance shall be regarded as constituting an agreement between the two Governments which shall enter into force on the date of Your Excellency's reply and shall remain in force until six months after the date of the receipt of notice of termination by either Government.

I avail myself of this opportunity to renew to Your Excellency the assurance of my highest consideration.

Koichiro Gemba
Minister for Foreign Affairs
of Japan

STATE DEPARTMENT DOCUMENT NUMBER: 12-199

AGREEMENT BETWEEN THE UNITED STATES OF AMERICA AND JAMAICA REGARDING THE CARIBBEAN BASIN SECURITY INITIATIVE AND THE PROVISION OF TECHNICAL SUPPORT FOR MARITIME SECURITY FORCES

EFFECTED BY EXCHANGE OF NOTES AT KINGSTON,
SEPTEMBER 24 AND NOVEMBER 6, 2012
ENTERED INTO FORCE NOVEMBER 6, 2012

CTIA DOCUMENT NUMBER: 18098.000

DIPLOMATIC NOTE

No. 456/12

The Embassy of the United States of America presents its compliments to the Ministry of Foreign Affairs and Foreign Trade of the Government of Jamaica and has the honor to refer to earlier discussions between representatives of the two Governments regarding the Caribbean Basin Security Initiative and the provision of technical support for maritime security forces through that initiative. The U.S. Government proposes to provide this type of support via a regional Technical Assistance Field Team to bolster the maintenance and logistics capabilities of Caribbean Basin Security Initiative partner nations' maritime forces through mentoring, training and development of partner nations' maintenance and logistics systems and processes. Support will be tailored to individual partner nations' requirements and could include, but is not limited to assessments, equipment, training, and technical support for maritime assets and maintenance and logistical systems.

In accordance with these discussions, it is proposed that the Government of Jamaica agree:

A. That unless the consent of the Government of the United States of America has been first obtained, the Government of Jamaica shall not:

(I) Permit any use of such defense articles, related training, including training materials, or other defense services by anyone not an officer, employee or agent of the Government of Jamaica;

(II) Transfer, or permit any officer, employee or agent of the Government of Jamaica to transfer, such defense articles, related training, including training materials, or other defense services by gift, sale or otherwise; or

(III) Use, or permit the use of, such defense articles, related training, including training materials, or other defense services for purposes other than those for which provided;

B. That such defense articles, related training, including training materials, or other defense services shall be returned to the Government of the United States of America when they are no longer needed for the purposes for which they were furnished, unless the Government of the United States of America consents to another disposition;

C. That the net proceeds of sale received by the Government of Jamaica in disposing of, with prior written consent of the Government of the United States of America, any defense article furnished by the Government of the United States of America on a grant basis, including scrap from any such defense article, shall be paid to the Government of the United States of America; and

D. That the Government of Jamaica shall maintain the security of such defense articles, related training, including training materials, and other defense services; that it shall provide substantially the same degree of security protection afforded to such defense articles, related training, including training materials, and other defense services by the Government of the United States of America; and that it shall, as the Government of the United States of America may require, permit continuous observation, scheduled inspections, physical inventories, and review by, and furnish necessary information to, representatives of the Government of the United States of America with regard to the use thereof by the Government of Jamaica.

The Ministry of Foreign Affairs and Foreign Trade's note stating that the foregoing is acceptable to the Government of Jamaica shall, together with this note, constitute an agreement between the two Governments, which shall enter into force on the date of the Ministry's note.

The Embassy of the United States of America avails itself of this opportunity to renew to the Ministry of Foreign Affairs and Foreign Trade of the Government of Jamaica the assurances of its highest consideration.

Embassy of the United States of America,
Kingston, Jamaica,
September 24, 2012.

Ref No.: 220/701/25

Embassy of the United States of America
Kingston, Jamaica
6th November, 2012

The Ministry of Foreign Affairs and Foreign Trade presents its compliments to the Embassy of the United States of America and has the honor to refer the Embassy's Note No. 456/12, dated 24th September, 2012. This Note refers to earlier discussions between representatives of the two (2) governments regarding the Caribbean Basin Security Initiative, and the provision of technical support for maritime security forces through that Initiative.

The United States government proposed to provide this type of support through a regional Technical Assistance Field Team to bolster the maintenance and logistics capabilities of the Caribbean Basin Security Initiative partner nations' maritime forces through mentoring, training and development of partner nations' maintenance and logistics systems and processes. Support will be tailored to the individual partner nations' requirements and could include, but is not limited to, assessments, equipment training and technical support for the maritime assets and maintenance and logistical systems.

In accordance with these discussions, the Government of Jamaica agrees that:

A. Unless the consent of the Government of the United States of America has been first obtained, the Government of Jamaica shall not:

(I) Permit any use of such defense articles, related training, including training materials, or other defense services by anyone not an officer, employee or agent of the Government of Jamaica;

(II) Transfer, or permit any officer, employee or agent of the Government of Jamaica to transfer, such defense articles, related training, including training materials, or other defense services by gift, sale or otherwise; or

(III) Use, or permit the use of, such defense articles, related training, including training materials, or other defense services for purposes other than those for which provided;

B. That such defense articles, related training, including training materials, or other defense services shall be returned to the Government of the United States of America when they are no longer needed for the purposes for which they were furnished, unless the Government of the United States of America consents to another disposition;

C. That, with prior written consent of the Government of the United States of America, the net proceeds of sale received by the Government of Jamaica in disposing of any defense article furnished by the Government of the Untied [*sic*] States of America on a grant basis, including scrap from any such defense article, shall be paid to the Government of the United States of America; and

D. That the Government of Jamaica shall maintain the security of such defense articles, related training, including training materials, and other defense services; that it shall provide substantially the same degree of security protection afforded to such defense articles, related training, including training materials, and other defense services by the Government of the United States of America; and that it shall, as the Government of the United States of America may require, permit continuous observation, scheduled inspections, physical inventories, and review by, and furnish necessary information to, representatives of the Government of the United States of America with regard to the use thereof by the Government of Jamaica.

Ministry of Foreign Affairs and Foreign Trade agrees that the foregoing is acceptable to the Government of Jamaica and that this Note together with the Diplomatic Note of the Embassy of the United States of America No. 456/12, dated 24th September, 2012 constitutes an agreement between the two (2) governments which shall enter into force on the date of this Ministry's Note.

The Ministry of Foreign Affairs and Foreign Trade of Jamaica avails itself of this opportunity to renew to the Embassy of the United States of America the assurances of its highest consideration.

JAMAICAN FOREIGN SERVICE

No. 5/503/10

The Ministry of Foreign Affairs and Foreign Trade presents its compliments to the Embassy of the United States of America and has the honour to acknowledge receipt of the latter's Note No. 456/12, dated 24 September 2012, pertaining to discussions between representatives of both Governments on the Caribbean Basin Security Initiative and the provision of technical support for Maritime Security Forces.

The Ministry of Foreign Affairs and Foreign Trade avails itself of this opportunity to renew to the Embassy of the United States of America, the assurances of its highest consideration.

Embassy of the United States of America
Kingston
29 October 2012

STATE DEPARTMENT DOCUMENT NUMBER: 12-200

ACQUISITION AND CROSS-SERVICING AGREEMENT (US-NZ-02) BETWEEN THE DEPARTMENT OF DEFENSE OF THE UNITED STATES OF AMERICA AND THE NEW ZEALAND DEFENCE FORCE, WITH ANNEXES

SIGNED AT SYDNEY, NOVEMBER 6, 2012
ENTERED INTO FORCE NOVEMBER 6, 2012

CTIA DOCUMENT NUMBER: 18099.000

PREAMBLE

The Department of Defense of the United States of America (U.S.) and the New Zealand Defence Force (NZ), hereinafter referred to as "the Parties", desiring to further the interoperability, readiness, and effectiveness of their respective military forces through increased logistic cooperation, have resolved to conclude this Acquisition and Cross-Servicing Agreement (this Agreement).

ARTICLE I. PURPOSE

This Agreement is entered into for the purpose of establishing basic terms, conditions, and procedures to facilitate the reciprocal provision of Logistic Support, Supplies, and Services as that term is defined in Article II of this Agreement.

ARTICLE II. DEFINITIONS

1. For the purposes of this Agreement and any Implementing Arrangements that provide specific procedures, the following definitions apply:

a. *Classified Information.* Official information that requires protection in the interests of national security and is so designated by the application of a security classification marking. This information may be in oral, visual, magnetic, or documentary form or in the form of equipment or technology.

b. *Equal-Value-Exchange.* Payment for a Transfer conducted under this Agreement in which it is agreed that the Receiving Party shall replace Logistic Support, Supplies, and Services that it receives with Logistic Support, Supplies, and Services of an equal monetary value.

c. *Implementing Arrangement.* A written supplementary arrangement that specifies the details, terms, and conditions for specific Logistic Support, Supplies and Services rendered pursuant to this Agreement.

d. *Invoice.* A document from the Supplying Party that requests reimbursement or payment for specific Logistic Support, Supplies, and Services rendered pursuant to this Agreement and any applicable Implementing Arrangement.

e. *Logistic Support, Supplies, and Services.* Food, water, billeting, transportation (including airlift), petroleum, oils, lubricants, clothing, communication services, medical services, ammunition, base operations support (and construction incident to base operations support), storage services, use of facilities, training services, spare parts and components, repair and maintenance services, calibration services, and port services. The term also includes the temporary use of general purpose vehicles and other nonlethal items of military equipment, where such lease or loan is permitted under the national laws and regulations of the Parties. The term "Logistic Support, Supplies, and Services" refers to support, supplies or services from any or all of the foregoing categories.

f. *Order.* A written request, in an agreed-upon format and signed by an authorized individual, for the provision of specific Logistic Support, Supplies, and Services pursuant to this Agreement and any applicable Implementing Arrangement.

g. *Point of Contact (POC).* An office or agency that is authorized by a Party to sign an Order requesting or agreeing to supply Logistic Support, Supplies, and Services under this Agreement, or to collect or make payments for Logistic Support, Supplies, and Services supplied or received under this Agreement. The POCs are listed in the POC Annexes of this Agreement or associated Implementing Arrangements.

h. *Receiving Party.* The Party ordering and receiving Logistic Support, Supplies, and Services.

i. *Replacement-In-Kind.* Payment for a transfer conducted under this Agreement in which it is agreed that the Receiving Party shall replace Logistic Support, Supplies, and Services that it receives with Logistic Support, Supplies, and Services of an identical, or substantially identical, nature under agreed conditions.

j. *Supplying Party.* The Party providing Logistic Support, Supplies, and Services.

k. *Transfer.* Selling (whether for payment in currency, Replacement-In-Kind, or Equal-Value-Exchange), leasing, loaning, or otherwise temporarily providing Logistic Support, Supplies, and Services under the terms of this Agreement.

ARTICLE III. APPLICABILITY

1. This Agreement is designed to facilitate reciprocal logistic support between the Parties to be used primarily during combined exercises, training, deployments, port calls, operations, or other cooperative efforts, or for unforeseen circumstances or exigencies in which one of the Parties may have a need for Logistic Support, Supplies, and Services.

2. This Agreement applies to the provision of Logistic Support, Supplies, and Services from the military forces of one Party to the military forces of the other Party in return for either cash payment or the reciprocal provision of Logistic Support, Supplies, and Services to the military forces of the Supplying Party.

3. All activities of the Parties under this Agreement and any Implementing Arrangements shall be carried out in accordance with their respective national laws and regulations. All obligations of the Parties under this Agreement and any associated Implementing Arrangements shall be subject to the availability of funds for such purposes. Unless otherwise agreed in advance, a Party shall not place an Order and receive support under this Agreement and any associated Implementing Arrangement unless it has funds or the resources to provide Replacement-in-Kind or Equal-Value-Exchange available to pay for such support. If a Party discovers that it does not have the funds or resources to fulfill its obligations, it shall promptly notify the other Party, which shall have the right to discontinue its provision of any support that was to be paid for with such funds or resources. This shall not affect the obligation of a Party to pay for support already received.

4. The following items are not eligible for Transfer under this Agreement, and are specifically excluded from its coverage:

a. Weapon systems;

b. Major end items of equipment (except for the lease or loan of general purpose vehicles and other nonlethal items of military equipment where such lease or loan is permitted under the national laws and regulations of the Parties); and

c. Initial quantities of replacement and spare parts associated with the initial order of major items of organizational equipment; however, individual replacement and spare parts needed for immediate repair and maintenance services may be transferred.

5. Also excluded from Transfer by either Party under this Agreement are any items the Transfer of which are prohibited by its national laws or regulations. In accordance with U.S. law and regulation, the United States currently may not transfer the following items under this Agreement:

i. Guided missiles;

ii. Naval mines and torpedoes;

iii. Nuclear ammunition (including such items such as warheads, warhead sections, projectiles, demolition munitions, and training ammunition);

iv. Guidance kits for bombs or other ammunition;

v. Chemical munitions or ammunition (which do not include riot-control agents);

vi. Source, byproduct, or special nuclear materials, or any other material, article, data, or thing of value the transfer of which is subject to the Atomic Energy Act of 1954 (Title 42, United States Code, Section 2011, et seq.); and

vii. Items of military equipment designated as Significant Military Equipment on the United States Munitions List (Part 121 of Title 22 of the U.S. Code of Federal Regulations), except as allowed under the definition of Logistic Support, Supplies, and Services under U.S. law.

ARTICLE IV. TERMS AND CONDITIONS

1. Each Party shall make its best efforts, consistent with national priorities, to satisfy requests from the other Party under this Agreement for Logistic Support, Supplies, and Services. However, when an Implementing Arrangement contains a stricter standard for satisfying such requests, the standard in the Implementing Arrangement shall apply.

2. Orders may be placed or accepted only by the Points of Contact, or their designees, identified by the Parties in Annexes B through I of this Agreement. When military forces of New Zealand require Logistic Support, Supplies, and Services outside the U.S. Pacific Command (USPACOM) Area of Responsibility (AOR), they may place Orders directly with the applicable POC or may seek the assistance of USPACOM, or a USPACOM component command, to place an Order with a non-USPACOM POC.

3. An Implementing Arrangement under this Agreement may be negotiated on behalf of the U.S. Department of Defense by Headquarters, USPACOM, the Headquarters of other U.S. Combatant Commands, or their designees. Implementing Arrangements may be negotiated on behalf of the New Zealand Defence Force by the Chief of Defence Force or his duly authorized designee. Implementing Arrangements shall identify POCs and their specific authorizations or limitations.

4. Prior to submitting a written Order, the Receiving Party should initially contact the Supplying Party' s POC, including by telephone, fax, or e-mail to ascertain availability, price, and desired method of repayment for required materiel or services. Orders shall include all the data elements in Annex A, as well as any other terms and details necessary to carry out the transfer. The standard Order form is attached as Annex J. The number of this Agreement, USNZ-02, should be annotated on all Orders and related correspondence.

5. Both Parties shall maintain records of all transactions.

6. The Receiving Party is responsible for:

a. Arranging pick-up and transportation of supplies acquired under this Agreement. This does not preclude the Supplying Party from assisting with loading supplies acquired under this Agreement onto the transportation conveyance.

b. Obtaining any applicable customs clearance and arranging other official actions required by national customs regulations.

7. The individual designated by the Receiving Party to receive the Logistic Support, Supplies, and Services on behalf of the Receiving Party shall sign the standard Order form (Annex J in the appropriate block as evidence of receipt. If the standard Order form is not available at the Supplying Party's point of issue, the individual receiving the Logistic Support, Supplies, and Services shall sign the receipt document provided by the Supplying Party as a substitute. The number of this Agreement, US-NZ-02, shall be entered on the receipt document.

8. The Supplying Party shall be responsible for:

a. Notifying the Receiving Party when and where Logistic Support, Supplies, and Services are available to be picked up; and

b. Forwarding the signed receipt document to the POC who is authorized to accept Orders under this Agreement. The signed receipt document shall be attached to the original Order Form.

9. Logistic Support, Supplies, and Services received through this Agreement shall not be retransferred, either temporarily or permanently, to any other country, international organization, or entity (other than the personnel, employees, or agents of the military forces of the Receiving Party) without the prior written consent of the Supplying Party obtained through applicable channels.

ARTICLE V. REIMBURSEMENT

1. For transfers of Logistic Support, Supplies, and Services under this Agreement, the Parties shall agree on payment either by cash ("reimbursable transaction"), or by Replacement-In-Kind or an Equal-Value-Exchange (both of which are exchange transactions). The Receiving Party shall pay the Supplying Party as provided in either paragraph 1.a. or paragraph 1.b. of this Article.

a. *Reimbursable Transaction.* The Supplying Party shall submit Invoices to the Receiving Party after delivery or performance of the Logistic Support, Supplies, and Services. Both Parties shall provide for the payment of all transactions, and each Party shall invoice the other Party at least once every three (3) months for all transactions not previously invoiced. Invoices shall be accompanied by necessary support documentation and shall be paid within sixty (60) days of the date prepared and entered upon the Invoice. Payment shall be made in the currency of the Supplying Party or as otherwise agreed in the Order. In pricing a reimbursable transaction, the Parties agree to the following reciprocal pricing principles:

(1) In the case of a specific acquisition by the Supplying Party from its contractors on behalf of a Receiving Party, the price shall be no less favorable than the price charged the military forces by the contractor of the Supplying Party for identical items or services, less any amounts excluded by Article VI of this Agreement. The price charged may take into account differentials due to delivery schedules, points of delivery, and other similar considerations.

(2) In the case of Transfer from the Supplying Party's own resources, the Supplying Party shall charge the same price charged its own military forces for identical Logistic Support, Supplies, and Services, as of the date delivery or performance occurs, less amounts excluded by Article VI of this Agreement. In any case where a price has not been established or charges are not made for one's own military forces, the Parties shall agree on a price in advance, reflecting reciprocal pricing principles, excluding charges that are precluded under these same reciprocal pricing principles.

b. *Exchange Transaction.* Exchange transactions may be by Replacement-In-Kind or Equal-Value-Exchange. The Receiving Party shall pay by transferring to the Supplying Party Logistic Support, Supplies, and Services that are agreed between the Parties to be identical (or substantially identical) or to be of equal monetary value to the Logistic Support, Supplies, and Services delivered or performed by the Supplying Party. When Equal-Value-Exchange is the agreed method of payment, both Parties will agree prior to the provision of the requested support, to the extent possible, on the goods and services that will be accepted for payment. The Receiving Party is responsible for arranging return transportation and delivery of the replacement Logistic Support, Supplies, and Services to the location mutually agreed between the Parties at the time the Order is signed. If the Receiving Party does not complete the exchange within the terms of a replacement schedule agreed to or in effect at the time of the original transaction, which may not exceed one year from the date of the original transaction, the transaction shall be deemed reimbursable and governed by paragraph 1.a. of this Article, except that the price shall be established using actual or estimated prices in effect on the date payment otherwise would have been due.

c. *Establishment of Price or Value.* The following pricing mechanisms are provided to clarify application of the reciprocal pricing principles. The price established for inventory stock materiel shall be the Supplying Party's stock list price. The price for new procurement shall be the same price paid to the contractor or vendor by the Supplying Party. The price for services rendered will be the Supplying Party's standard price, or, if not applicable, the costs directly associated with providing the services. Prices charged shall exclude all taxes and duties that the

Receiving Party is exempted from paying under other agreements or arrangements concluded between the Governments of the Parties. Upon request, the Parties agree to provide information sufficient to verify that these reciprocal pricing principles have been followed and that prices do not include waived or excluded costs.

2. When a definitive price for the Order is not agreed to in advance, the Order, pending agreement on final price, shall set forth a maximum liability to the Party ordering the Logistic Support, Supplies, and Services. Then the Parties shall enter into negotiations promptly to establish the final price.

3. POCs for payments and collections for each Party are identified in the Annexes to this Agreement.

4. The price for Logistic Support, Supplies, and Services under this Agreement shall not be higher than the price for the same Logistic Support, Supplies, and Services available under any other Agreement between the Parties or their Governments.

ARTICLE VI. WAIVED OR EXCLUDED COSTS

Insofar as national laws and regulations permit, the Parties shall ensure that any readily identifiable duties, taxes, and similar charges are not imposed on activities conducted under this Agreement. The Parties shall cooperate to provide proper documentation to maximize tax and customs relief. The provisions of any applicable tax and customs relief Agreements also shall apply under this Agreement. The Parties shall inform each other whether the price charged for Logistic Support, Supplies, and Services includes taxes or duties. In determining whether duties, taxes, or similar charges should be levied, the pricing principles in Article V govern the value of the Logistic Support, Supplies, and Services provided by the Supplying Party.

ARTICLE VII. SECURITY OF INFORMATION

All Classified Information and material exchanged between the Parties shall be in accordance with their respective national disclosure policies. Any Classified Information and material provided or generated pursuant to this Agreement shall be protected in compliance with the General Security Agreement covering the exchange of classified information between the Government of the United States of America and the Government of New Zealand, which entered into force November 17, 1961, as amended.

ARTICLE VIII. INTERPRETATION, AMENDMENTS, AND REVISION OF INFORMATION

1. Any disagreements regarding the interpretation or application of this Agreement, any Implementing Arrangements, or transactions executed hereunder shall be resolved through consultation between the Parties and shall not be referred to any national or international tribunal, or third party for settlement.

2. Either Party may, at any time, request amendment of this Agreement by providing written notice to the other Party. In the event such a request is made, the Parties shall enter into negotiations promptly. This Agreement may be amended only by written agreement between the Parties. Replacement of Annexes B through I, which list POCs, may be done by a Party transmitting the replacement Annex to the other Party through military channels, without formal amendment of this Agreement.

ARTICLE IX. ENTRY INTO FORCE AND TERMINATION

This Agreement, which consists of a Preamble, Articles I-IX, and Annexes A through J, shall enter into force upon the date of the last signature. This Agreement shall remain in force unless terminated by the mutual written agreement of the Parties or by either Party giving not less than 180 days notice in writing to the other Party of its intent to terminate. Notwithstanding termination of this Agreement, all reimbursement obligations incurred pursuant to its terms shall remain binding on the responsible Party until satisfied.

ARTICLE X. SUCCESSION

1. The Arrangement between the Department of Defense of the United States of America and the New Zealand Defence Force Concerning Acquisition and Cross-Servicing signed on November 2, 2000 ("the 2000 ASCA"), as amended, shall be superseded by this Agreement on the date that this Agreement enters into force.

2. Upon entry into force, this Agreement applies to all new Orders for Logistic Support, Supplies, and Services. Any references in other U.S.- New Zealand documents to the 2000 ACSA, or Implementing Arrangements between the U.S. and New Zealand made pursuant to the 2000 ACSA that are in effect on the date this Agreement enters into force, shall be construed as referring to this successor Agreement for the purposes of Orders issued after this Agreement enters into force. Unless otherwise agreed by written amendment to a specific Order, the 2000 ACSA and any Implementing Arrangements made pursuant to the 2000 ACSA that are in effect on the date this Agreement enters into force shall continue to apply to all Orders issued prior to entry into force of this Agreement. Any financial obligations, transactions, Orders, or requests for Logistic Support, Supplies, or Services executed prior to the entry into force of this Agreement under the authority of the 2000 ACSA, or any Implementing Arrangements made pursuant to the 2000 ACSA that are in effect on the date this Agreement enters into force, shall remain binding.

IN WITNESS WHEREOF, the undersigned, being duly authorized by their respective Governments, have signed this Agreement.

DONE, in duplicate, in the English language.

FOR THE DEPARTMENT OF DEFENSE OF THE UNITED STATES OF AMERICA

[Signature]

SAMUEL J. LOCKLEAR, III
Admiral, United States Navy
Commander, U.S. Pacific Command

at: Sydney, Australia

on: 6 November 2012

FOR THE NEW ZEALAND DEFENCE FORCE

[Signature]

RICHARD R. JONES
Lieutenant General
Chief of Defence Force

at: Sydney, Australia

on: 6 November 2012

LIST OF ANNEXES

TAB B—AFSOUTH (Air Force)

TAB C—USARSO (Army)

TAB D—USNAVSOUTH (Navy)

TAB E—USMARFORSOUTH (Marine Corps)

TAB F—SOCSOUTH (Special Operations)

ANNEX H—USNORTHCOM POCs

ANNEX I—USTRANSCOM POCs

ANNEX J—USAFRICOM POCs

TAB A—U.S. Africa Command (AFRICOM)

TAB B—U.S. Air Forces Africa (USAFAF)

TAB C—U.S. Army Africa (USARAF)

TAB D—U.S. Naval Forces Africa (USNAVAF)

TAB E—U.S. Marine Forces Africa (USMARFORAF)

TAB F—Combined Joint Task Force—Horn of Africa (CJTF-HOA)

TAB G—U.S. Special Operations Command Africa (USSOCAF)

ANNEX A
MINIMUM ESSENTIAL DATA ELEMENTS

1) Implementing Arrangements or support Arrangement

2) Date of Order

3) Designation and address of office to be billed

4) Numerical listing of stock numbers of items, if any

5) Quantity and description of material/services requested

6) Quantity furnished

7) Unit of Measurement

8) Unit price in currency of billing country, or as otherwise agreed to in the Order

9) Quantity furnished (6) multiplied by unit price (8)

10) Currency of billing country, or as otherwise agreed to in the Order

11) Total Order amount expressed in currency of billing country, or as otherwise agreed to in the Order

12) Name (typed or printed), signature, and title of authorized Ordering or requisitioning representative

13) Payee to be designated on remittance

14) Designation and address of office to receive remittance

15) Recipient's signature acknowledging service or supplies received on the Order or requisition or a separate supplementary document

16) Document number of Order or requisition

17) Receiving organization

18) Issuing organization

19) Transaction type

20) Fund citation or certification of availability of funds when applicable under Parties' procedures

21) Date and place of original transfer; in the case of an exchange transaction, a replacement schedule including time and place of replacement transfer

22) Name, signature and title of authorized acceptance official

23) Additional special requirement, if any, such as transportation, packaging, etc.

24) Limitation of government liability

25) Name, signature, date and title of Supplying Party official who actually issues supplies or services.

ANNEX A/TAB A
STANDARD FORM

ACQUISITION AND CROSS-SERVICING AGREEMENT (ACSA)/
MUTUAL LOGISTICS SUPPORT (MLS)
ORDER FORM

1. Requisition No.	2. Support Agreement	3. Operation/ Theater	4. Order Date
5. Requesting Unit	6. Requesting Nation	7. Providing Unit	8. Providing Nation
9. Deliver to Unit	10. Deliver to Country	11. Deliver Place	12. Deliver Time

13. REQUESTED LINE ITEM SUMMARY (SEE ATTACHED LINE ITEM DETAIL SHEET)

No.	Sub	Attch	Stock No. & Description	Unit of Mes	Quantity Request (Less Previously Received)	Quantity Received	Unit Price	Total

14. Method of Payment ☒ Cash ☐ Replacement-in Kind (RIK) ☐ Equal-Value-Exchange (EVE)		15. Currency	16. Not to Exceed Amount	17. Line Item Cost
22. Authorized Requestor		23. Authorized Supplier		18. Trans Costs
Signature		Signature		19. Other Costs
Name (Last, First MI Rank/Title)	Date	Name (Last, First MI Rank/ Title)	Date	20. Total Claimed

Unit/Office	Nation/Organization	Unit/Office	Nation/Organization	21. Agreed Return Date
24. Purchase Order No.	25. Fund Citation	26 Bill To	30. Remarks	
27. Invoice No.	28. Acct No./Finance Tracking No.	29. Pay To		
31. Receipt			32. Invoice I Certify that the amount invoiced is exclusive of all taxes to which exemption has been granted under provisions of existing agreements and that the invoice is correct.	
Signature			Signature	
Name (Last, First MI Rank/Title)	Date	Name (Last, First MI Rank/ Title)	Date	20. Total Claimed
Unit/Office	Nation/Organization	Unit/Office	Nation/ Organization	21. Agreed Return Date

ANNEX B
NEW ZEALAND POINTS OF CONTACT

MAIN POINT OF CONTACT IN RESPECT OF THIS AGGREEMENT [*sic*]:

Staff Officer One Multinational Logistics Policy
HQ Defence Logistics Command
Private Bag 39 997
Wellington
New Zealand

Phone (644) 496 0248

Fax (644) 496 0159
Mobile +64 27441 5567
E-mail bruce.wooller@nzdf.mil.nz

ALTERNATIVE POINT OF CONTACT/ ORDERING AND FINANCIAL RESPONSIBILITIES:

J4 Branch, HQ JFNZ is responsible for both:

a. approving, placing, and accepting orders; and

b. collecting and making payments for support, supplies, and services.

a. Unit:	J4 Branch, HQ JFNZ
b. Telephone:	Unclassified Commercial (+644) 529-6400
c. Facsimile:	Unclassified Commercial (+644) 529-6409
d. E-mail:	stephen.goodman@nzdf.mil.nz (unclassified only)
e. Message Address:	HQ JFNZ
f. Mailing Address:	J4 Branch HQ JFNZ 2 Seddul Bahr Road, Upper Hutt, NEW ZEALAND

ANNEX C
USCENTCOM
POINTS OF CONTACT, ORDERING AND FINANCIAL RESPONSIBILITIES

TAB A—HQ USCENTCOM

TAB B—USARCENT (Army)

TAB C—USNAVCENT (Navy)

TAB D—USAFCENT (Air Force)

TAB E—USMARCENT (Marine Corps)

TAB F—SOCCENT (Special Operations)

ANNEX C/TAB A
HQ U.S. CENTRAL COMMAND (USCENTCOM)

1. The USCENTCOM POC for coordinated **placement and acceptance of Orders** under this Agreement is the USCENTCOM J4, Multinational Logistics Branch (CCJ4-MNL)

a. Unit:	CCJ4-MNL
b. Telephone:	Com'l: 813-529-4085/4084 DSN: 529-4085/4084
c. Fax:	
d. Message Address:	USCENTCOM//J4/MNL//
e. Mailing Address:	USCENTCOM ATTN: CCJ4-MNL 7115 South Boundary Boulevard MacDill AFB, FL 33621-5101

2. The USCENTCOM agency responsible for **payments and collections** under this Agreement is the USCENTCOM Comptroller Office.

a. Unit:	CCJ8-FM
b. Telephone:	Com'l: 813-827-5884 DSN: 651-5884
c. Fax:	Com'l: 813-827-4218/4648 DSN: 651-4218 /4648
d. Message Address:	USCENTCOM//CCJ8//
e. Mailing Address:	USCENTCOM ATTN: CCJ8-FM 7115 South Boundary Boulevard MacDill AFB, FL 33621-5101

ANNEX C/TAB B
THIRD U.S. ARMY/U.S. ARMY FORCES CENTRAL COMMAND (USARCENT)

1. The USARCENT POC responsible for **placement and acceptance of Orders** is the G-4, Logistics Sustainment Division.

Primary (Operational Command Post-Kuwait)

a. Unit:	Third U.S. Army, G-4
b. Telephone:	Comm: (011) 965-2389-7603 DSN: (318) 430-7603

Alternate (Main Command Post-Shaw, AFB)

a. Unit:	Third U.S. Army, G-4
b. Telephone:	Comm: (803) 885-7407 DSN: (312) 889-7407
c. Fax:	Comm: (803) 895-7392
d. Mailing Address:	Third U.S. Army ATTN: G-4, MNL 1 Gabreski Street Shaw Air Force Base, Sumter, SC 29152

2. The USARCENT agency responsible for **payments and collections** under this Agreement is the USARCENT Comptroller.

a. Unit:	Third Army/U.S. Army Central
b. Email:	3aacsca@arcent.army.mil
c. Telephone:	Com'l: 803-885-8945/8044 DSN: 889-8945/8044
d. Message Address:	USARCENT G8
e. Mailing Address:	Third Army/U.S. Army Central ATTN: USARCENT G8 1 Gabreski Drive, Bldg 1947 Shaw Air Force Base, SC 29152

ANNEX C/TAB C
U.S. NAVAL FORCES CENTRAL COMMAND (USNAVCENT)

1. The USNAVCENT POC for coordinated **placement and acceptance of Orders** under this Agreement is the USNAVCENT N4.

a. Unit:	COMUSNAVCENT-BAHRAIN Code: N4/Coalition Logistics Officer
b. Telephone:	Com'l: (CC) 973-1785-3721/4183 DSN: 318-439-9432/4183
c. Fax:	Com'l: 973-1785-4350 DSN: 318-439-4350 Com'l: 973-1785-4579 (Classified) DSN: 318-439-4579 (Classified)
d. Message Address:	COMUSNAVCENT//N4//COALITION LOGISTICS OFFICER//
e. Mailing Address:	COMUSNAVCENT Code: N4/LRC/Coalition Logistics Officer/ FPO, AE 09501-6008

2. The USNAVCENT agency responsible for **payments and collections** under this Agreement is the COMUSNAVCENT COMPTROLLER.

a. Unit:	COMUSNAVCENT Comptroller, CODE NOOCF
b. Telephone:	Com'l: 973-1785-3029 DSN: 318-439-3029
c. Fax:	Com'l: 973-1785-4350 DSN: 318-439-4350
d. Message Address:	COMUSNAVCENT//N00CF//
e. Mailing Address:	COMUSNAVCENT Code: NOOCF FPO, AE 09501-6503

ANNEX C/TAB D
U.S. AIR FORCES CENTRAL COMMAND (USAFCENT)

1. The USCENTAF POC for coordinated **placement and acceptance of Orders** under this Agreement is the USAFCENT/A4, Director of Logistics.

a. Unit:	US CENTAF/ A4–LGXP
b. Telephone:	Com'l: 803-895-4457/44344 DSN: 965-4457/4344
c. Fax:	Com'l: 803-895-2932 DSN: 965-2932
d. Message Address:	COMUSCENTAF SHAW AFB SC//A4//
e. Mailing Address:	USAFCENT/ A4–A4XP 524 Shaw Drive, Suite 135 Shaw AFB, SC 29152-5029

2. The USCENTAF agency responsible for **payments and collections** under this Agreement is the 9th Air Force Financial Management Analysis Branch.

a. Unit:	9 AF/USAFCENT/FMA
b. Telephone:	Com'l: 803-895-6690 DSN: 965-6690
c. UNCLASSIFIED Fax:	Com'l: 803-895-6877 DSN: 965-6877
d. Message Address:	USAFCENT SHAW AFB SC//FMA//
e. Mailing Address:	9 AF/USAFCENT/FMA 411 Myers Street, Building 1049 Shaw AFB, SC 29152-5029

ANNEX C/TAB E
U.S. MARINE FORCES CENTRAL COMMAND (USMARCENT)

1. The USMARCENT POC for coordinated **placement and acceptance of Orders** under this Procedural Agreement is the USMARCENT G-4:

a. Unit:	USMARCENT G4
b. Telephone:	Com'l: 813-827-7098 DSN: 651-7098
c. Fax:	Com'l: 813-827-7037 DSN: 651-7037
d. Message Address:	COMUSMARCENT G4 (MC)
e. Mailing Address:	USMARCENT, G-4, MacDill AFD 7115 South Boundary Boulevard, Bldg 535 Tampa, FL 33621-5101

2. The USMARCENT agency responsible for **payments and collections** under this Agreement is the USMARCENT G-8:

a. Unit:	USMARCENT G-8
b. Telephone:	Com'l: 813-827-7319 DSN: 651-7319
c. Fax:	Com'l: 813-827-7037 DSN: 651-7037
d. Message Address:	COMUSMARCENT G8 (MC)
e. Mailing Address:	USMARCENT, G-8, MacDill AFB, 7115 South Boundary Boulevard, BLDG 535 Tampa, FL 33621-5101

ANNEX C/TAB F
SPECIAL OPERATIONS COMMAND CENTRAL (SOCCENT)

1. The Special Operations Command Central (SOCCENT) POC for coordinated **placement and acceptance of Orders** under this Agreement is the SOCCENT, J4.

a. Unit:	SOCCCENT, J4
b. Telephone:	Com'l: 813-828-0297 DSN: 968-0297
c. Fax:	Com'l: 813-828-4826 DSN: 968-4826 Com'l: 813-828-8372 (Classified) DSN: 968-8372 (Classified)
d. Message Address:	COMSOCCENT MACDILL AFB FL//J4//
e. Mailing Address:	HQ, SOCCENT ATTN: SOCCENT, J4 7115 South Boundary Boulevard MacDill AFB, FL 33621-5101

2. The Special Operations Command Central (SOCCENT) agency responsible for **payments and collections** under this Agreement is the SOCCENT Comptroller.

a. Unit:	SOCCENT, Comptroller
b. Telephone:	Com'l: (813) 828-4614//DSN: 968-4614
c. Fax:	Com'l: 813-828-8747 DSN: 968-8747 Com'l: 813-828-1894 (Classified) DSN: 968-1894 (Classified)
d. Message Address:	COMSOCCENT MACDILL AFB FL//SOCCO//
e. Mailing Address:	HQ SOCCENT ATTN: SOCCO 7115 South Boundary Boulevard MacDill AFB, FL 33621-5101

ANNEX D
USPACOM/USFJ/USFK
POINTS OF CONTACT, ORDERING AND FINANCIAL RESPONSIBILITIES

TAB A—USPACOM

TAB B—COMPACFLT (Navy)

TAB C—USARPAC (Army)

TAB D—MARFORPAC (Marines)

TAB E—PACAF (Air Force)

TAB F—SOCPAC (Special Operations Command)

TAB G—HQ USFJ

TAB H—USARJ (Army)

TAB I—MARFORJ (Marines)

TAB J—USAFJ (Air Force)

TAB K—HQ USFK

TAB L—HQ USAFK (Air Force)

ANNEX D/TAB A
COMMANDER, U.S. PACIFIC COMMAND (CDRUSPACOM)

1. The USPACOM POC for coordinated **placement and acceptance of Orders** under this Agreement is the J42, Logistics Readiness Division, International Logistics & Sustainment Branch:

a. Unit:	HQ USPACOM J4
b. Telephone:	Com'l: (808) 477-9400 or DSN: 315-477-9400
c. Fax:	Com'l: (808) 477-0936 or DSN: 315-477-0936
d. Message Address:	CDRUSPACOM HONOLULU HI//J4//
e. Mailing Address:	HQ USPACOM J42 Bldg 700, Box 64028 Camp H. M. Smith, HI 96861-4028

2. The USPACOM POC responsible for **payments and collections** under this Agreement is the Comptroller:

a. Unit:	HQ USPACOM J05
b. Telephone:	Com'l: (808) 477-1175 or DSN: 315-477-1175
c. Fax:	Com'l: (808) 477-0535 or DSN: 315-477-0535
d. Message Address:	CDRUSPACOM HONOLULU HI//J05//
e. Mailing Address:	HQ USPACOM J05 Bldg 700, Box 64037 Camp H. M. Smith, HI 96861-4037

ANNEX D/TAB B
COMMANDER, U.S. PACIFIC FLEET (COMPACFLT)

1. The COMPACFLT POC responsible for **placement and acceptance of Orders** under this Agreement is:

a. Unit:	COMPACFLT (N403)
b. Telephone:	DSN: 315-474-6915 or Com'l: (808) 474-6915
c. Fax:	DSN: 315-474-5464 or Com'l: (808) 474-5464
d. Message Address:	COMPACFLT PEARL HARBOR HI//N403//
e. Mailing Address:	Commander, U.S. Pacific Fleet Code N403 250 Makalapa Drive Pearl Harbor, HI 96860-3131

2. The COMPACFLT POC for **payments and collections** under this Agreement is:

a. Unit:	COMPACFLT (N00F)
b. Telephone:	DSN: 315-471-8215 or Com'l: (808) 471-8215
c. Fax:	DSN: 315-474-6937 or Com'l: (808) 474-6937
d. Message Address:	COMPACFLT PEARL HARBOR HI//N00F//
e. Mailing Address:	Commander, U.S. Pacific Fleet Code N00F 250 Makalapa Drive Pearl Harbor, HI 96860-3131

ANNEX D/TAB C
U.S. ARMY PACIFIC (USARPAC)

1. The USARPAC POC responsible for **placement and acceptance of Orders** under this Agreement is Headquarters USARPAC Logistics Plans and International Programs:

a. Unit:	USARPAC/APLG-PEPM
b. Telephone:	DSN: 315-438-8621 or Com'l: (808) 438-8621
c. Fax:	DSN: 315-438-3460 or Com'l: (808) 438-3460
d. Message Address:	CDRUSARPAC FT SHAFTER HI//APLG-PEPM//
e. Mailing Address:	Commander, U.S. Army, Pacific Attn: APLG-PEPM, Plans, Exercises, Policy/ Programs and Multinational Interagency Ft. Shafter, HI 96858

2. The USARPAC POC responsible for **payments and collections** under this Agreement is the Defense Finance and Accounting Service, Honolulu Operating Location:

a. Unit:	DFAS
b. Telephone:	DSN: 315-472-3760 or Com'l: (808) 472-3760
c. Fax:	DSN: 315-472-8250 or Com'l: (808) 472-8250
d. Message Address:	DFAS HONOLULU HI//
e. Mailing Address:	DFAS Box 77, Building 1392 Pearl Harbor, HI 96860-7552

ANNEX D/TAB D
MARINE FORCES PACIFIC (MARFORPAC)

1. The MARFORPAC POC responsible for **placement and acceptance of Orders** under this Agreement is:

a. Unit:	MARFORPAC, G4
b. Telephone:	Com'l: (808) 477-8595/8341 or DSN: 315-477-8595/8341
c. Fax:	Com'l: (808) 477-8710 or DSN: 315-477-8710
d. Message Address:	COMMARFORPAC G4 (UC)
e. Mailing Address:	MARFORPAC, G4 Attn: Multinational Logistics Branch Box 64118 Camp H. M. Smith, HI 96861-4118

2. The MARFORPAC POC responsible for **payments and collections** under this Agreement is:

a. Unit:	MARFORPAC, G8
b. Telephone:	Com'l: (808) 477-8397 or DSN: 315-477-8397
c. Fax:	Com'l: (808) 477-8702 or DSN: 315-477-8702
d. Message Address:	COMMARFORPAC G8 UC
e. Mailing Address:	MARFORPAC, G-8 Box 64112 Camp H. M. Smith, HI 96861-4112

ANNEX D/TAB E
PACIFIC AIR FORCES (PACAF)

1. The PACAF POC responsible for **placement and acceptance of Orders** under this Agreement is Headquarters PACAF Logistics Directorate, Resource Integration Division:

a. Unit:	PACAF/A4P
b. Telephone:	DSN: 315-449-3778 or Com'l: (808) 449-3778
c. Fax:	DSN: 315-449-4778 or Com'l: (808) 449-4778
d. Message Address:	HQ PACAF HICKAM AFB HI//A4P//
e. Mailing Address:	HQ PACAF/A4P 25 E. Street, Suite H-302 Hickam AFB, HI 96853-5427

2. The PACAF POC responsible for **payments and collections** under this Agreement:

a. Unit:	DFAS-Indianapolis
b. Telephone:	Com'l: 317-510-8548 DSN: 699-8548
c. Fax:	Com'l: 317-275-0304 DSN 510-366-0304

d. Mailing Address:

For checks, make payable to "U.S. Treasury" and forward to:

DFAS-IN
3801 Remittances
P.O. Box 269339
Indianapolis, IN 46226-0670

For payment through wire transfer, the following info is required:

United States Treasury
New York, New York
ABA (Bank routing) number: 021 030 004
Agency Name: DFAS-ADY/DE
Agency Location Code: 00003801
Norfolk, VA 23551-2488

3. The PACAF POC responsible for **receiving supporting documentation** used to bill the recipient of Logistic Support, Supplies, and Services under this Agreement is:

a. Unit:	DFAS Limestone
b. Telephone:	DSN: 312-220-1400 or Com'l: (207) 328-1400
c. Fax:	DSN: 312-220-1414 or Com'l: (207) 220-1414
d. Message Address:	DFAS Limestone// ME//

e. Mailing Address: DFAS Limestone
Suite 207
27 Arkansas Road
Limestone, ME 04751-6216

ANNEX D/TAB F
SPECIAL OPERATIONS COMMAND PACIFIC (SOCPAC)

1. The SOCPAC POC responsible for **placement and acceptance of Orders** under this Agreement is:

a. Unit:	SOCPAC/SOJ4
b. Telephone:	DSN: 315-477-0616 or Com'l: (808) 477-0616
c. Fax:	DSN: 315-477-2908 or Com'l: (808) 477-2908
d. Message Address:	COMSOCPAC HONOLULU HI//SOJ4//
e. Mailing Address:	HQ SOCPAC/SOJ4 Box 64046 Camp H. M. Smith, HI 96861-4046

2. The SOCPAC POC responsible for **payments and collections** under this Agreement is:

a. Unit:	SOCPAC/SOJ08
b. Telephone:	DSN: 315-477-2603 or Com'l: (808) 477-2603
c. Fax:	DSN: 315-477-1574 or Com'l: (808) 477-1574
d. Message Address:	COMSOCPAC HONOLULU HI//SOJO8//
e. Mailing Address:	HQ SOCPAC/SOJO8 Bldg 700, Box 64046 Camp H. M. Smith, HI 96861-4046

ANNEX D/TAB G
HQ U.S. FORCES JAPAN (HQ USFJ)

1. The HQ USFJ POC responsible for **placement and acceptance of Orders** under this Agreement is:

a. Unit:	USFJ/J43
b. Telephone:	Com'l: 0425-52-2511 ext. 5-2445 DSN: 315-225-2445
c. Fax:	Com'l: 0425-52-2511 ext. 5-4709 DSN: 315-225-4709
d. Message Address:	COMUSJAPAN YOKOTA AB JA//J4//
e. Mailing Address:	Headquarters, United States Forces, Japan Logistics Directorate/J4, Yokota Air Base Fussa-Shi, Tokyo 197

2. The HQ USFJ agency responsible for **payments and collections** under this Agreement is:

a. Unit:	DFAS-J
b. Telephone:	Com'l: 0425-52-2511, ext. 5-9838 DSN: 315-225-9838
c. Fax:	Com'l: 0425-52-2511, ext. 5-9841 DSN: 315-225-3213
d. Message Address:	DFAS JAPAN YOKOTA JA//
e. Mailing Address:	DFAS-J, Unit 5220, Bldg 206 Yokota Air Base Fussa-Shi, Tokyo 197

ANNEX D/TAB H
U.S. ARMY JAPAN (USARJ)

1. The USARJ POC responsible for **placement and acceptance of Orders** under this Agreement is:

a. Unit:	USARJ, DCS, G4
b. Telephone:	Com'l: 0462-51-1788 ext. 263-7204 DSN: 315-263-5471
c. Fax:	Com'l: 0462-51-1788 ext. 263-8372 DSN: 315-263-8372
d. Message Address:	CDRUSARJ 9th TSC CP ZAMA JA//DSCLOG//
e. Mailing Address:	HQ, USARJ/DCS, G4 ATTN: APAJ-GD-LOG, (ACSA POC) Camp Zama, Zama-Shi Kanagawa-Ken, 288-0000

2. The USARJ POC responsible for **placement and acceptance of Orders** for the **836th U.S. Army Transportation Battalion** under this Agreement is:

a. Unit:	836th U.S. Army Transportation Bn
b. Telephone:	Com'l: 0454-53-4840 ext. 269-6630 DSN: 315-269-6330
c. Fax:	Com'l: 0454-53-4840 ext. 269-6246 DSN: 315-269-6739
d. Message Address:	CDR 836TH TRANS BN YOKOHAMA JA//SDPC-YO-XO//
e. Mailing Address:	836th U.S. Army Transportation Bn ATTN: SDPC-YO-XO Mizuho Sanbashi Kanagawa-Ku Yokohama-Shi, 221-0034

3. The USARJ POC responsible for **placement and acceptance of Orders** for the **835th U.S. Army Transportation Bn** under this Agreement is:

a. Unit:	835th U.S. Army Transportation Bn
b. Telephone	Com'l: 098-857-3844 DSN: 315-648-7729
c. Fax:	Com'l: 098-892-5111 ext. 648-7731 DSN: 315-648-7731
d. Message Address:	CDR 835TH TRANS BN OKINAWA JA//MTPC-OK-XO//

e. Mailing Address:	835th U.S. Army Transportation Bn ATTN: MTPC-OK-XO Shisetsu, Bldg, 305 Nahagunko-Nai, Kakinohana-Cho Naha-Shi, Okinawa 900

4. The USARJ agency responsible for **payments and collections** under this Agreement is:

a. Unit:	DFAS-J (Army Accounting)
b. Telephone:	Com'l: 042-552-2511 ext. 5-5340 DSN: 315-225-5340
c. Fax:	Com'l: 042-552-2511 ext. 5-3523 DSN: 315-225-3523
d. Message Address:	DFAS JAPAN YOKOTA JA//
e. Mailing Address:	DFAS-J (Army Accounting) Unit 5220 ATTN: AAOA Yokota Air Base Fussa-Shi, Tokyo 197

ANNEX D/TAB I
MARINE FORCES JAPAN (MARFORJ)

1. The MARFORJ POC responsible for **placement and acceptance of Orders** for the **III MEF** under this Agreement is:

a. Unit:	III Marine Expeditionary Force (G-4/Supply)
b. Telephone:	Com'l: 0988-92-5111 ext. 622-7137 DSN: 315-622-7137
c. Fax:	Com'l: 0988-92-5111 ext. 622-9019 DSN: 315-622-9019
d. Message Address:	CG III MEF//G4//
e. Mailing Address:	Commanding General ATTN: AC/S G4/MRB/SUP Unit 35601 FPO, AP 96606-5061

2. The MARFORJ POC responsible for **placement and acceptance of Orders** for **Marine Forces Japan, Camp Butler** under this Agreement is:

a. Unit:	Marine Corps Base, Camp S.D. Butler (G-4/)
b. Telephone:	Com'l: 0988-92-5111 ext. 645-7223 DSN: 315-645-7223
c. Fax:	Com'l: 098-892-5111 ext. 645-7231 DSN: 315-645-7231
d. Message Address:	CG MCB CP BUTLER JA//G4//SUPPLY//
e. Mailing Address:	Commanding General, Marine Corps Base, Camp S.D. Butler (G4) ATTN: ACSA POC Unit 35001 FPO AP 96373-5001, Central Post Office Naha-shi, Okinawa-ken 900

3. The MARFORJ agency responsible for **payments and collections** under this Agreement is:

a. Unit:	Marine Forces Japan, Camp Butler (Comptroller)
b. Telephone:	Com'l: 098-892-5111 ext. 645-7310 DSN: 315-645-7310
c. Fax:	Com'l: 098-892-5111 ext. 645-7351 DSN: 315-645-7759
d. Message Address:	DMS CG MCBUTLER COMPT JA//COMPT//

e. Mailing Address:	Commanding General, Marine Forces Japan (Comptroller) Unit 35001 ATTN: ACSA POC FPO AP 96373-5001 or Commanding General, Marine Forces Japan (Comptroller) Unit 35001 ATTN: ACSA POC Central Post Office, Naha-shi, Okinawa-ken 900

ANNEX D/TAB J
U.S. AIR FORCES JAPAN (USAFJ)

1. The USAFJ POC responsible for **placement and acceptance of Orders** under this Agreement is:

a. Unit:	HQ 5AF/ A4A7 (Logistics and Engineering)
b. Telephone:	Com'l: 011-81-311-755-4527 Japanese phone: 0425-52-2511, ext. 5-4527 DSN: 315-225-4527
c. Fax:	None
d. Message Address:	5AF YOKOTA AB A4/A4A7//
e. Mailing Address:	HQ 5AF/A4A7, Unit 5087, Bldg 714 Logistics and Engineering Directorate ATTN: ACSA POC Yokota Air Base, Fussa-Shi, Tokyo 197
f. Email	5af.a4a7@yokota.af.mil

2. The USAFJ agency responsible for **payments and collections** under this Agreement is:

a. Unit:	DFAS-J
b. Telephone:	Com'l: 0425-52-2511, ext. 5-9838 Com'l out of country: 011-81-311-755-9838 DSN: 315-225-9838
c. Fax:	Com'l: 0425-52-2511, ext. 5-3553 DSN: 315-225-3553
d. Message Address:	DFAS JAPAN YOKOTA JA//
e. Mailing Address:	DFAS-J, Unit 5220, Bldg 104 APO, AP 96328-5220 (or Yokota Air Base, Fussa-Shi, Tokyo, Japan 197-0001)

ANNEX D/TAB K
U.S. FORCES KOREA (HQ USFK)

1. The HQ USFK POC for coordinated **placement and acceptance of Orders** under this Agreement is the USFK J45, Multinational Logistics Division:

a. Unit:	USFK J4
b. Telephone:	Com'l: +82 (0) 505-723-6078 or DSN: 315-723-6078
c. Fax:	Com'l: +82 (0) 505-723-8477 or DSN: 315-723-8477
d. Message Address:	
e. Mailing Address:	USFK J4 ATTN: MLD MLSA Mgr Unit 15273 APO AP 96204

2. The HQ USFK POC responsible for **payments and collections** under this Agreement is the Comptroller:

a. Unit:	175th FMC, Unit #15300
b. Telephone:	Com'l: +82 (0) 505-723-7793 or DSN: 315-723-7793
c. Fax:	Com'l: +82 (0) 505-723-3165 or DSN: 315-723-3165
d. Message Address:	
e. Mailing Address:	175th FMC, Unit #15300 ATTN: EAFC-CPA-AOG APO AP 96205-0073

ANNEX D/TAB L
U.S. AIR FORCES KOREA (HQ USAFK)

1. The HQ USAFK POC for coordinated **placement and acceptance of Orders** under this Agreement is:

a. Unit:	HQ 7AF A4/A4RX (International Agreements—Plans and Resources Branch)
b. Telephone:	Com'l: 011-82-31-661-7503/7701 DSN: 315-784-7503/7701
c. Fax:	Com'l: 011-82-31-661-1103 DSN: 315-784-1103
d. Message Address:	7AF OSAN AB ROK/A4//
e. Mailing Address:	HQ 7AF/A4/A4RX Unit 2117 (Attn: A4RX Chief) APO, AP 96278-2117

2. The HQ USAFK POC for **payments and collections** under this Agreement is:

a. Unit:	DFAS Japan
b. Telephone:	Com'l: 011-81-311-755-6049
c. Fax:	None provided
d. Message Address:	None provided
e. Mailing Address:	DFAS Japan Unit 5220 APO AP 96328-5220

ANNEX E
USEUCOM
POINTS OF CONTACT, ORDERING AND FINANCIAL RESPONSIBILITIES

TAB A—USEUCOM

TAB B—USAFE (Air Force)

TAB C—USAREUR (Army)

TAB D—USNAVEUR (Navy)

TAB E—USMARFOREUR (Marine Corps)

TAB F—SOCEUR (Special Operations)

TAB G—USAREUR KFOR

ANNEX E/TAB A
HQ U.S. EUROPEAN COMMAND (HQ USEUCOM)

1. The HQ USEUCOM POC for coordinated **placement and acceptance of Orders** under this Agreement is the ECJ4 Logistics Support Division, Multinational Agreements Branch:

a. Unit:	HQ USEUCOM ECJ4-LS-MNA
b. Telephone:	Com'l: 49-711-680-7474 or 1490 DSN: 314-430-7474 or 1490
c. Fax:	Com'l: 49-711-680-7476 DSN: 314-430-7476
d. Mailing Address:	(Commercial) HQ USEUCOM-ECJ4 G.E.B. 2304 Patch Barracks 70569 Stuttgart-Vaihingen, Germany (Military) HQ USEUCOM-ECJ4 Unit 30400 APO AE 09131

2. The HQ USEUCOM agency responsible for policy issues regarding **payments and collections** under this Agreement is the Comptroller:

a. Unit:	HQ USEUCOM-ECCM
b. Telephone:	Com'l: 49-711-680-5985 DSN: 314-430-5985
c. Fax:	Com'l: 49-711-680-6350 DSN: 314-430-6350
d. Mailing Address:	(Commercial) HQ USEUCOM-ECCM G.E.B. 2304 Patch Barracks 70569 Stuttgart-Vaihingen, Germany (Military) HQ USEUCOM-ECCM Unit 30400 APO AE 09131

ANNEX E/TAB B
U.S. AIR FORCES EUROPE (USAFE)

1. The HQ USAFE POC responsible for **placement and acceptance of Orders** under this Agreement is Headquarters USAFE Logistics Readiness Division, International Logistics Branch:

a. Unit:	HQ USAFE/A4RI
b. Telephone:	Com'l: 49-(0)6371-47-6788 DSN: 314-480-6788
c. Fax:	Com'l: 49-(0)6371-47-9255 DSN: 314-480-9255
d. Email Address:	usafe.a4ri@ramstein.af.mil
e. Message Address:	HQ USAFE RAMSTEIN AB GE//A4RI//
f. Mailing Address:	(Commercial) HQ USAFE/A4RI Gebäude 528 Zimmer 102 Flugplatz 66877 Ramstein, Germany (Military) HQ USAFE/A4RI Unit 3050 Box 105 APO AE 09094-0105

2. The HQ USAFE agency responsible for **payments and collections** under this Agreement is the Defense Finance and Accounting Service, Ramstein AB:

a. Unit:	DFAS-DJF-ARER
b. Telephone:	Com'l: 49-(0)6371-47-2068/7573 DSN: 314-480-2068/7573
c. Fax:	Com'l: 49-(0)6371-47-7582 DSN: 314-480-7582
d. Email Address:	usafe.dfas.ce@ramstein.af.mil
e. Message Address:	HQ USAFE RAMSTEIN AB GE//FM-DFAS//
f. Mailing Address:	(Commercial) HQ USAFE/FM-DFAS Gebäude 413 Zimmer 116 Flugplatz 66877 Ramstein, Germany (Military) HQ USAFE/FM-DFAS Unit 3050 Box 5 APO AE 09094-0505

ANNEX E/TAB C
U.S. ARMY EUROPE (USAREUR)

1. The USAREUR agencies responsible for **placement and acceptance of Orders** are:

For Logistics Support, Supplies, and Services in connection with training at **Grafenwoehr and Hohenfels:**

a. Unit:	Commander 7th U.S. Army JMTC
b. Telephone:	Com'l: +49-9641-83-7159 DSN: 314-475-7159
c. Fax:	Com'l: +49-9641-83-8416 DSN: 314-475-8416
d. Mailing Address:	(Commercial) Commander, 7th U.S. Army JMTC ATTN: AETT-RM-MGT Grafenwoehr Lager D-92655 Grafenwoehr, Germany (Military) Commander, 7th U.S. Army JMTC ATTN: AETT-RM-MGT Unit 28130 APO AE 09114-8130

For all other Logistics Support, Supplies, and Services:

a. Unit:	Commander, HQ USAREUR/7A
b. Telephone:	Com'l: +49-6221-57-6375 DSN: 314-370-6375
c. Fax:	Com'l: +49-6221-57-4002 / 6194 DSN: 314-370-4002/6194
d. Mailing Address:	(Commercial) Commander, HQ USAREUR/7A ATTN: AEAGF-IA Roemerstrasse 168 D-69126 Heidelberg, Germany (Military) Commander, HQ USAREUR/7A ATTN: AEAGF-IA Unit 29351 APO AE 09014

For **placing and executing Purchase Orders (contracts) over $25,000:**

a. Unit:	U.S. Army Contracting Center, Europe (USACCE)
b. Telephone:	Com'l: +49 611-816-2148 / 2153 DSN: 314-336-2148 / 2153
c. Fax:	Com'l: +49 611-816-2175 DSN: 314-336-2175
d. Mailing Address	(Civilian) U.S. Army Contracting Command, Europe Konrad Adenauer Ring 39 D-65187 Wiesbaden, Germany (Military) U.S. Army Contracting Command, Europe APO AE 09096 MR 410, Box 744

Office for **Making Payments for HQ USAREUR/7A (including payments for BALKANS AREA of OPERATIONS):**

a. Unit:	Defense Finance & Accounting Service-Europe (DFAS-EUROPE)
b. Telephone:	Com'l: +49-631-411-6443 / 6520 / 6521 / 6522 DSN: 314-483-6443 / 6520 / 6521 / 6522
c. Fax:	Com'l: +49-631-411-6362
d. Mailing Address:	(Commercial) DFAS-Europe Vendor Pay Kleber Kaserne, Gebaeude 3200 ATTN: LW Mannheimer Strasse 218/219 D-67657 Kaiserslautern, Germany (Military) DFAS-Europe Vendor Pay, ATTN: LW Unit 23122 APO AE 09227

Office for **Collecting Payments for HQ USAREUR/7A (including collections for BALKANS AREA of OPERATIONS):**

a. Unit:	Defense Finance and Accounting Service- Jacksonville/Indianapolis
b. Telephone:	Com'l: +01 317-510-1416 DSN: 312 699-1416
c. Fax:	Com'l: +01 317 510-4181 DSN: 312 699-4181
d. Mailing Address:	(Civilian) 3801 Collections DFAS-JAX/IN PO Box 269490 Indianapolis, IN 46226-9490, USA

ANNEX E/TAB D
U.S. NAVY EUROPE (USNAVEUR)

1. The USNAVEUR agency responsible for **placement and acceptance of Orders** under this Agreement is:

a. Unit:	COMUSNAVEUR (CNE)-COM SIXTH FLEET (C6F) (N4)
b. Telephone:	Com'l: 39-081-568-1832/1840 DSN: 314-626-1832/1840
c. Fax:	Com'l: 39-081-568-1272 DSN: 314-626-1272
d. Message Address:	COMUSNAVEUR NAPLES IT//N4 ACSA//
e. Mailing Address:	(Commercial) COMUSNAVEUR-C6F N4 LOGISTICS PLANS (ACSA) Marina Militaire Americana Viale Fulco Ruffo Di Calabria Aereoporto Capodichino Napoli, Italia 80144 (Military) COMUSNAVEUR-C6F N4 LOG PLANS (ACSA) PSC 817, Box 70 FPO, AE 09622

2. The USNAVEUR agency for **payments and collections** for Logistics Support, Supplies, and Services is:

a. Unit:	COMUSNAVEUR (COMPTROLLER)
b. Telephone:	Com'l: 39-081-568-3817 DSN: 314-626-3817
c. Fax	Com'l: 39-081-568-3143 DSN: 314-626-3143
d. Message Address:	COMUSNAVEUR NAPLES IT//N02F//
e. Mailing Address:	(Commercial) COMUSNAVEUR-C6F COMPTROLLER Marina Militare Americana Viale Fulco Ruffo Di Calabria Aereoporto Capodichino Napoli, Italia 80144

(Military)
COMUSNAVEUR-C6F
COMPTROLLER
PSC 817, Box 70
FPO, AE 09622

ANNEX E/TAB E
MARINE FORCES EUROPE (MARFOREUR)

1. The MARFOREUR agency responsible for **placement and acceptance of Orders** under this Agreement is:

a. Unit:	HQ MARFOREUR/G4
b. Telephone:	Com'l: 49-703-115-3141 DSN: 314-431-3141
c. Fax:	Com'l: 49-7031-15-519 DSN: 314-431-2519
d. Mailing Address:	Commanding Officer Headquarters Marine Forces Europe Panzer Kaserne APO AE 09046

2. The MARFOREUR agency responsible for **payments and collections** under this Agreement is:

a. Unit:	HQ MARFOREUR/G4
b. Telephone:	Com'l: 49-7031-15-438 DSN: 314-431-5438
c. Fax:	Com'l: 49-7031-15-519 DSN: 314-431-5519
d. Mailing Address:	Commanding Officer Headquarters Marine Forces Europe Panzer Kaserne APO AE 09046

ANNEX E/TAB F
SPECIAL OPERATIONS COMMAND EUROPE (SOCEUR)

1. The SOCEUR agency responsible for **placement and acceptance of Orders** under this agreement is:

a. Unit:	SOCEUR/J4
b. Telephone:	Com'l: 49-711-680-4963 DSN: 314-430-4963
c. Fax:	Com'l: 49-711-680-577 DSN: 314-430-0577
d. Mailing Address:	HQ USEUCOM SOCEUR/SOJ4 Unit 30400 APO AE 09131

2. The SOCEUR agency responsible for **payments and collections** under this Agreement is:

a. Unit:	SOCEUR/J8
b. Telephone:	Com'l: 49-711-680-7249 DSN: 314-430-7249
c. Fax:	Com'l: 49-711-5771 DSN: 314-430-5771
d. Mailing Address:	HQ USEUCOM SOCEUR/SOJ8 Unit 30400 APO AE 09131

ANNEX E/TAB G
U.S. ARMY EUROPE (USAREUR) Kosovo Forces (KFOR) (KOSOVO AO)

1. The USAREUR KFOR agency responsible for **placement and acceptance of Orders** is:

a. Unit:	Task Force Falcon / AST Balkans, Camp Bondsteel
b. Telephone:	Com'l: +49-621-730-781-3083 / 3892 / 6401 DSN: 314-781-3083 / 3892 / 6401
d. Commercial Fax:	Com'l: +49-621-730-781-3891 DSN: 314-781-3891
e. Mailing Address:	AST Balkans, Camp Bondsteel ATTN: Multi-National Support Cell APO AE 09340

2. The 266th Theater Finance Command agency responsible for **payments and collections** for Logistics Support, Supplies, and Services is:

a. Unit:	Finance Office
b. Telephone:	Com'l: +49-621-730-781-5133 / 4272 / 3721 DSN: 314-781-5133 / 4272 / 3721
c. Fax:	Com'l: +49-621-730-781-5465 DSN: 314-781-5465
d. Mailing Address:	Finance Office Camp Bondsteel, Kosovo Task Force Falcon / KFOR # APO AE 09340

ANNEX F
JOINT STAFF J4, Joint and Coalition Warfighting (JCW)
POINTS OF CONTACT, ORDERING AND FINANCIAL RESPONSIBILITIES

The Joint Staff agencies responsible for Joint and Coalition Warfighting(JCW) ACSA/AGATRS management are:

a. Unit	JSJ4HR ACSA Program Manager
b. Telephone	Com'l: (703) 571-9787 DSN: 671-9787
c. Fax	Com'l:703-697-2024 DSN: 671-2024
d. Mailing Address:	4000 Joint Staff The Pentagon, Room 2C937 Washington, DC 20318-4000

1. The Joint Staff Hampton Roads POC for coordinated **placement and acceptance of Orders** under this Agreement is the J7 Readiness, Requirements and Initiatives Division:

a. Unit:	JSJ7 Hampton Roads
b. Telephone:	Com'l: (757) 203-5438 DSN: 668-5438
c. Fax:	Com'l: (757) 203-6058 DSN: 668-7238
d. Mailing Address:	Joint Staff J7 Hampton Roads (ACSA Mgr) 116 Lake View Parkway Suffolk, VA 23435-0697

2. The JS Hampton Roads agency responsible for **payments and collections** under this Agreement is the Comptroller:

a. Unit:	Joint Staff JSSE Comptroller
b. Telephone	Com'l: (757) 203-5438 DSN: 668-7238
c. Fax:	Com'l: (757) 203-5300 DSN: 668-5300
d. Mailing Address:	Joint Staff JSSE Comptroller 116 Lake View Parkway Suffolk, VA 23435-0697

ANNEX G
USSOUTHCOM
POINTS OF CONTACT, ORDERING AND FINANCIAL RESPONSIBILITIES

TAB A—HQ USSOUTHCOM

TAB B—AFSOUTH (Air Force)

TAB C—USARSOUTH (Army)

TAB D—USNAVSOUTH (Navy)

TAB E—USMARFORSOUTH (Marine Corps)

TAB F—SOCSOUTH (Special Operations)

ANNEX G/TAB A
HQ U.S. SOUTHERN COMMAND (HQ USSOUTHCOM)

1. The HQ USSOUTHCOM POC for coordinated **placement and acceptance of Orders** under this Agreement is the ES-LOG Joint Logistics Operations Center:

a. Unit:	SOUTHCOM ES-Log
b. Telephone:	Com'l: (305) 437-1427 or 1400 DSN: 567-1427 or 1400
c. Fax:	Com'l: (305) 437-1443 DSN: 567-1443 Com'l: (305) 437-1444 (Classified) DSN: 567-1444 (Classified)
d. Message Address:	CDR USSOUTHCOM MIAMI FL//ES-LOG//(CM)
e. Mailing Address:	COMMANDER HQ USOUTHCOM-ES-LOG 3511 NW 91st Ave. Miami, FL 33172-1217

2. The HQ USSOUTHCOM agency responsible for coordinating **payments and collections** under this Agreement is the Comptroller:

a. Unit:	USSOUTHCOM-R&A
b. Telephone:	Com'l: (305) 437-1814 or 1811 DSN: 567-1814 or 1811
c. Fax:	Com'l: (305) 437-1840 DSN: 567-1840
d. Message Address:	CDR USSOUTHCOM MIAMI FL//R&A//(CM)
e. Mailing Address:	COMMANDER HQ USSOUTHCOM (Attn: R&A) 3511 NW 91st Ave. Miami, FL 33172-1217

ANNEX G/TAB B
AFSOUTH
AIR FORCES SOUTHERN (AFSOUTH)

1. The AFSOUTH POC for coordinated **placement and acceptance of Orders** under this Agreement is the AFSOUTH A4:

a. Unit:	AFSOUTH A4X
b. Telephone:	Com'l: 520-228-3022 DSN: 228-3022
c. Fax:	Com'l: 520-228-3015 DSN: 228-3015 Com'l: N/A (Classified) DSN: N/A (Classified)
d. Message Address:	AFSOUTH DAVIS MONTHAN AFB AZ//A4X//
e. Mailing Address:	COMMANDER 12 AF (AFSOUTH) 2915 S. 12th AF Dr., Suite 144B ATTN: A4X DMAFB, AZ 85707

2. The AFSOUTH agency responsible for coordinating **payments and collections** under this Agreement is the Financial Management Office:

a. Unit:	12 AF (AFSOUTH)/FM
b. Telephone:	Com'l: 520-228-6406 DSN: 228-6406
c. Fax:	Com'l: 520-228-7129 DSN: 228-7129
d. Message Address:	AFSOUTH DAVIS MONTHAN AFB AZ//FM//
e. Mailing Address:	12 AF (AFSOUTH) FM 2915 S. Twelfth AF Dr., Suite 233 DMAFB, AZ 85707-4100

ANNEX G/TAB C
USARSO
U.S. ARMY SOUTH (USARSO)

1. The USARSO POC for coordinated **placement and acceptance of Orders** under this Agreement is USARSO DCS G-4:

a. Unit:	USARSOUTH DCS G-4
b. Telephone:	Com'l: 10-295-6713 DSN: 421-6713
c. Fax:	Com'l: 210-295-6369 DSN: 421-6369
d. Message Address:	HQ USARSO G4 FT SAM HOUSTON TX
e. Mailing Address:	Deputy Chief of Staff, G-4, U.S. Army South Attn: ARSO-LG 2450 Stanley Road, Suite 301 Ft. Sam Houston, TX 78234-7517

2. The USARSO agency responsible for coordinating **payments and collections** under this Agreement is the USARSO DCS G-8:

a. Unit:	USARSO G-8
b. Telephone:	Com'l: 210-295-6031 DSN: 312-421-6031
c. Fax:	Com'l: 210-295-6306 DSN: 312-421-6306
d. Message Address:	HQ USARSO G8 FT SAM HOUSTON TX
e. Mailing Address:	Deputy Chief of Staff, G-8, U.S. Army South Attn: ARSO-RM-FS 2450 Stanley Road, Suite 303 Ft. Sam Houston, TX 78234-7517

ANNEX G/TAB D
USNAVSOUTH
U.S. NAVAL FORCES SOUTH (USNAVSOUTH)

1. The USNAVSOUTH POC for coordinated **placement and acceptance of Orders** under this Agreement is the USNAVSOUTH (N41A):

a. Unit:	USNAVSOUTH/COMUSNAVSO
b. Telephone:	Com'l: 904-270-4037, ext. 3207/3232 DSN: 960-1037, ext. 3207/3232
c. Fax:	Com'l: 904-270-4055 DSN: N/A Com'l: N/A (Classified) DSN: N/A (Classified)
d. Message Address:	COMUSNAVSO
e. Mailing Address:	COMMANDER HQ USNAVSOUTH (Attn: N41A) BLDG 1878 NAVAL STATION Mayport, FL 32228-0003

2. The USNAVSOUTH agency responsible for coordinating **payments and collections** under this Agreement is the Comptroller:

a. Unit:	USNAVSOUTH/COMUSNAVSO
b. Telephone:	Com'l: 904-270-4037, ext. 3207/3232 DSN: 960-1037, ext. 3207/3232
c. Fax:	Com'l: 904-270-4055 DSN: N/A
d. Message Address:	COMUSNAVSO
e. Mailing Address:	COMMANDER HQ USNAVSOUTH (Attn: N41A) BLDG 1878 NAVAL STATION Mayport, FL 32228-0003

ANNEX G/TAB E
USMARFORSOUTH
U.S. MARINE FORCES SOUTH (USMARFORSOUTH)

1. The USMARFORSOUTH POC for coordinated **placement and acceptance of Orders** under this Agreement is the USMARFORSOUTH Comptroller:

a. Unit:	USMARFORSOUTH Comptroller
b. Telephone:	Com'l: 305-437-2604 DSN: 567-2604
c. Fax:	Com'l: 305-437-2542 DSN: 567-2542 Com'l: N/A (Classified) DSN: N/A (Classified)
d. Message Address:	COMMARFORSOUTH
e. Mailing Address:	COMMANDER HQ USMARFORSOUTH/Comptroller 8420 NW 52nd St. Suite 100 Miami, FL 33166

2. The USMARFORSOUTH agency responsible for coordinating **payments and collections** under this Agreement is the USMARFORSOUTH Comptroller:

a. Unit:	USMARFORSOUTH Comptroller
b. Telephone:	Com'l: 305-437-2604 DSN: 567-2604
c. Fax:	Com'l: 305-437-2542 DSN: 567-2542
d. Message Address:	COMMARFORSOUTH
e. Mailing Address:	COMMANDER HQ USMARFORSOUTH (Attn: Comptroller) 8420 NW 52nd St. Suite 100 Miami, FL 33166

ANNEX G/TAB F
SOCSOUTH
SPECIAL OPERATIONS COMMAND SOUTH (SOCSOUTH)

1. The SOCSOUTH POC responsible for coordinated **placement and acceptance of Orders** under this Agreement is the SOCSOUTH J4:

a. Unit:	SOCSOUTH
b. Telephone:	Com'l: 305-224-6403 DSN: 791-6403
c. Fax:	Com'l: 305-224-6415 DSN: N/A Com'l: N/A (Classified) DSN: N/A (Classified)
d. Message Address:	COMSOCSOUTH //J4//
e. Mailing Address:	HQ SOCSOUTH 29350 CORAL SEA BLVD BOX 6 HOMESTEAD, FL 33035

2. The SOCSOUTH POC responsible for coordinating **payments and collections** under this Agreement is the SOCSOUTH J8:

a. Unit:	SOCSOUTH
b. Telephone:	Com'l: 305-224-6380 DSN: 791-6380
c. Fax:	Com'l: 305-224-6386 DSN: 791-6386
d. Message Address:	COMSOCSOUTH //J8//
e. Mailing Address:	HQ SOCSOUTH 29350 CORAL SEA BLVD BOX 6 HOMESTEAD, FL 33035

ANNEX H
USNORTHCOM
POINTS OF CONTACT, ORDERING AND FINANCIAL RESPONSIBILITIES
U.S. NORTHERN COMMAND (USNORTHCOM)

1. The USNORTHCOM POC for coordinated **placement and acceptance of Orders** under this Agreement is:

a. Unit:	NORAD-USNORTHCOM/J4
b. Telephone:	Com'l: (719) 554-5585 DSN: 692-5585
c. Fax:	Com'l: (719) 554-3062 or 0813 DSN: 692-3062 or 0813
d. Message Address:	NORAD-NORTHCOM PETERSON AFB CO//J4//
e. Mailing Address:	250 Vandenberg St. St. B016 Peterson AFB CO 80914-3816

2. The USNORTHCOM agency responsible for **payments and collections** under this Agreement is:

a. Unit:	NORAD-USNORTHCOM/J8
b. Telephone:	Com'l: (719) 556-6032 DSN: 834-6032
c. Fax:	Com'l: (719) 556-0334 DSN: 834-0334
d. Message Address:	NORAD-NORTHCOM PETERSON AFB CO//J8//
e. Mailing Address:	250 Vandenberg St. Rm 1031 Peterson AFB CO 80914-3816

ANNEX I
USTRANSCOM
POINTS OF CONTACT, ORDERING AND FINANCIAL RESPONSIBILITIES
U.S. TRANSPORTATION COMMAND (USTRANSCOM)

1. The USTRANSCOM POC for coordinated **placement and acceptance of Orders** under this Agreement is the TCJ3 Deployment and Distribution Operations Center (DDOC):

a. Unit:	USTRANSCOM-TCJ3-O
b. Telephone:	Com'l: (618) 229-1747 or 4946 DSN: 779-1747 or 4946
c. Fax:	Com'l: (618) 256-1363 DSN: 576-1363 Com'l: (618) 256-6859 (Classified) DSN: 576-6859 (Classified)
d. Message Address:	USTRANSCOM SCOTT AFB IL//TCJ3-O//
e. Mailing Address:	USTRANSCOM TCJ3-O (DDOC) 508 Scott Drive Bldg. 1900 Scott AFB IL, 62225-5357
f. E-mail Address:	USTC-DDOCCHIEF@ustranscom.mil

2. The USTRANSCOM agency responsible for **payments and collections** under this Agreement is the TCJ8 Program Analysis and Financial Management Directorate:

a. Unit:	USTRANSCOM-TCJ8
b. Telephone:	Com'l: (618) 229-5358 DSN: 779-5358
c. Fax:	Com'l: (618) 256-4477 DSN: 576-4477
d. Message Address:	USTRANSCOM SCOTT AFB IL//TCJ8//
e. Mailing Address:	HQ USTRANSCOM—TCJ8 203 West Losey Bldg. 1700 Scott AFB IL, 62225-5233
f. E-mail Address	ustcj8@ustranscom.mil

ANNEX J
USAFRICOM
POINTS OF CONTACT, ORDERING AND FINANCIAL RESPONSIBILITIES

TAB A—U.S. Africa Command (AFRICOM)

TAB B—U.S. Air Forces Africa (USAFAF)

TAB C—U.S. Army Africa (USARAF)

TAB D—U.S. Naval Forces Africa (USNAVAF)

TAB E—U.S. Marine Forces Africa (USMARFORAF)

TAB F—Combined Joint Task Force—Horn of Africa (CJTF-HOA)

TAB G—U.S. Special Operations Command Africa (USSOCAF)

ANNEX J/TAB A
HQ U.S. AFRICA COMMAND (USAFRICOM)

The USAFRICOM J4/J8 agencies responsible for COCOM ACSA/AGATRS management are:

a. Unit:	HQ USAFRICOM J45 ACSA
b. Telephone:	Commercial: 49-711-729-3746 DSN: 314-421-3746
c. Fax:	Commercial: 49-711-729-8964 DSN: 314-421-8964
d. Message Address:	africom-oplog-ls@africom.mil
e. Mailing Address:	HQ USAFRICOM J45 ACSA Unit 29951 APO AE 09751-9951
	AND
a. Unit:	HQ USAFRICOM J8 ACSA
b. Telephone:	Commercial: 49-711-729-3632 DSN: 314-421-3632
c. Fax:	Commercial: 49-711-729-3637 DSN: 314-421-3637
d. Message Address:	AFRICOM RES-IN-J81@usafricom.mil
e. Mailing Address:	HQ USAFRICOM J8 ACSA Unit 29951 APO AE 09751-9951

ANNEX J/TAB B
U.S. AIR FORCES AFRICA (USAFAF)

1. The USAFAF POC responsible for **placement and acceptance of Orders** under this Agreement is Headquarters USAFE Logistics Readiness Division, International Logistics Branch:

a. Unit:	HQ USAFE/A4RI
b. Telephone:	Commercial: 49-(0)6371-47-6788 DSN: 314-480-6788
c. Fax:	Commercial: 49-(0)6371-47-9255 DSN: 314-480-9255
d. Email Address:	usafe.a4ri@ramstein.af.mil
e. Message Address:	HQ USAFE RAMSTEIN AB GE//A4RI//
f. Mailing Address:	Commercial: HQ USAFE/A4RI Gebäude 528 Zimmer 102 Flugplatz 66877 Ramstein, Germany Military: HQ USAFE/A4RI Unit 3050 Box 105 APO AE 09094-0105

2. The USAFAF agency responsible for **payments and collections** under this Agreement is the Defense Finance and Accounting Service, Ramstein AB:

a. Unit:	DFAS-DJF-ARER
b. Telephone:	Commercial: 49-(0)6371-47-2068/7573 DSN: 314-480-2068/7573
c. Fax:	Commercial: 49-(0)6371-47-7582 DSN: 314-480-7582
d. Email Address:	usafe.dfas.ce@ramstein.af.mil
e. Message Address:	HQ USAFE RAMSTEIN AB GE//FM-DFAS//
f. Mailing Address:	Commercial: HQ USAFE/FM-DFAS Gebäude 413 Zimmer 116 Flugplatz 66877 Ramstein, Germany Military: HQ USAFE/FM-DFAS Unit 3050 Box 5 APO AE 09094-0505

ANNEX J/TAB C
U.S. ARMY AFRICA (USARAF)

1. The HQ USARAF G4 agencies responsible for approving, placing and accepting orders are:

a. Unit:	HQ USARAF, G4 SOD, MNIA
b. Telephone:	Commercial: +39-0444-71-4871 DSN: 314-635-4871
c. Fax:	Commercial: N/A DSN: N/A
d. Message Address:	mail.USARAF.G4MNIA@EUR.ARMY.MIL
e. Mailing Address:	Commercial: Caserma Ederle USARAF G4 SOD, MNIA 196 Viale Della Pace, Bldg. 3 36100, Vicenza, Italy Military: USARAF ATTN: G4 SOD, MNIA Unit 31401, Box 1 APO AE 09630

2. The HQ USARF G8 agency responsible for coordinating payments and collections for this agreement is:

a. Unit:	HQ USARAF G8 Support Agreements (ACSA)
b. Telephone:	Commercial: 39-04444-71-7383 DSN: 314-634-7383
c. Fax:	Commercial: 39-04444-71-7744 DSN: 314-634-7744
d. Message Address:	Richard.b.piercy@eur.army.mil
e. Mailing Address:	Military: HQ USARAF G8 Support Agreements (ACSA) Unit 31401, Box 3 APO AE 09630

ANNEX E*/TAB D
U.S. NAVAL FORCES AFRICA (USNAVAF)

1. The USNAVAF N4 agency responsible for approving, placing, and accepting orders is:

a. Unit:	COMUSNAVEUR (CNE)—COM SIXTH FLEET (C6F) (N4)
b. Telephone:	Commercial: 39-081-568-1849/1840 DSN: 314-626-1849/1840
c. Fax:	Commercial: 39-081-568-1272 DSN: 314-626-1272
d. Message Address:	COMUSNAVEUR NAPLES IT//N4 ACSA//
e. Mailing Address:	Commercial: COMUSNAVEUR-C6F N4 LOGISTICS PLANS (ACSA) Marina Militaire Americana Viale Fulco Ruffo Di Calabria Aereoporto Capodichino Napoli, Italia 80144 Military: COMUSNAVEUR-C6F N4 LOG PLANS (ACSA) PSC 817 BOX 70 FPO AE 09622

2. The USNAVAF N8 agency for coordinating payments for support, supplies, and services is:

a. Unit:	COMUSNAVEUR (COMPTROLLER)
b. Telephone:	Commercial: 39-081-568-3817 DSN: 314-626-3817
c. Fax:	Commercial: 39-081-568-3143 DSN: 314-626-3143
d. Message Address:	COMUSNAVEUR NAPLES IT//N02F//
e. Mailing Address:	Commercial: COMUSNAVEUR-C6F COMPTROLLER Marina Militare Americana Viale Fulco Ruffo Di Calabria Aeroporto Capodichino Napoli, Italia 80144 Military: COMUSNAVEUR-C6F COMPTROLLER PSC 817 BOX 70 FPO AE 09622

* Editor's Note: The original reads "ANNEX E", but "ANNEX J" was probably intended.

ANNEX J/TAB E
MARINE FORCES AFRICA (USMARFORAF)

1. The HQ MARFORAF G4 agency responsible for approving, placing, and accepting orders under this agreement is:

a. Unit:	Marine Forces Africa
b. Telephone:	Commercial: +49 (0) 703 115 2094 DSN: 314-431-2094
c. Fax:	Commercial: +49 (0) 703 115 2392 DSN: 314-431-2392
d. Message Address:	MFAWatch@mfe.usmc.mil
e. Mailing Address:	Marine Forces Africa Unit 30401 APO-AE 09107-0401

2. The HQ MARFORAF G8 agency responsible for coordinating payments and collections in support of this agreement is:

a. Unit:	Marine Forces Africa
b. Telephone:	Commercial: +49 (0) 703 115 2746 DSN: 314-431-2746
c. Fax:	Commercial: +49 (0) 703 115 2392 DSN: 314-431-2392
d. Message Address:	MFAWatch@mfe.usmc.mil
e. Mailing Address:	Marine Forces Africa Unit 30401 APO-AE 09107-0401

ANNEX J/TAB F
COMBINED JOINT TASK FORCE—HORN OF AFRICA (CJTF-HOA) (Navy)

1. The CJTF-HOA J4 agency responsible for approving, placing, and accepting orders is:

a. Unit:	Joint Logistics Plans Center, CJ-4
b. Telephone:	Commercial: 00-253-359-034 DSN: 311-824-4535
c. Fax:	Commercial: N/A DSN: N/A
d. Message Address:	CJTF-HOAJ4JLPCGROUP@usafricom.mil
e. Mailing Address:	Commercial: N/A Military: PSC 831 BOX 0036 FPO AE 09363-0036

2. The CJTF-HOA J8 agency for coordinating payments for support, supplies, and services is:

a. Unit:	J8 Deputy Director/Comptroller CJTF-HOA
b. Telephone:	Commercial: 00-253-341-588 DSN: 311-824-4478
c. Fax:	Commercial: N/A DSN: N/A
d. Message Address:	HOA_RESOURCE_ADVISORS@usafricom.mil
e. Mailing Address:	Commercial: N/A Military: PSC 831 BOX 0036 FPO AE 09363-0036

ANNEX J/TAB G
SPECIAL OPERATIONS COMMAND AFRICA (USSOCAF)

1. The HQ SOCAF J4 agency responsible for approving, placing, and accepting orders under this agreement is:

a. Unit:	Special Forces Command Africa
b. Telephone:	Commercial: +49 (0) 711 7293340 DSN: 314-421-3340
c. Fax:	Commercial: +49 (0) 711 7293705 DSN: 314-421-3705
d. Message Address:	SOCAFRICA.JOC@africom.mil
e. Mailing Address:	Commercial: Kelly Kaserne GEB.3304 Plieningstr. 289 70567 Stuttgart, GE Military: SOCAFRICA Unit 30401 APO AE 09107

2. The SOCAF J8 agency responsible for coordinating payments and collections in support of this agreement is:

a. Unit:	Special Forces Command Africa
b. Telephone:	Commercial: +49 (0) 711 7295252 DSN: 314-421-5252
c. Fax:	Commercial: +49 (0) 711 7293705 DSN:314-421-3705
d. Message Address:	SOCAFRICA.JOC@africom.mil
e. Mailing Address:	Commercial: Kelly Kaserne GEB.3304 Plieningstr. 289 70567 Stuttgart, GE Military: SOCAFRICA Unit 30401 APO AE 09107

State Department Document Number: 12-201

Extension of the Mutual Logistics Support Agreement (RP-US-01) of November 8, 2007 Between the Department of Defense of the United States of America and the Department of National Defense of the Republic of the Philippines

Signed at Sydney, November 6, 2012
Entered into force November 6, 2012

CTIA Document Number: 13647.001

The Department of Defense of the United States of America and the Department of National Defense of the Republic of the Philippines (the "Parties") entered into the Mutual Logistics Support Agreement (MLSA), signed at Quezon City on November 8, 2007, with a five year term.

Per the terms of Article IX (Effective Date and Termination) of the MLSA, the Parties hereby agree to extend the MLSA for an additional five (5)-year term through November 8, 2017.

This extension will enter into force on the date of last signature.

IN WITNESS WHEREOF, the undersigned, being duly authorized by their respective governments, sign this extension. DONE, in duplicate, in the English language at Sydney, Australia, this 6th day of November, 2012.

FOR THE DEPARTMENT OF NATIONAL DEFENSE OF THE REPUBLIC OF THE PHILIPPINES

[Signature]

JESSIE D. DELLOSA
General, Philippine Army
Chief of Staff of the Armed Forces of the Philippines

FOR THE DEPARTMENT OF DEFENSE OF THE UNITED STATES OF AMERICA

[Signature]

SAMUEL J. LOCKLEAR, III
Admiral, United States Navy
Commander, U.S. Pacific Command

State Department Document Number: 12-202

Amendment to and Extension of the Agreement of June 7 and July 16, 2012 Between the United States of America and the North Atlantic Treaty Organization (NATO) Concerning the Provision of Services and Commodities on an Advance-of-Funds or Reimbursable Basis

Signed at Brussels, November 15, 2012
Entered into force November 15, 2012

CTIA DOCUMENT NUMBER: 18045.001

PREAMBLE

The United States of America ("the United States"), and the North Atlantic Treaty Organization ("NATO"), hereinafter referred to as the Parties,

On the part of the United States, acting under the authority of section 607 of the Foreign Assistance Act of 1961, as amended;

On the part of NATO, acting in accordance with the mandate of the North Atlantic Council and relevant financial regulations and rules;

Recalling the exchange of letters between the United States of America and NATO of May 15 and 16, 2012 (the "Exchange of Letters"), and the Agreement between the United States of America and the North Atlantic Treaty Organization (NATO) Concerning the Provision of Services and Commodities on an Advance-of-Funds or Reimbursable Basis, signed at Baghdad and Brussels on June 7 and July 16, 2012 (the "Agreement"), which together established arrangements concerning the presence of the NATO Transition Cell (the "Cell") in Baghdad, Iraq;

Desiring to extend such arrangements until July 1, 2013;

Have agreed as follows:

ARTICLE I

The understanding between the United States of America and NATO that was effected by the Exchange of Letters is hereby extended to remain effective until July 1, 2013.

ARTICLE II

Pursuant to Article VII.2 of the Agreement, the Agreement shall be extended to remain in force until July 1, 2013.

ARTICLE III

Article III.7 of the Agreement shall be replaced by the following:

> NATO shall provide reimbursement for all charges on invoices from the U.S. Department of State and the U.S. Department of Defense by Electronic Funds Transfer to the bank account identified in writing in each invoice.

DONE at Brussels, this 15th day of November, 2012, in duplicate.

FOR THE UNITED STATES OF AMERICA:	FOR THE NORTH ATLANTIC TREATY ORGANIZATION:
[Signature]	[Signature]
Ivo H. Daalder	Alexander Vershbow
U.S. Ambassador to NATO	Deputy Secretary General

STATE DEPARTMENT DOCUMENT NUMBER: 12-203

EXTENSION OF THE AGREEMENT OF JANUARY 25, 2008 BETWEEN THE UNITED STATES OF AMERICA AND THE REPUBLIC OF HONDURAS REGARDING THE STATUS OF UNITED STATES PERSONNEL WHO MAY BE TEMPORARILY PRESENT IN HONDURAS IN CONNECTION WITH MILITARY EXERCISES AND TRAINING

EFFECTED BY EXCHANGE OF NOTES AT TEGUCIGALPA,
OCTOBER 17 AND NOVEMBER 19, 2012
ENTERED INTO FORCE NOVEMBER 19, 2012

CTIA DOCUMENT NUMBER: 18061.001

DIPLOMATIC NOTE

Note No. 372

The Embassy of the United States of America presents its compliments to the Ministry of Foreign Affairs of the Republic of Honduras and has the honor to refer to the exchange of diplomatic notes (No. 34 and No. 29 – DT, respectively), dated January 25, 2008, that constitute an agreement between the Government of Honduras and the Government of the United States of America regarding the status of members of the armed forces of the United States and civilian personnel of the Department of Defense of the United States who may be temporarily present in Honduras in connection with military exercises and training, United States security assistance programs, and other agreed purposes.

The January 25, 2008, Agreement was to remain in force for one year and was to be automatically extended for additional periods of one year, up to a maximum combined duration of five years, thereby expiring on January 24, 2013. To continue without interruption the military assistance and other programs our two governments have established, the Embassy requests an amendment to provide for extensions to the Agreement until January 24, 2018, such that the penultimate paragraph of the Agreement reads as follows:

> "If the foregoing is acceptable to the Government of Honduras, the Embassy proposes that this note, together with the Foreign Ministry's reply to that effect, shall constitute an agreement between the two governments which shall enter into force on the date of the Foreign Ministry's reply and shall remain in force for an initial term of one year and shall be automatically extended for additional periods of one year, up to a maximum combined duration of ten years. During the initial one-year term or any extended one-year term, either government may terminate this Agreement by giving the other party six months' prior written notice of its intent to terminate the Agreement."

If this proposal is acceptable to the Government of the Republic of Honduras, the Embassy proposes that this note, and a note containing a reply to that effect from the Ministry, shall constitute an agreement between the two governments.

The Embassy of the United States of America avails itself of this opportunity to renew to the Ministry of Foreign Affairs of the Republic of Honduras the assurances of its highest consideration.

Embassy of the United States of America
Tegucigalpa, October 17, 2012

True and faithful copy of the
original or certified copy the same
having been carefully examined by
me and compared with said
document and found to agree
therewith word for word and
figure for figure

Dated: Oct/17/2012

[Signature]
Gregory Pearman
Vice-Consul of the
United States of America
Tegucigalpa, Honduras

U.S. Department of State
Office of Language Services
Translating Division

LS No. 11-2013-0292
Spanish/English
BBM/ALK

TRANSLATION

Ministry of Foreign Affairs
Republic of Honduras

Tegucigalpa, November 19, 2012

Embassy of the United States of America
Tegucigalpa, Honduras

Note Verbale No. 254-DGTC

The Ministry of Foreign Affairs, Office of Treaties and Agreements, presents its compliments to the Embassy of the United States of America and has the honor to refer to its note No. 372 of October 17, 2012 regarding the exchange of diplomatic notes constituting an **agreement between the Government of the Republic of Honduras and the Government of the United States of America regarding the status of members of the armed forces of the United States** who may be temporarily present in Honduras in connection with military exercises and training, United States security assistance programs, and other purposes.

The Ministry of Foreign Affairs has the honor to inform the Embassy of the United States of America that it hereby agrees to extend the above-mentioned Agreement and that the Embassy's note and this note in reply shall constitute an agreement between our two governments.

[Complimentary close]

[Initialed] [Seal of the Ministry of Foreign Affairs]

APPENDIX I
INDEX BY COUNTRY

Canada

Narcotics

Framework Agreement on Integrated Cross-border Maritime Law Enforcement Operations Between the United States of America and Canada. Signed at Detroit, May 26, 2009. Entered into force October 11, 2012. **12-5 CTIA 303, DOS 12-192.**

China

Satellites

Memorandum of Understanding Between the United States Geological Survey of the Department of the Interior and the Center for Earth Observation and Digital Earth (CEODE) of the Chinese Academy of Sciences (CAS) for Cooperation in the Use of U.S. Land Remote Sensing Satellite Data, with Annexes. Signed at Reston and Beijing, October 10 and 20, 2012. Entered into force October 20, 2012. **12-5 CTIA 323, DOS 12-195.**

Colombia

Defense

Acquisition and Cross-Servicing Agreement (US-CO-2) Between the Department of Defense of the United States of America and the Ministry of National Defense of the Republic of Colombia, with Annexes. Signed at Bogota and Miami, June 27 and 30, 2012. Entered into force June 30, 2012. **12-5 CTIA 205, DOS 12-185.**

Council of Europe Development Bank (CEB)

Refugees

Adherence Agreement Between the United States of America and the Council of Europe Development Bank with Respect to the Regional Housing Programme Fund, with Annexes. Signed at Washington D.C., and Paris, August 26 and September 24, 2012. Entered into force September 24, 2012. **12-5 CTIA 139, DOS 12-177.**

Ecuador

Diplomatic Relations

Agreement Between the Department of Defense of the United States of America and the Ministry of Defense of the Republic of Ecuador Concerning Health Care for Military Members and Their Dependents. Signed at Quito and Washington D.C., September 27 and October 5, 2012. Entered into force October 5, 2012. **12-5 CTIA 299, DOS 12-191.**

Ghana

Economic Cooperation

Development Agreement Between the United States of America and the Republic of Ghana for Improved Reading Performance in Primary School. Signed on September 26, 2012. Entered into force September 26, 2012. **12-5 CTIA 273, DOS 12-186.**

Development Agreement Between the United States of America and the Republic of Ghana for Equitable Improvements in Health Status. Signed on September 26, 2012. Entered into force September 26, 2012. **12-5 CTIA 279, DOS 12-187.**

Development Agreement Between the United States of America and the Republic of Ghana for Sustainable and Broadly Shared Economic Growth. Signed on September 26, 2012. Entered into force September 26, 2012. **12-5 CTIA 285, DOS 12-188.**

Honduras

Military Operations

Extension of the Agreement of January 25, 2008 Between the United States of America and the Republic of Honduras Regarding the Status of United States Personnel Who May Be Temporarily Present in Honduras in Connection with Military Exercises and Training. Effected by Exchange of Notes at Tegucigalpa, October 17 and November 19, 2012. Entered into force November 19, 2012. **12-5 CTIA 433, DOS 12-203.**

India

Economic Cooperation

Second Amendment to the Partnership Agreement of September 30, 2010, as Amended, Between the United States of America and India, for Health, with Addendum and Attachment. Signed at New Delhi, September 28 and October 1, 2012. Entered into force October 1, 2012. **12-5 CTIA 177, DOS 12-181.**

Indonesia

Satellites

Implementing Arrangement Between the United States Geological Survey of the Department of the Interior and the National Institute of Aeronautics and Space (LAPAN) of the Republic of Indonesia for Cooperation in the Use of U.S. Land Remote Sensing Satellite Data, with Annexes. Signed at Reston and Jakarta, October 10 and November 2, 2012. Entered into force November 2, 2012. **12-5 CTIA 339, DOS 12-197.**

Ireland

Crimes and Criminals

Agreement Between the United States of America and Ireland on Enhancing Cooperation in Preventing and Combating Serious Crime. Signed at Dublin, July 21, 2011. Entered into force October 19, 2012. **12-5 CTIA 183, DOS 12-182.**

Jamaica

Defense

Agreement Between the United States of America and Jamaica Regarding the Caribbean Basin Security Initiative and the Provision of Technical Support for Maritime Security Forces. Effected by Exchange of Notes at Kingston, September 24 and November 6, 2012. Entered into force November 6, 2012. **12-5 CTIA 357, DOS 12-199.**

Japan

Defense

Extension of the Agreement of October 24, 1996, as Amended, Between the United States of America and Japan Concerning Cooperation on the Advanced Spaceborne Thermal Emission and Reflection Radiometer (ASTER) Program. Effected by Exchange of Notes at Washington D.C., October 19, 2012. Entered into force October 19, 2012, effective October 24, 2012. **12-5 CTIA 193, DOS 12-183.**

Agreement Between the United States of America and Japan Concerning a Program for Cooperative Research on Hybrid Electric Propulsion. Effected by Exchange of Notes at Tokyo, November 2, 2012. Entered into force November 2, 2012. **12-5 CTIA 351, DOS 12-198.**

Jordan

Nuclear Materials and Safety

Arrangement Between the United States Nuclear Regulatory Commission and the Jordan Nuclear Regulatory Commission for the Exchange of Technical Information and Cooperation in Nuclear Safety Matters, with Addendums. Signed at Vienna, September 20, 2012. Entered into force September 20, 2012. **12-5 CTIA 129, DOS 12-176.**

Kenya

Economic Cooperation

Twenty-seventh Amendment to the Development Assistance Grant Agreement of August 19, 2003 Between the United States of America and the Republic of Kenya for Reduced Fertility and the Risk of HIV/AIDS Transmission Through Sustainable, Integrated Family Planning and Health Services. Signed on September 28, 2012. Entered into force September 28, 2012. **12-5 CTIA 167, DOS 12-179.**

Eighteenth Amendment to the Development Assistance Grant Agreement of August 19, 2002, as Amended, Between the United States of America and the Republic of Kenya for Increased Rural Household Income. Signed on September 28, 2012. Entered into force September 28, 2012. **12-5 CTIA 171, DOS 12-180.**

Korea

Nuclear Materials and Safety

Arrangement Between the United States Nuclear Regulatory Commission and the Nuclear Safety and Security Commission of the Republic of Korea for the Exchange of Technical Information and Cooperation in Nuclear Safety Matters, with Addendums. Signed at Vienna, September 18, 2012. Entered into force September 18, 2012. **12-5 CTIA 93, DOS 12-173.**

Liberia

Economic Cooperation

Development Objective Agreement Between the United States of America and the Republic of Liberia for USAID Development Objective 2: Sustained, Market-Driven Economic Growth to Reduce Poverty, with Annexes. Signed on September 29, 2012. Entered into force September 29, 2012. **12-5 CTIA 1, DOS 12-165.**

Development Objective Agreement Between the United States of America and the Republic of Liberia for USAID Development Objective 1: More Effective, Accountable and Inclusive Governance, with Annexes. Signed on September 29, 2012. Entered into force September 29, 2012. **12-5 CTIA 19, DOS 12-166.**

Development Objective Agreement Between the United States of America and the Republic of Liberia for USAID Development Objective 4: Better-Educated Liberians, with Annexes. Signed on September 29, 2012. Entered into force September 29, 2012. **12-5 CTIA 43, DOS 12-167.**

Mali

Cultural Property

Extension of the Agreement of September 19, 1997 Between the United States of America and the Republic of Mali Concerning the Imposition of Import Restrictions on Archaeological Material from Mali from the Paleolithic Era (Stone Age) to Approximately the Mid-Eighteenth Century, with Attachment. Effected by Exchange of Notes at Bamako, August 15 and September 5, 2012. Entered into force September 5, 2012, effective September 19, 2012. **12-5 CTIA 75, DOS 12-171.**

Mexico

Nuclear Materials and Safety

Arrangement Between the Nuclear Regulatory Commission of the United States of America and the Comision Nacional de Seguridad Nuclear y Salvaguardias of the United Mexican States for the Exchange of Technical Information and Cooperation in Nuclear Safety and Research Matters, with Addendums. Signed at Vienna, September 18, 2012. Entered into force September 18, 2012. **12-5 CTIA 105, DOS 12-174.**

Netherlands

Defense

Extension of the Agreement of May 3, 2005, as Extended, Between the United States of America and the Kingdom of the Netherlands Concerning the Status of Military and Civilian Personnel of the United States Department of Defense Temporarily Present in the Netherlands Antilles and Aruba in Connection with Military Exercises and Training. Effected by Exchange of Notes at The Hague, October 17 and 29, 2012. Entered into force October 29, 2012. **12-5 CTIA 335, DOS 12-196.**

New Zealand

Defense

Acquisition and Cross-Servicing Agreement (US-NZ-02) Between the Department of Defense of the United States of America and the New Zealand Defence Force, with Annexes. Signed at Sydney, November 6, 2012. Entered into force November 6, 2012. **12-5 CTIA 363, DOS 12-200.**

North Atlantic Treaty Organization - NATO

North Atlantic Treaty Organization (NATO)

Amendment to and Extension of the Agreement of June 7 and July 16, 2012 Between the United States of America and the North Atlantic Treaty Organization (NATO) Concerning the Provision of Services and Commodities on an Advance-of-Funds or Reimbursable Basis. Signed at Brussels, November 15, 2012. Entered into force November 15, 2012. **12-5 CTIA 431, DOS 12-202.**

Panama

Military Operations

Agreement Between the United States of America and the Republic of Panama Regarding the Status of United States Personnel Who May Be Temporarily Present in Panama in Connection with a Visit by Thirty-one Officials from the U.S. Navy Mobile Security Detachment. Effected by Exchange of Notes at Panama City, October 1 and 16, 2012. Entered into force October 16, 2012. **12-5 CTIA 319, DOS 12-194.**

Philippines

Defense

Extension of the Mutual Logistics Support Agreement (RP-US-01) of November 8, 2007 Between the Department of Defense of the United States of America and the Department of National Defense of the Republic of the Philippines. Signed at Sydney, November 6, 2012. Entered into force November 6, 2012. **12-5 CTIA 429, DOS 12-201.**

Scientific Cooperation

Agreement Between the United States of America and the Republic of the Philippines on Scientific and Technological Cooperation, with Annex. Signed at Washington D.C., June 8, 2012. Entered into force October 15, 2012. **12-5 CTIA 313, DOS 12-193.**

Qatar

Defense

Agreement Between the United States of America and the State of Qatar Concerning Security Measures for the Protection of Classified Military Information, with Appendix. Signed on July 17, 2012. Entered into force August 15, 2012. **12-5 CTIA 67, DOS 12-170.**

Switzerland

Nuclear Materials and Safety

Arrangement Between the United States Nuclear Regulatory Commission and the Swiss Federal Nuclear Safety Inspectorate of Switzerland for the Exchange of Technical Information and Cooperation in Nuclear Safety Matters, with Addendums. Signed at Vienna, September 19, 2012. Entered into force September 19, 2012. **12-5 CTIA 117, DOS 12-175.**

Tanzania

Economic Cooperation

Amendment Number Thirteen to the Strategic Objective Grant Agreement of August 23, 2005, as Amended, Between the United States of America and the United Republic of Tanzania for Strategic Objective No. 11, Health Status of Tanzanian Families Improved, with Annex. Signed on September 24 and 26, 2012. Entered into force September 26, 2012. **12-5 CTIA 291, DOS 12-189.**

Amendment Number Thirteen to the Strategic Objective Grant Agreement of July 26, 2005, as Amended, Between the United States of America and the United Republic of Tanzania for Strategic Objective No. 12: Incomes of Small Farmers Increased in Selected Agricultural Commodity Sub-sectors, with Annex. Signed on September 22 and 26, 2012. Entered into force September 26, 2012. **12-5 CTIA 295, DOS 12-190.**

Turkey

Nuclear Materials and Safety

Arrangement Between the United States Nuclear Regulatory Commission and the Turkish Atomic Energy Authority for the Exchange of Technical Information and Cooperation in Nuclear Safety Matters, with Addendums. Signed at Vienna, September 18, 2012. Entered into force September 18, 2012. **12-5 CTIA 81, DOS 12-172.**

Zambia

Economic Cooperation

Implementation Letter Amending the Development Cooperation Agreement of September 27, 2011 Between the United States of America and the Republic of Zambia. Signed at Lusaka, September 25, 2012. Entered into force September 25, 2012. **12-5 CTIA 163, DOS 12-178.**

APPENDIX II
INDEX TO MULTILATERAL AGREEMENTS

Defense

Amendment One to the Memorandum of Understanding of August 23 and September 23, 2005 Among the Department of Defence of Australia and the Department of National Defence of Canada and the Ministry of Defense of the Republic of Finland and the Ministry of Defense of the State of Kuwait and the Ministry of Defense of the Kingdom of Spain and the Federal Department of Defense, Civil Protection and Sports of the Swiss Confederation and the Department of Defense of the United States of America Concerning the Cooperative Framework for the F/A-18 Program. Signed at Arlington, Ottawa, Williamtown, Madrid, Bern, Kuwait, Tikkakoski, and Kuala Lumpur, June 14, 22, 24 and 28, July 8, August 19 and 24, 2010. Entered into force August 24, 2010. **12-5 CTIA 197, DOS 12-184.**

APPENDIX III
TOPICAL INDEX

Documents are listed by topic and, within each topic, by the country which is the other party to the agreement. References are to page numbers within this volume and to Department of State numbers or Senate Treaty document numbers.

The manufacturer's authorised representative in the EU for product safety is Oxford University Press España S.A. of El Parque Empresarial San Fernando de Henares, Avenida de Castilla, 2 - 28830 Madrid (www.oup.es/en or product.safety@oup.com). OUP España S.A. also acts as importer into Spain of products made by the manufacturer.
Printed and bound by CPI Group (UK) Ltd, Croydon, CR0 4YY
14/09/2026
02216304-0020